Offenc

Offences and Defences

Selected Essays in the Philosophy of Criminal Law

JOHN GARDNER

OXFORD
UNIVERSITY PRESS

OXFORD
UNIVERSITY PRESS

Great Clarendon Street, Oxford OX2 6DP

Oxford University Press is a department of the University of Oxford.
It furthers the University's objective of excellence in research, scholarship,
and education by publishing worldwide in

Oxford New York

Auckland Cape Town Dar es Salaam Hong Kong Karachi
Kuala Lumpur Madrid Melbourne Mexico City Nairobi
New Delhi Shanghai Taipei Toronto

With offices in

Argentina Austria Brazil Chile Czech Republic France Greece
Guatemala Hungary Italy Japan Poland Portugal Singapore
South Korea Switzerland Thailand Turkey Ukraine Vietnam

Oxford is a registered trade mark of Oxford University Press
in the UK and in certain other countries

Published in the United States
by Oxford University Press Inc., New York

British Library Cataloguing in Publication Data

Data available

Library of Congress Cataloging in Publication Data

Gardner, John (John B.)
Offences and defences: selected essays in the philosophy of criminal law / John
Gardner.
    p. cm.
Includes index.
ISBN 978-0-19-923935-1 (hardback)—ISBN 978-0-19-923936-8 (pbk.)
1. Criminal law—Philosophy. 2. Justification (Law) 3. Criminal
liability. 1. Title
K5018.G37 2007
345.001—dc22   2007034284

Typeset by Newgen Imaging Systems (P) Ltd., Chennai, India
Printed in Great Britain
on acid-free paper by
Biddles Ltd., King's Lynn

ISBN 978-0-19-923935-1
ISBN 978-0-19-923936-8 (Pbk.)

1 3 5 7 9 10 8 6 4 2

In memory of
WRW Gardner 1924–2004

Preface

In this book I republish a selection (around half) of my 16 years of published writings on the philosophy of criminal law. The main criterion of selection was personal affection. In general, I stand by the omitted essays no less than by the included ones. But for a variety of reasons I have come to like the included ones more and the omitted ones less. The ones I like more are also, in my view, those that benefit most from being read together. They vary a bit in style but they share many themes. Instead of being sequenced chronologically, they are arranged here to bring out their thematic interrelations. So the book can be read, more or less, as a book. Each essay develops at least some ideas more cursorily introduced in the previous one.

Several of the essays in the book have been subject to extensive and formidable criticism. Although I have not had cause to disown any of the lines of thought assembled here, I have often been persuaded that I was guilty of oversight or overstatement. Yet in the preparation of this book, I have resisted the temptation to tamper or tinker. I have also opted not to adjust for any subsequent changes in the law. The essays appear here much as they originally appeared in print. I have limited myself to a few stylistic changes and some added cross-referencing in the footnotes. I have saved up discussion of objections and difficulties to the end of the book where I have included a reply to some of my critics. Those in search of a thematic overview might find this a good place to look.

I was lucky, as a graduate student in Oxford, to share my philosophical interests with many of my peers. As a BCL student, I benefited most from talking to Annalise Acorn, Tom Dimitroff, Timothy Macklem, and Alan Summers, all of whom helped to stir up in me an interest in problems of agency and responsibility as well as compounding my enthusiasm for intellectual pursuits in general. Later, when I was a DPhil student, Stephen Shute and Jeremy Horder became my closest academic collaborators. Shute, Horder and I were jointly and severally inspired, particularly by the innovative work of Antony Duff, to devote ourselves to the philosophical study of the criminal law. Our shared view was that the subject had been too dominated by anxieties about the justifiability of punishment. We often talked into the night about problems in the criminal law that were insufficiently visible to punishment theorists. We went on to convene an annual seminar series on the subject for later generations of BCL students, and to edit a book based on it. Many of the essays in the present volume, especially the ones from the 1990s, display the very powerful influence of Shute and Horder, two of the smartest legal thinkers that I have ever had the pleasure to know. The essays 'Rationality and the Rule of Law in Offences Against the Person' (Chapter 2) and 'The Gist of Excuses' (Chapter 6) were inspired by conversations with Jeremy Horder. 'The Wrongness of Rape' (Chapter 1), meanwhile, was co-written with Stephen Shute. I am very grateful to Steve for kindly permitting me to include this joint work here, as well as for numerous other acts of friendship.

Later, decamping from Oxford to King's College London, at the instigation of Andrew Ashworth and Ian Kennedy, I found myself happily reunited with Timothy Macklem. As well as teaching together, and undertaking home improvement works together, he and I embarked on various joint writing projects in the theory of value and the theory of rationality. My large debt to Macklem is evident in several of the papers that follow, especially those written from 1999 onwards. He pursues every question to a depth that would intimidate lesser scholars. He has often helped me to see how much more there is to uncover. The essay 'Complicity and Causality' (Chapter 3) bears all the hallmarks of Macklem's inspiration, even though there is much in it with which I am sure he disagrees. 'Provocation and Pluralism' (Chapter 8), meanwhile, was a co-authored piece first conceptualized by him rather than me. There are also a couple of paragraphs in the 'Reply to Critics' (Chapter 12) that are derived from one of our co-authored pieces. Many thanks to Tim for his characteristic generosity in letting me include this material here, as well as for doing so much to improve my thinking and being.

Many other friends and colleagues gave me the benefit of their comments on drafts or oral presentations of the essays that follow. Readers with the energy can go back to the originally published versions to see who exactly helped with what. But let me settle here for a consolidated list in alphabetical order: Andrew Ashworth, Michael Bratman, Jules Coleman, Antony Duff, Lindsay Farmer, Simon Gardner, Stephen Gough, Scott Hershovitz, Tony Honoré, Tatjana Hörnle, Barbara Hudson, Doug Husak, Nils Jareborg, Heike Jung, Sandy Kadish, Frances Kamm, Chris Kutz, Nicola Lacey, Grant Lamond, Derek Parfit, Joseph Raz, Paul Roberts, Samuel Scheffler, Scott Shapiro, Andrew Simester, Jonathan Simon, Michael Smith, Hamish Stewart, John Tasioulas, Stuart Toddington, Andrew von Hirsch, Jay Wallace, and Emma Young.

I would like to renew my gratitude to all these fine people, without whom I would have made even more and even worse mistakes. Thanks also to the many unlisted colleagues and students whose diverse questions and challenges helped me to make whatever progress I have made with the subject over the years.

John Gardner
1 May 2007

Acknowledgements

'The Wrongness of Rape' was co-written with Stephen Shute and is taken from J Horder (ed), *Oxford Essays in Jurisprudence, Fourth Series* (2000). It is reprinted with the kind permission of Stephen Shute.

'Rationality and the Rule of Law in Offences Against the Person' appeared in *Cambridge Law Journal* 53 (1994), 502, copyright © 1994 The Cambridge Law Journal and contributors. It is reprinted with the kind permission of The Cambridge Law Journal.

'Complicity and Causality', which started life as the Kadish Lecture 2004 at the University of California, Berkeley, was first published in *Criminal Law and Philosophy* 1 (2007), 127, copyright © 2006 Springer Science+Business Media BV. It is reprinted with the kind permission of Springer Science+Business Media.

'In Defence of Defences' first appeared in *Flores Juris et Legum: Festskrift till Nils Jareborg* (2002). It is reprinted courtesy of Iustus Förlag AB.

'Justifications and Reasons' is reprinted from A Simester and ATH Smith (eds), *Harm and Culpability* (1996).

'The Gist of Excuses' was first published in *Buffalo Criminal Law Review* 1 (1998), 575, copyright © 1998 The Regents of the University of California. It is reprinted with the kind permission of University of California Press.

'Fletcher on Offences and Defences' appeared in *Tulsa Law Review* 39 (2004), 817. It is reprinted courtesy of the Tulsa Law Review.

'Provocation and Pluralism' was co-written with Timothy Macklem and is drawn from *Modern Law Review* 64 (2001), 815, copyright © 2001 The Modern Law Review Limited. It is reprinted with the kind permission of Timothy Macklem and Blackwell Publishing (on behalf of the Modern Law Review).

'The Mark of Responsibility', my inaugural lecture in Oxford, first appeared in *Oxford Journal of Legal Studies* 23 (2003), 157, copyright © 2003 Oxford University Press. The version reprinted here, with an added postscript, is taken from M Dowdle (ed), *Public Accountability: Designs, Dilemmas and Experiences* (2006), postscript copyright © 2006 Cambridge University Press and used with permission.

'The Functions and Justifications of Criminal Law and Punishment' was previously available only in German, in B Schünemann, A von Hirsch and N Jareborg (eds), *Positive Generalprävention: Kritische Analysen im Deutsch-Englischen Dialog* (1998), German version copyright © 1998 CF Mueller Verlag. It is translated and reused with permission.

'Crime: in Proportion and in Perspective' is reprinted from A Ashworth and M Wasik (eds), *Fundamentals of Sentencing Theory* (1998).

'Reply to Critics' is previously unpublished but includes some material adapted from J Gardner and T Macklem, 'No Provocation Without Responsibility: A Reply to Mackay and Mitchell', *Criminal Law Review* [2004], 213. It is adapted courtesy of Timothy Macklem and Thomson Publishing Services (on behalf of Sweet & Maxwell Ltd).

Table of Contents

1

The Wrongness of Rape

1. Philosophizing rape

That rape is wrong, and seriously wrong at that, can scarcely be doubted. Arguably, rape is among those wrongs which are never excusable. Probably, it is among those wrongs which are never justifiable. Certainly, it is among those wrongs which ought to be forbidden and punished by the criminal law. Joel Feinberg is right to place it on his short list of wrongs which are crimes 'everywhere in the civilised world' and the decriminalization of which 'no reasonable person could advocate.'[1]

In view of all this, one might expect it to be obvious to every reasonable person *what* is wrong with rape. Many writers and commentators, including Feinberg, seem to imagine that this is indeed obvious, and do not give the question detailed attention. Some writers, for example, just take rape as a settled paradigm of wrongdoing in need of no explanation, and work towards the conclusion that certain other actions are wrong simply by pointing out their resemblance to rape. But unless we know what exactly is wrong with rape, how do we know whether such a resemblance is resemblance in a relevant respect—that is to say, in a respect which makes the rape-resembling action wrong too? Other writers concentrate on difficult test cases which seem to lie at or near the borderline of rape. Of a fascinating and burgeoning recent philosophical literature on rape, a very large proportion has been concerned with tricky issues about the precise demarcations of consent in rape, or the difficulties of relying on the concept of consent to settle particular classes of case (e.g. those involving false promises or emotional blackmail on the part of the alleged rapist).[2] Even if it were plausible to think that good philosophy

---

[1] Feinberg, *Harm to Others* (1984), 10.

[2] For example, D Archard, *Sexual Consent* (1998), 130ff. Likewise, most of the contributions to the two special issues on 'Sex and Consent' in *Legal Theory* 2 (1996). Another recent substantial philosophical contribution—K Burgess-Jackson's *Rape: A Philosophical*

could remove borderline cases of rape (or borderline cases of anything else) from their borderline—and that is very doubtful—it seems odd that anyone would try to settle such cases by studying the moral logic of consent without giving detailed thought to the prior questions of whether and why consent matters to rape in the first place. And that depends, of course, on what exactly is wrong with rape.

One can understand, of course, why there might be some reluctance to tackle this last question as a purely philosophical puzzle. Might a philosopher, starting from the professional presumption that nothing is quite as obvious as it appears, seem to be doubting that rape is wrong at all, or at any rate casting doubt on its seriousness? Might a philosopher, for whom no aspect of a subject can ultimately be left unspoken if the subject is chosen for study, be guilty of serious insensitivity in taking up the study of unspeakable experiences? Let us not forget that some victims of rape have had unspeakable experiences.[3] Some, like Lucretia, may even come to regard their lives after rape as not worth living. It may be said that the proper way to make such experiences morally vivid, and to bring out their moral significance, is not through intellectual dissection, in which the horror is reduced to the clinical banality of its component parts. Shouldn't it instead be done through drama, poetry, sculpture, and other more purely expressive, as well as more effectively therapeutic, media? Or, at least through study of a less abstract kind, led perhaps by the attempts of those who have experienced being raped to bring their experiences to life? This anti-philosophical line of thought is compounded, for male philosophers, by the fact that the experiences in question are often held to be paradigmatically, and are certainly preponderantly, the experiences of women rather than those of men. The resulting sense that the experiences in question are not even ours to dissect may make the subject seem philosophically uncomfortable, not to say unsafe.

But even in the confession of these anxieties, one finds questionable philosophical assumptions. The most obvious is the assumed centrality

---

Investigation (1996)—tries to proceed with various definitional or borderline questions while deliberately equivocating about what is wrong with rape (see his remarks at 58).

[3] The word 'unspeakable' has been put to all sorts of uses by philosophers. Here it means what it commonly means, namely the property which something might have of being so appalling that at least some rational agents might not be able to bring themselves to speak of it. On the very closely connected concept of 'unthinkability', see H Frankfurt, 'Rationality and the Unthinkable' in Frankfurt, *The Importance of What We Care About* (1988).

of the *experience* of rape to an understanding of what makes rape wrong.[4] Consider, for example, Catharine MacKinnon's definition: 'Politically, I call it rape whenever a woman has sex and feels violated.'[5] Politically, maybe, but philosophically? Does the *feeling* of sexual violation capture what's wrong with rape? Or is it, rather, the violation itself? And if so, what counts as 'violation' in the relevant sense? We can see at once that a focus on consent alone doesn't tell us the answer. It doesn't tell us what is wrong with rape *in particular*. Many other acts which would be wrong in the absence of consent are perfectly innocent in the presence of consent— handshaking, for example, or stripping someone's wallpaper while they are out at work. Why should rape be regarded as a different wrong from, say, non-consensual handshaking? Why should it be a *separate* entry on Feinberg's short list of crimes which nobody should decriminalize? Consent doesn't give the answer, since many other wrongs prohibited by the criminal law, such as vandalism, theft, and assault, might equally be defined in terms of absence of consent. Why aren't these all handily collapsed into one crime of 'doing to another that to which they do not consent'? Why aren't they all just one and the same wrong? You may still think that the answer is obvious: rape is a worse violation than mere vandalism, theft, and assault. True enough. But in what respect, in what dimension, is rape worse? Wherein does its 'worseness' lie? What exactly, in other words, is wrong with rape?

2. Harmless rape as pure rape

The view that associates rape with feelings of violation is one of a larger family of views which make the wrongfulness of rape a function of the harmfulness of rape. Such views are represented daily in the media through accounts of the trauma of rape and the sense of insecurity or loss of trust which the experience of it generates. These are harms because they change someone's life for the worse. Some unpleasant episodes in our lives are, by contrast, harmless. There is the pain and discomfort of being under the (competent) dentist's drill, or the fleeting but intense irritation of reading an objectionable letter from some foolish bigmouth in my local newspaper. These examples of harmless pain and offence are not

---

[4] But cf JH Bogart, 'Reconsidering Rape: Rethinking the Conceptual Foundations of Rape Law', *Canadian Journal of Law and Jurisprudence* 8 (1995), 159, 168–170.

[5] MacKinnon, *Feminism Unmodified* (1987), 82.

intended to suggest that every pain or offence is necessarily harmless. The torturer uses pain to do a great deal of harm, often scarring his victims physically and psychologically, often breaking down his victims' sense of their own humanity, often forcing them into betrayals which undermine their lives. The buffoon who wields his smutty sense of humour around the office can be inflicting harm on the colleagues he offends by lessening their confidence, their self-esteem, or their sense of ease with their work and their working environment. In these examples the essential added feature on top of the pain or offence is the diminution of someone's prospects, the change for the worse in his or her life, which the pain or offence brings with it.[6] That prospective dimension is the dimension of harm, and the first place people normally look for the wrongfulness of rape is in this dimension.

In focusing on the harmfulness of rape, liberal-minded lawyers have tended to make common cause with many of their radical feminist critics. In the case of the former, the focus on harm is a natural consequence of the application of the liberal 'harm principle', which forbids the attaching of legal sanctions to wrongdoing except to the extent that this is necessary to prevent harm and proportionate to the harm thereby prevented. Meanwhile, many of their radical feminist critics, politicians to the end, have tended to urge not that the harm principle is mistaken but that the list of harms to which the law and its liberal-minded defenders are typically sensitive, in thinking of rape and other offences mainly perpetrated against women, is a myopic, not to say facile, one.[7] The focus is too narrowly on physical harms, or on harms with a medical diagnosis, and not enough on women's own experiences of rape—the way that a victim's life is changed *for her* by the fact of having been raped, or the way that women's lives are changed *for them* by the risk of being raped. No doubt these challenges to the narrow legalistic approach to harm have a great deal of merit. But they share with the views that they challenge a mistaken starting-point. The harm principle sets certain constraints on the legal proscription of wrongs, but it does not prevent the law from showing sensitivity to other features of those wrongs in defining or classifying them for legal purposes. It does not say that the only wrongfulness

---

[6] The main source of this view of the nature of harm is J Raz, 'Autonomy, Toleration and the Harm Principle' in R Gavison (ed), *Issues in Contemporary Legal Philosophy* (1987).

[7] See e.g. MacKinnon, *Feminism Unmodified*, above n 5, 166; Burgess-Jackson, *Rape: A Philosophical Investigation*, above n 2, 56–57.

legal systems may attend to lies in harmfulness.[8] The law may proscribe breach of contract (whether by making it actionable in the civil courts or punishable in the criminal courts) and when it does so it complies with the harm principle. Breaches of contract tend to do harm even when they do not specifically harm the plaintiff by losing her the advantage (if any) of the contract, because even under those circumstances they tend to erode the practice of maintaining reliable voluntary obligations, thereby harming everyone who has reason, or might come to have reason, to enter into such obligations. But breach of contract is wrongful because it is the breach of a voluntary obligation, not because of these various harms which accompany the breach (including the damage to the practice). Focusing on the harms tends to occlude the wrongfulness of the act itself.

The same holds for rape. It is possible, although unusual, for a rapist to do no harm. A victim may be forever oblivious to the fact that she was raped, if, say, she was drugged or drunk to the point of unconsciousness when the rape was committed, and the rapist wore a condom. To those who object that this is physiologically impossible—that the rape must involve damaging or painful force, which will inevitably bring it to light later—the answer is that this objection neglects the important fact that, as those who have drawn attention to the phenomenon of 'date-rape' have highlighted, one may be raped while sexually aroused, even while sexually aroused by the attentions of the rapist, and one may be sexually aroused, of course, while drunk or drugged. Then we have a victim of rape whose life is not changed for the worse, or at all, by the rape. She does not, in MacKinnon's phrase, 'feel violated'. She has no feelings about the incident, since she knows nothing of it. Indeed, the story has no prospective dimension for the victim, except possibly a hangover in the morning; otherwise the victim's life goes on exactly as before. Not even, for that matter, a prospective dimension for others, who might be put in fear of midnight rape by tales of soporific victims taken unawares. Remember—in our example the incident never comes to light at all. (Let's add, for complete insulation, that the rapist, who told no one of what he did, is run over by a bus as he leaves the house, and that this would have been no less likely to happen to him even if he had not perpetrated the rape, since that didn't either delay or precipitate his leaving. So the rape doesn't even make a difference to *his* prospects.)

---

[8] See further S Shute and J Horder, 'Thieving and Deceiving: What is the Difference?', *Modern Law Review* 56 (1993), 548.

It is no objection that the question of the wrongfulness of this rape will never arise in any practical deliberation, such as the deliberation of a court, since *ex hypothesi* the rape will never come to light. Acts which never come to light are not rendered innocent by that fact alone. So one is left with the question of what is wrong with this particular rape. Its wrongfulness cannot lie in its harmfulness. For it does no harm. *Ex hypothesi* nobody's prospects are diminished, or indeed affected at all, by the rape. Yet this atypical, but absolutely unequivocal, feature does not make any difference to the rape's being wrongful.

There are various ways to sideline the example, to regard its atypicality as making it philosophically hazardous to rely upon it. After all, doubts were already raised above about the difference that philosophical argument can make at the borderline. Isn't this just another borderline case? Not so. On the contrary, the case is, in the sense which matters here, the central case of rape. For it is the *pure* case, entirely stripped of distracting epiphenomena. In more typical cases, rape is of course harmful. Much of the harm is typically harm to the victim, and sometimes, as already mentioned, unspeakable harm. Some of it may be physical injury, but apart from that kind of injury any harm to the victim depends on the victim's evaluations of what has been done to her.[9] She may be traumatized, lose her trust in men, be deprived of her sense of her own security, suffer from a reduction in her self-esteem, feel humiliated and/or dirty, etc. All these reactions depend on the victim's own evaluation of her ordeal. Are we to regard all these evaluation-dependent harms as reflecting the victim's irrationality, her superstition, her oversensitivity, etc.? Are we to think of them as mere manifestations of her weakness?[10] Barring exceptional pathological cases, no. To avoid the consequence that these are irrational reactions on the victim's part, one must explain what it is about the act of rape that gave the victim a reason to react this way. If nothing was wrong with being raped apart from the fact that one reacted badly

---

[9] Psychiatric injury may be a borderline case. Arguably it is harm *to* the victim's evaluative powers rather than harm depending on her evaluations. This is not the place to explore this point.

[10] One reaction to this question may be to ask why irrationality is assumed to be a weakness. One strand in academic feminism, sympathetically critiqued in G Lloyd's *The Man of Reason* (1984), regards rationality itself—not just the following of particular reasons but the very idea of following reasons—as a 'male norm', and therefore questions whether the expectation that women should meet it isn't itself an element of patriarchal oppression. This strand of feminism should be resisted. The claim that women's reactions should not be judged by the simplest canon of rationality (i.e. should not be judged according to whether women have sufficient valid reasons for reacting as they do) plays straight into the hands of misogynists, and indeed rapists. See n 36 below for further explanation.

afterwards, then one had no reason to react badly afterwards. So such reactions, to be rational, must be epiphenomenal, in the sense that they cannot constitute, but must shadow, the basic, or essential, wrongness of rape. This is not to deny that these reactions may count as grossly aggravating factors. There can be no doubt that a rape is made worse, perhaps immeasurably worse, by the humiliation of its victim, by the fact that she blames herself, etc. It is also true that the rapist is more of a moral monster if he sets out to humiliate, or callously adds to his victim's suffering by playing on her worst fears, etc. The point is only that what these (actual or intended) harms aggravate is the wrongfulness of rape, a wrongfulness which remains even in the absence of these harms. The alternative view, that these harms are what make rape wrong, turns the victim of rape, in a way, into a victim twice over: for she is now, in her reactions to the rape, additionally a victim of irrationality, a pathological case. She has no reason to react the way she does since, absent that reaction, she was not wronged by the rapist. Here is the basic philosophical objection to MacKinnon's (admittedly 'political') proposal that rape occurs 'whenever a woman has sex and feels violated'. *Pace* MacKinnon, the victim's feeling of violation must be epiphenomenal to rape, or else there is nothing in rape to give her cause to feel violated. Presumably what there is in rape to give her cause to feel violated is the fact that, in some special way, she was violated by the rapist. And the crucial problem is to identify wherein exactly that violation lies, and hence to explain the (evaluation-dependent) harmful consequences of rape by first explaining what, exactly, is wrong with rape.

So the case of the utterly harmless rape—perpetrated on a sexually aroused but somatic victim and leaving no trace on her memory or her body (or indeed any other trace)—is the pure case because it strips out the epiphenomena. It strips out not only the physical injuries but also the victim's evaluation-dependent reactions to the rape. It is rape pure and simple. Those who accept the purity of the case, and hence the need to rehabilitate it into the centre of the moral terrain of rape even as it languishes at the statistical periphery, may feel moved to try adjusting their account of harm to include it. They may feel moved to devise a way in which the victim of our supposedly harmless rape is harmed after all, perhaps in the mere fact of her violation.[11] As a violated woman, some might say, she is somehow now a less than perfect specimen. The harm is

---

[11] Bogart speaks of this violation as a 'formal' or 'abstract' harm. This idea is obscure. See Bogart, 'Reconsidering Rape', above n 4, 170 and 173. Similarly, HE Baber, 'How Bad is Rape?' *Hypatia* 2 (1987), 125.

that she has been defiled. This conclusion, and indeed the urge to move towards it, has sinister affinity with older, and one hopes long since discredited, views of female sexuality. The talk here—it is not?—is of fallen women. But beyond that moral question mark which hangs over the search for a harm in the pure case, there lies the question of what would be the *gain* in adjusting one's account of harm to transform this into a harmful rape. Why would one want this pure and simple rape to be accredited as harmful? Some might say that only in this way can the pure case pass through the filter of the liberal harm principle. It is a mistake to think that the liberal harm principle excludes legal prohibition of rape in the pure case, and we will return to this point towards the end of this essay. But in any case, the question of whether a certain wrong can properly be prohibited by law is a secondary question. One should not baulk at the possibility that there could be wrongs which are in general open to legal prohibition, but some morally significant instances of which cannot legitimately be prohibited by law. In such cases the moral considerations which bear on the wrongness of the action apart from the law do support legal prohibition, but additional moral considerations of an institutional character—including the harm principle—preclude prohibition as a legitimate means of eradicating the wrong. Perhaps, then, the pure case of rape is bound to be legally marginal. In fact, that is what one might expect, given that (*ex hypothesi*) the rape in this case is never detected and never prosecuted. For the law to focus on it might well be regarded as fatuous. But be it ever so legally marginal, the pure case as sketched above remains morally central, for the reasons given above. The alternative is to dismiss the outraged victims of more typical rapes as suffering pathological reactions. This suggestion adds insult to injury. The wrongfulness of rape cannot, therefore, lie in the harmfulness of rape.

3. Infringing the proprietor's rights

One can say, of course, that the wrongfulness of rape lies in the violation of its victim's rights. But which rights? Let's say, for a start, her right not to be raped. Since the victim has a right not to be raped if and only if raping her wrongs her, this introduction of the category of a right doesn't take us much further. It does have the virtue of introducing the thought that rape is not only a wrong but a wrong *against the person raped*, which means that it is based on her interest. That seems correct. But we are still left with the question of which interest of hers it is based on. And that question, it could be said, still represents little advance over the question with which we started, namely the question of what is wrong with rape. Phrasing the question in terms of rights and interests does, however, prompt a certain kind of more helpful, although nevertheless mistaken, reply to our original question. The wrongness of rape, according to this reply, comes of the fact that the victim of rape has a proprietary interest in, and derived from that a proprietary right over, her own body. It is her body, she owns it, nobody else may use it without her say-so. Rape is none other than the non-consensual 'borrowing of sexual organs'.[12] So the right not to be raped is, at base, a property right or an aspect of a property right.

What is our interest in property? Only some brief remarks are possible here. Those who focus on productivity are, fundamentally, on the right track—so long as 'productivity' is construed widely enough to include the provision of shelter, security, comfort, amusement, and other benefits to the property holder. The importance of property lies basically in the valuable things we can do with that property that we can't so easily do without it. This can be called its *use-value*.[13] Aspects of property rights, other than the right to use property, are basically derivative of the use-value of property. The value of being able to acquire and transfer property, for example, is basically the value of the property ending up where it can best be used. In conditions of global and indiscriminate abundance, property rights may lose their basic moral purchase, because in these conditions everyone has more than they can use. The question of whether something could best be used by a person other than the person who holds it is less prone to arise, for there is always plenty left to go round. But in times of scarcity or of merely local or discriminate

---

[12] GA Cohen, *Self-Ownership, Freedom and Equality* (1995), 244. Cohen comments that one may believe in ownership of the body while conceding that property rights might not provide the *whole* explanation of rape's wrongness. Nevertheless, his definition of rape as a 'borrowing' is as purely proprietarian a definition as one could conceive. For less equivocal renderings of the proprietarian approach, see G Calabresi and A Douglas Melamed, 'Property Rules, Liability Rules, and Inalienability: One View of the Cathedral', *Harvard Law Review* 85 (1972), 1089 at 1124–1127; or else DA Dripps, 'Beyond Rape: An Essay on the Difference between the Presence of Force and the Absence of Consent', *Columbia Law Review* 92 (1992), 1780.

[13] The mistake in many productivity accounts of the value of property holding is to focus too narrowly on *further* productivity (i.e. the use of things with use-value for the production of *other* things with use-value). This mistake lies at the heart of both Marx's and Locke's so-called 'labour theories' of property value, on the comparison of which see Cohen, *Self-Ownership, Freedom and Equality*, above n 12, 165–194.

abundance (i.e. abundance from which some are excluded, leaving them in conditions of scarcity), the question is always live: could this thing be better used by someone else? The idea of a property right to such things is that, up to a point, the question of where something is better used can least wastefully be settled by leaving the question to the person who already holds the thing. This means that, again up to a point, people are left free to hold property that they do not use. It is still theirs and cannot be taken without their say-so.[14] If others were to take it away from them this might yield a better use for it, but the suboptimal use of a particular thing is justified, up to a point, by the general gains in use-value that are made from a co-ordinating system based on consensual transactions.

Up to a point. But the question on everybody's lips is: up to which point? In the long history of property rights the point has been located in different places by different civilizations and regimes. Some things have been regarded at some times and in some places as incapable of being subject to property rights, or incapable of being subject to certain kinds of strong property rights such as ownership. The tendency to wasteful-ness by property holders, their refusal to let things be put to their best use, has often been regarded (no doubt sometimes rightly) as too high a price to pay for the avoidance of the costs associated with alternative methods of distribution and allocation. Some things, the value of which is basically their use-value, have therefore on occasions been taken out of a fully-fledged property regime. Thus, at some times and in some places, housing has been publicly provided for tenancy but not for ownership, TV stations or take-off slots at airports have not been capable of being owned, etc. Meanwhile, some things have been owned but with spe-cial regulation inhibiting their use and disposal, such as rent control legislation, restrictions on inheritance, rules against predatory pricing or monopolization, and official scrutiny of hostile takeovers. Since the basic value of property is instrumental, different policies and practices may serve that value more or less effectively at different times and places, depending on other prevailing conditions—for instance, the extent of

---

[14] Actually, the 'say-so' or consent condition is not a universally necessary element of respect for property rights. One can imagine a system in which things stay with the cur-rent holder unless complex bureaucratic measures are followed to secure a transfer. Even if these bureaucratic measures do not require the consent of the current holder, it is not misleading to regard this holding as a kind of property right. However, for simplicity, we can stick here to the familiar protective measure of requiring consent to transfers, which is common to most modern systems where the consideration mentioned in the next-but-one paragraph looms large.

the public tendency towards decadence, the sluggishness of competition, the degree of scarcity, or the extent of globalization.

However, one observation that may be made regarding large parts of the inhabited world today is that property rights are tending to campaign, in a sense, for their own augmentation and deregulation. The rise of public faith in property holding as a pat solution to the co-ordination problems associated with the use of things under conditions of scarcity, combined with people's increasing alienation from other human beings, leads people to attach great and ever-growing symbolic importance to the acquisition and holding of property. Increasingly, they come to identify with at least some things they hold as extensions of themselves, tokens of their own personality. The idea of 'sentimental value' has always highlighted this aspect of property holding. But it extends nowadays to much else besides the inherited keepsakes of the past or the gifts of friends and family. In fact, it is increasingly associated more with self-chosen than with other-chosen things. Insofar as people regard themselves as autonomous beings, their own choice of property—which house to buy, which ties to wear, which CDs to collect—has an ever more important place in their self-expression. The result is the cultural condition which has come to be known as 'consumerism'. No doubt it has got wildly out of hand. But up to a point—and again the point cannot be settled out of local context—consumerism does effect the moral change which its participants seem to presuppose. They regard property as meaning more, as carrying more significance, than just the significance imported by its use-value. Their regarding it as carrying that significance actually endows it with that significance by changing its social meaning. People are increasingly *identifying* with what they have. So on top of its basic use-value, much more of what people hold now has what we might call *identification-value*. When property is taken away without the proper consensual process, it is not merely (or even) that the system of optimal use-value is disrupted. It is that people are metaphorically violated by the removal of a part of their extended selves.

Some think that identification-value, and particularly the value which comes of investing autonomous choice in property, suffices on its own to explain why property rights continue to reside in those who make suboptimal use of their property. But property rights can persist even when use-value and identification-value are *both* missing. Consider what might be regarded as the pure case of burglary. Suppose an estate agent who has keys to my house lets himself in while I am on holiday and takes a pile of my old clothes from the attic, passing them on to a charity shop. I had long since forgotten that the clothes were there, and I had no further use, anyway, for loon pants and kipper ties. The burglary goes forever undiscovered. (The estate agent, who told nobody of what he was doing, falls under a bus as he leaves the charity shop, as he would have done anyway even if my clothes had not been among those he delivered.) Yet my property right is violated. Why is this? After all, I have no interest in these old long-forgotten clothes that comes of *either* my use of them *or* my identification with them. But on top of that, as already indicated, there is the co-ordinating value of property rights in securing use-value and identification-value *at large* (i.e. for people in general). My having this property right over my old clothes, which is violated by the intruding estate agent, does not come of any use-value or identification-value *to me* but of the contribution which my having such a property right makes to the perpetuation of a *system* of optimal use-value coupled, so far as possible, with optimal identification-value. So I have an interest in this property which is basically derivative of the public interest in my having such an interest. We could call this the pure case for the same reason that we called the pure case of rape the pure case. It is the case of the wrong and nothing but the wrong.

The analogies between rape and burglary here are startling, and may seem to support the idea that rape is wrong because we own our own bodies. But in fact the above remarks tend to undermine this view. Neither the use-value nor the identification-value which support our proprietorial relations with things can apply straightforwardly to our relationship with our own bodies. We will come to the use-value in the next section ('4. Use and abuse'). But the main point can be seen through the lens of the identification-value. The identification-value of property holding is the symbolic value of artificially extending oneself out into the world. But regarding our bodies, there is no question of such an artificial self-extension. There is a long-standing tradition in Western philosophy which diminishes the centrality of the body. The body becomes something like an arbitrary receptacle in which the real business of human life—that special inner thing called 'the self'—just happens to live.[15] This is a barely intelligible view. People are, in part, their bodies and their relationship with their bodies cannot, barring strange pathological cases (schizophrenia?) or conceptually testing science fiction (brains in vats?),

---

[15] This is the Cartesian tradition. But notice that one could follow Descartes's famous 'dualist' views about the *relations* between mind and body without adding that the body is the inferior partner. For two self-styled 'Cartesian friends of the body' taking this line, see the exchange between S Shoemaker and G Strawson under the title 'Self and Body' in *Proceedings of the Aritotelian Society (Supp Vol)* 73 (1999), 287.

be that of artificial self-extension. The embodied self is not the extended self; in the distinction between self and world the body already belongs to the 'self' side without any need for, or possibility of, self-extension into it. It is true that one may play with the boundaries of the body, deliberately blurring the line between the self and its extension into the world. Some kinds of body-piercing and tattooing fit this profile. They are ways of expressing a kind of continuity between self and world which can, under certain cultural conditions, be a symbol of rank or alternatively a symbol of individuality and even rebellion. But these boundary-blurring practices, and others, presuppose that the body is already part of the self and cannot, again barring pathological conditions or sci-fi fantasies, be alienated from it. It is not merely that the self cannot survive outside it, like a patient who cannot live without an artificial lung. It is that without the body there is no complete self to survive.

Some people nowadays say that the experience of being burgled was like that of being raped. Others may well resent this suggestion: have the people in question ever actually been raped? If not, how do they know that the experience of burglary was like the experience of rape? The answer lies in the way in which property rights, particularly under modern conditions, and particularly in the immediate living environment, operate as self-extensions. Even someone who has not been raped but whose house has been burgled, may experience a kind of violation of the self, because they understood their home as a projection of their identity, a kind of larger, more artificial body. The mistake comes in when one tries to reverse the analogy, when one tries to think of one's body as a kind of smaller, more natural house.[16] Anyone who had been raped and said it was like being burgled would be committing a serious travesty. It would show extraordinary moral insensitivity. This is not, or at any rate not merely, because they would be diminishing or trivializing their rape. It is primarily because property rights are necessarily the derivative or shadow case. One can analogize what happens to what one owns to what happens to oneself, because what one owns can be an extension of oneself. But one cannot in the same way analogize what happens to oneself to what happens to what one owns, because oneself cannot be an addition to what one owns. This is the first and major flaw in all self-ownership doctrines, including but not restricted to those that focus on ownership of one's own body. They render one's relationship to oneself

---

[16] The mistake is made, we think, by M Davis in 'Setting Penalties: What Does Rape Deserve?', *Law and Philosophy* 3 (1984), 61 at 78.

contingent in such a way that there is no longer any self to do any own-
ing, of itself or of anything else.

4. Use and abuse

One consequence of the modern philosopher's alienation of the body
from the self, is to sever the value of the body from the value of the self.
The body, like other tools and receptacles and artefacts, is basically use-
valuable, its use-value augmented, in some cases, by the expressive value
of the inhabiting self's contingent identification with it. Once the intelligibility of this latter expressive value is called in question, a question
mark also appears above the idea that the body's value is mainly its use-
value. Use-value for whom? Who is the user? The possibilities are self or
others. If the body is part of the self, then the idea that it is *used* by the self
becomes harder to understand.[17] At any rate that cannot be its most basic
value. In very rough terms, the explanation goes something like this.
Use-value is value for people. Why should what is valuable for people be
valuable *tout court*? The ultimate answer, although it may take a number
of precise forms, cannot but include the premiss that people are valuable.
To avoid vicious circularity, this further value cannot be use-value. So people
may have their use-value, perhaps, but that cannot be the only, nor the most
ultimate, value they have. To use people without at the same time respecting
this further non-use value involves treating them as something other than
people. It means treating them as things. In principle, this applies as much to
the use of the self as to the use of others. And because the (living) body is part of
the self, part of the person, it applies equally to the use of (living) bodies.[18]
   The most famous articulation of this argument is Kant's. In simple
terms it shows that there is no value in objects unless there is some more
ultimate value in subjects. It shows, therefore, that those who would tie
the wrongness of rape to ownership of one's own body not only miss, but
positively invert, the basic element of rape's wrongness. The value of the
body becomes, in this view, basically its use-value. So what is the rapist

---

[17] This consideration is also at the basis of the account of rape's wrongness offered
by CM Shafer and M Frye, in their classic paper 'Rape and Respect' in M Vetterlin-
Braggin, F Elliston, and Jane English (eds), *Feminism and Philosophy* (1977), 333 at 337.
Our position mirrors that of Shafer and Frye in many respects, but not in all. For the most
important divergence, see below n 22 and accompanying text.
[18] 'Living' is in parentheses so as not to prejudge the interesting question of whether
it can ever be demeaning, on the same grounds, to use someone's body after his or her
death.

doing wrong, in our pure case of rape, when he uses someone else's body for sexual pleasure? The answer may be that it is not his to use. But this answer, in a way, plays into the rapist's hands. It makes it intelligible for him to respond with the objection that he can make better use of this unconscious body than can the person whose body it is. After all, he is only harmlessly borrowing this body, or some of its components, while its regular user is not using it, or not using those components. Relative to that alternative non-use, this use optimizes use-value. On the proprietarian model one can resist this as a final answer by observing that owners still get to decide even when they decide against optimal use. Remember the clothes in the attic. But this resistance concedes to the rapist too much of the moral high ground. It concedes to him that in principle the body of a person is there to be used. This is a kind of use of a person, a kind of *objectification* of a subject. That a rapist objectifies his victim by treating her as a mere repository of use-value is what is basically wrong with rape. In making arguments which ultimately rest on the sheer use-value of people and their bodies, the proprietarian approach not only fails to make sense of the wrongness of rape; it actually gives succour to rapists.

The claim that certain practices objectify women lies, as is well known, at the heart of Catharine MacKinnon's and Andrea Dworkin's joint critique of pornography. The critique has been subjected to searching philosophical study by Martha Nussbaum.[19] As Nussbaum shows, 'objectification' is a term which, in the work of MacKinnon and Dworkin, tends to equivocate between a cluster of related ideas:

(1) the conversion of subjects into instruments or tools;
(2) the denial of subjects' autonomy;
(3) treating subjects as inert or inactive;
(4) treating subjects as fungible (i.e. interchangeable with other subjects or objects);
(5) breaking into subjects or breaking down the boundaries between subjects;
(6) asserting ownership over subjects; and
(7) refusing to regard subjects as beings with their own feelings and experiences (i.e. as subjective).

While Nussbaum agrees that categories 2 to 7 can have their moral moment in the debate about sexual representation, she stresses category 1 (instrumentalization) as the crucial entry on the list, the one that best captures what

---

[19] Nussbaum, 'Objectification', *Philosophy and Public Affairs* 24 (1995), 249.

objectification must be if it is to be generally objectionable.[20] That seems right. One should merely add that category 1 is closely bound up with category 6 (ownership), and that those who base arguments against objectification on ownership or other property relations, including those who assert inalienable self-ownership, encourage instrumentalization.

The extension of this 'objectification' argument from pornography to rape helps to bring out what some feminists are getting at when they claim that pornography is bound up with rape irrespective of whether the consumption of pornography makes any causal contribution to the incidence of rape.[21] For present purposes, however, the main importance of the 'objectification' argument lies in the way that it begins to differentiate rape, or at any rate the pure case of rape, from other paradigms of criminal wrong, including paradigms of non-sexual criminal violence. There are interesting and no less problematic questions about what is wrong with murder, or with common assault, or with kidnapping, or with torture, or with threatening to kill, or with blackmail, etc. All are wrong in different ways, by virtue of different lines of argument. Arguably, the wrongness of at least some of these wrongs is fully explicable only by invoking the Kantian argument somewhere along the line. But none of these wrongs instantiates the central moral importance of the Kantian argument so clearly and unequivocally as rape. Rape, in the pure case, is the sheer use of a person. In less pure, but statistically more typical cases, this use is accompanied by violence, terror, humiliation, etc. The important point is that when someone feels terrified or humiliated by rape itself this feeling is justified. Rape is terrifying and humiliating even when unaccompanied by further affronts, because the sheer use of a person, and in that sense the objectification of a person, is a denial of their personhood. It is literally dehumanizing.

5. Delimiting rape

So all sheer use of human beings, all treatment of them merely as means, is *ab*use; and rape is the central case of such abuse. This is the line of

---

[20] 'Objectification', above n 19, 265.
[21] This is one sympathetic way to interpret A Dworkin's remark in *Pornography: Men Possessing Women* (1979), 137, that 'a rape [is] repeated each time the viewer consumes the [pornographic] photographs'. For more study of the point, see D Cameron and E Fraser, 'On the Question of Pornography and Sexual Violence: Moving Beyond Cause and Effect' in C Itzin, *Pornography: Women, Violence and Civil Liberties* (1992).

thought that generates the basic distinction between rape and (most) non-sexual offences against the person (as well as some sexual offences). But does it fix, even approximately, the boundaries of rape? Does it help to explain the modern focus on *lack of consent* as the touchstone of rape? Does it help us to establish the focus on *penetrative* sexual abuse (or certain forms of penetrative sexual abuse) which is still typical of the law of rape in most jurisdictions which have retained the offence separately? And does this line of thought help us to settle how *mistakes* as to consent should be dealt with by the law of rape? Let's look at each of these familiar problems in turn.

(a) Lack of consent At the deepest level, the Kantian argument echoed above does not distinguish between use by self and use by others. It resists the objectification of subjects either by those subjects or by other subjects. In other words, the evil in question is *agent-neutral*: it consists in the use of people as a mere means, irrespective of which people are doing the using. So at the deepest level, the Kantian argument makes no exception for self-abuse. *A fortiori* it makes no exception for self-licensed abuse by others. How, then, can consent make all the difference between the paradigmatic use of a person (rape) and the paradigmatic treating of a person as a person which is the opposite of that use (sexual intercourse)? One suggestion is that only a subject can consent, and so, by being astute to another's consent, someone who has sexual intercourse with that other is not treating that other any more *merely* as a means, and hence is not objectifying her.[22] She may be treating herself as a mere means, but then again she is not the one accused of rape. This suggestion makes *astuteness to consent* of the essence. But in most familiar legal systems the first question about consent in a rape trial is not: was the accused astute to the complainant's consent? The first question is: did she actually consent? Only if the answer is 'no' does the further question arise (depending on the mens rea requirements for rape in that legal system) of how astute the accused was to whether the complainant consented. One may say that this is an institutional oddity, that the explanation lies in some technical consideration about the criminal process or the structure of criminal offences. But in fact it goes deeper.

If the argument from astuteness worked to show how consent comes to be pivotal in rape, it would do so only at the price of eliminating the

---

[22] This is roughly the line taken by Shafer and Frye in 'Rape and Respect', above n 17, and here we have the main point at which the position in this essay diverges from theirs.

accusation of objectification against consent-astute users of consenting subjects, including many clients of prostitutes and many consumers of pornography. To put the point crudely, it would deflect blame from clients to prostitutes, and from consumers of pornography to those appearing in it. Consenting prostitutes and pornographic performers would be objectifying themselves (objectionable), while their clients and consumers, assuming the latter were astute to the presence of consent, would be treating them as subjects (unobjectionable). This conclusion lets clients of prostitutes and users of pornography slip too easily off the moral hook.

Two obvious ways of avoiding the conclusion have often been favoured by those who want to keep that moral hook in place, both of which have been adduced from time to time by MacKinnon and Dworkin. One way to keep the moral hook in place is to deny that the consent of workers in the sex industry is genuine. In denying that this kind of consent is genuine, one may point to some other objectifier in the background—a pimp or a pornographer, say, or an insidious sex industry system, or indeed an insidious *sex* system—to mitigate the accusation of self-objectification against the prostitute or model. She was coerced or manipulated or exploited into submission by that other objectifier, and the client or consumer is complicitous because he is astute only to that submission, and not to any genuine consent.[23] This line of argument carries serious risks, not least the risk that one ultimately ends up accusing those prostitutes or models who *claim* to be genuinely consenting as suffering from a false consciousness, and hence as less than fully functional moral agents who can speak for themselves, and hence as not fully human. In other words, one risks objectifying sex industry workers oneself in order to make it seem to be the case that they are objectified by their consumers and clients and other participants in their industry. To avoid such risks one may alternatively regard the consent of women who participate in the sex industry as genuine, and hence as capable of forestalling the accusation that these women were *personally* objectified by their clients and consumers, while holding that women *in general* were objectified by being represented in that way.[24] This introduces Nussbaum's category 4 (fungibility) into the story, and requires us to show that the sex industry puts

---

[23] R West, 'A Comment on Sex, Consent and Rape', *Legal Theory* 2 (1996), 232 at 242; MacKinnon, *Feminism Unmodified*, above n 5, 179–183; Dworkin, *Pornography: Men Possessing Women*, above n 21, 207.

[24] MacKinnon, *Feminism Unmodified*, above n5, 170–174; Dworkin, *Pornography: Men Possessing Women*, above n21, 224.

every woman, and not only the women who work in it, under prurient, instrumentalizing gaze. This may well be so, but the objectification element in the use of pornography or the resort to prostitutes does not depend on it. Nor does one need to show that women in the sex industry are not genuinely consenting in order to keep their clients and consumers on the moral hook. For the fact that women working in the sex industry may give their genuine and effective consent, and even the astuteness of their clients and consumers to that consent, does not make it the case that they are not being personally objectified in the relevant sense by their clients and consumers.

On the contrary, such sex industry workers typically are being objectified by their clients and consumers, and this is indeed an attack on their humanity. They are being used purely for sexual gratification. But the sex workers' right to sexual autonomy, where their consent is genuine, serves to license the abuse.[25] The argument for drawing the line at consent is roughly the same regarding the right to sexual autonomy as it is regarding property rights. With property rights the argument was that even if, regarding a particular piece of property, use-value was in suboptimal combination with identification-value, the value of having a system in which people control by consent the uses of their own property optimally co-ordinates, within limits, the pursuit of use-value and identification-value. With the right to sexual autonomy the argument is that even if, in a particular sexual encounter, the ultimate value of a person was denied (i.e. that person was used merely as a means), the value of having a system of sexual relations in which people control by consent the treatment of their own bodies secures optimally respect for the ultimate value of people. An obvious objection to this argument is that it depends on a contingency, namely the contingency of whether people generally grant their consent wisely (i.e. in ways that do not constitute self-abuse). The proliferation and permeation of sex industry values in, for example, mainstream advertising, may seem to show that this assumption cannot be

---

[25] Thanks to some familiar practices of pimps and pornographers, it is likely that in many cases the consent is not freely given, in which case the considerations which follow do not apply. Nor of course do they apply to children. Our argument assumes only that sometimes consent is real enough and that on those occasions it matters. One reason, among many, why pimps and pornographers get away with practices that remove the reality of consent is that they inhabit a shady world of questionable legality in which employment protection, etc. cannot be guaranteed. This creates an extra instrumental argument against the criminalization of aspects of the sex industry. But this argument is distinct from, and supplementary to, the one pursued here.

upheld today. But it must be remembered that in constructing and honouring people's rights, those people must be given a certain kind of moral credit. By much the same argument which condemns rapists, those of us who are discussing, legislating, implementing, and enforcing people's rights must also regard them as people, as beings with value other than use-value. In particular, we must regard them as moral agents capable of understanding their own value and making up their own minds about their relationships with others. We must work on the assumption that they respect themselves or else we do not ourselves respect them. It follows that even when people betray that assumption they must enjoy some latitude to do so. They must have some moral space to go wrong and to permit others to go wrong with them.

This consideration is reinforced, in modern conditions, by the general value of personal autonomy which applies to all kinds of options, including but not restricted to sexual options, and pushes for avenues of experimentation to be opened up. But the value we have been learning about is not the value of personal autonomy. It is the distinct value of allowing particular kinds of options to be pursued, including various sexual options, which may at first sight appear dehumanizing. The truth is that these options often *are* dehumanizing, and therefore to be avoided by the person who is confronted with them. But allowing people nevertheless to pursue them is, up to a point, rehumanizing, because it credits them with moral agency, without which credit their dehumanization is only compounded. This rehumanizing value combines with the general value of personal autonomy to yield a right to sexual autonomy. Rape, understood in the modern way as non-consensual sexual intercourse, is a wrong against the person raped because it is a violation of this right.[26] The resort to prostitutes and the use of pornography is also wrong, because it objectifies the prostitute or model even when her consent is genuine. But when her consent is genuine such resort or use is not a violation of the prostitute's or model's right to sexual autonomy, and so not a wrong *against* the prostitute or model. Or at any rate it is not a wrong against the prostitute or model *under the same heading* as

---

[26] This right is structurally different from a property right in that, regarding this right, the consent condition cannot be replaced with a condition licensing non-consensual access by bureaucratic procedures, of the type which we suggested may be consistent with property rights in n 14 above. The marital rape exemption purported to do this—to by-pass the woman's say-so with a bureaucratic method for allocating sex—but it would be seriously misleading to present this as a protection of a married woman's rights, let alone her right to sexual autonomy. It was clearly a protection of a married man's rights against the sexual autonomy of his wife.

that under which rape is a wrong against its victim. For a person's consent is capable of licensing, in the name of sexual autonomy itself, some suboptimal sexual relationships, which in this case means depressingly dehumanizing relationships, relationships of objectification.[27]

(b) Penetration In many jurisdictions what counts as sexual intercourse for the purposes of the crime of rape is limited to (one or another kind of) penetrative violation. Why is penetration so special? Does it count as a special way of using another person? The natural answer, of course, is that it counts as an especially humiliating way of using them. But again the special humiliation seems epiphenomenal. There was no special humiliation in the pure case because there was no humiliation at all in the pure case: the rape was never discovered. If, in more everyday cases, penetrative violations *are* particularly humiliating (or terrifying, confidence-sapping, etc.) in the eyes of those who experience them, then as usual we want to know the reason why. Why do violations of *this* kind have such special import for those who suffer them? One might say, of course, that the law itself contributes something to the special significance of penetration by historically reserving the name of 'rape' for that class of violations. Certainly there is something in that: the historic legal names of some criminal offences have gathered moral import with age, and often do contribute to structuring people's moral thinking. The thinking is as follows: rape is (particularly) terrible; rape is non-consensual penetration; so non-consensual penetration is (particularly) terrible. But this cannot serve *by itself* to justify the law's maintaining its insistence on penetration. Perhaps the old focus on penetration was superstitious or corrupt and the modern law should now be doing its utmost to change the confused moral thinking which that old focus left in its wake. Some aspects of the law of rape or the practice of rape prosecution, such as the marital rape exemption and the institutional blindness to date-rape, as well as the accompanying interest in evidence of the victim's sexual

---

[27] You can see here where the right to sexual autonomy favoured here differs from the alternative 'right to sexual integrity' advanced by N Lacey in 'Unspeakable Subjects, Impossible Rights: Sexuality, Integrity and Criminal Law', *Canadian Journal of Law and Jurisprudence* 47 (1989), 47. The depressingly dehumanizing relationships we mentioned do not involve anything recognizable as integrity. They are self-betraying, and usually on both sides. Nevertheless, so long as there is mutual consent, those who engage in them have a right to do so under the heading of sexual autonomy. In spite of this disagreement, however, Lacey's paper has greatly influenced this essay. With the removal of unhappy Cartesian and Lockean overtones from the relevant idea of autonomy, the distance between us is considerably reduced.

history, are now widely acknowledged to have left a false trail, and hence a false understanding of rape, in public consciousness. Isn't the penetration condition, with its crude phallocentrism, in the same camp? Doesn't it hang over from an era of obsession with female virginity and overbearing preoccupation with the sin of bearing illegitimate children, an era in which women were *officially* regarded as objects (chattels of their fathers and husbands) rather than subjects? So shouldn't we dump this condition now? The answer is not quite so simple.

What is true is that the justification of the penetration condition in the modern law of rape does involve some attention to social meaning. Some associate the Kantian argument adopted above with a view of morality as a body of eternal verities which one abandons on pain of self-contradiction. In places, this was how Kant himself presented the applications of the argument. But in fact the applications of the argument depend on many contingencies, including the social meaning of many actions. Which actions count as paradigms of sheer use-and-abuse of human beings varies, even though the Kantian argument against the sheer use-and-abuse of human beings has enduring force. Often, the special symbolism of a particular act or class of acts is tied to the particular symbolism of acts which are regarded as their moral opposites. The special symbolism of penetrative violation is closely associated, in our culture, with the special symbolism of penetrative sexual activity. That latter symbolism may be over-romanticized. It may come of an aspiration to an impossible perfect union of two selves through two bodies, by making the two bodies, in a sense, just one (recall Shakespeare's 'beast with two backs'). Be that as it may, the fact that penetrative sex is regarded as having that significance actually endows it with that significance by changing its social meaning. The social meaning of the subversion of penetrative sex—its subversion in rape—tends to mirror the social meaning of penetrative sex. If the latter is thought of as a perfection of subject-subject relations—through the most complete and literal intertwining of selves—then the former may well come to represent a paradigm of subject-object relations. This is relevant to explaining and justifying the reactions even of those who do not share the aspiration to intertwine selves in this literal way (e.g. those who eschew or avoid penetrative sexual relationships, or those who see them as purely functional). The use of penetration can be a special weapon even against these people, perhaps *especially* against these people. It can become a peculiarly dramatic way of objectifying them, of turning them into mere things to be used, mere means to another's ends. That being so, there is reason for all those who suffer such violations to feel humiliated, whether or not they see particular value, or any value, in consensual penetrative sexual activity. The social meaning of consensual sexual penetration is not necessarily the meaning it has for them, and it is the social meaning of consensual sexual penetration which the rapist exploits by subverting it.

This is not a case against expanding the legal definition of rape to include some kinds of non-penetrative violations, or for discriminating among various kinds of penetration. In fact, it is not an argument for any particular legal definition of rape. It merely points out that the reactions of those who attach particular significance to penetrative violations, or to certain penetrative violations, need not be irrational. They may be supported by symbolic values. Much is left to law-makers and law-interpreters in deciding how best to embody and reflect such symbolic values in a given legal system. Social meanings are often ambiguous, and always have grey areas. Rarely do they set definite boundaries to moral wrongdoing without additional instrumental arguments, and instrumental argument also introduces many contingencies which can affect legal classifications. This was already revealed when we were discussing the 'lack of consent' requirement. The instrumental question of what system of sexual relations would lead to the least use-and-abuse of human beings was an element of the argument. No doubt similar instrumental issues arise in the case of the penetration condition. The point is that although the mere use of people is a timeless evil, the elevation of penetrative non-consensual sexual violation to the status of special paradigm is a long-standing, but culturally conditioned application.

These remarks on the importance of social meaning merit the attention of those who are uneasy about the tendency to associate rape with sex, and in particular the tendency to think of it as a 'sexual offence'. Many campaigners and social researchers tell us that rape typically has nothing to do with sexual desire, and everything to do with a male desire for power over women. Surely it should be regarded as a crime of misogynist aggression, a hate-crime, rather than a sexual offence? One should be uneasy about the essentialist view of sexual desire which this critique seems to harbour: why can't a misogynist desire to subordinate women be a sexual desire? (Is it because sex is wonderful and misogyny is vile?) But even if we grant the integrity of the assumed contrast between sexual desire and other kinds of desire, the main objection to this line of thought is that it assumes that 'sexual offences' are those offences which are differentiated by the offender's motivations. The real reason for thinking of rape as a sexual offence has nothing to do with the offender's motivations. It is that rape is a weapon against its victim which trades on the social meaning of sexual penetration. It is a way of taking a paradigm subject-subject relationship—a possibly over-romanticized conception of sexual intimacy—and turning it against someone to make a mere object of her.[28] This is perfectly compatible with the possibility and indeed may well suggest, that the perpetrator hates the victim, or what she represents. It is not necessary to deny the connection between rape and sex in order to make this clear. On the contrary, if the connection with sex is dropped and rape is simply labelled as, say, 'aggravated assault', then it seems that (for better or worse) we have decided no longer to recognize in law what is *particularly* wrong with rape. True, a rape can *accurately* be labelled as a kind of assault (as the police often label it when conducting their investigations) since the unifying theme of assault crimes is invasion by one of another's personal space, and the rapist clearly does invade his victim's personal space. But this is a wrong incidental to, and usually rather trivial when placed alongside, the most fundamental element of wrongdoing in rape. So the description of rape as an assault, though accurate, is reductive and unrevealing.[29] That most fundamental element of wrongdoing in rape, which differentiates rape from (most) assaults and gives rape a separate theme from the family of assault crimes, is the *sheer use* of the

[28] Contrast the approach taken by L Pineau in her 'Date Rape: A Feminist Analysis', *Law and Philosophy* 8 (1989), 217. Pineau argues that sex should be understood, paradigmatically, as 'ongoing communication', and sex outside this paradigm should be understood as presumptively rape. Here Pineau *endorses* a particular idealized view of sex, and hence becomes what we just labelled an 'essentialist'. The view defended here, by contrast, is not essentialist about sex. It only trades on the mere fact that an idealized view of sex—which we did not endorse and which indeed may not be endorsed very widely nowadays—nevertheless still colours the social meaning of various actions, including, most notably, actions which appropriate and subvert that ideal.

[29] Contrast M Davis, 'Setting Penalties: What Does Rape Deserve?', above n 16, 79. Davis's reduction of rape to assault relies not only on the fact that rape must (incidentally) involve assault, but also on the claim that all assault involves objectification. But that is not true. Someone who threateningly presses his face up to mine, or grabs me by the arm to get my attention (both paradigm assaults), doesn't, by these moves alone, treat me as an object. An object, after all, doesn't respond to intimidation or to attention-grabbing. The wrongness of assault is only very indirectly related to the Kantian considerations we adduced, which lie at the heart of the wrongness of rape. (Davis also errs in thinking that an objectification argument like ours must rely on the rapist *seeing* his victim as an object. It does not. It is about his *treating* her as an object, however he may see her. He may see women as vulnerable child-like creatures in need of a masterly knight in shining armour to protect them. This isn't seeing women as objects, but it is compatible with—and may well indeed be conducive to—treating them as such. That is one important lesson of the feminist critique of patriarchy: patriarchy is a *delusional* mode of oppression in which dehumanizing behaviour is often misconceived by its perpetrators as humanizing behaviour.)

person raped, whether that is how the rapist saw what he was doing or otherwise. To understand how rape counts as sheer use, the social meaning of sexual penetration has to be kept in focus.

Whatever the offender means by it, and indeed whatever it means to its victim, rape is a crime of sexual violation according to its social meaning; and that social meaning is the meaning which is at the heart of rape's wrongness. One may still insist that 'violence' would be a better word here than 'violation'. Wouldn't it at least have more political bite? It is doubtful whether even this is true. Assimilation of rape to the category of 'violent crime' in the media and in public discussion of crime has perhaps done more than almost anything else to maintain the public myth that rapists are strangers waiting in dark alleys who subdue their victims by force.[30] But rapists work by many more insidious methods than this and they still wrong their victims by non-consensual objectification of them. As the pure case of rape serves to remind us, and many more common kinds of case amply illustrate, the violation that is rape need not be associated with any kind of violence.[31] Nor are the worst rapes necessarily the most violent rapes. Rapes in breach of trust using subtle threats or surreptitiously administered drugs to forestall any resistance can, in some cases, represent an even more egregious abuse of the person raped and can therefore be worse *qua* rapes (and this still remains true whether or not these are the rapes that involve the worst experiences for the person raped[32]).

[30] In 'Coercion and Rape: The State as a Male Protection Racket' in *Feminism and Philosophy*, above n 17, 360 at 364, SR Peterson draws attention to a countervailing pragmatic consideration: classifying rape as a sexual offence may contribute to the shocking but still prevalent tendency to see a complainant's sexual history as relevant to the issue of consent, and indeed (even more outrageously) to the issue of her veracity on the issue of consent, in a rape trial. This problem of 'the second rape in the courtroom'—a rather apt metaphor, since such lines of questioning themselves make objectifying assumptions about female sexuality—should be addressed head-on, by making evidence of a complainant's sexual history inadmissible and by reforming and improving accessibility to the law of libel for those women who are represented in the press as 'asking for it'. Distorting the wrongness of rape to avoid the problem means throwing out the baby with the bathwater.

[31] Matters are made worse here by the confused assumption in much of the literature that assault is a crime of violence—so that, if rape is a kind of assault, then rape is by that token a crime of violence. See e.g. S Brownmiller, *Against Our Will* (1975), 377 or R West, 'A Comment on Sex, Consent and Rape', above n 23, 242. On the differences between assaults and crimes of violence, see J Gardner, 'Rationality and the Rule of Law in Offences Against the Person', *Cambridge Law Journal* 53 (1994), 502 (Chapter 2 in this volume).

[32] cf Alan Wertheimer, 'Consent and Sexual Relations', *Legal Theory* 2 (1996), 101, wherein the seriousness of a rape is regarded as a function of its harmfulness.

(c) Mistakes as to consent Academic criminal lawyers often worry about the correct response, in the law of rape, to misunderstandings regarding consent. Should the defendant in a rape trial be given the benefit of his genuine mistakes as to consent? Or are there other conditions which need to be satisfied before mistakes as to consent will exonerate? The basic answer has already been hinted at. The key is the astuteness of the defendant to consent.[33] For the reasons given above, being astute to consent is not a sufficient condition for avoiding the accusation of objectification. But it is nevertheless a necessary condition. Being astute to consent means not only paying attention to, but also taking seriously, the responses of another person to what one is doing to them. If one fails to pay attention to these responses or to take them seriously, it doesn't matter whether one's failure comes of malice, callousness, selfishness, misogyny, insensitivity, or sheer stupidity. Criminal lawyers, in rape trials and elsewhere, have a strange tendency to regard stupidity as exculpating rather than inculpating. But stupidity is a vice, not an excuse. Where risks are complex, some degrees of obliviousness to them may, of course, be excusable. It all depends on how much sophistication can reasonably be expected of human beings in general, without special expertise. But the risk that one is using another human being by sexual violation of them without their consent is not complex, does not call for special expertise, and attention to it can reasonably be expected of all adult human beings unless they are seriously mentally ill. That is why, as suggested at the outset, rape is arguably inexcusable.[34] Barring serious mental illness, if one is not paying attention to the consensuality of some sexual activity one is embarking on, then it is not hyperbolic to regard one as morally beyond the pale—an animal, as the tabloids might put it. Likewise, if one is paying attention but, as in the famous *Morgan* case, one concludes or assumes that the protestations of one's victim are not to be taken seriously.[35] The *Morgan* defendants were animals *par excellence*. For, however they saw it themselves, they treated their sexual 'conquest' as something less than a subject, as something less than a self-respecting human being

---

[33] See text at n 22 above.
[34] Serious mental illness is not an excuse. It eliminates the mentally ill person's responsibility for (some or all of) her actions and this means that there can be no requirement, and no possibility, for those actions to be justified or excused.
[35] *DPP* v *Morgan* [1976] AC 182. Interestingly, the defendants' claim that this was the conclusion they drew was, according to the House of Lords, regarded as a 'pack of lies' by the jury.

fit to decide and speak for herself when it came to her own sexuality.[36] She was just a sex-aid for their gratification. That is the clearest imaginable objectification of her. And since she did not in fact consent to the objectifying sexual penetration, it was the clearest imaginable way of violating her right to sexual autonomy, and the clearest imaginable case of rape.

These remarks, particularly those about stupidity, will likely be regarded by many criminal lawyers as supporting a rather radical form of 'objectivism' about mens rea. But in the face of this suggestion, three important caveats need to be entered.

First, as they stand, the above remarks bear only on the mens rea for the crime of rape. The question of what should be the mens rea for a particular crime is a question which calls, at least in the first instance, for a local answer specific to that crime. For it depends, as the foregoing remarks were meant to illustrate, on what exactly is wrong, or is supposed to be wrong, with perpetrating that particular crime. That what was just called 'astuteness to consent' is a necessary condition of not being a rapist where there is non-consensual sexual intercourse comes of the fact that rape is, fundamentally, a crime of objectification, a crime of using a person as a thing. It should not be assumed that similar mens rea requirements would necessarily be suitable for other crimes which are wrong in other ways—that is to say, thanks to other arguments or other clusters of arguments.

Secondly, the remarks above about mistakes as to consent are 'objectivist' only in the sense that they hold the defendant's mentality, as well as his conduct, up to the appropriate moral standard. Since morality governs reasons for action, it governs not only what we do but also why we do it. Some criminal lawyers may wonder whether the criminal law has a role in requiring us to reason acceptably. The simple answer is that it does if and when we proceed to *act* on the unacceptable reasons. Any mens rea standard in criminal law is, at base, a standard which bears on the reasoning by which certain actions may acceptably be performed. The one suggested above is no exception. Thus the proposal here is not an 'objectivist' proposal in the rather different sense, familiar from some corners of

---

[36] Here is where the consideration of women's rationality stressed in n 10 above has its most important bite. Since women are rational agents, a woman who rejects sexual advances must be taken to have her reasons for doing so, and these reasons (thanks to the right to sexual autonomy) must be regarded by the person making the advances as sufficient reasons against persisting. It is not morally open to him to regard the word 'no' as rationally arbitrary (e.g. as a pathological reaction owed to sex-role conditioning) and therefore as presenting no rational obstacle to persistence.

private law, of making nothing turn on the defendant's state of mind at the time of the offence. The defendant's attitude, the way he looks upon others, is at the heart of the proposed approach to his mistakes.[37]

Finally, the remarks above on astuteness to consent do not strictly speaking end the matter of what should be the mens rea for rape in law. There are some more general institutional considerations which need to be brought to bear before the task of specifying a suitable mens rea standard for rape can be completed. There may be many such considerations, and they are prone to vary from time to time and from jurisdiction to jurisdiction. They may include considerations relating to ease of explanation to and application by lay people who may be involved in certain kinds of trials, as well as considerations of statutory drafting, proof, precedent, procedure, etc. These considerations are such that different legal systems which include crimes of rape may go their different ways on this and other aspects of the definition of rape, especially at or near the borderlines. And some legal systems may be such that they have more than one acceptable way to go, especially at or near the borderlines. All that needs to be added on this score is that there is one important institutional consideration which often bears on the specification of mens rea elements for crimes, but which has very little purchase in the law of rape. Quite apart from their independent moral salience, it is a further part of the job of mens rea requirements in the criminal law to help put potential defendants on notice that they are about to enter the realms of possible criminality. If it is a condition of criminal liability that one actually noticed what one was doing, then, assuming one can be taken to know the law, one also knows whenever one is dicing with criminal liability. This supports a kind of 'subjectivist' twist in the mens rea for many crimes.[38] Not, however, in the case of rape. Barring bizarre conditions calling for the use of an insanity or automatism defence, it is hard to see how sexual penetration could be unwitting.[39] That being so, the institutional 'notice' requirement is fully satisfied in the requirement of sexual penetration, and there is no need for a further element of notice in shaping the law's attitude to mistakes regarding consent.

[37] For a similar approach to the mens rea of rape, see RA Duff, 'Recklessness and Rape', *Liverpool Law Review* 3 (1981), 49. However, Duff erred in generalizing his analysis of recklessness as to consent in rape to many other crimes without separate analysis of their moral structure: see his *Intention, Agency and Criminal Liability* (1990), 139ff.

[38] See J Gardner, 'On the General Part of the Criminal Law' in RA Duff (ed), *Philosophy and the Criminal Law: Principle and Critique* (1998), 242–244.

[39] For a discussion of this issue and English law's approach to it, see S White, 'Three Points on Pigg', *Criminal Law Review* [1989], 539.

Anyone who knows the law knows that when they embark on sexual penetration, lack of consent could carry them across the boundary into rape. And one can scarcely make a plausible defence of mistake of *law* in such a case, since (as we have established) rape is *malum in se* rather than *malum prohibitum*. Morality itself—that is to say, the moral doctrine defended in this essay—puts one on notice.[40] Even if lack of consent did not turn sexual penetration into a crime in law, any tolerably morally sensitive adult realizes that lack of consent makes sexual penetration of another's body wrongful, because it amounts to the most straightforward breach of that other's right to sexual autonomy. It is morally unlicensed objectification.

6. The role of the law

You may say that it is enough, to justify the criminalization of rape, that it violates people's right to sexual autonomy, and enough to justify the criminalization of rape *as such* that it violates that right in a special symbolically significant way. Perhaps so. It is commonly thought, however, that justifying criminalization means, among other things, passing the test of the harm principle. Yet it is not true in any familiar jurisdiction that rape is a crime only when harmful. Even the pure case is classified as rape, and criminally so. One could sideline it by saying that the harm principle is a rule of thumb, and tolerates some departures from its standard. One could also sideline the pure case by observing that the harm principle's standard is met if the class of criminalized acts is a class of acts which *tend* to cause harm, and that is true of rape in spite of the possibility of the pure case. But, although there is much to be said for these two qualifications, suitably refined, the argument of this paper teaches a different lesson about the harm principle.

It is no objection under the harm principle that a harmless action was criminalized, nor even that an action with no tendency to cause harm was criminalized. It is enough to meet the demands of the harm principle that, if the action were not criminalized, *that* would be harmful. This test is passed by the pure case of rape with flying colours. If the act in this case were not criminalized, then, assuming at least partial efficacy on the

---

[40] On this way of delimiting the scope for a 'mistake of law' defence to criminal charges, see the introduction to S Shute, J Gardner, and J Horder (eds), *Action and Value in Criminal Law* (1994), 10–12.

part of the law, people's rights to sexual autonomy would more often be violated. This would be a harm, not only to those people (if they were conscious and became aware of the rape), but also to a broader constituency of people (in our culture mainly women) whose lives would then be even more blighted than at present by violations of their right to sexual autonomy and, more pervasively still, by their justifiable *fear* of violations of their right to sexual autonomy.[41] These blights are harms which the legal prohibition on rape, if it is functioning properly, helps to reduce. For the purposes of the harm principle that is all that is needed. There is no need to show, in addition, that a given rape caused, or was likely to cause, harm.

These remarks yield two general conclusions about the moral scope and functions of the criminal law. Some have wanted to broaden the traditional interpretation of the harm principle to remove its instrumental cast. They have wanted to shift the focus of the principle away from the diminution of people's prospects, the change for the worse in their lives. They have thought this necessary to bring 'Kantian', non-instrumental wrongs, into the fold of the criminal law.[42] In fact, the traditional instrumental reading of the harm principle is correct. But non-instrumental wrongs, such as pure rapes and pure burglaries, can readily be brought under the umbrella of the harm principle. They are brought under that umbrella because the harm principle does not say that only harmful wrongs may be criminalized. It says that the criminalization of wrongs is justified only in order to prevent harm. Non-instrumental wrongs, even when they are perfectly harmless in themselves, can pass this test if their criminalization diminishes the occurrence of them, and the wider occurrence of them would detract from people's prospects—for example, by diminishing some public good, such as people's sense of ease with their living environment, the prospects for them to enjoy loving and trusting sexual relationships, their ability to go out and enjoy themselves at night or in strange places, or the degree of mutual respect which prevails in public culture at large.

---

[41] Thus SR Peterson is right to emphasize the way that rape 'restrict[s] the freedom of bodily movement for women': 'Coercion and Rape', above n 30, 360. But Peterson is wrong to regard this as what is primarily *wrong* with rape. It is because rape is wrong anyway that women justifiably fear it, and therefore become especially restricted in their use of some kinds of public transport, their access to certain neighbourhoods, and many other valuable options. This restriction is one of the key kinds of harm which makes it alright, according to the harm principle, to use the law to control the wrong of rape. But the wrongness of rape is independent of, and prior to, this harm.

[42] See e.g. RA Duff, *Intention, Agency and Criminal Liability*, above n 37, 111–112.

This brings us to the second conclusion. Some writers have thought that the criminal law could be characterized as a system of fundamentally public wrongs, in which the key interest is the interest of the public at large represented by the State, as opposed to private law in which the wrongs committed are fundamentally wrongs against individuals, who are therefore given the right to control enforcement and remedy.[43] Indirectly, this essay has attacked this view. If there is any fundamental difference between crimes and torts, except for the procedures and remedies associated with them, then it is not the difference between a fundamentally public interest and a fundamentally private interest. Crimes and torts alike may protect or reflect similar mixtures of public and private interests. The wrong of rape is a wrong against the person raped, even when she is unaware of it and suffers no harm as a result. The criminal law protects her rights as an individual. Nevertheless, the criminal law may be, and often is, concerned with public goods. These include, for example, the public goods of property holding and sexual autonomy, as well as those of tolerant co-existence, a clean and aesthetically acceptable environment, a decent social security system, etc. In some parts of the criminal law, the harm to these public goods which is done by violations of the rights of an individual, is the harm which justifies criminalization of those violations so far as the harm principle is concerned, even though the wrong done is a wrong against a particular individual right holder. The same holds in the law of tort, which is equally subject to the requirements of the harm principle and may equally involve wrongs against particular people which are publicly harmful rather than harmful to those people. The law of trespass and the law of libel, as well as the law relating to breach of contract, take this form. The wrong in each case is against an individual, but the wrong is actionable even when the individual wronged was not harmed by the wrong (in which case damages are nominal). In such cases the harm which justifies making the wrong actionable in law is the public harm of loss of respect for property, reputation, or voluntary undertaking, as the case may be. There may be differences between trespass, libel and breach of contract on the one hand, and rape and burglary on the other, such that the former are nowadays normally actionable only in private law, and only the latter are crimes. But the difference does not lie in the difference between public and private interests in the subject-matter of the legal proceedings. In

---

[43] See e.g. LC Becker, 'Criminal Attempt and the Theory of the Law of Crimes', *Philosophy and Public Affairs* 3 (1974), 262.

fact, these examples show that the contrast between public and private wrongs is, fundamentally, a misleading one. Many familiar individual rights, including those supported by these legal categories, are in large measure justified by the public good which is nurtured in their existence and recognition.[44] As we have just seen, the right to sexual autonomy, the right at the centre of the modern law of rape, is no exception.

[44] On this broader point about rights, see J Raz, 'Rights and Individual Well-Being' in his *Ethics in the Public Domain* (1994).

2

Rationality and the Rule of Law in Offences Against the Person

1. The charges against the 1861 Act

The Offences Against the Person Act 1861 ('the 1861 Act') is much disparaged by today's criminal lawyers. Its provisions have been described as 'impenetrable' by the Court of Appeal.[1] The House of Lords could not conceal its dissatisfaction with what it called 'the irrational result of this piecemeal legislation'.[2] Andrew Ashworth has written of the 'antiquated and illogical structure'[3] of an Act which the Law Commission regards as 'unsatisfactory in very many respects'.[4] Most recently, Brooke J, launching the latest version of the Commission's reform package, lambasted the operation of the 1861 Act as 'a disgrace', and claimed that this hostile view is shared in every corner of the criminal justice system.[5]

Although the Act as a whole is often found guilty by association, these serious accusations are being levelled, for the most part, at just a few of its provisions. These are the provisions dealing with what have come to be regarded as the core, workaday offences against the person of a non-fatal and non-sexual kind, namely sections 18, 20 and 47. The charges against these provisions fall under two broad headings. Some charges are laid against the three provisions individually, stressing difficulties of comprehension and adaptation. The language is archaic, the preoccupations are quaint, miscellaneous alternatives are herded uncomfortably together

---

[1] *R v Parmenter* [1991] 2 All ER 225 at 233 *per* Mustill LJ.
[2] *R v Savage, R v Parmenter* [1991] 4 All ER 698 at 721 *per* Lord Ackner.
[3] A Ashworth, *Principles of Criminal Law* (1991), 281.
[4] Law Commission, *Legislating the Criminal Code: Offences Against the Person and General Principles* (Law Com No 122, 1992), para 7.8. Hereafter referred to as 'LCCP 122'.
[5] 'Call for New Law on Assault', *The Guardian*, 17 November 1993. The occasion was the publication of Law Commission, *Legislating the Criminal Code: Offences Against the Person and General Principles* (Law Com No 218, 1993). Hereafter referred to as 'LC 218'.

within single definitions, redundant verbiage is included while essential specifications are left out, interpretations have been forced to ever more absurd technicality in the struggle to maintain a semblance of applicability to modern circumstances, etc. To these are added charges against the three provisions collectively, stressing the peculiarities of their interrelation. The provisions have miscellaneous elements in common and miscellaneous differences, leave inexplicable gaps, overlap in arbitrary ways, are chaotically dispersed through the Act, etc. These latter deficiencies obviously cannot be remedied merely by clarifying and updating the definitions of the relevant offences taken one at a time; what is required is a wholesale reorganization of this part of the criminal law.

The Law Commission has for some time advocated such a wholesale reorganization, supported and informed by arguments falling under both of the headings just identified. Against the provisions individually, the Commission has principally urged what I will call the rule of law argument. Owing to their unclarity, sections 18, 20 and 47 can no longer serve as adequate guides to those whose actions and decisions are supposed to conform to them. The rule of law is thus violated. Against the provisions collectively, meanwhile, the Commission's main argument has been what I will call the rationality argument. The offences differ from each other in ways which defy any rational explanation, and for that reason fail between them to provide tolerably systematic coverage of the basic range of aggressions with which the law ought to be concerned. My own view is that neither of these arguments yields anything like as strong a case against the 1861 Act as the Law Commission wants us to believe. Over the following pages, indeed, the relevant provisions will be defended against both of the Commission's arguments. Whatever may be their deficiencies, individually or collectively, and however strong may be the case for their reform, the deficiencies are not those identified by the Commission, and the case for reform is not that upon which the Commission relies. And the result of mistaking the problems, as we will see, is the mistaking of the solutions. The Commission's reform proposals promise a statutory regime which would possibly do more to damage the law relating to offences against the person than it would do to improve it.

2. The rationality argument

The rationality argument figures less prominently in the Law Commission's latest report than it does in the consultation paper which preceded it. One can only speculate as to the causes of its demotion, but its spirit certainly lives on in the draft Bill. The spirit of the argument is captured in the Commission's comment that 'sections 18, 20 and 47 of the 1861 Act... were not drafted with a view to setting out the various offences with which they deal in a logical or graded manner'.[6] The assumption is that the three offences can, in substance, be graded, and that this would be the logical way to define and organize them. Between them they deal with matters which would most naturally be dealt with in a hierarchy of more and less serious offences all conforming to a standard definitional pattern. The irrationality of the 1861 Act lies in its failure to take this natural path, its failure to carry the underlying hierarchy of seriousness over into the actual definition and organization of the offences. Thus section 18 should be regarded, in substance, as an aggravated version of section 20; and yet there are miscellaneous differences between the two sections which do not appear to bear any rational relation to the aggravation. Likewise, section 20 should be regarded, in substance, as the more serious cousin of section 47; and yet the two offences are drafted in quite different terms, so that the essential difference in point of seriousness is obscured by a mass of other, utterly irrelevant differences. If the sections were properly graded in definition as they are in substance, then section 18 would surely cover a narrower class of cases than section 20 which would cover a narrower class of cases than section 47; and yet section 47 is, in at least one respect, the narrowest offence of the three, while section 18 is, in at least one respect, broader than section 20. That is surely irrational. The law on such matters should be thoroughly governed, in the Law Commission's words, 'by clear distinctions... between serious and less serious cases'.[7]

That a section 18 offence should be regarded, in substance, as a more serious version of a section 20 offence is easy enough to understand. Section 20 covers malicious wounding and the malicious infliction of grievous bodily harm. Section 18 covers malicious wounding and maliciously causing grievous bodily harm, when these things are done with an intention to do grievous bodily harm or to prevent or resist arrest. The extra element of intention required for a section 18 offence obviously accounts for the difference between the sentencing maxima (five years' imprisonment under section 20 and life under section 18), and marks a difference in point of seriousness (or potential seriousness) which the Law Commission is rightly anxious to retain in its new hierarchy

---

[6] LCCP 122, para 7.4.   [7] LCCP 122, para 7.40.

of replacement offences. The Commission has not even felt the need to explain its decision, however, to eliminate the difference in the causal elements of sections 18 and 20. Section 20 requires that grievous bodily harm be inflicted, whereas for section 18 it need only be caused. The law at present tells us that infliction requires violent force. One may cause grievous bodily harm by, for example, passing on an infection or poisoning. But one may not inflict grievous bodily harm in that way.[8] If that is right, one may commit a section 18 offence without using violent means, but a section 20 offence requires such means. This, the Commission apparently holds to be a self-evidently irrational point of distinction between the two offences. One may glean the reasons. In the first place the distinction between 'causing' and 'inflicting', as the law presents it, fails the test which the Commission uses to determine what factors may affect the seriousness of a crime in this area of the law. For the Commission, seriousness varies only 'according to the type of injury that [the defendant] intended or was aware that he might cause'.[9] In the second place, and more straightforwardly, the distinction we are looking at appears to operate back to front. The extra element of violence is required for the less serious offence, not the more serious. The distinction is not merely irrational, it may be said, but perverse.

Not so. The distinction is easy enough to understand. One must begin by thinking of section 20 as the basic offence, and infliction as the basic mode of causation with which the two offences together are concerned. That is not hard to do. Only someone who mistakes the harm in section 20 for the wrong in section 20 would think it irrelevant how the harm came about. For the wrong is that of bringing the harm about in that way. In morality, as in law, it matters how one brings things about. It matters, first and foremost, in deciding which wrong one committed. You have not been mugged, although you have been conned, if I trick you into handing over your money by spinning some yarn. You have not been coerced, although you have been manipulated, if I get you to do something by making you think you wanted to do it all along. You have not been killed, although you have been left to die, if a doctor fails to prescribe life-saving drugs. These are matters of intrinsic moral significance. The fact that one inflicted harm rather than merely causing it can be, likewise, a matter of intrinsic moral significance. It is this, among other things, which distinguishes the torturer, who continues to enjoy

---

[8] *R* v *Wilson* [1983] 1 All ER 448 at 454–455.
[9] LC 218, para 13.5.

a distinctive offence all of his own in the Law Commission's proposals, and an offence, moreover, which is still explicitly defined in terms of 'infliction'.[10] The old section 20 builds on the same moral significance, although without restricting attention to the special case of the torturer. Under section 20, that is to say, one does not merely end up grievously harmed. One is a victim of violence. This is the common factor, moreover, which unites the infliction of grievous bodily harm with wounding, accounting for the fact that these sit side by side in a single offence.[11] Thus section 20 is correctly regarded, not merely as a core offence against the person, but as a core crime of violence. Violence is the basic section 20 theme which has to be adapted for the purposes of the more heinous offence under section 18.

That the process of adaptation involves extending the crime to cases where grievous bodily harm comes about other than by violence—cases where it is caused without being inflicted—may sound paradoxical, but it is in fact a natural move to make. The move is connected with the familiar maxim that intended consequences are never too remote. That maxim paints a somewhat exaggerated picture, but to the extent that it speaks the truth it proceeds from the thought that those who intend some result could otherwise enjoy a bizarre kind of mastery over their own normative situation. They could evade a moral or legal rule which is means-specific simply by adopting different means. Since the very fact that one adopts means to some result entails that one intends it, this kind of evasion is by definition unavailable to those who do not intend the result. So there is good reason, other things being equal, to withdraw some or all of the means-specificity from a moral or legal rule where its violation consists in the intentional pursuit or achievement of some result.[12] That is precisely what section 18 does. Lest the fact that it does this be summarily

[10] Section 10 of the Commission's draft Bill, LC 218, at 94, proposes a wider version of an offence already in force under section 134 of the Criminal Justice Act 1988. The demands of the torture scenario make it clear that the law relating to 'infliction' as stated in the *Wilson* case (in n 8 above) needs to be modified slightly to accommodate the possibility of psychological violence. Since section 20 is concerned with *bodily* harm only, that possibility passed the court by.

[11] On the element of violence in wounding, see *R v Beckett* (1836) 1 Mood & R 526; *R v Spooner* (1853) 6 Cox CC 392.

[12] There is no associated reason, however, to withdraw the protection of *novus actus interveniens*, which, being a doctrine concerning the effects on liability of the unexpected, cannot by its nature be manipulated. This explains why I rejected 'intended consequences are never too remote' as an exaggerated maxim. But see further on in this section of the chapter (below) for a situation, involving unintended consequences, in which even the doctrine of *novus actus interveniens* arguably falls to be modified.

dismissed as a mere slip of the draftsman's pen, it is worth noting that section 18 explicitly confirms the profound importance of the point by including the words 'by any means whatsoever' in its definition, words which contrast neatly with section 20's infliction-oriented proviso 'with or without any weapon or instrument'.[13] So whether or not one believes that there should be specific crimes of violence among the most basic offences against the person, as soon as one appreciates that section 20 creates such a crime, one can at once grasp the rational explanation for the differences between it and section 18.

None of this contradicts the Commission's view that section 18 should be regarded as the more serious version of section 20. On the contrary, it confirms that view. It merely casts doubt on the Commission's reductive assumption about the kind of variations one should expect to find between the definitions of more serious offences and those of less serious offences. These need not be restricted, as a matter of principle, to variations in the configuration of mens rea and resulting harm. That is the clear message of the relationship between sections 18 and 20. When we come to relate sections 18 and 20 to section 47, however, the message is quite different. What needs to be uprooted here is the assumption that the former relate to the latter, in substance, as more serious offences to less serious. That assumption needs to be replaced with a sensitivity to the essential qualitative differences between section 47 offences and those covered by sections 18 and 20. They are incomparably different types of offences, with different basic themes. Looking at the 1861 Act one might have thought this obvious. In the first place, section 47 has the same maximum sentence as section 20. That instantly alerts one to the possibility that offences under sections 20 and 47 should be regarded like those under sections 1 and 17 of the Theft Act 1968 (i.e. theft and false accounting), as offences which are, in essence, neither more serious nor less serious than each other.[14] In the second place, section 47 belongs

---

[13] The draftsman of the 1861 Act explains his use of the expression 'by any means whatsoever' differently. It was needed, he says, to bring section 18 into line with the law of attempted murder as consolidated elsewhere in the 1861 Act: CS Greaves, *The Criminal Law Consolidation and Amendment Acts* (2nd edn, 1862), at 52. But that does not detract from my point, since the reason I give for this expression's presence in section 18 is also the reason for its presence in the old statutory provisions on attempted murder which the draftsman of the 1861 Act was consolidating.

[14] The point about sections 1 and 17 of the Theft Act 1968 only stands since the maximum penalty for theft was reduced by the Criminal Justice Act 1991. Before that change, the same point could have been made concerning sections 1 and 15 of the Act (theft and obtaining by deception).

clearly to its own family of offences, namely those of assault (sections 38 to 47). Since the rest of that family is not treated as having some simple scalar relation to section 18 and 20 offences, one may ask why section 47 should be thought to be any different.

The answer lies, once again, in mistaking the harm for the wrong. Section 47 prohibits assault occasioning actual bodily harm. Because actual bodily harm is plainly a less serious variant of grievous bodily harm, too much focus on the harm can lead one to think that section 47 is, in substance, a less serious variant of section 20. And the harm is obviously where one focuses, at the outset, if one adopts the Law Commission's view that seriousness varies in this context only 'according to the type of injury that [the defendant] intended or was aware that he might cause'. But in fact one should pay attention first, in section 47, to the assault, not the harm. Here we find a major point of distinction between section 47 and section 20. For in spite of the fact that most assaults do involve violence, assault is not a crime of violence. Its essential quality lies in the invasion by one person of another's body space. As every law student knows, such an invasion may take one of two forms. It may take the form of a mere assault, an invasion of body space without bodily contact but with the apprehension of its imminence, or it may take the form of a battery, when the contact between the two bodies actually takes place. The Law Commission's own proposed redefinition of assault makes it sound as if the contact, apprehended or actual, must be violent. Their draft provisions speak of 'force' and 'impact'. But this has never been the common law's emphasis, and it distorts the substance of the offence. One may assault someone without violence: by removing their coat or shoes, by sitting too close to them, by stroking their hair, etc.[15] Conversely, one may subject another to violence without assaulting them: by luring someone into the path of an express train, for example, or by leaving a brick where it will fall on someone's head.[16] These are not peripheral but central cases. They reveal how far the subject-matter of sections 38 to 47 of the 1861 Act differs, in substance as well as in detail, from that of section 20. The accident of drafting is not so much that the assault crimes in sections 38 to 47 diverge from the crimes

---

[15] See, for example, *R* v *George* [1956] Crim LR 52, or *Faulkner* v *Talbot* [1981] 3 All ER 468.

[16] But cf *DPP* v *K* [1990] 1 All ER 331, in which an analogous mischief (leaving a dangerous chemical in a hot air drier where it might blow out onto someone's skin) was misconstrued as an assault for the purposes of a section 47 charge. The case does illustrate the need for some new endangerment offences to be devised roughly along the lines of the railway offences in sections 32–34 of the 1861 Act.

of violence in sections 18 and 20. The accident, on the contrary, is that they ever coincide.

It is, of course, no accident that section 47 adds a harm requirement to the element of assault. That is precisely what distinguishes a section 47 assault from an assault *simpliciter*, and from the various other special categories of assault specified in the 1861 Act and elsewhere. It would be a mistake to jump to the conclusion, however, that the harm plays the same logical role in section 47 that it plays in sections 18 and 20. In common with other aggravated assault provisions, but quite unlike sections 18 and 20, section 47 creates a crime of constructive liability, i.e. a crime which one commits by committing another crime. Committing a certain crime, e.g. assault or dangerous driving, may always carry the risk of harm, or other primary risks. But in a constructive liability context, it also exposes one to secondary risks, risks of additional liability, which one would not have faced but for one's commission of the original crime. Under section 47, those who commit the crime of assault take the risk, not only that it will occasion harm (the primary risk), but also that, if it does, they will have committed a more serious crime (the secondary risk). They likewise take the risk, under section 51 of the Police Act 1964, that their assault will be upon a police officer in the execution of his duty (the primary risk), and that, if it is, they will again have committed the more serious crime of assaulting a police officer in the execution of his duty (the secondary risk). And so on. By committing an assault, one changes one's own normative position, so that certain adverse consequences and circumstances which would not have counted against one but for one's original assault now count against one automatically, and add to one's crime.

Constructive offences, although common enough even in modern legislation,[17] are not easily accommodated within the criminal law principles espoused by many contemporary criminal lawyers, and taken for granted by the Law Commission. In particular, such offences violate what Andrew Ashworth calls the 'correspondence principle', whereby every element of the actus reus must carry with it a corresponding element of mens rea.[18] Fortunately, this 'correspondence principle' is not

---

[17] A perennial favourite is the offence of causing death by dangerous driving (previously by reckless driving), now found in the Road Traffic Act 1988, s1.

[18] A Ashworth, *Principles of Criminal Law*, above n 3, 129–130. Notice that, although liability under sections 18 and 20 is not constructive, these provisions also violate Ashworth's principle in a small way by virtue of the doctrine in *R* v *Mowatt* [1967] 3 All ER 47 that one may be convicted of a section 18 or 20 offence without foreseeing the grievous bodily harm one did, so long as one forsesaw *some* harm.

and never has been a principle of English law. The relevant principle of English law is *actus non facit reum nisi mens sit rea*: no guilty act without a guilty mind.[19] Constructive offences, when they are properly conceived and designed, do not violate this principle. The more basic offences with which they are associated require mens rea, and that mens rea is naturally carried over into the constructive offence. The guilty act must therefore still be attended by a guilty mind, in line with *actus non facit reum nisi mens sit rea*. What need not be attended by any mens rea are the consequences and circumstances, the risk of which one bears because one committed the original crime. For if these were attended by mens rea, that would make a nonsense of the idea, at the heart of all constructive liability, that those who embark on crimes, or at least certain risky crimes, change in the process their own normative positions regarding the risks they take. That is why there is no grand departure from principle in the House of Lords' recent, and I would say overdue, confirmation that section 47 of the 1861 Act has no mens rea requirement apart from the mens rea of assault.[20] It also explains the causal element in section 47, the element of 'occasioning'. The chain of 'occasioning' should be regarded as very elastic, stretching to harms rather more remote than any which are caused or inflicted. You lunge towards me, I step backwards, somone's umbrella trips me up, I fall backwards, a cyclist runs me over. The assault occasions the resulting harm even though it does not cause it.[21] Section 47 liability may therefore arise even though the actual bodily harm comes about by a very indirect route, perhaps involving successive coincidences. In committing an assault, on this view, one bears not only the risk that harm will come about, but also, up to a point, the risk of how it will come about. In respect of the harm, then, some of the protection of the doctrine of *novus actus interveniens* is forfeited by the assaulter, along with some of the protection of the doctrine of mens rea.

In line with its general principle of offence seriousness, the Law Commission would restore both of these protections. In the process it would remove the section 47 offence from the assault family, drop its constructive elements, and replace it with an offence in the same family as those offences which would serve as replacements for sections 18 and 20. Yet this move is not a replacement of less rational organization with more, as

<hr />

[19] *R v Tolson* [1886–90] All ER Rep 26. cf G Williams, *Textbook of the Criminal Law* (2nd edn, 1983), who misinterprets *Tolson* as authority for the correspondence principle, and so regards it as militating against a constructive interpretation of section 47.
[20] *R v Savage, R v Parmenter* [1991] 4 All ER 698.
[21] But cf *R v Roberts* (1971) 56 Cr App Rep 95, in which the distinction is neglected.

we can now see, but a choice between two possible rational arrangements in the law of non-sexual and non-fatal offences against the person. After all, we have just supplied a perfectly rational explanation for the main features of the section 47 offence, understood as a variation on the assault theme. There are also, as the Law Commission shows, rational explanations for the features of the proposed replacement for section 47, understood as a variation on the theme of sections 18 and 20. The point is, however, that one cannot have it both ways, since the assault theme (invasion of body space) is not the same as the theme of sections 18 and 20 (personal violence). The Law Commission can make its proposed arrangements seem to have it both ways only by diluting the two themes so that they become harder to distinguish. The violence theme is weakened in the replacements for sections 18 and 20 by the eradication of the 'infliction' paradigm. At the same time, the spatial invasion theme is weakened in the restatement of assault by concentration on 'force' and 'impact'. But this two-way rapprochement generates a regrettable loss of discrimination in the law of offences against the person which no amount of rational reordering can compensate. It represents a triumph of reductive thinking. Codification need not be like this. In the law of offences against property, excellently codified during the 1960s and 1970s, we find many different offences involving much the same harms. Whether one is a victim of theft, deception, criminal damage or making off, one is harmed by being deprived of one's belongings. Yet this codification did not seek to eradicate the different themes of the different offences, and turn out some general scale of seriousness. On the contrary, it went out of its way to capture these different themes in precise and differentiated language. That is because, in the realm of property offences, the harm does not capture all that is interesting, or rationally significant, about the wrong. Nor are things any different in the law of offences against the person. In substance, the wrong of an assault crime is different from the wrong of a section 20 crime much as the wrong of theft is different from the wrong of fraud. The two may happen to overlap, even across a large proportion of their terrain, but one cannot in principle unify them into a neatly scaled family of crimes. Indeed the Law Commission recognizes this, in spite of its own inclinations, by preserving distinct offences of poisoning and torture, and by hiving off the sexual offences to a different corner of the codification agenda.[22] One may ask why the basic

---

[22] It is a relief to see that the Commission does not fall into the trap of mistaking rape for a crime of violence, as it does with assault. Some suppose that we would appreciate

thematic separation of sections 18 and 20 from section 47 does not also deserve preservation. Certainly the rationality argument does not supply the answer; for there is nothing irrational, to speak of, in either section 47 or sections 18 and 20.

3. The rule of law argument

Part of the answer is to be found, perhaps, in the Commission's second main argument for the reform of the 1861 Act, which I call the rule of law argument. This argument is, if anything, bolstered in the transition from consultation document to final report. In the latter, particular stress is laid on the extent to which the guiding light of the law has been dimmed by the antiquity of the legislation. Firstly, the provisions need to be translated into entirely different language to make them clear enough to use.[23] Secondly, this linguistic unclarity opens the law up to judicial development and redevelopment on a scale which seriously hinders the certainty of the law.[24] The Commission is most explicitly concerned about the effect of this on juries and magistrates and police officers who are trying to apply the law. But we are plainly supposed to take it for granted that, if there is a rule of law problem for juries and magistrates, there must be a rule of law problem for those who may be on the law's sharp end, i.e. potential offenders.[25] If the law cannot even be a source of reliable guidance in the courtroom, how can it be a source of reliable guidance in the pub or in the street? The Law Commission's proposed simplification and systematization of the non-fatal and non-sexual offences against the person is therefore held out as being not only in the interests of the administration of justice, but also in the interests of

what it wrong with rape more if we stopped seeing it as a 'sexual offence' and started seeing it as a straightforward crime of violence. But it strikes me that the reverse is true. It is precisely the tenacity of the courts in perpetuating the old idea that rape is a crime of violence that has done more than anything else to blunt public appreciation of the rapes which take place under the cover of manipulative and exploitative relationships. Rape is a crime of sexual invasion, not a crime of violence. To focus on the use of violence is to detract from the centrality of the invasion.

[23] LC 218, para 12.9.
[24] LC 218, para 12.11.
[25] LC 218, para 12.6, bemoans the 1861 Act's 'complete unintelligibility to the layman'. Meanwhile, LCCP 122, para 7.11, refers us back, for supporting argument, to the earlier report, *A Criminal Code for England and Wales* (Law Com No 177, 1989), paras 2.2–2.7, in which much is made of 'the idea that the law should be known in advance to those accused of violating it'.

crime prevention and avoidance, which only a straightforward, publicly ascertainable framework of criminal law can secure.

The Commission is obviously right to think that the law in this area must be clear if it is to provide satisfactory guidance. But it would be a mistake to suppose that all interests in clarity will be served, in the context of the law relating to offences against the person, by the same kind of clarity. To be sure, that may be a reasonable expectation in some areas of the law. The very same clarity in the law of contract which will help courts in their interpretation and enforcement of contracts, for example, will also help many of those who want to make or terminate contracts to do so without recourse to the courts. The same may be true in some areas of criminal law, e.g. trading standards or food hygiene offences. In the specialized pursuits with which such offences are concerned, it is proper to expect and encourage some degree of specialized acquaintance with the relevant law, and the same clarity which will help juries and magistrates and the police to acquire that specialized acquaintance for the purpose of determining whether offences have been committed will also help shopkeepers and restaurateurs do the same for the purpose of avoiding the commission of offences. That is also the case in those areas of the criminal law where one is explicitly told of the crime one is about to commit whenever one is about to commit it, e.g. when one is making declarations on tax forms or social security forms. Here again, the very clarity which would help a jury or magistrate to apply the law will also help the potential offender not to fall foul of it. In all of these situations, what is needed on all sides, and what the rule of law unequivocally demands, is what we might call textual clarity. The law is textually clear if it is stated in straightforward, unornamented language, avoiding great technicality or complexity of drafting, and minimizing the scope for conflicting interpretations.

In other areas of the law, however, the textual clarity which helps the court, including its lay members, is not the same clarity which helps with ordinary public understanding and conformity. After all, there are many parts of the law, including much of the general criminal law, which are rarely encountered in textual form, except by police officers, lawyers and those participating in trials. Nor should we wish it to be otherwise. The presumption that everyone knows the law, or at any rate knows the general criminal law, becomes untenable if we insist that people can only know the law by its texts, and we proceed to design the law accordingly. Most people have better things to do than acquaint themselves with a mass of legal materials, however easy to read and understand. Most people, most of the time, need to know roughly what the law says on non-specialist matters without knowing, or caring, how the law says it. Textual clarity is an irrelevance. The clarity which is needed here, we may call moral clarity. Moral clarity is secured, not by the use of straightforward and unornamented language in legal texts, but by the adequate replication in the law of clear distinctions and significances which apply outside the law, together with reasonably clear indication (in the titles of Acts, the common names and classifications of offences, etc.) of which cluster of distinctions and significances people can expect to find replicated where.

Now it may be thought that, if and to the extent that the rule of law does demand this moral clarity, its ambitions must be contained within the limits prescribed by what has come to be known as the 'harm principle'. For the harm principle, like the rule of law, reflects the importance of making the law compatible with people's need to be, to a substantial degree, the authors of their own lives; and while the rule of law makes its contribution to this aim by requiring the law to advertise its own restrictions, so that legal liability and the resulting disruption do not take people unawares, the harm principle makes its parallel contribution by limiting the types of moral considerations to which the law may have regard in shaping its restrictions, so that over a wide range of issues people have freedom to decide for themselves even if they do not decide rightly. So one may be tempted to conclude that the rule of law can consistently demand the legal replication of moral distinctions and significances only if they are moral distinctions and significances admissible within the terms of the harm principle, i.e. those that relate to the nature or degree of the harm. This idea resonates with the Law Commission's view, already mentioned more than once, that offences against the person should be divided up only 'according to the type of injury that [the defendant] intended or was aware that he might cause'. But it is based, all the same, on a misinterpretation of the harm principle. The harm principle says that the law should not be used to restrict or punish harmless activities. Perhaps it adds that the law should not restrict or punish harmful activities in ways which are disproportionate to the harm.[26] But beyond this, it says nothing about how, or even when, harmful activities should be dealt with by the law. Such matters remain to be settled on other grounds. Sometimes the law may legitimately decline to deal with certain harmful activities at all. On other occasions the law may legitimately elect to deal with them only on certain terms, attaching

---

[26]   J Raz, *The Morality of Freedom* (1986), 420–421.

limitations and provisos and conditions which have nothing much to do with the nature or degree of the harm. That explains why one should not, in the words of the previous section, reduce the wrong to the harm. It also explains, more to the immediate point, why there need be no significant conflict between the demands of the harm principle and the demand for moral clarity which is, at least where the general criminal law is concerned, a central demand of the rule of law. For without violating the harm principle one may rely on countless moral distinctions and significances in the definition of a crime, including those that have little or nothing to do with the nature or degree of harm, so long as the activity being criminalized is indeed harmful and the means used to suppress it are not disproportionate to the harm in question.

It should already be fairly clear how these observations engage with the remarks I made in the previous section ('2. The rationality argument') about the rationality of the 1861 Act. For this Act, like the Theft Acts 1968 and 1978, strives for moral clarity by dividing up the offences which fall within its scope into strikingly different moral categories, distinguished not, or not only, by the degree of harm involved, but rather by how the harm is brought about. Crimes of violence, in particular, are distinguished from assault crimes, where invasion of body space is the central theme, even though bodily harm may be equally at stake in both scenarios. The original text of the 1861 Act, casually amended over the intervening century, went even further in its moral discriminations. The possible modes of violence, in particular, were further divided up. Section 18 spoke, in the alternative, of intents to 'maim, disfigure or disable' as well as the generic intent to do grievous bodily harm. Lesser-known provisions of the 1861 Act still preserve this further degree of moral specificity. Section 21 deals with choking, suffocating, or strangling; section 22 deals with the use of stupefactants and overpowering substances, sections 23 and 24 with poisoning, section 26 with starving and exposing to the elements; sections 28 to 30 deal with burning, maiming, disfiguring and disabling by use of explosives, and in the case of section 29 by use of corrosive substances; section 31 deals with spring guns and man traps, sections 32 to 34 with endangering railway passengers by various finely specified means, and so forth. These different crimes, some crimes of violence and some not, are notable for the moral clarity with which they are differentiated.[27]

---

[27] At this point I should mention my debt to Jeremy Horder, a draft of whose paper 'Rethinking Non-Fatal Offences Against the Person' in *Oxford Journal of Legal Studies* 14 (1994), 335, first alerted me to the need to defend the fine-grained differentiations of the 1861 Act. My defence is on a different basis from Horder's, which stresses the

Like the differences marked in the Theft Acts between theft, obtaining by deception, false accounting, making off without payment, handling stolen goods, and so on, these provisions single out for specific prohibition some, although not all, of the many different modes of wrongdoing in which the harms with which the Act is concerned may be at stake. And they single them out in ways which resonate in the moral imagination of the ordinary people to whom the law must provide its clear guidance.

Notice that there are two separate but related points here. The distinctions in the 1861 Act between different ways of causing harm are being held up as genuine moral distinctions, possessing the rational appeal of which I made a great deal in the previous section. They are also being held up as distinctions which appeal to the popular moral imagination, so that they are accessible and vivid to people in search of the law's guidance. The two points should not be collapsed. Morality certainly should not be confused with anybody's beliefs about it. On the other hand, the independence of the two points should not be exaggerated. The relationship of the popular moral imagination to the moral distinctions embodied in the 1861 Act is not merely the ordinary relationship of beliefs to their objects. The popular moral imagination also has, within limits, a constitutive role to play. Remember that we are talking about distinctions, not between different types or degrees of harm, but between different ways of bringing harm about. These distinctions relate, not to the effects of the relevant criminal actions, but to the very nature of the actions themselves. It is a matter of intrinsic rather than instrumental differentiation, differentiation not in terms of what the actions cause or bring about but rather in terms of what they express or convey.[28] This is where we come to the important move. For to speak of what an action expresses or conveys is to speak of its meaning, and the meaning of an action is its public meaning. If an act of race discrimination is an act

---

importance of fair labelling rather than clear guidance. The two defences, however, are for the most part complementary.

[28] Of course, there may be an interaction between intrinsic and instrumental differentiation, since what actions express or convey may give them further consequences. That rape expresses a view of women as less than human, for example, explains why rape is a particularly humiliating mode of violation. But in order to understand where rape gets its particular wrongness, one should not leap straight to the humiliation. Even if it is missing because, e.g., the victim was drugged and never learns of the violation, or has been rendered insensitive to her own humanity by persistently brutal treatment, there still remains the baseness of expressing the base attitude that the violation expresses, independently of any consequence which that expression may have for the victim herself or for others. I am grateful to Andrew von Hirsch for reminding me to stress this point.

expressing contempt, for example, that is not because the discriminator means it to be contemptuous nor because the person discriminated against reads it that way. It is because that is the meaning which acts of race discrimination have in the public culture in which this race discrimination takes place.[29] This does not mean that race discrimination is only as bad as it is thought to be by people in that culture. For people may underestimate how bad it is to express the contempt which, by virtue of its public meaning, race discrimination necessarily expresses, or may fail to see the additional instrumental factors, some of them independent of public meaning, which buttress its undesirability. Yet the authentic rational significance of discrimination, and the possibility of rationally distinguishing between discriminatory and non-discriminatory actions, still depends in part on the fact that race discrimination has the public meaning it has. Likewise, the intrinsic differentiation between violent and non-violent means, between deceptive and non-deceptive means, between terrorists and poisoners, between rapists and philanderers, etc. These depend on the public meanings of the different actions involved. And those public meanings are not only reflected but also constituted in the collective moral imagination of those who inhabit the public culture in which the acts being differentiated take place. So the claims about the rationality of the 1861 Act made in the previous section are not related in some merely coincidental way to the claims about its moral clarity which are being made in the present section. On the contrary, they share the same foundations. Both the Act's rationality and the Act's moral clarity depend, at least in part, on the fact that it reflects distinctions between actions which even now differ in the popular imagination, hence have different public meanings, and hence have different intrinsic moral significances.

In itself this does not show that the 1861 Act is superior in any way to the Law Commission's proposals for replacing it. It does show, however, that the Commission's rule of law argument against the 1861 Act is every bit as overstated as its rationality argument. Not only do the main provisions of the 1861 Act still represent a perfectly rational way of organizing the law relating to offences against the person, but they also live up to

---

[29] I am not denying that the public meaning of some actions may itself have some sensitivity to the intentions or perceptions of the particular people involved. Although this is not true of discrimination, it is true of, e.g., acts of deception and betrayal as well as some physical violations and acts of violence. It is this sensitivity which explains the importance of many mens rea distinctions in the criminal law, including the distinction between the mens rea of section 20 and that of section 18.

the demands of the rule of law in at least one vital respect, in that they have a good dose of the moral clarity which makes them accessible to the ordinary people who must be guided by them. But it may still be asked whether this moral clarity really has to be so much at the expense of textual clarity, which is also an important demand of the rule of law. Do the two really need to conflict? The Law Commission could point to its draft provisions on poisoning and torture, at least, to show that morally clear distinctions and significances need not be couched in the ornamented, arcane and technical language of the 1861 Act. So one may well wonder why sections 18, 20 and 47 should not be translated into similarly clear and simple modern language, so that the interest of ordinary people in the moral clarity of the general criminal law can be reconciled with the interest in textual clarity of those who participate in trials and others who must actually consult the law's texts.

The answer to this comes in two parts. The first part begins with a concession that the language of sections 18, 20 and 47 is in places arcane and ornamented, so that there are indeed some marked deficiencies of textual clarity. And some of these could indeed be removed without detracting from the moral clarity of the sections. The word 'malicious' in sections 18 and 20, for example, while it is certainly not redundant,[30] has probably outstayed its welcome. The job which it now does, and is rightly asked to do, is not one which it does particularly well. It is an ordinary straightforward word, to be sure, with an ordinary straightforward meaning, but if it were used in sections 18 and 20 to convey that meaning, then those sections would not only compromise much of the moral clarity which I have claimed for them but would also gratuitously violate other sound principles of criminal law, such as the principle that the law does not look to an offender's motive. The word is now fanciful, and we can certainly find a clearer way of saying what it is now supposed to say. The same is not true, however, of all the arcane and ornamented expressions in sections 18, 20 and 47. I am thinking in particular of the expressions 'grievous bodily harm' and 'actual bodily harm'. These are certainly quaint, and you might say unnecessary. Everybody knows that grievous bodily harm is serious[31] and actual bodily harm need not be.[32] Why not dump the ornamental terms 'grievous' and 'actual'? The Law Commission itself has the answer. Throughout the draft codification

---

[30]   *Pace* Diplock LJ in *R* v *Mowatt* [1967] 3 All ER 47 at 50.
[31]   *DPP* v *Smith* [1960] 3 All ER 161.
[32]   Although it must be more than *de minimis*: *R* v *Jones* [1981] Crim LR 119.

process, arcane and ornamental words have been preserved from the common law. 'Rape', 'murder', 'manslaughter', 'assault', 'riot' and 'affray' are still to be with us. 'Assault', in particular, still figures in the definition of certain proposed aggravated offences, as it currently does in section 47. The reason is simple. These words carry their moral force with them. Whether or not they began as legal terms of art, and some of them are now so ancient that one cannot be sure how they began, they are now words which help to constitute the very intrinsic moral significances and distinctions which, in law, they exist to capture. They represent justified departures from the textual clarity of the law in the name of moral clarity. The Law Commission evidently does not think that the expressions 'grievous bodily harm' and 'actual bodily harm' have the same pedigree. But I beg to differ. These expressions (and even their abbreviations 'GBH' and 'ABH') have entered the popular moral imagination, and now help to constitute the very moral significances which they quaintly but evocatively describe.[33] One cannot therefore remove the quaintness, the arcane and ornamented language, without detracting from the moral clarity which it carries with it and constitutes. One must choose, to this extent at least, between moral clarity and textual clarity. And in this case, as with murder and rape, one should choose moral clarity. That is because, here at least, the price of the textual unclarity is minimal. Unlike the term 'malicious', the expressions 'actual bodily harm' and 'grievous bodily harm', arcane and ornamented though they may be, have never given much trouble to those who must deal with the law in its textual manifestations. The deficiency of textual clarity here has barely cast a fleeting shadow across the guiding light of the law.

So much for the first part of the answer, the confession and avoidance part. Now we come to the denial. For the language of sections 18, 20 and 47 is not in all respects so ornamented, arcane and technical as the Law Commission's observations suggest, and thus the deficiencies of textual clarity are by no means comprehensive. In particular, the causal words 'inflict' and 'occasion' in sections 20 and 47, like the word 'cause' in section 18, are ordinary English words which in the 1861 Act carry, even after a century of interpretation, much of their ordinary English meanings. It is hard to believe that these words give juries and magistrates problems because of

---

[33] I think back to Alan Bleasdale's successful television serial *GBH* (1991). Can one imagine a drama called, in the words of the Law Commission proposals, *Serious Injury*? It is not a trivial question. One should not underestimate the role of drama (including soap operas, sitcoms, etc.) in supporting and reflecting public appreciation of the law in a complex and alienating modern society.

their unclarity, and equally hard to believe (since the proposed definition of torture contains the very word 'inflict') that the Law Commission sincerely found these words unclear. What creates problems with these words, if anything does, is the assumption of some criminal lawyers, particularly academic criminal lawyers, that they need to provide definitions of these words which specify all the necessary and sufficient conditions of their application. This cannot but lend an unnecessary veneer of technicality to the terms. It is an unnecessary veneer because one does not need to be able to articulate the necessary and sufficient conditions of something in order to understand it perfectly well. Sound understanding does not dispense with grey areas. For many grey areas are not the product of any defect of understanding, or even failure of articulation, but part of the very thing being understood and articulated, which is constituted in part by the role it plays in our more global understanding and articulation of the world around us. Even criminal lawyers now accept this, I hope, when they are dealing with the word 'appropriation' in the Theft Act 1968, the word 'intention' in its many appearances in statute and at common law, and many other important legal words.[34] It is time they got used to the same thing where causal terms are concerned, and stopped regarding the variety of causal relations in terms of which our world is organized as some kind of failure of clarity in our thinking and language. The word 'wounding' in sections 18 and 20 affords another example of the same point. Here the courts have, it must be admitted, gone doubly astray, attempting to define wounding principally by defining a wound, which has in turn been defined by stating a supposedly necessary and sufficient condition, viz a 'puncturing of the skin'.[35] But the mistakes here do not lie in the choice of the ordinary and clear word 'wounding' to do its ordinary English job in the 1861 Act. The mistakes lie in the spurious demand for a further definition which sharpens the unsharp periphery of a word, when the very thing to which the word applies has an unsharp periphery which the unsharp periphery of the word clearly and accurately replicates. This shows that one should not mistake even the fullest textual clarity for maximal certainty in the law. Textual clarity requires the avoidance of arcane, ornamented language, the avoidance of great technicality and complexity of drafting,

---

[34] See *R v Gomez* [1993] 1 All ER 1 for a competent and insightful discussion of 'appropriation' without resort to, or hope of, a comprehensive definition. The discussion of 'intention' in *R v Moloney* [1985] 1 All ER 1025, although in some respects less competent, correctly concludes that the grey area at the margins of 'intention' cannot be excised by sharper definition except at the price of excessive technicality.

[35] *C (a minor) v Eisenhower* [1983] 3 All ER 230.

and a minimization of the scope for conflicting interpretation. But some of what lawyers regard as 'conflicting interpretation' has nothing to do with unclarity of language, and everything to do with the structure of the world which the language attempts to capture. To iron out the grey areas of that world for the sake of certainty is not necessarily to enhance textual clarity, but on occasions, as the case of wounding nicely illustrates, to retard textual clarity by adding extra legal technicality. If certainty and textual clarity are both demands of the rule of law, then here we have, questions of moral clarity apart, a real source of conflict within that ideal.

It is partly the Law Commission's ambition to maximize both certainty and textual clarity at the same time which leads it into what I earlier called its reductive thinking. For these two aspects of the rule of law often work against one another. Beyond a certain point, the sharper one tries to make the law's distinctions at the margins, the more technical terms one must tolerate. To reduce such conflict the Commission's codification team have come up with two strategies. The first is to cut down the number of elements in each criminal offence so that the opportunities for both unclarity of word and uncertainty of world are minimized. The second is to insist that the elements of each offence are chosen, wherever possible, from a relatively limited palette of approved elements which are either defined in the statute or thought to be relatively free of greyness in both world and word. But this is unfortunately no solution. For to the extent that it does resolve the conflict between certainty and textual clarity, it does so at the expense of other important aspects of the rule of law.[36] Of these the demand for moral clarity is the most important, and it demands what the Law Commission normally refuses to supply, namely offences differentiated by the very nature of the action, and not only by the harm done or the mens rea conditions associated with that harm. The Commission refuses to supply these, I venture, because once intrinsic action classifications are involved, the prospects for reconciling maximal certainty and maximal textual clarity are minimal. One is dealing with aspects of the world which invariably have extensive peripheries as well as cores, and from which the peripheries can only be eliminated by the use of technical terms and complex drafting, thereby compromising textual

[36] This adds a new dimension to Raz's remark in *The Authority of Law* (1979), at 222, that 'complete conformity [to the rule of law] is impossible'. It is impossible not only because, as Raz points out, 'some vagueness is inescapable', but also because the 'vagueness' of law may take different forms, and the elimination of one form, pursued to extremes, may be the triumph of another. The rule of law conflicts, not only with other important moral principles, but also with itself.

clarity. But the Commission's argument for textual clarity is itself compromised by reliance on demands of the rule of law, demands for public ascertainment and access, which in fact often militate against it.

4. A special verdict

This last conclusion, like that of the section before, lives up to the ambitions with which the paper began. Those ambitions, let me say again, were modest. The aim was only to show how the two arguments upon which the Law Commission mainly relied in criticizing the 1861 Act, and in building its own alternative legislative package, were flawed. It has not been suggested that there is nothing wrong with the 1861 Act, but only that whatever may be wrong with it does not reside, as the Commission has repeatedly charged, in the rationality of its core provisions or in the degree of its respect for the rule of law. Nor has it been claimed that the Commission's proposals for replacement of these core provisions represent no advance, but only that they represent no decisive advance over the 1861 Act in the particular respects in which they are claimed to represent a decisive advance, i.e. in respect of their rationality and their degree of respect for the rule of law.

This very limited defence of the 1861 Act does, however, help to expose a tension of wider significance. Throughout its long-running codification project, the maxim *actus non facit reum nisi mens sit rea* has been very prominent in the Law Commission's thinking, and almost religiously observed. Indeed it has been fortified considerably, buttressed both by Ashworth's 'correspondence principle'[37] and by a further demand that mens rea be 'subjective', i.e. that nobody be held liable on the basis of things done or brought about to which he or she did not advert.[38] If this latter fortification of the *actus non facit reum* principle is justified, it is justified on rule of law grounds. It is justified, in other words, not because there is any general moral divide between the advertent and

[37] Law Commission, *Report on the Mental Element in Crime* (Law Com No 89, 1978), para 86; *Codification of the Criminal Law* (Law Com No 143, 1985), paras 8.29–8.33; *A Criminal Code for England and Wales*, above n 25, para 8.27.

[38] Law Commission, *Report on the Mental Element in Crime*, para 59; *Codification of the Criminal Law*, para 8.20; *A Criminal Code for England and Wales*, paras 8.19–8.20; LCCP 122, para 7.22. This explains the Commission's insistence that offence seriousness should vary, not simply according to the type of injury caused, but 'according to the type of injury that [the defendant] *intended or was aware* that he might cause'.

the inadvertent wrongdoer apart from the law, which there is not, but because (if they can be presumed to know the law) those who advert to the relevant features and consequences of their actions also advert to, or can be presumed to advert to, the legal liability to which they are exposing themselves. Those who do not advert to the relevant features and consequences, on the other hand, are then subject to the unexpected disruption of criminal liability, with all that being criminalized means for the course of their lives. If the demand for subjective mens rea is justified, in other words, it is justified by the way in which it helps people to steer their lives around the criminal law rather than running straight into it. This is one rule of law reason why the criminal law should not replicate the general negligence liability found in private law, and one to which the Law Commission obviously gives great weight.

But it is not the only rule of law reason why the criminal law should not replicate such a general negligence liability, nor the most important. For the general negligence liability that we know of from private law is also, as we might put it, action-unspecific. It governs the doing of anything—just about anything at all—without due care. This means that one is not alerted to the fact that one may be risking negligence liability by the mere fact that one is performing actions of a certain kind, e.g. shooting guns rather than building houses, driving cars rather than playing golf, etc. In criminal law we should normally demand this extra source of alertness. We should expect the criminal law to attach itself to particular actions, so that one has, by virtue of this as well as by virtue of one's advertence, a good idea of when one is running into trouble. As the draftsman of the 1861 Act himself put it, specifying 'each and every act intended to be subjected to any punishment ... has the advantage of calling direct attention to all the acts that are made penal'.[39] To this extent, a prohibition on, say, negligent driving or negligent shooting is superior to a prohibition on negligent actions generally. The Law Commission, however, neglects this axis of differentiation in its proposals to recodify the law relating to offences against the person. The new replacements for sections 18 and 20—'intentionally causing serious injury' and 'intentionally or recklessly causing serious injury'—lack the

---

[39] CS Greaves, *The Criminal Law Consolidation and Amendment Acts*, above n 13, xxxvii. This consideration did not make Greaves himself an enthusiast for action-specificity. Indeed, he regretted the action-specificity of the 1861 Act, and did his best, he tells us, to circumvent it by sneaking in catch-all provisions where possible. But he is more candid than the Law Commission, I think, in explaining why. It had nothing to do with rationality or the rule of law. It was simply that such definitions collectively leave holes in the law which 'afford the artful a chance of evading punishment'.

characteristic action-specificity of the 1861 Act's offences, which focus on acts of violence. The new replacement for section 47—'intentionally or recklessly causing injury'—likewise lacks the action-specificity of the existing offence, which warns one off assaults, and makes liability for the aggravated assault turn on whether one failed to heed the warning. By engineering these shifts, the Law Commission fails to carry through the robust support for the rule of law which drives its most dearly held 'subjectivist' principle.

Let me spell the irony out in simpler terms by dwelling a little more on section 47. As far as conformity to the rule of law is concerned, this provision is in one respect worse than the Commission's proposed replacement for it, and in one respect better. It is worse because, since one need not appreciate the risk of actual bodily harm in order to be liable, one admittedly cannot rely on any such appreciation to give one warning of the liability one faces. On the other hand, section 47 is better because, since one needs to commit an assault in order to commit an assault occasioning actual bodily harm, one is warned of the risk of such constructive liability by the very fact that one engages in the original assault. This argument does not always work to defend constructive liability against challenges based on the rule of law. But it does work to defend constructive liability, and defend it well, when certain further conditions are met. Of these the most important by far is the one of which I have made so much in the preceeding pages, and which the crime of assault occasioning actual bodily harm meets, viz responsiveness to the rationally significant intrinsic differences between actions which play such a large role in, and are structured by, the popular moral imagination.[40] Even if constructive, an offence specification which meets this condition of responsiveness can do more, I venture, to address the concerns underlying 'subjectivism' than does the pursuit of 'subjectivism' itself. And yet the Law Commission, for all it is wedded to 'subjectivism', eschews such responsiveness altogether in its treatment of the core offences against the person. In the process, it underestimates the resources of rationality, and takes the risk of retarding the very ideal of the rule of law which its reforms are claimed to advance.

---

[40] Andrew Simester has pointed out to me another important and complementary factor that may sometimes further strengthen this defence of constructive liability. It is that the basic offence, onto which the constructive liability is grafted, is itself partly justified by the fact that it helps to prevent the very harms, the occurrence of which activates the constructive liability. This is arguably true of a section 47 offence, and certainly true of the offence under section 1 of the Road Traffic Act 1988.

3

Complicity and Causality

1. Solzhenitsyn's puzzle

And the simple step of a simple courageous man is not to take part in the lie, not to support deceit. Let the lie come into the world, even dominate the world, but not through me.[1]

It is natural to read Solzhenitsyn's remark as splitting morality into two parts. The first part concerns making a difference, changing the world, having a causal influence. It would be best if the world contained no wrongs, so it would be best if nobody committed them. If one can do anything to prevent the wrongs, or some of them, then so much the better. But what if the wrongs have been or will be committed no matter what one does? What if it is out of one's hands? That is where the second part of morality comes into play. The second part is concerned with one's own participation in wrongdoing. The wrongs are going to be committed anyway; there is nothing to be done about that. But one must not be implicated in them. One's own hands must remain clean even as the world falls.

There is something puzzling about this way of dividing up morality. How does one come to be implicated in something without having made any difference to it? How can wrongs conceivably come 'through' me, to use Solzhenitsyn's vivid expression, except by my making a causal contribution to their commission? How do my hands get dirty if the wrongdoing is out of my hands? Is there another mode of participation in wrongdoing other than by causal contribution? We should begin by setting aside a possible distraction. Arguably, it is possible to get one's hands dirty on the wrongs of another by profiting from them, or by helping to conceal them, or in various other *ex post facto* ways. If a country employs slave labour to build its infrastructure, multinational companies that

---

[1] Alexander Solzhenitsyn, *One Word of Truth* (1972).

take advantage of the cheapness of the infrastructure to increase their returns are arguably committing a moral wrong that involves compounding another person's moral wrong. It is possible, although it can also be misleading, to think of this as a kind of complicity. We can think of complicity broadly as including any kind of wrongdoing that consists in any kind of association with the wrongs of another. But Solzhenitsyn already narrows the topic down to exclude so-called 'complicity after the fact'. He is interested only in how the wrong comes into the world, not what is done with it once it is there. His suggestion is that there is a way that a wrong can come into the world *through* me, and make my hands dirty in the process, without my having made any difference to it.

In this paper I will suggest that there is no such way of participating in (being complicit in, being an accomplice to, being implicated in) the wrongdoing of another. A common worry is that causal contribution is what characterizes a principal wrongdoer, i.e. a wrongdoer who is not an accomplice. So if complicity is not going to collapse into principalship, some other mode of contribution—a non-causal mode—must characterize a wrongdoer who is an accomplice. I will suggest, on the contrary, that the difference between principals and accomplices is a causal difference, i.e. a difference between two types of causal contribution, not a difference between a causal and a non-causal contribution. And I will suggest that there is a moral difference that supervenes upon this causal difference. So I will agree with Solzhenitsyn's view that morality can be divided into two parts: principalship and complicity. I will merely draw the line in a different place. Both principals and accomplices make a difference, change the world, have an influence. The essential difference between them is that accomplices make their difference through principals, in other words by making a difference to the difference that principals make.

2. Principals and accomplices

Let me come to the topic of complicity through another topic, at first sight only very remotely connected. Are there any wrongs that are unjustifiable and inexcusable in principle? For instance, can we imagine any adequate justifications or excuses for raping a child or massacring prisoners of war? Isn't it the case that if one commits these wrongs, even in terrible fear of the alternatives, even in the thrall of terrible ignorance, one is automatically thereby exposed as a coward or a knave? Shouldn't one

Complicity and Causality

submit to death, even to one's own death and the death of all around one, even to the extinction of all life on earth, rather than do it? Perhaps. It is hard to know how to go about comparing the extinction of life on earth with the rape of a child or the massacre of prisoners of war. Fortunately, one doesn't need to be able to make such comparisons to come up with a general argument to challenge the idea that the commission of these latter wrongs cannot imaginably be justified or excused.

After all, one can always imagine a scenario in which one needs to commit a certain wrong in order to avoid more and/or worse commissions of the *very same wrong*. My sadistic kidnappers warn me (and they are not bluffing) that if I don't torture one innocent person agonizingly to death then they will torture a hundred even more innocent people even more agonizingly to death. And if I don't fly a large plane into a large skyscraper full of people, they will have 50 even larger planes flown into 50 even larger skyscrapers even more full of people. When all this even greater wrongdoing is perpetrated, my kidnappers tell me, it will be my fault.[2] Although they are not speaking the whole truth in saying this— obviously it will also be *their* fault—they are surely speaking the truth. For surely there is only one justified thing for me to do in such a case, and no apparent excuse for not doing it. I must commit the single wrong myself and thereby avoid the multiple and/or worse commissions of the same wrong by them. If that is true then there are no wrongs that cannot imaginably be justified or excused. Of every wrong it is true that one can imagine extreme circumstances in which one would be justified in committing it, and *a fortiori* extreme circumstances in which one would be excused. To say that a certain wrong is unjustifiable (or inexcusable) is only an emphatic way of saying that the relevant justifying (or excusing) circumstances do not in fact obtain. It is not to say that they never imaginably could.

There is much to be said about this argument before its success can be adjudicated. Here I will raise only one issue. It is the issue of whether it can be morally relevant, in determining what if anything I am justified or excused in doing, whether *I* would be flying the plane into the sky-scraper, whether *I* would be doing the torturing of innocents, and so on. All else being equal, shouldn't I care more about what *I* do, about my own wrongs, than about other people's? So shouldn't I give the avoidance of

[2] Their strategy of persuasion is essentially that of the militia commander in Bernard Williams's famous 'Jim in the Jungle' example: see 'A Critique of Utilitarianism' in JJC Smart and B Williams, *Utilitarianism: For and Against* (1973), at 98–99.

my own wrongdoing, all else being equal, more weight in my reasoning than the avoidance of wrongdoing by others? Agent-relativists are those who say that I should. Agent-neutralists are those who say that I should not. All else being equal, say agent-neutralists, it is self-indulgent or squeamish to care more about one's own wrongs than about those of other people, just as it is self-righteous or hypocritical to care more about the wrongs of other people than about one's own. Some agent-neutralists are strict consequentialists who think that actions can only ever be made wrong by their consequences, e.g. pain, misery, or death. But one may also believe, more plausibly, that actions such as torture and massacre are intrinsically wrong (wrong irrespective of their consequences), and yet still be an agent-neutralist about their avoidance. One may still think that what each of us should care about, and aim to achieve, is that there be less torture and less massacre in the world, never mind whether it is perpetrated by ourselves or by someone else. Under such a doctrine we are still interested in the consequences of wrongdoing, to be sure, but the consequences we are interested in are further wrongs, which are not made wrong by *their* consequences (and the wrongness of which is therefore missed or misrepresented by strict consequentialists).

Now an agent-neutralist can of course admit that one's own wrongs are the ones for which one is responsible, i.e. for which one owes a justification or an excuse and in respect of which one can be at fault.[3] But even though I may not owe a justification or excuse for other people's wrongs as such, the agent-neutralist story goes on, I may still owe a justification or excuse for my own failure to prevent other people's wrongs. I may still be responsible for other people's wrongs as an accomplice, a secondary wrongdoer who contributed to the commission of their wrongs. The real debate is then about whether, given the choice between my being an accomplice in wrongdoing (by failing to prevent its commission by others) and my being a principal in wrongdoing (by committing it myself), I should care more about, and hence give extra rational weight to, not committing it myself. The agent-neutralist offers a negative answer. It is no good replying on behalf of the agent-relativist that merely failing

---

[3] For simplicity, I am bracketing (and will not discuss here) the special case of vicarious responsibility. Vicarious responsibility is sometimes confused with responsibility as an accomplice. But the two are quite different. Being vicariously responsible means owing a justification or excuse for another's wrongs *irrespective of one's own participation in them*. One reason why the two are often confused is that, once institutionalized in the law, they may offer rival techniques for pursuing some of the same legal policies. On the legal policies (and with some symptoms of the confusion), see G Fletcher, *Rethinking Criminal Law* (1977), 642–644.

to prevent wrongdoing is not enough to make one an accomplice in that wrongdoing. The agent-neutralist will only point out that whether failing to prevent wrongdoing is enough to make one an accomplice in that wrongdoing must depend, *inter alia*, on whether one should care as much about the wrongs of others as one should care about one's own wrongs—and that, of course, is exactly what is at issue.

My own sympathies have always been with the agent-neutralist. It seems to me that the avoidance of wrongdoing by anyone is fundamentally everyone's concern.[4] So there is no general boundary of responsibility such that merely failing to prevent another's wrong cannot make one an accomplice. And yet a paradox seems to emerge as soon as we begin to think of the issue in terms of responsibility and fault. If I should not care about my own wrongs any more than I care about the wrongs of others, why should I care about my own responsibility or fault any more than I care about the responsibility or fault of others? 'Torture that innocent person,' say my kidnappers in an agent-neutralist spirit, 'or we will torture a hundred. If the hundred get tortured, it will be your fault.' I don't have to be an agent-relativist to resist this line of persuasion. Instead I can simply out-agent-neutralize my captors. I can reply: 'My fault or your fault, it's all the same to me. After all I don't care about what I do any more or less than I care about what you do, and that extends not only to wrongs but also to justifications and excuses. I don't care whether I am justified or excused any more or less than I care whether you are justified or excused. I don't care whose fault it all is. I'm not squeamish about such things.'

If this reply really contains a consistent extension of the agent-neutralist thought, then agent-neutralism has a big problem. Because now it turns out that an agent-neutralist *can't* tell the story that I suggested she could 'of course' tell about responsibility. She can't after all say that my morally salient connection with the wrongs of my kidnappers is as an accomplice, a secondary wrongdoer who contributes to the commission of their wrongs by failing to prevent those wrongs. It turns out that this way of looking at the problem was an agent-relativist Trojan horse. For thinking about the problem in terms of complicity by failing to prevent already assumes an agent-relative standpoint. It assumes that I should care about my wrongs in a way that I shouldn't care about the wrongs of others. Otherwise, why is it morally salient that, by failing to prevent

[4] J Gardner and T Macklem, 'Reasons' in J Coleman and S Shapiro (eds), *The Oxford Handbook of Jurisprudence and Philosophy of Law* (2002).

other people's wrongs, *I too do wrong*? As an agent-neutralist I should simply care to prevent wrongs; whether they are mine is irrelevant. Only an agent-relativist can be animated to avoid wrongdoing by the thought of her own involvement in it, by the thought that at least some of the wrongdoing would be her own.

So it begins to look like we are forced to agent-relativism by agent-neutralism itself. It looks like my kidnappers can't get any hold over me with their agent-neutralist arguments unless I am agent-relativist enough to care especially about my own involvement; but if I am agent-relativist enough to care especially about my own involvement, their agent-neutralist arguments anyway lose their hold over me. To put it another way, it looks like one cannot be a consistent agent-neutralist. Fortunately, it only looks that way. The foregoing remarks build a paradox out of an ambiguity. There are two different senses in which particular wrongs might be 'especially mine to care about'. Consider my promise to submit this paper for publication. My promise creates a duty on me that only I can fulfil. Of course, this doesn't necessarily mean that only I can do the actual submitting. Maybe that can be done for me by an assistant. Whether that is true depends on how exactly we interpret the promise. But what it does mean is that, however we interpret the promise, there is some action of promise-keeping that is mine to perform (either submitting the essay myself or having it submitted for me). If I don't do this thing, the promise wasn't kept, and the duty it created wasn't fulfilled. So the reason that my promise gives me to keep my promise is, as I will put it, *personal in respect of conformity*. Thanks to my promise there is a reason for me to conform to. What does not follow is that the reason is also *personal in respect of attention*, that only I should feel the force of the reason in my practical reasoning. On the contrary, it may be that everyone in the world owes my reason the same rational attention that I do. It may be that my keeping my promise is everyone's business, so that everyone should, all else being equal, help me to do so with the same vigour as if the promise were theirs. They could in principle do this by encouraging me in my promise-keeping, or by facilitating me, reminding me, coercing me, etc. There are many possible ways for other people to give my reason the full attention it deserves, assuming that the reason is impersonal in respect of attention. The only principled limit to what they can do to help me is that they can't actually keep the promise for me. For, to reiterate, my reason to keep my promise is personal in respect of conformity.

The debate between agent-relativists and agent-neutralists is a debate about whether reasons (or some of them) are personal in respect of attention. Agent-relativists say 'yes'; agent-neutralists say 'no'. Agent-relativists say that, all else being equal, others have less reason (or less compelling reason) than I have to contribute to my keeping my promise; agent-neutralists say that, all else being equal, others have as much reason (and as compelling reason) as I have to contribute to my keeping my promise.[5] But both sides can readily admit that keeping my promise is something that only I can do. Even those who insist that all reasons are impersonal in respect of attention can still consistently accept that at least some reasons are personal in respect of conformity. So the agent-neutralist victim of the sadistic kidnappers can still say that her actions are her responsibility and the actions of her kidnappers are their responsibility. All that this means is that there are some reasons for her to conform to, and other reasons for them to conform to. This is not an agent-relativist Trojan horse. She is not saying, or suggesting, that in deciding what she should do she should give more emphasis or weight to what she does than to what the kidnappers do. Indeed, she could consistently assert that her main responsibility for the time being is to stop her kidnappers carrying out their nefarious plan. If she fails, she might say, she is responsible for failing to stop them committing their wrongs. She is then asserting her responsibility as an accomplice. But she is not asserting her responsibility as a principal. For the wrong she admits to is a wrong of contributing to the kidnappers' wrongs (by failing to prevent them). It is a secondary wrong. It is her wrong but it is her wrong of failing to minimize the wrongdoing of all.

Another way of saying this is to say that, for agent-neutralists and agent-relativists alike, the distinction between principals and accomplices is embedded in the structure of rational agency. As rational beings we cannot live without it. I am responsible for what I do, and you are responsible for what you do. But on any credible view I need to give attention, in what I do, to what you will do in consequence. And you need to give attention, in what you do, to what I will do in consequence. In that sense, there are two parts of morality. There is what I should do *simpliciter*, and then there is what I should do by way of contribution to what you do. If I fail in the first I am a principal. If I fail in the second

---

[5] Many hold mixed views according to which some reasons are agent-neutral and other are agent-relative. See, e.g., Nagel's 'The Fragmentation of Value' in his *Mortal Questions* (1979), or Scheffler's *The Rejection of Consequentialism* (1982).

I am an accomplice. The truism 'I am responsible for my actions' cannot mean that I am responsible for my actions, never mind your actions. For my own actions inevitably include my actions of contributing to your actions. This much is (or should be) uncontentious. What is contentious is the further issue of how, in thinking about which actions I should perform, I should *count* those actions of yours to which I would thereby be contributing. Agent-relativists say that, all else being equal, I should count your actions for less—give them less rational attention—than I would count my own actions. Agent-neutralists say that, all else being equal, I should count them just the same.

In principle, an agent-neutralist view creates greater scope for wrongful complicity than does an agent-relativist view. On an agent-neutralist view, those who contribute to the wrongs of others can claim no allowance in respect of rational attentiveness for the mere fact that those wrongs are not their own. All else being equal, on an agent-neutralist view, I should not prefer my failing to prevent you committing a grisly murder than over my committing the same grisly murder myself. All else being equal, I shouldn't care whether it will be you or me holding the knife. All else being equal, I am complicit in murder—*in effect* a murderer myself—if I don't prevent you from murdering.

But all else is rarely equal. For by and large, I am better-placed to prevent my own wrongs than I am to prevent yours. Of course there are many contingencies involved in working out how well-placed I am to prevent your wrongs. Something depends on who you are to me, what kind of wrong you are planning, where you are physically located, whether I can trust you to keep your side of the deal, how much I know about what is going on, etc. The point is only that it would *often* be an inefficient use of rational energy for me to pay the same rational attention to your wrongs as I pay to my own. I would be more productively employed, as the saying goes, keeping my own house in order.

This is the main consideration that militates against a radically expanded scope for complicity, even on an agent-neutralist view. It explains, in agent-neutral terms, the conspicuous element of superficial agent-relativity in everyday moral experience. Often—but not always—a mere failure to prevent a wrong committed by another is not enough to make me an accomplice to that wrong. Some more active contribution is required. This reflects the fact that, to put it crudely, stepping in to prevent another's wrong typically has more costs and fewer benefits, even in terms of wrongdoing-avoidance itself, than does refusing to procure or enable the commission of another's wrong. The reasons at stake here—the reasons to avoid wrongdoing—are ultimately agent-neutral. But they include agent-neutral reasons for people to reason and react agent-relatively over a range of cases.[6] So they yield derivative agent-relative reasons. There are agent-neutral reasons why, sometimes, we should regard other people's wrongdoing (agent-relatively) as being less our business, and less worthy of our rational attention, than our own wrongdoing would be. And these reasons are reflected, quite properly, in how we judge people and their actions morally, and in particular whether and when we judge them to have been wrongdoers by their complicity in the wrongdoing of others.

Doesn't the case against a radically expanded domain of complicity have more to do with freedom than it has to do with the efficient use of rational energy? Doesn't respect for our freedom require that we be counted as accomplices only in a narrow range of cases? Certainly, freedom is important in deciding how much of the morality of complicity we should institutionalize in the law (in the same way that freedom is important in deciding how much of the morality of anything we should institutionalize in the law). But freedom has little bearing on the morality of complicity apart from the law. True, in order to avoid being complicit, one might sometimes have to stop someone committing a wrong by coercing him or manipulating him, both of which would invade his freedom. But that consideration has already been implicitly folded into our discussion under the heading of rational efficiency. Imagine that the wrong about to be committed is one of coercion or manipulation, and it is a wrong I could possibly prevent by coercion or manipulation. Then the simple question we have been addressing is whether, given that there is going to be coercion or manipulation either way, I should prefer not to be the coercer or the manipulator myself. For an agent-relativist the basic answer is 'yes'. For an agent-neutralist the basic answer is 'no'. The main qualification for the agent-neutralist is the one I mentioned already. Am I best-placed to intervene? Sometimes yes, sometimes no. Sometimes it would be better, agent-neutrally, for me to leave the business of wrong-prevention to others, such as the wrongdoer himself, or his mother, or his teacher, or the law. That being so, it might be better for me to think agent-relatively, to downgrade the wrong in respect of the rational attention I give it. So there need be no differences in eventual moral judgment—in determining who counts as an accomplice and who does not—as between those who start from an agent-neutral position and those who start from an agent-relative position. The only essential difference lies in whether

---

[6] See D Parfit, *Reasons and Persons* (1984), 112–114.

the element of agent-relativity in ordinary moral experience (which is what admittedly limits the domain of complicity) calls for, or does not call for, a deeper agent-neutral defence.

3. Causality and the elimination of complicity

So there are two parts of morality. There is what I should do *simpliciter* (the morality of principalship), and then there is what I should do by way of contribution to what you do (the morality of complicity). 'Contribution' here means 'causal contribution'. What is at stake in the debate between agent-neutralists and agent-relativists is how to count, in determining what each of us should do, what others do *in consequence* or *as a result*.[7] If what I do has no consequences or results for what anyone else will do, there is nothing for agent-neutralists and agent-relativists to disagree about. My action is not linked to anyone else's actions in such a way as to raise the question of how anyone else's actions are to be counted in determining what I am to do.

Spelling this feature out may lead some to think that the discussion has gone down the wrong path. For shouldn't this feature lead us to doubt whether the examples we have been discussing so far need be analysed in terms of complicity at all? Consider the story in which my captors will have 50 planes flown into 50 skyscrapers if I don't fly one plane into one skyscraper. For simplicity's sake, let's assume agent-neutrality. And for simplicity's sake, let's assume that there is a wrong of killing *per se*, a wrong with no other ingredient but killing. In the example, there is admittedly killing on both sides. It is a case in which my responsibility for the higher number of killings (where the planes are flown by other people) would be as accomplice, whereas my responsibility for the lower number of killings (where I fly the plane myself) would be as principal. But why can't it be the ordinary responsibility of a principal on both sides? After all, my refusal to kill just a few hundred people will admittedly have the deaths of all those thousands of people among its consequences. In other words, I will have caused all those thousands of deaths. In other words again, I will have killed all those thousands of people, as

---

[7] Results are outcomes of actions that are also constituents of them; consequences, by contrast, are non-constitutive outcomes. This useful terminology is owed to GH von Wright, *Norm and Action* (1963), 39ff. Probably, in cases of complicity, the principal's action should be regarded as a result rather than a consequence of the accomplice's action. But we need not settle the question here.

surely as if I had flown the planes myself. That being so, the choice that my kidnappers give me is simply a choice between my killing a smaller number of people and my killing a larger number. Either way, I am a principal, a killer. It's true that my killing the larger number is by omission (my not flying and crashing a plane), whereas my wrongfully killing the smaller number is by positive act (my flying and crashing a plane). But this distinction can clearly be accommodated within the scope of principalship. On any credible analysis of killing, there can be killing by omission as well as by positive act. That being so, complicity can be eliminated from the story altogether.[8]

This strategy of elimination works for some imaginable wrongs but not for others. If there is a wrong *per se* of acting with fatal consequences, then clearly anybody who procures the commission of that wrong also commits the wrong as a principal. With some provisos, the same can be said of the wrong of causing death, if causing death is a wrong *per se*. But the same can't be said of the wrong of killing. Killing is not merely causing death, and causing death, in turn, is not merely acting with fatal consequences. In saying this I am not relying on the idea that to be a killer one must have a mens rea of some kind, or be at fault. I am assuming that it is possible to be an accidental and faultless killer. What I mean is that killing is *causally* different from merely causing death and that causing death, in turn, is *causally* different from occasioning death. Roughly, killing is causing death other than by making a causal contribution to a killing by someone else; causing death, in turn, is making a causal contribution to a death other than by making a causal contribution to an abnormal action or event (often known as a *novus actus interveniens*) that itself makes a causal contribution to the death.[9]

You can see at once, even in these rough renditions, what I mean by saying that the differences are causal differences. Causing death is a causally refined way of causally contributing to death. It requires a distinctive causal route from causer to death, free of any *novus actus interveniens*. Killing in turn is a causally refined way of causing death. It requires a distinctive causal route from killer to death, not mediated through a killing by someone else. This is consistent with the observation that it is possible to kill by omission. If I go away for a month and leave my toddler locked

[8] For a nice application of this line of thought, see *Empress Car Company (Abertillery) Ltd* v *National Rivers Authority* [1999] 2 AC 22.

[9] On *novus actus interveniens*, and the classification of causal contributions more generally, the most important contribution was made by HLA Hart and T Honoré in *Causation in the Law* (2nd edn, 1984).

in the house without food, I kill her by failing to feed her. I am clearly a principal in her killing, a killer. The causal route from me to the death is not interrupted by a *novus actus interveniens* nor is it mediated through killing by another. But things are quite different if I fail to stop someone else from poisoning my toddler. Then my causal contribution is mediated by someone else's act of killing. It follows that I do not commit the wrong of killing myself, assuming always that there is such a wrong, but am at most complicit in its commission by failing to prevent it. Failing to prevent a child being killed is not the same as killing a child by failing to prevent her death. In fact the two are mutually exclusive. Either I killed the child myself or I contributed to someone else's doing the killing; it can't be both. (We may say, when I contributed to someone else's doing the killing, that I was a killer 'in effect'. I used this idiom myself above. But a killer in effect is not a killer. It is a person whose actions had the same result or consequence as those of a killer.)

This intriguing causal refinement that distinguishes killing from causing death also distinguishes various other nominate action-types from their less causally refined neighbours. To take another example from my own earlier discussion: the causal element of torture is not merely causing pain, let alone acting with painful consequences. It is *inflicting* pain. Inflicting pain is causing pain other than by making a causal contribution to an infliction of pain by someone else; causing pain, in turn, is making a causal contribution to pain other than by making a causal contribution to an abnormal action or event that itself makes a causal contribution to the pain. So when I fail to prevent or procure the torture of a hundred people, I am not myself their torturer. Following Sandy Kadish, I will call actions like these 'nonproxyable'.[10] Kadish uses the label to refer to actions (such as having sex and eating) that do not consist in making a causal contribution to anything. Since they do not consist in making a causal contribution to anything, one obviously cannot engage in them oneself by contributing causally to another person's engaging in them. But what Kadish does not notice is that there are many actions that *do* consist in making a causal contribution to something, but which also have the feature of being non-proxyable, because the requisite causal contribution is a refined one. This is true of not only killing and torturing, but also of coercing, enslaving, inducing, destroying, igniting, and countless other action-types. Just leaf through the dictionary for plentiful

[10] S Kadish, 'Complicity, Cause, and Blame: A Study in the Interpretation of Doctrine', *California Law Review* 73 (1985), 323 (at n 162).

examples. Where non-proxable actions are wrongs *per se* or necessary ingredients of more complex wrongs, one cannot be a principal in these wrongs by making one's causal contribution through another principal. In such cases, whoever acts through a principal must be an accomplice.[11] So in such cases, the attempt to eliminate complicity from the moral landscape, in favour of a more capacious domain of principalship, fails.

Why, we may wonder, are so many common-or-garden nominate action-types non-proxable? Part of the answer surely lies in the fact that such action-types are often wrongs *per se* or at least necessary ingredients of more complex wrongs. Where the wrongs in question are common, it saves a lot of time if such action-types have names of their own. But that answer just invites a restatement of the question. Why are there so many wrongs that have actions of non-proxable types as necessary ingredients? Why, in other words, are our moral classifications so often organized around keeping principals segregated from accomplices? We already know the answer. The distinction between principals and accomplices, as we discovered, is embedded in the structure of rational agency. As rational beings we cannot live without it. It enters our thought as soon as we begin to think about responsibility. I am responsible for my actions, and you are responsible for yours. My actions are mine to justify or excuse, and your actions are yours to justify or excuse. And yet my actions include my actions of contributing to your actions. So there is a sense in which my responsibility for my actions can extend out to your actions. I can be accused of failing to attend to reasons that are yours to conform to even though I cannot be accused of failing to conform to them myself. I fail to attend to them, in the relevant sense, by contributing to your non-conformity with them. The question which divides agent-relativists and agent-neutralists is merely how much of this kind of rational attention I should be giving to your reasons. Which contributions to your non-conformity make me complicit in it? The two sides differ in their response. But they can do so without disagreeing about what counts as principalship.

This much is repetition. It repeats the explanation of why the contrast between principals and accomplices is embedded in the structure of rational agency. The pay-off that we have just discovered is that the distinction between principals and accomplices is therefore often marked in

---

[11] Notice, interestingly, that some wrongs of complicity may themselves involve non-proxable actions. Inducing a wrong is a possible way of being an accomplice. But one cannot be an inducer of a principal by acting through another inducer, because inducing is a non-proxable action.

morality. Many moral wrongs, such as torture and rape and betrayal and deceit, are committed only by performing non-proxyable actions, such that anyone who contributes to their commission through another person's commission of them is an accomplice, not a principal, in their commission. If moral theory has lost sight of this distinction in recent times, we have the consequentialist revolutionaries to thank. Strict consequentialists insist that it matters only what consequences my action has, not how those consequences come about (where this has no further consequences). We have just found one reason why they cannot be right about this. They cannot be right because if they were right, an elementary truth about responsibility would be falsified. The elementary truth is that I am responsible for my actions, while you are responsible for yours. Each of us has a different relationship to our own actions from the relationship that we have to the actions of others. The relationship we have to our own actions is direct: we answer for them as such. The relationship we have to the actions of others is indirect: we answer for them only inasmuch as, by our own actions, we contribute to them. If strict consequentialists want to abandon the distinction between these two modes of responsibility for actions, they need to abandon not merely agent-relativism, but also the idea that we each have a special relationship to our own actions. In the process, strict consequentialists take their own moral position to the edge of intelligibility. Who is strict consequentialism addressed to, if not to each of us in respect of our own actions? How does it survive as a moral view without presupposing the elementary truth that we are each responsible for our own actions?

Many people, bending over backwards to avoid this strict consequentialist error, are tempted to say that people, as responsible agents, have free will and defy causality. Causal chains therefore cannot run to or through their actions. One wipes people out of the story, as responsible agents, if one insists on subjecting their actions to causal explanations or on running causal explanations through their actions. So it is often said. But this strikes me as an equal and opposite mistake, a way of fending off strict consequentialism that throws the baby out with the bathwater. For the strict consequentialist clearly has one thing right. When I pay a hitman to kill an enemy, it is a straightforward consequence of what I do that the hitman kills my enemy, and hence that my enemy dies. Barring the special case of *novus actus interveniens*, I procure the killing and I also cause, through the hitman, the death. There is a straightforward causal explanation of how it all unfolds, action and reaction, antecedent and consequent. None of this wipes out the hitman's part in the story as a responsible agent. On the contrary, it presupposes it. The hitman's part in the story as a responsible agent is wiped out only if we go on to claim that I was myself a killer (not just a killer in effect, but a killer). The reason why this wipes out the hitman's part in the story as a responsible agent is not that the hitman has free will and can change his mind after I give him the go-ahead. His change of mind after I give him the go-ahead is no different, causally speaking, from a change in the wind after I throw a ball. No—the reason why claiming that I was the killer wipes out his part in the story as a responsible agent is that he was the killer—and only one of us can be the killer.[12] He committed the primary and non-proxyable wrong. My part in the causal story was not as principal but as accomplice. In fact I straightforwardly caused him to commit the wrong. To say that is to confirm, not to deny, his responsible agency.

4. Complicity beyond causality?

Procuring or causing or inducing someone to commit a wrong; failing to prevent or permitting or enabling the commission of a wrong: these are straightforwardly causal modes of complicity. Where these modes of complicity are concerned, the principal would not have committed her wrong but for the accomplice's intervention. The accomplice clearly made a difference to the overall incidence of wrongdoing; the world clearly contains extra wrongs thanks to her. But there are other modes of complicity (for example, assisting and encouraging the commission of a wrong) which are prone to fail this test. I lend someone the tools that she uses to break into a house; but she didn't exactly *need* them; she would have got in by other means even without my tools. I egg the kidnapper on with reminders of the great rewards his crime may bring; but he didn't exactly need my encouragement; he was going ahead with the kidnap plan anyway. English law says, and I think rightly, that I am complicit in these cases only because my assistance actually assists and my encouragement actually encourages.[13] A failed attempt at assistance or encouragement is just that. It may still be wrongful but it is not complicity, any more than a failed attempt at murder is murder. It is a failed attempt because it has no effect, no impact, on the principal. This helps us to see that there must be *something* causal going on in these cases. I am making

---

[12] Of course, there could be more than one killer in a case involving joint principals. See J Gardner, 'Reasons for Teamwork', *Legal Theory* 8 (2002), 495.

[13] *Clarkson* [1971] 3 All ER 344.

some kind of causal contribution to the principal's wrong that serves to turn my attempt into a success. But the problem is that I don't seem to have made a difference to the overall incidence of wrongdoing; the world contains no extra wrongs thanks to me. This may make us think again of Solzhenitsyn's way of dividing up morality. The wrongdoing is coming into the world anyway; perhaps one can't change that; and yet there remains a sense (doesn't there?) in which the wrongdoing comes into the world through the accomplice—with his assistance or encouragement—and that is what implicates him in it as an accomplice.

Granted that I made some kind of causal contribution to the principal's wrong, why is it a problem for the causal view of complicity (as we may call the view defended in this paper) if I didn't thereby make a difference to the *overall incidence* of wrongdoing? It is a problem because it seems odd that someone should be expected to pay attention (in her practical reasoning) to features of the world that will come out no better whatever she does. Whether one is an agent-neutralist or an agent-relativist about the avoidance of wrongdoing, shouldn't one advocate (under the heading of the efficient use of rational energy) that people aim to make differences to wrongdoing they *can* make rather than differences they *can't* make? Of course, one may reply that assistance and encouragement often do make all the difference between commission and non-commission of the principal wrong. Often they tip the balance. The risk that one will tip the balance in any particular case arguably justifies a general rule against providing assistance or encouragement to potential wrongdoers, a general rule that applies even to cases where the help or encouragement proves unnecessary, because the wrong will be committed anyway. No doubt this consideration is valid and important. It figures not only in justifying the law of complicity, but also in explaining the morality of complicity apart from the law. But there is also a deeper consideration in play that has nothing to do with the risk of tipping the balance. For there is a sense in which, even when the assistance or encouragement furnished to a wrongdoer is unnecessary, it does (in spite of appearances) make a difference to the overall incidence of wrongdoing, a difference that warrants attention in the accomplice's practical reasoning.

As a first step towards seeing this deeper consideration, think about the infamous 'arms dealer' defence: 'If I don't do it, somebody else will.'[14] This defence strikes most of us as lame. But why? Surely the arms dealer

---

[14] For excellent discussion, see J Glover, 'It Makes No Difference Whether or Not I Do It', *Aristotelian Society Supp Vol* 49 (1975), 171.

has a point. Surely it makes no difference to the overall incidence of arms dealing whether this particular dealer deals in arms or not. There are plenty of others waiting in the wings. Maybe they will even be able to deliver the same arms on the same day at the same price. If this arms dealer were shot today, there would scarcely be a blip in the statistics for arms dealing this year. So the arms dealer doesn't really change anything. Or does he? We are invited to think of the problem impersonally, perhaps calculating the net number of arms dealt, or the net number of arms deals done. Possibly this arms dealer makes no difference to those impersonal figures. But it is important to remind ourselves that the arms dealer himself has no business thinking of the problem so impersonally. After all, some of the arms deals in question are his arms deals and this makes him responsible for them as a principal. They are his to justify or excuse. Other deals that might take place if he did not deal would not be his. At most he would be responsible for them as an accomplice. This certainly opens up the question that arose, *mutatis mutandis*, in the case of the sadistic kidnappers: whether and when the avoidance of (complicity in) arms dealing by others is capable of justifying one in dealing arms oneself. In answering this question, it clearly matters how much arms dealing is involved on each side, and how bad the arms dealing is. But notice that it also matters *why* one engages in the arms dealing. One justifies one's own arms dealing by pointing to the arms dealing of others thereby avoided only if one deals in arms *in order to* avoid arms dealing by others. So one needs to pay attention (in one's practical reasoning) to the facts upon which one relies for justification.[15] That is why the 'arms dealer' defence seems so lame. The arms dealer who makes it clearly does not deal in arms to avoid arms dealing by others.

As I said before, it is not obvious that someone should pay attention (in her practical reasoning) to features of the world that will come out no better whatever she does. But it is obvious that she must pay such attention if she relies on those features *by way of justification* for what she does. Justifying one's wrongs is not cancelling them; it is showing that one committed them for a sufficient reason, that one was not unreasonable in committing them. That being so, we should not allow the arms dealer to get away with the idea that, by dealing arms, he made no difference to the overall incidence of wrongdoing. In the relevant sense of 'overall

---

[15] For detailed explanation, see J Gardner, 'Justifications and Reasons' in AP Simester and ATH Smith (eds), *Harm and Culpability* (1996) (reprinted as Chapter 5 in this volume).

difference', he did make an overall difference. He added his own arms dealings. True, he also subtracted like arms dealing by others, by competitors of his who would have filled the space in the arms market if he had moved into another line of work. But he cannot be allowed simply to treat the subtraction as cancelling out the addition, as yielding a zero sum. That is an abdication of responsibility. It is an abdication of responsibility because it is a refusal to accept that the relationship he has to his own wrongs is different from the relationship that he has to his competitors' wrongs; in particular, that he can rely upon theirs to justify his only if he commits his in order to avoid theirs.

How does this help us understand cases in which the accomplice's assistance or encouragement is, so to speak, surplus to the principal's requirements? There are some dissimilarities. But all the cases teach the same lesson. In the assistance and encouragement cases, as in the case of the arms dealer, we should resist the idea that the accomplice made no difference to the overall incidence of wrongdoing, in the relevant sense of 'overall incidence'. She added the wrongs (of the principal) to which she (as an accomplice) made a contribution. True, she also subtracted wrongs to which she did not make a contribution, wrongs which, *ex hypothesi*, would have been committed without her assistance or encouragement. But the wrongs that she subtracted cannot be regarded as literally cancelling out the wrongs that she added. By virtue of her contribution to them, she stands in a different relationship to the wrongs that were added. It is an abdication of responsibility for her to rely on the wrongs thereby subtracted unless she is pointing to them by way of justification or excuse for her own contribution. In which case she has to explain how the avoidance of those subtracted wrongs figured in her practical reasoning. So she cannot help herself to the proposal that she need not attend (in her practical reasoning) to features of the world that will come out no better whatever she does. She needs to have attended, in her practical reasoning, to whatever features of the world she relies upon to justify her own acts. If they did not figure in her practical reasoning, they also do not help her to defend her contribution to the principal's wrongs.

You may say that this line of thought is question-begging. It assumes that our assister or encourager is an accomplice in order to explain why, on the causal view, she is an accomplice. But that is not quite true. The argument certainly assumes that the assister or encourager contributes to the wrongs of the principal. But that assumption was built in at the start. We followed English law in insisting that it is a necessary condition of being an assister or encourager that (as the case may be) one's assistance actually assists or one's encouragement actually encourages. The fact that one made such a contribution already gives one something to justify. Does it already make one complicit? The issue is tricky. Of course, there are tricky issues of intention and knowledge to settle. But that is not the area of trickiness I have in mind. The trickiness I have in mind is this: should we consider someone's justification for performing an act before or after deciding that the someone in question is an accomplice? Is complicity the thing to be justified or the unjustified thing? In surveying the debate between agent-neutralists and agent-relativists in section 2 above ('Principals and accomplices'), I sided with the view that at least some questions of justification need to be settled first, before classifying an agent as an accomplice. That is why (I claimed) agent-neutralism throws, in principle, a wider net of complicity than agent-relativism: it allows each of us fewer *justified* abstentions from preventing the wrongs of others. If this view is right, then the argument of this section was not question-begging. It certainly assumed that an assister or encourager contributes to the principal's wrong. But the argument did not assume that an assister or encourager was thereby made complicit in the principal's wrong. Rather, before classifying her as complicit, it allowed her the opportunity to justify her assistance or encouragement of the principal's wrongs by reference to the alternative wrongs that were thereby avoided: in other words, by reference to the difference that she made to the overall incidence of wrongdoing. So we are still in part one of Solzhenitsyn's two-part morality. We are still talking about those who make a difference to the state of the world.

5. After Solzhenitsyn

Solzhenitsyn's remark makes us think of the defensive arms dealer in the following way. The arms dealer doesn't really make a difference to the incidence of wrongdoing. The arms dealing that he is about to embark upon will 'come into the world' whatever he does. The only question for him is whether to be implicated in this particular arms trading, whether it is to 'come through him'. How is he implicated in this particular arms deal given that he makes no difference to it? The puzzle vanishes if we think of the principal wrongdoer as something much bigger than him, say the arms *industry* as a whole. It is the arms industry that is necessary for any particular arms to be dealt. One arms trader is just a tiny cog in the huge machine of wrongdoing. It is being a cog that makes him

complicit. The question then becomes: does he need to make any difference at all, anywhere in the industry, to be implicated? Does he have to
make at least a tiny marginal difference? Or is it enough that he is just
part of it, dealing arms, joining in the industry's ventures, albeit making
not even a marginal difference to the extent of arms trading? Can one
perhaps even be a wrongdoer simply by association?[16]
    I have already suggested how to approach these questions. No doubt
there are plenty of cases where the principal is a collectivity and the
individuals who make up the collectivity are accomplices. Perhaps they
throw up special difficulties connected with the marginality of individual contributions.[17] But such cases proliferate out of control if one begins
as Solzhenitsyn begins. In Solzhenitsyn's vein, one thinks of the problem
in two parts, beginning with the moral shape of the world—the wrongs
that will be there anyway, with or without my personal influence. One
shifts afterwards to thinking about *my* moral position, and that of other
particular people. Given that the wrongs will come into the world anyway, how can I avoid getting my hands dirty on them? In place of this
way of dividing up morality, I have been trying to lay the groundwork
for a different picture in which the moral shape of the world is simply
the moral position of the people in it. Wrongdoing never just 'comes
into the world' and accomplices never just get their hands dirty on it on
the way past. Accomplices themselves bring wrongdoing into the world.
So too do principals. The essential difference between accomplices and
principals is that accomplices bring wrongdoing into the world through
principals. And that is where morality cleaves in two. An accomplice is
one who acts with the consequence or result that the principal commits
the wrong. I see no reason to believe that there is any other way of being
complicit in another's wrongdoing than by making such a difference.

    [16] Of course, associating with wrongdoers could itself be a principal wrong. I don't
mean to raise any question mark over that possibility.
    [17] Some of them are discussed with great profit by C Kutz in *Complicity: Law and
Ethics for a Collective Age* (2000). I tend to think that Kutz is too quick to abandon the
causal view defended above. For some brief remarks, see my review of his book in *Ethics*
114 (2004), 827.

4

In Defence of Defences

1. Wrongdoing and justification

According to a view of wrongdoing that I will call the 'closure' view, no action is wrong unless it is wrong *all things considered*, i.e. taking account of both the reasons in favour of performing it (the pros) and the reasons against performing it (the cons). This view was promoted in its simplest and most accessible form by the utilitarians. Yet its appeal was never distinctively utilitarian. It was espoused no less vigorously by Kant. From his anti-utilitarian view that it is always morally wrong to fail do what any moral reason would have one do, Kant concluded that there can be no moral reasons in favour of performing an action if there are moral reasons against performing it.[1] For otherwise, some morally wrong actions would not be morally wrong all things considered, and that would be inconsistent with the closure view of wrongdoing, which Kant treated as axiomatic.

The closure view of wrongdoing obviously takes a lot of philosophical weight off the shoulders of the idea of *justification*. What calls for justification, we can all presumably agree, is that to which there is some rational objection. One might think that the fact that an action is wrong yields a powerful rational objection to its performance, and that wrongdoing therefore calls for justification if anything does. But according to the closure view, wrongdoing can't possibly call for justification, because the reasons in favour of performing the action that would be relied upon to justify it have already been counted in settling whether the action was wrong. Talk of 'justified wrongdoing' therefore turns out to be oxymoronic. Naturally one may still say something more circumspect. Even on the closure view, one may say that an action was 'prima facie' wrong, and yet justified. But the words 'prima facie', as used by supporters of the closure view, carry the connotation that the action was not really wrong

---

[1] Kant, *The Metaphysic of Morals* (trans Gregor, 1996), 16–17.

at all. It only seemed to be wrong, on the strength of incomplete information. When all the pros and cons of performing it were known, it turned
out not to be wrong at all.[2]

Opponents of the closure view sometimes also speak of 'prima facie
wrongs', but they mean something quite different by the expression. For
them, prima facie wrongdoing is simply wrongdoing.[3] It is therefore
something to which there is a rational objection, and which accordingly
calls for justification. The words 'prima facie' are added only as a warning
against the tendency to interpret the word 'wrong' in line with the more
prevalent closure view. Clearly, the words 'prima facie' are an unhappy
choice for this role, since they may just as readily be interpreted as casting
doubt on whether the action is really wrong at all, and hence as confirming the preconceptions of subscribers to the closure view.[4] Nevertheless,
they are intended to have the opposite effect. Calling an action 'prima
facie wrong' is intended to affirm that the action really is wrong, while
leaving open the further question of whether the wrongdoing is justified.
By the same token, an action that is 'all things considered wrong' is not
merely a wrong action. It is a wrong action and also (a quite separate matter) an unjustified one. If it were justified, that would not stop it being
wrong. It would merely make it wrong but justified, a conclusion which
might be conveyed by saying that it was 'all things considered alright' to
perform it. Or so say the opponents of the closure view.

So the contrast between the two views could be brought out nicely by
saying that on the closure view, one cannot understand what a 'prima
facie' wrong is without first understanding what an 'all things considered' wrong is. A prima facie wrong, on this view, is merely an action
that appears to be (all things considered) wrong until the full facts are
known. But on the rival view that I have just set out, the reverse is true.

---

[2] D Lyons, *Forms and Limits of Utilitarianism* (1965), 19–22; RB Brandt, 'Morality
and its Critics', *Am Phil Q* 26 (1989), 89.
[3] See J Searle, 'Prima Facie Obligations' in J Raz (ed), *Practical Reasoning* (1978);
AJ Simmons, *Moral Principles and Political Obligation* (1979), 24–28. Both Searle and
Simmons go on to abandon the 'prima facie' terminology.
[4] The problem started with WD Ross, who first coined the terminology. Ross could
never decide whether, in calling some wrongs 'prima facie', he meant to commit himself
to the closure view of wrongdoing or on the contrary to repudiate that view. Sometimes
he said that prima facie wrongs are simply actions of a type that *tend* to be wrong but need
not always be: *The Right and the Good* (1930) at 28. But sometimes he said they remained
'morally unsuitable' (i.e. wrong) on all occasions, even when all things considered they
ought to be committed: *Foundations of Ethics* (1939), 85. His official definition of a
'prima facie duty' on page 20 of the former book tries to walk a non-existent line between
the two interpretations.

One cannot understand what an 'all things considered' wrong is without first understanding what a 'prima facie' wrong is. A prima facie wrong is just a wrong, while an all things considered wrong is a wrong *with an added feature*, namely absence of justification.

Which view is right? One finds a great deal of ambivalence in contemporary writings, and nowhere more so than in the work of contemporary criminal lawyers. Criminal lawyers retain in their analytical armoury the distinct concepts of 'offence' and 'defence'. For some purposes and on some occasions they present defences, including justificatory defences, as constituting a weapon on the defendant's side that is distinct from, and additional to, a mere denial of the offence. By pleading a justification, the story goes, the defendant does not *deny* but rather *concedes* criminal wrongdoing, which is the very thing that he then tries to justify (e.g. by arguing that he acted in reasonable self-defence). Here the closure view is denied.[5] But for other purposes and on other occasions, the closure view reasserts itself. The distinction between offences and defences is then played down as a technicality, a specialized lawyers' distinction that may bear in some way on evidence or procedure, say, but is of no *substantive* importance. To say that the defendant committed a criminal wrong but was justified comes to the same thing, in the end, as saying that she committed no criminal wrong.[6] Whichever way one expresses it, the criminal law has no wish to condemn, deter, or punish such actions. And that is all that ultimately matters. In this vein, many criminal lawyers end up concurring with HLA Hart's conclusion that 'killing in self-defence is an *exception* to the general rule'.[7] That is to say: once the definition of the criminal wrong is fully spelled out, with all of its little nooks and crannies, it already automatically anticipates the so-called 'justificatory' case, and leaves the killer with nothing to justify. The closure view strikes back.

Inverting the conventional textbook wisdom, I tend to think that criminal lawyers are thinking in a more shallow and technical way when they side with Hart and endorse the closure view, and in a deeper way when they rebel against the closure view and assert the substantive importance of their distinction between offences and defences. It is true that this distinction between offences and defences can be difficult to place in particular cases. Regarding some arguments available to criminal defendants it is admittedly unclear, morally as well as legally, whether

---

[5] See e.g. G Williams, *Textbook of Criminal Law* (2nd edn, 1983), 50–51.

[6] ibid, 138 (and especially n 6 on that page).

[7] HLA Hart, 'Prolegomenon to the Principles of Punishment' in his *Punishment and Responsibility* (1968), at 13.

they are to be regarded as denials of wrongdoing, or rather as concessions of wrongdoing coupled with assertions of justification. That is because, morally as well as legally, some wrongs (notably wrongs defined in terms of negligence) do admittedly anticipate, in their very definitions, various arguments that would otherwise count as justificatory. But these are special, complicated cases.[8] Denying the closure view does not mean denying that there are cases of this type. It means insisting that cases of this type are complicated variations on cases of a simpler and more basic type in which assertions of justification are distinct—in a morally as well as legally significant way—from denials of the wrong.

That Hart and many other writers on criminal law do not see this distinctness comes, I suspect, of the fact that their account of what counts as moral and legal *significance* in the criminal law is impoverished. They regard distinctions as being of moral and legal significance in the criminal law only if those distinctions make a constitutive difference to the proper incidence of condemnation, deterrence, or punishment. But the criminal law is only secondarily a vehicle for condemnation, deterrence, and punishment. It is primarily a vehicle for the public identification of wrongdoing (by certain standards of evidence and procedure) and for responsible agents, whose wrongs have been thus identified, to *answer for* their wrongs by offering justifications and excuses for having committed them. By calling this latter function 'primary' I do not mean to suggest that it is socially more important. I mean that the proper execution of the other functions depends upon it. Criminal law can be a proper vehicle for condemnation, deterrence and punishment only because it is a vehicle for responsible agents to answer for their wrongs.

You may say that this claim begs the question against the closure view. It assumes, rather than argues, that wrongs can be correctly identified and yet that their justification can be left open. True enough. All I meant to do so far was to point out that a rather superficial grasp of what the criminal law is for could lead criminal lawyers to privilege the closure view too hastily. To see why that would be not only hasty but mistaken, one naturally needs to look beyond the narrow debate over the criminal law's functions to broader debates in moral philosophy. The most important of these debates concerns the role of our rational faculties in our acting successfully, and hence living well. What led Kant and the utilitarians (and

---

[8] To understand these complicated cases, one must understand that wrongs are not the only things that call for justification. This opens the logical space for actions which it would be wrong to perform without justification yet not wrong to perform with justification. I will not explore this category here.

many other modern moral philosophers following in their footsteps) to endorse the closure view was a shared but misplaced optimism about the extent to which perfection of our rational faculties would entail perfection of our lives. The problem they had with the idea of an action that was wrong and yet justified was that it seemed to give the seal of full rational approval to that course of action (by agreeing that it was justified) while still insisting that the same course of action left a blemish on one's life (by persisting in identifying it as wrong). A more classical picture of rationality, far from baulking at this possibility, had embraced it as a key defining aspect of the human predicament. According to the classical picture, if one does wrong it is some consolation that one does so with justification (for one thereby exhibits one's competence as a rational being) but it would be better still if one does no wrong in the first place and hence *needs* no justification. Never mind that sometimes (in so-called 'moral dilemma' cases in which failing to take the justified path would *also* be wrong) this leaves one in the unlucky position that one's life will be blemished by wrongdoing whatever one does and hence irrespective of one's competence as a rational being. That's the way the cookie crumbles, according to the classical view. But not so according to the optimistic view of the Enlightenment revisionists. They were prepared to admit that one's life could be damaged *as a consequence* of things that one did that were all things considered alright. They admitted that such deeds might be misunderstood or envied, for example, and thus might be held against one by other people (or even by oneself) in such a way that one's life was ruined by misplaced resentment or regret. Yet they refused to admit that one's life might already have been ruined—or even so much as blemished—by the mere fact that one performed such a deed (and hence they refused to admit that the resentment or regret in question might *not* be entirely misplaced). They refused, in sum, to leave logical space for the classical idea of the tragic, which is the idea of a life unluckily blemished by wrongful actions that were performed without the slightest rational error, and may even have been rationally inescapable.[9]

My own view, you will not be surprised to hear, is that the elimination of this classical category of the tragic, and the concomitant embrace of the closure view of wrongdoing, was a major mistake in the history of

---

[9] The leading study of this idea, tracking it through a great deal of ancient literature and philosophy, is M Nussbaum's *The Fragility of Goodness* (1986). Her analysis of Aristotle's examples from myth and history, at 327–342, is particularly choice.

moral philosophy.[10] This is obviously not the place to do the detailed work necessary to bear this claim out. So let me instead conclude this brief survey by returning to the more familiar concerns of criminal lawyers.

Lawyers may protest that it is one thing to hold, with Aristotle and Aeschylus, that justified wrongdoing still leaves some kind of blemish on the wrongdoer's life, but quite another to endow it with normative consequences of the kind that are commonly administered by the law. But the two cannot be prized apart. I don't mean, of course, that people should be exposed to *punishment* for their justified wrongs. There are, however, many types of normative consequences apart from liability to punishment, including a duty to show regret, to apologize, to make restitution, to provide reparation, and so on. These duties often arise in respect of fully justified wrongs. More to the point, so far as criminal lawyers are concerned, the acquisition of a moral duty to offer some justification for what one did is *itself* a normative consequence of doing it. In the institutional setting of the criminal trial, different legal systems naturally handle this duty differently. Not all convert it into a legal duty on the defendant to explain himself personally, and not all put the burden of proof for a justification (as opposed to the burden of adducing preliminary evidence) on the defendant's side. Be that as it may, all presuppose that even fully justified wrongdoing has at least one normative consequence. It makes it the wrongdoer's job to offer up what justification she can, as a responsible agent who answers for her own wrongs.

2. Responsibility and excuse

The closure view of wrongdoing deflates, I think mistakenly, the independent significance of justifications. A closely related view deflates the independent significance of *excuses*. In criminal law scholarship, the view I have in mind is associated most closely with JL Austin. According to Austin's view, just as offering a so-called 'justification' is really a matter

---

[10] In his book, *Punishment, Responsibility and Justice: A Relational Critique* (2000), Alan Norrie mounts a many-pronged, and often penetrating, attack on what he calls the 'Kantian character' of criminal-law thinking. However, when he comes to my critique of the closure view of wrongdoing, he suddenly and without warning changes sides and claims, against me, that 'if [a reason] is defeated then it is indeed undermined, and ... cancelled' (at 153). If Norrie is right about this then the power of reason to overcome the adversity of human life is given a massive boost. It is hard to imagine a more Kantian dream, or a more surprising author to be dreaming it.

of denying that one did anything wrong, so offering a so-called 'excuse' is really a matter of denying *responsibility* for one's wrongdoing.[11]

Admittedly, it is not an abuse of language to say that those who are excused are not responsible for their wrongs.[12] Like the words 'wrong' and 'wrongdoing', the word 'responsible', applied to an agent, can mean various subtly different things. It sometimes means no more than 'apt to incur adverse normative consequences in the event of wrongdoing'. If treated as basic, this usage yields what I will call the 'residual' view of responsibility. This view groups together under the heading of 'factors bearing on responsibility' a ragbag of factors that are still effective, even when wrongdoing has been established, to forestall the wrongdoing's adverse normative consequences (meaning, according to context, a liability to be punished, a duty to make reparations or to apologize, etc.). If one believes as I do that establishing wrongdoing in the relevant sense means leaving the question of justification open, then this residual view of responsibility turns *both* justifications *and* excuses into factors bearing on responsibility. But if one shares Hart's closure view of wrongdoing, according to which establishing wrongdoing already means establishing absence of justification, then the residual view of responsibility designates excuses but not justifications as factors bearing on responsibility. Combining the closure view of wrongdoing with the residual view of responsibility, a simple and appealing framework emerges according to which: (a) justifications are denials of wrongdoing; (b) excuses are denials of responsibility; and (c) wrongdoing and responsibility combine (jointly exhaustively and mutually exclusively) to yield adverse normative consequences such as a liability to be punished for one's wrongs.

I do not know whether Austin himself endorsed the residual view of responsibility. But he certainly gave succour to it when he characterized excuses as (full or partial) denials of responsibility, which is a seriously misleading characterization. The most basic problem of the residual view is apparent on its face. It threatens the role that the concept of responsibility is normally presumed to play in moral and legal argument. The fact that someone is responsible is normally held to play

---

[11] JL Austin, 'A Plea for Excuses' in his *Philosophical Papers* (1961), at 124. Austin's view on this point may also have influenced Hart's treatment of the same topic in a paper written a few months later, viz 'Legal Responsibility and Excuses' in his *Punishment and Responsibility*, above n 7.

[12] This fact doubtless weighed heavy for Austin, who was much moved by the thought that 'our common stock of words embodies all the distinctions men have found worth drawing': 'A Plea for Excuses', n 11 above, at 130.

some role in *explaining why* her wrongdoing carries or would carry certain adverse normative consequences for her. But the residual view of responsibility transparently disables it from doing any more than *asserting that* her wrongdoing carries certain adverse normative consequences for her, never mind why. It is mere placeholder for a leftover ragbag of factors and does nothing to explain why those factors are relevant to punishment, reparation, apology, etc. It does not point to anything interesting that these factors have in common apart from the fact that they are all conditions for adverse normative consequences to attach to wrongdoing. This leads one to the suspicion that the use of the word 'responsible' simply to mean 'apt to incur adverse normative consequences in the event of wrongdoing' is a shadow or derivative use. The more basic use must be to designate some independently significant property or set of properties that *make* someone apt to incur such adverse normative consequences.

I have already made one suggestion, in the previous section ('1. Wrongdoing and justification'), for understanding the notion of responsibility compatibly with this constraint. I suggested that responsible agents are those who are in a position to *answer for* their wrongs, or in other words to venture justifications and excuses for what they did. You may object that while this suggestion technically meets the objections to the residual view, it does so in a supremely unhelpful way. In the first place, it isn't transparent why being in a position to answer for one's wrongs should be thought relevant to anyone's exposure to adverse normative consequences of the kind we are considering. In the second place, it isn't revealed what is supposed to be 'independently significant' about being in this position, i.e. why it matters apart from the fact that it opens the way to adverse normative consequences.

Do these objections bite? I think not. I indicated already what is independently significant about being able and willing to justify what one does. This is none other than being able and willing to explain one's action as a manifestation of one's rational competence. One made no rational error in performing the action—and one cares to explain why.[13] One reveals thereby one's participation in the most basic human goods of reason

---

[13] The fact that being responsible means being in a position both to *have* and to *make* a relevant explanation leads to English criminal law's doctrine of 'unfitness to plead', which grants an acquittal to those who cannot answer for themselves at trial even if they were fully in command of their faculties when the crime was committed. I agree with Antony Duff's view that the acquittal of such people is justified by the fact that—just like those who are acquitted because of mental illness at the time of their crimes—they are not responsible for their crimes: RA Duff, *Trials and Punishments* (1986), 119ff.

and speech.[14] Isn't this fact independently significant by any plausible standards? And it is not hard to see how the possession of this distinctively human capacity—or should I say conjunction of capacities—might come to bear on one's exposure to certain adverse normative consequences. For the consequences we have in mind here, are all of them of a distinctive kind that *symbolize* one's participation in the basic human goods of reason and speech? It is not as if, because one did wrong, the way is open to just any form of retaliation, preventive detention, quarantine, etc. Rather, the way is open to punishing one, extracting compensation or apology from one, and similar (partly) symbolic transactions, which all address one as a being who grasps and listens to reason rather than a mere object to be manipulated for some other being's good. The latter point naturally needs to have a lot of details filled in. Writers on punishment, especially, vary in the extent to which they expect the speech-and-reason-affirming aspect of the practice to dominate it and drive it as opposed to merely setting constraints on it.[15] That is a subject for a different paper. But the general point is clear.

In two closely connected ways, these observations turn the residual view of responsibility on its head. According to the residual view, one's responsibility is something to be regretted and (if possible) avoided. For it is none other than a vulnerability to adverse normative consequences in the event of wrongdoing. Since the consequences are adverse, they are (analytically) to be avoided. But according to the rival view just presented (which is obviously not the *only* rival to the residual view), one's responsibility is something to be proud of and (if possible) to defend. One's responsibility is closely bound up with the one's humanity, and to have it called into question is, with the best will in the world, degrading.[16] Naturally one may still regret, and seek to avoid, the adverse normative consequences that one's responsibility sometimes brings with it. But the self-respecting way to avoid these is not by denying one's responsibility. Rather it is by offering a

---

[14] On which, see J Gardner and T Macklem, 'Reasons' in J Coleman and S Shapiro (eds), *The Oxford Handbook of Jurisprudence and Philosophy of Law* (2002).

[15] Antony Duff's recent book *Punishment, Communication and Community* (2001) is the most sustained and dramatic available rendition of the 'dominate and drive' view. Personally, however, I lean towards the less exciting 'constraint' view. See J Gardner, 'Bemerkungen zu den Functionen und Rechtfertigungen von Strafrecht und Strafe' in N Jareborg, A von Hirsch and B Schünemann (eds), *Positive Generalprävention als letzte Auskunft oder letzte Verlegenheit det Straftheorie* (1998) (translated as Chapter 10 in this volume).

[16] I say 'with the best will in the world' because people often degrade each other through misplaced attempts to be humane, to make concessions to weakness, etc. See J Gardner and T Macklem, 'Compassion without Respect? Nine Fallacies in *R v Smith*', *Criminal Law Review* [2001], 623.

justification or an excuse. And this brings us to the second inversion of the residual view. On the view I sketched, unlike the residual view, offering an excuse is not a way of denying, but rather a way of *asserting*, one's responsibility. For having an excuse, like having a justification, is by its nature an affirmation of one's rational competence. Both justifications and excuses are rational explanations for wrongdoing. They explain why the agent acted as she did by pointing to reasons that she had at the time of her action.

So what is the difference between them? Writers sometimes lose sight of the distinction between excuses and factors negating responsibility because they are worried about losing sight, otherwise, of the distinction between excuses and justifications. Justifications are rational explanations for wrongdoing. Surely excuses must be non-rational ones? This neglects the fact that there are two kinds of rational explanations for wrongdoing. A rational explanation is a justificatory one to the extent that it cites reasons that the agent had *for doing whatever she did*. It points to features of her situation that militated in favour of the action she took. An excusatory explanation falls short of this. It relies on reasons the agent had *for thinking* that she had reasons to do as she did, or reasons she had *for being inclined or inspired or driven* (etc.) to do as she did. Excuses point to features of one's situation that do not militate in favour of the action one took, but nevertheless *do* militate in favour of the beliefs or emotions or attitudes (etc.) on the strength of which one took that action.[17] The defendant did not have reason to kill her husband, for instance, but she certainly had reason to be so terrified by his obnoxious behaviour that night that she was driven to kill him. The action is excused thanks to the fact that it was performed on the strength of justified terror. The element of justification is still there, notice, but at one remove from the action. In that respect the explanation remains rational, and the agent who offers it claims rational competence. And this, in turn, is where an excuse differs fundamentally from a denial of responsibility. One can imagine a terror that is not explained by any features of one's situation. One's terror is in no way lessened when one has less to be terrified of and one knows it. If one kills in the grip of this terror then one has left the realm of excuses behind, let alone the realm of justifications. For not only the killing but even the terror itself is no longer apt to be rationally explained. One can only explain it pathologically, as an affliction. In the process one casts doubt—most regrettably—on one's responsibility for one's actions.

---

[17] Strictly speaking, this covers only character-based excuses and not skill-based excuses, which focus on the way in which the action was approached.

The same Enlightenment turn of thought, that I mentioned earlier, as lending credence to the closure view of wrongdoing also tends to obscure the basic difference in point of rationality on which the distinction between justifications and excuses turns. Recall that Kant and the utilitarians shared a misplaced optimism about the extent to which perfection of our rational faculties would entail perfection of our lives. This has given rise in many quarters to a related optimism about the extent to which perfection of our theoretical rationality entails perfection of our practical rationality. If there could be cases in which it would be perfectly rational to φ and yet perfectly rational to conclude that it would not be rational to φ, that would raise the spectre of our lives being blemished by wrongdoing without our being able to prevent its being so blemished by even the most impeccable conceivable exercise of our rational faculties. Our practical rationality is, after all, epistemically bounded. We can only act on reasons that we are aware of and (*qua* rational) we can only be aware of reasons that we have reason to be aware of. To bring the blemishing of our lives by wrongdoing back under our rational control, what is needed, the story goes, is some epistemic tweak built into the very fabric of practical rationality, such that those who act on what they rationally hold to be the balance of reasons should be regarded as acting on the balance of reasons (and as doing no wrong). Or something like that. Again you will not be surprised to learn that I regard this tweaking as a serious mistake. It is one thing to have a reason to defend oneself and quite another to have every reason to believe one has a reason to defend oneself that in reality one does not have (e.g. because one has strayed accidentally and without any warning onto the set of an action movie). The first opens the way to justifying one's act of self-defence. The second opens the way to excusing it. Thus, sometimes, even though we are epistemically faultless, we cannot be aware of what we would need to be aware of in order to perform a justified action. In that case the most we can hope for is an excuse. That takes us down a peg, morally speaking, because although it testifies to our rational competence, it also points to a rational error. We acted for a non-existent reason, albeit one that we were justified in holding to exist.

3. Jareborg's ladder

According to the picture I have sketched—which I believe applies as much in the criminal law context as in other contexts of moral thinking—it is best of all if we commit no wrongs. If we cannot but commit wrongs, it is best if we commit them with justification. Failing justification, it is best if we have an excuse. The worst case is the one in which we must cast doubt on our own responsibility. When I say 'best' and 'worst' here I mean best and worst for us: for the course of our own lives and for our integrity as people. So far as avoiding liability to punishment is concerned, denials of wrongdoing, justifications, excuses and denials of responsibility may all in principle be as good as each other. Lawyers sometimes say that this makes them all as good as each other 'in practice'. But the lawyer's idea of 'practice' here is distorted. We should care not only about limiting our liabilities but also about the kind of argument that we rely upon to avoid those liabilities. That has been my main thesis.

This thesis owes much to Nils Jareborg, whose typically modest and unpretentious essay 'Justification and Excuse in Swedish Criminal Law' influenced me greatly when I first read it some years ago.[18] Although he quotes without dissent (or indeed comment) a passage from Hart in which the closure view of wrongdoing is espoused and a passage from Austin encouraging the residual view of responsibility, Jareborg himself does not seem to endorse either view. On the contrary, he writes:

If it is important to distinguish between

(a) a deed is criminalized, but not unlawful (because it is justified); and
(b) a deed is unlawful, but not a crime (because the actor is excused)

it is even more important to distinguish between

(1) an unlawful deed is not a crime (because the actor is excused); and
(2) an unlawful deed is a crime, but the actor cannot legally be punished.[19]

I do not agree with the way that Jareborg allocates certain specific criminal defences to these various categories. For instance, he promptly allocates mental incapacity to the 'excuse' category, when (to my way of thinking) it belongs to the 'cannot legally be punished' category. But Jareborg's general structure strikes me, all the same, as absolutely correct. Excising the specialized criminal lawyer's terminology: it is important to distinguish between actions that are not wrong at all, and actions that are wrong but justified; between actions that are wrong but justified and those that are wrong and unjustified but excused; and between unjustified but excused wrongs and those which are neither justified not excused but are nevertheless not punishable. The last category includes, but is broader than, the category of wrongs which are committed without responsibility. It

---

[18] In N Jareborg, *Essays in Criminal Law* (1993).
[19] ibid, at 13.

also includes some specifically *legal* or *institutional* defences such as diplomatic immunity, abuse of process, etc. Thus one could usefully subdivide Jareborg's final contrast (2) into two parts: (2a) an unlawful deed is a crime but the actor is not responsible; and (2b) an unlawful deed is a crime, and the actor is responsible, yet he or she enjoys protection against prosecution or conviction. I have not said anything here about the (2b) defences, which raise fascinating problems of their own. However, I have said a few things, I hope usefully, about all of Jareborg's other classes of defences. In particular, I have tried to explain why, as Jareborg says, it is important to distinguish between them—even when the distinctions do not make a 'practical' difference according to the impoverished lawyer's perception of practicality.

5

Justifications and Reasons

1. Isolating the issue

Nobody seriously denies that there is a close relationship between justifications and reasons. To claim that one has justification for doing or believing as one does is to claim, at the very least, that one has reasons for so doing or so believing. The question which arouses disagreement is merely how the reference to 'reasons' here is to be interpreted. For reasons may be either *guiding* or *explanatory*.[1] Guiding reasons are reasons which apply to one. They bear on what one ought to do or believe. One may, however, overlook or ignore these reasons. Then, even though one acts or believes exactly as the guiding reasons would have one act or believe, they are not the reasons *for* which one so acts or believes. They are not, in other words, the explanatory reasons. Explanatory reasons are logically related to guiding reasons, for it is necessarily true of every explanatory reason that the person who acts on it, or holds beliefs on the basis of it, also believes it to be a guiding reason for the action or belief in question.[2] But it may or may not be the guiding reason that she believes it to be. Just as guiding reasons need not be explanatory reasons, in other words, so explanatory reasons need not be guiding reasons. Thus there arises an issue, current in epistemology as well as moral and legal philosophy, about whether justification depends on guiding reasons or on explanatory reasons. Are one's actions and beliefs justified by the reasons which actually applied to one, or by the reasons which, perhaps mistakenly,

---

[1] See J Raz, *Practical Reason and Norms* (2nd edn, 1990), 16–20.

[2] Or, strictly speaking, believes it to *disclose* or *reflect* a guiding reason. Some apparent counter examples to this are mentioned by EJ Bond in *Reason and Value* (1983), 29. They cannot be dealt with here. But I should stress that 'believes' here, and throughout this paper, carries its widest connotations. It covers everything from the firmest conviction to the merest inkling, everything from knowing to imagining, and everything from explicit awareness to latent or subconscious recognition. cf the remarks on 'vindication' in n 39 below.

one thought applied to one and accordingly treated, in one's acting or believing, as if they were reasons which actually applied to one? Faced with this question, some have come to the view that there are two different perspectives or points of view from which one's actions or beliefs may be justified. On the one hand, there is so-called 'subjective' justification, which depends on explanatory reasons, and hence bows to one's mistakes about the applicable guiding reasons when these mistakes affect what one believes or how one acts. Then there is 'objective' justification, which depends on guiding reasons, and hence extends justification even to some who had no inkling of those reasons, let alone acted or believed anything on the basis of them.[3] In the eyes of some writers, these two modes of justification simply represent irreconcilably different ways of looking at our actions and beliefs. For some purposes or in some contexts we may favour one perspective, while for other purposes and in other contexts we resort to the other.

The terminology of 'subjective' and 'objective' which is used to draw this contrast is notoriously treacherous. It is particularly likely to be misleading for criminal lawyers, who also customarily use these labels to mark a number of quite different distinctions. One of these distinctions needs to be mentioned at this stage in order to move it out of the way. It is a distinction between those who attach justificatory importance to how our actions turn out, and those who decline to do so. In the lingo of some criminal law scholarship and commentary, an 'objectivist' might say that murder is harder to justify than attempted murder, because a death actually comes about; a 'subjectivist' would have to demur.[4] It is a profound and interesting disagreement. But it is not the same as the disagreement about whether justification depends on explanatory reasons or guiding reasons. Rather, it is an internecine dispute, among those who accept that justification turns in part on guiding reasons, about what kinds of guiding reasons there can be. Some hold that: (a) there can in principle be no guiding reasons for or against doing what cannot be done (thus the proposition 'ought implies can'); and (b) the most we can ever do is try, with no guarantee of success. It means that they insist on regarding all guiding reasons as merely reasons

³ See e.g. A Goldman, *Epistemology and Cognition* (1986), 73; J Kvanig, 'Subjective Justification', *Mind* 93 (1984), 71; WP Alston, 'Concepts of Epistemic Justification', *The Monist* 68 (1985), 71. This is also, I believe, the distinction with which Paul Robinson is mainly concerned in his 'Competing Theories of Justification: Deeds vs Reasons' in AP Simester and ATH Smith (eds), *Harm and Culpability* (1996), 45.

⁴ See e.g. A Ashworth, 'Taking the Consequences' in S Shute, J Gardner and J Horder (eds), *Action and Value in Criminal Law* (1993), 107 at 109–110, or A Duff, 'Subjectivism, Objectivism and Criminal Attempts' in *Harm and Culpability*, above n 3, 19.

for or against trying, not as reasons for or against succeeding.[5] But in fact there may be reasons to succeed as well as reasons to try. Moreover, the two do not automatically go hand in hand. Sometimes I have reasons to try without having reasons to succeed. Suppose that people will mistakenly take against me if I do not try to help with an unjust war effort. Then I have a perfectly obvious reason to try, but (other things being equal) no reason to succeed. Conversely, I may have reason to succeed but no reason to try. Suppose that, since I cannot swim a stroke, it would be pointless for me to try to rescue someone from a stormy sea. Then (other things being equal) I have no reason to try to rescue them, but it scarcely means that I have no reason to rescue them.[6] If I had no reason to rescue them, after all, I would not be so horrified at the realization that it is pointless for me to try. I could walk past without compunction. That shows why we should give short shrift to 'ought implies can': my horror as I look on helplessly reflects the fact that I ought to save this life even though I cannot. But it also shows why, if the justification of an action depends in part on the guiding reasons for performing that action, the justification of an action may sometimes be partly hostage to the action's results and sometimes not. It simply depends on what particular action the reasons in question are reasons to perform, i.e. whether they are reasons to get or avert certain results or merely reasons to try to get or avert those results. That, however, does not suggest for a moment that sometimes, in relation to some actions, one should look to explanatory reasons rather than guiding reasons to do the justificatory work. On this issue, so far as I can see, the justificatory role of explanatory reasons is neither here nor there.

In what follows, my central concern will not be with the question of what guiding reasons there are in favour of particular actions or

⁵ This appears to be the argument of WD Ross in *Foundations of Ethics* (1939), 160, relied upon by A Ashworth in 'Sharpening the Subjective Element in Criminal Liability' in A Duff and N Simmonds (eds), *Philosophy and the Criminal Law* (1984), 79.
⁶ Some who accept that I have reason to save in this case may doubt whether I have no reason to try. They picture me momentarily wavering on the cliff's edge, incapacitated by indecision, now leaning forward to jump, now pulling back. Does this not suggest the impetus of a reason to try to save? It may do: it may suggest that I believe myself, contrary to fact, to be capable of effecting a rescue, and so think there is a reason to try, and feel its pull. But my wavering may also be interpreted as the action of a man who is, in momentary defiance of logic, trying to succeed without trying, because he has reason to succeed but no reason to try. This interpretation presupposes that sound practical reasoning follows what Anthony Kenny calls 'the logic of satisfactoriness' (by which one automatically has reason to do whatever is sufficient to achieve what one has reason to achieve) and not 'the logic of satisfaction' (by which one automatically has reason to do whatever is necessary to achieve what one has reason to achieve). For argument, see A Kenny, 'Practical Inference', *Analysis* 23 (1966), 65.

particular kinds of actions, but with the more fundamental conceptual question of whether justification depends upon guiding reasons or explanatory reasons. The answer, irritating but unavoidable, is that it depends upon both. No action or belief is justified unless it is true *both* that there was an applicable (guiding) reason for so acting or so believing *and* that this corresponded with the (explanatory) reason why the action was performed or the belief held. It follows that the common view that there are two different perspectives on justification, a 'subjective' (explanatory reason) perspective and an 'objective' (guiding reason) perspective, must be rejected. To cite explanatory reasons as well as guiding reasons is not to provide justifications from two different points of view, nor even to provide two partial justifications, but merely to provide the two essential parts of one and the same (partial or complete) justification. Of course, this is not to deny that some actions and beliefs may be justified from one point of view and not from another. A certain belief may be justified from my point of view and not from yours, or justified from the Benthamite point of view but not from the Kantian. A certain action may be justified from the point of view of a Christian but not from the point of view of a Muslim, or justified from the point of view of the army's rules of engagement but not from the point of view of the criminal law. My only proviso is that, from whatever point of view one claims justification for one's actions or beliefs, one claims justification only if one claims *both* that there were, from that point of view, reasons for one to act or believe as one did *and* that one's reasons for performing the act or holding the belief were among these reasons. Notice that this is perfectly compatible with a recognition that, within certain systematic points of view or perspectives, the word 'justification' may sometimes be appropriated to do other jobs, e.g. to refer to something falling short of, or going beyond, justification. The legal point of view, in particular, is widely noted for putting its own specialized glosses on everyday words. But English criminal law, at any rate, has not yet paid that particular compliment to the word 'justification'. So far as I can see, our judges persist in using the word 'justification' to refer mainly to legal justifications proper, i.e. to legally recognized reasons for acting which were also the relevant agent's reasons for acting in the case under consideration. This is the essence of the famous *Dadson* doctrine.[7] But even if English criminal

---

[7] *R* v *Dadson* (1850) 4 Cox CC 358. *Per* Erle J: 'The prosecutor not having committed a felony known to the prisoner at the time when he fired, the latter was not justified in firing at the prosecutor.' There are two conditions of justification implicit in this: (1) that the prosecutor must have been a felon and (2) that the prisoner firing upon him must

law were found to use the word 'justification' in some different, technical sense, that would be a matter of little concern for present purposes. Our interest is not in the legal meaning of the word 'justification'. Our interest is in the ordinary phenomenon, that of justification, which still plays a major role in the thinking of most criminal courts, and indeed in evaluative thinking at large, whatever the local lawyers and legal commentators may choose to call it.

2. Pros and cons: the basic asymmetry

What calls for justification? I already mentioned actions and beliefs, and we may add to the list a wide range of phenomena which are logically related to actions and beliefs, such as emotions, attitudes, desires, decisions, practices, and rules. But in a way, that is not an answer to the question. We still need to know whether such things *always* call for justification, or only *sometimes* do. The answer has to be an equivocation. In a loose sense, justification is always called for. That is just to say that actions, beliefs, etc. are always answerable to reason. One may always ask 'why?' But in the stricter and more important sense which concerns us here, justification is called for only when one also has some reason *not* to act, believe, etc. as one does. The unobjectionable, in other words, is in no need of justification. In this stricter sense, justification may be either partial or complete. What one claims if one claims *partial* justification is that the prima facie reasons against one's action or belief are countered by some reasons in favour. What one claims if one claims *complete* justification is that the reasons in favour are, moreover, strong enough to prevail over the reasons against. Thus by claiming full justification one denies that the prima facie judgment against performing the action or accepting the belief should be elevated to the status of an 'all things considered' judgment against its performance or acceptance. All things considered, the action or belief was alright in spite of the prima facie objections to it.

---

have known (or, more broadly, believed) this at the time when he fired. Condition (1) specifies the necessary guiding reason, while (2) is needed to ensure that it is also the explanatory reason. It is true that believing that the prosecutor is a felon is not the same as acting because he is a felon. But the former is a necessary condition of the latter, and since the court in *Dadson* expresses the doctrine negatively, the absence of this necessary condition is all that is needed to dispose of the case. It does not mean that the knowledge condition is being elevated to the status of a sufficient condition—*pace* P Robinson, 'Competing Theories of Justification: Deeds vs Reasons', n 3. See further *R* v *Thain* [1985] NI 457, in which the distinction between beliefs and reasons becomes pivotal.

Criminal lawyers should already be at ease with this distinction
between prima facie and all things considered judgments, and should
quickly be able to see its relevance to the idea of a justification. For this
distinction is highly visible, as Kenneth Campbell has observed, in the
familiar demarcation between criminal offences and (justificatory) criminal defences.[8] In classifying some action as criminal, the law asserts
that there are prima facie reasons against its performance—indeed reasons sufficient to make its performance prima facie wrongful. In providing a justificatory defence, the law nevertheless concedes that one may
sometimes have sufficient reason to perform the wrongful act, all things
considered. Yet the very familiarity of this point has led many criminal lawyers to underestimate its significance. They have looked upon
it rather shame-faced as a kind of artificial legalistic divide. Some have
thought that it can only be a matter of expository convenience whether
one treats a certain issue as going to the presence of an offence or the
absence of a defence.[9] Others have conceded at most an evidential significance to the demarcation, relating it only to the question of who
should normally bear the burden of adducing initial evidence.[10] Things
are not helped here by the fact that criminal lawyers are also accustomed
to use the label 'prima facie' itself to mark an evidential classification. To
say that an action was prima facie wrongful normally signals, to the legal
mind, that there is some reason to believe that a wrong was committed,
but that it may yet, once more evidence is presented, turn out not to be
so. But in the sense which matters for an understanding of the demarcation between offences and justificatory defences, to identify a prima facie
wrong is to identify an *actual* wrong, not just an apparent or putative
wrong.[11] It is to claim that there were indeed legally recognized reasons against an action, not merely that there are now legally admissible
reasons to believe that there were such reasons. To be sure, the reasons
against the action, which are also the reasons for its criminalization, may
all have been defeated in the final analysis. It may have been alright for
the defendant to act against them all things considered. But it does not
mean that they dropped out of the picture. That a reason is defeated does
not mean that it is undermined or cancelled. It still continues to exert its

---

[8] K Campbell, 'Offence and Defence' in I Dennis (ed), *Criminal Law and Justice*
(1987), 73. Campbell does not seem to limit the point, as I do, to *justificatory* defences.
[9] G Williams, 'Offences and Defences', *Legal Studies* 2 (1982), 233 at 233–234.
[10] See MS Moore, *Act and Crime: the Philosophy of Action and its Implications for
Criminal Law* (1993), 179.
[11] For further discussion of this point, see J Searle, 'Prima Facie Obligations' in J Raz
(ed), *Practical Reasoning* (1978), 81.

rational appeal. It may indeed be a matter of bitter regret or disappointment that, thanks to the reasons which justified one's action, one nevertheless acted against the prima facie reasons for avoiding that action. It may even be a matter of regret or disappointment to the criminal law. The law certainly need not welcome it. But by granting a defence the law concedes that any regret or disappointment must be tolerated, and that no liability can attach to the person who by her prima facie wrongful actions occasioned it. By granting a *justificatory* defence the law concedes that this is true by virtue of the fact that the defendant had, at the time of her prima facie wrongful action, sufficient reason to perform it.[12]

Whether one accepts this account of the role of justification in the law and beyond is not a matter of merely academic importance. It has far-reaching practical implications. One implication is of immediate significance to us. It stems from the fact that, as I have explained them, claims of justification cannot but exhibit one of the most striking asymmetries in all human thought and experience. This is the asymmetry between the pursuit of positive value and the avoidance of negative value, between reasons in favour and reasons against, or, as we might say in ordinary conversation, between *pros* and *cons*. The asymmetry is brought to the surface by claims of justification only because such claims implicate both reasons in favour of and reasons against the justified action or belief. If the role of justification were that of cancelling or undermining the reasons against an action or belief—if it were, in lawyers' terms, a matter of 'negating an element of the offence'—then no question of the relationship between reasons for and reasons against would arise in cases of justification, since in such cases all reasons against would be 'negated', i.e. cancelled or undermined, and would not exert any countervailing force. But since a justification merely defeats the reasons against an action or belief without cancelling or undermining them, the conflict between pros and cons, and hence its asymmetrical structure, is very much at the centre of attention when claims of justification are made.

---

[12] cf P Robinson, 'A Theory of Justification: Societal Harm as a Prerequisite for Criminal Liability', *UCLA Law Review* 23 (1975), 266 at 274: 'Justified behaviour is correct behaviour and therefore is not only tolerated but encouraged.' Robinson assumes that a justification operates to cancel or undermine the countervailing considerations rather than to defeat them. So the law has nothing to regret. It is surprising that Robinson apparently remains attached to this position to this day in spite of his own highly effective attack on it in 'Criminal Law Defences: A Systematic Analysis', *Columbia Law Review* 82 (1982), 199 at 220: 'Where conduct is covered by an offence modification, it is not in fact a legally recognised harm ... Justified conduct, on the other hand, causes a legally recognised harm or evil ... It is tolerated only when, by the infliction of the intermediate harm or evil, a greater societal harm is avoided or benefit gained.'

To understand the asymmetry of rational conflict properly, one must begin by thinking a little about the logic of guiding reasons. The first question is: what are guiding reasons there to guide? It may seem like a silly question. Surely it goes without saying that guiding reasons for and against action are there to guide action, guiding reasons for and against belief are there to guide belief, guiding reasons for and against emotion are there to guide emotion, and so on. But there is an alternative view. Perhaps guiding reasons of all kinds are merely there to guide reasons. Thus reasons for or against action are there to guide the reasons for which we act, reasons for or against belief are there to guide the reasons for which we believe, etc. It is not a circular or regressive proposal so long as one remembers the distinction between guiding reasons and explanatory reasons. The suggestion that guiding reasons guide reasons is the suggestion that the real point of there being a guiding reason is that one should act, believe, etc. *on the basis of that reason,* i.e. that it should also be the explanatory reason for one's so acting or believing. Thus if one merely acts or believes as the guiding reason would have one act or believe, but one's explanatory reasons are quite different, then strictly speaking one did not follow the guidance. Some have thought that guiding reasons do indeed work in this way by default, or at least that they work in this way by default if they belong to certain families, e.g. moral reasons, reasons of duty, altruistic reasons, etc.[13] If this were true then it would immediately introduce a very radical asymmetry between reasons for and reasons against action and belief. That is because, as I have pointed out elsewhere, explanatory reasons are necessarily reasons *for* action or belief rather than reasons *against.*[14] Explanatory reasons explain. They are the reasons that the agent or believer had for acting or believing as she did. To say that she also acted or believed *in spite of* certain countervailing reasons is necessarily to return to the discourse of guiding reasons, and to leave the discourse of explanatory reasons behind. For the whole point of what one says is that these reasons, since the agent or believer did not act or believe on the basis of them, do not explain her action or belief.[15]

---

[13] See, famously and starkly, Kant's *Groundwork of the Metaphysic of Morals* (trans Paton, 1964), 65–68. For interpretation and discussion of Kant's point, see e.g. B Williams, 'Persons, Character and Morality' in his *Moral Luck: Philosophical Papers 1973–1980* (1981), 1 at 16–19; B Herman, 'Integrity and Impartiality', *The Monist* 66 (1983), 233; S Scheffler, *Human Morality* (1992), 19ff.

[14] 'Action' and 'belief', at this point and throughout this paper, must be interpreted widely enough to include inaction and disbelief.

[15] See J Gardner and H Jung, 'Making Sense of Mens Rea: Antony Duff's Account', *Oxford Journal of Legal Studies* 11 (1991), 589 at 569–573.

The effect of this, if we share the view that guiding reasons exist to guide explanatory reasons, is that guiding reasons against action and belief are to a large extent a debased currency. They can only exert their purchase in a derivative way. After all, to the question 'for what reason should I act?', the answer 'here's a reason not to' is, to say the least, evasive. One cannot, as a matter of logic, act for reasons against so acting (unless, of course, one mistakes them for reasons in favour). The most one can do is modify one's reasons for so acting in the light of reasons against. This endows reasons against with at most an indirect motivational role, subsidiary to that of reasons in favour. The claim is not, I should stress, that reasons against an action cannot be appreciated, considered, taken into account, given their due weight, etc. alongside reasons in favour. The point is only that they cannot, *qua* reasons against one's action, be the reasons for which one acted. It means that, on any view according to which the point of guiding reasons is to guide explanatory reasons, reasons against action and belief are bound to be poor relations which lack the independent rational force of their positive cousins.

If it were accurate, this broadly Kantian account would make it easy to explain how justifications come to take the form I claimed for them. Since on this account one follows reasons in favour of an action only if one actually acts for those reasons, there is no justificatory ground to be gained by citing a guiding reason in favour of what one did if one did not act for that reason. On the other hand, one can readily lose justificatory ground by citing a guiding reason against one's action without claiming to have acted on it, since reasons against action are merely reasons to modify the reasons for which one acted, and cannot themselves be acted on.[16] Unfortunately, however, the Kantian account quickly descends into confusion. It is not surprising that those who have espoused it, including Kant himself, have had great difficulty understanding the nature of moral, legal, and other rational conflict. For this view of theirs, by debasing the independent rational force of negative guiding reasons, ultimately forces them to reinterpret such reasons as mere cancelling conditions on positive guiding reasons.[17] Thus it turns out that the correct view, for once, is the obvious one. Fundamentally, guiding reasons for and against action are there to guide *actions*, not to guide explanatory

[16] *Qua* reasons against. They may of course be reasons for some other action as well as reasons against this one.
[17] Needless to say, some regard this as a positive merit of the Kantian line of thought: see B Herman, 'Obligation and Performance: A Kantian Account of Moral Conflict' in O Flanagan and A Rorty (eds), *Identity, Character, and Morality* (1990), 311.

reasons for actions. This is the grain of truth in Paul Robinson's view that a 'deeds' account of justification should be preferred to a 'reasons' account.[18] It means that negative guiding reasons retain in full their independent rational force. Although one cannot in principle act for these reasons, one can act as they would have one act, and other things being equal that is all that guiding reasons, be they positive or negative, envisage that one should do. But does it follow that explanatory reasons do not matter at all so far as guiding reasons are concerned? Do guiding reasons wash their hands of the quality of our reasoning, so long as we do the right thing in the end? Not a bit of it. In a moment we will come to the special 'second-order' cases of reasons to act for reasons, and reasons not to do so. But even before we come to these, there are two ways in which ordinary guiding reasons for action and belief necessarily have something to say on the subject of explanatory reasons. The first point is permissive. Other things being equal, the fact that such-and-such is a reason for a given action or belief makes it *alright* for this to be the reason why one performs the action or holds the belief. The second point of contact is rather more prescriptive. For it is a basic principle of practical rationality, which is at the root of the whole pros/cons asymmetry, that one should always act for *some* undefeated reason, i.e. that at least one of the (guiding) reasons in favour of doing as one did should have been one's (explanatory) reason for doing it.

You may well be suspicious of any appeal to the 'basic principles of practical rationality'. Is this not just a device to win an argument by fiat, to make its conclusion sound incontrovertible when in fact it should be vigorously interrogated? I sincerely hope not. In one way, it is true, principles of practical rationality are more fundamental than other practical principles. For they apply across the boundaries between different fields of practical reasoning. They apply equally in legal reasoning, moral reasoning, strategic reasoning, etc., and do so just by virtue of the fact that these are fields of practical reasoning. This may mean that they have a slight air of the *a priori* about them. But in fact this air is deceptive. Principles of rationality have a rather more mundane, *a posteriori* basis than many ordinary moral and legal principles. For principles of rationality exist purely to guide us towards conformity with moral reasons, legal reasons, and so on, whatever those reasons may happen to be. They are sound or valid principles of rationality if it is true that, when we conform our reasoning to them, we also better conform our actions and

[18] See his 'Competing Theories of Justification: Deeds vs Reasons', above n 3.

beliefs to whatever reasons for action and belief apply to us. Thus principles of rationality stand or fall, in large measure, on their straightforwardly instrumental merits.[19] The basic principle of practical rationality that tells us always to act for some undefeated reason is no exception. For while it is true that, by default, guiding reasons are there to guide actions and beliefs rather than to guide explanatory reasons for actions and beliefs, it is also important to remember that the only way in which actions and beliefs can be guided is through the guidance of explanatory reasons. Reasons can only move us, if you like, by motivating us. And the principle that we should always act for some undefeated reason is a principle which identifies what we should be looking for, in the way of motivation, if we are to maximize our prospects of acting as reason demands. We should look for an undefeated reason to act as we do. There is no point in going further and looking for *all* the undefeated reasons to act in that way.[20] That would be ridiculous overkill. The very fact that the reason for which one acts is undefeated is enough by itself to guarantee that, all things considered, it is on the winning side in the whole overarching conflict of reasons.[21] Thus the basic principle of rationality which I cited, although modest, is as strong a principle as we need to ensure that our explanatory reasons for action reliably push us towards an action that ought, all things considered, to be performed.

[19] That explains why, in the work of some philosophers, the label 'principles of rationality' has been appropriated to designate the principles we should adopt if we are better to secure whatever ends we each happen to have, without touching on the intrinsic merit of those ends. See e.g. D Parfit, *Reasons and Persons* (1984), 4. This also underlies the popular use of 'rational' when associated with the calculating pursuit of personal advancement.

[20] But isn't it necessary to survey all the reasons, if only in order to *work out* that the reason for which one acts is indeed undefeated? Not necessarily. On the view defended here, the fact that one acted for an undefeated reason by instinct or habit need not in any way detract from one's justification. Sometimes we identify undefeated reasons better without stopping to think. There is no basis for the view that fully deliberated action is more reliably sound than spontaneous action: often, the more we think about it, the worse our predicament gets. That is one reason (among many) why such things as emotions, passions, and raw desires are so crucial to any well-rounded life. It incidentally helps to dispel another criminal lawyers' myth: that justifications are more at home in situations where there is proper scope for clear thinking, while in situations of emergency, calling for immediate reactions, we must make do with excuses.

[21] Or perhaps we should say, to accommodate cases of incomparability, 'not on the losing side'. In some cases one acts on undefeated reasons whichever way one acts, and one is justified either way, since incomparability prevents the reasons in favour from defeating the reasons against or vice versa. Where the undefeated reasons on both sides are *protected* reasons (on which see below) these are normally known as 'dilemma' cases. For a good account of which, see R Marcus, 'Moral Dilemmas and Consistency', *Journal of Philosophy* 77 (1980), 121.

These claims cut against a familiar model of rational conflict. On this model, the reasons for and the reasons against some action or belief are always up to a point mutually defeating. Some of the reasons in favour of an action or belief devote their entire motivating energy to defeating the reasons against that action or belief, and in the process become spent forces, so that the only undefeated reasons in the end are those which were not needed for the battle, the reasons which make up, so to speak, the *net advantage* which the pros had over the cons in terms of their rational force. These are therefore the only reasons left for us to act upon, if it is true that one should always act for an undefeated reason. But my claims in defence of the principle that one should always act for some undefeated reason suggest an alternative picture, according to which, if the reasons in favour of some action defeat the reasons against, then in the ordinary case it is only the reasons against which end up defeated. The reasons in favour are *all of them* undefeated, i.e. they are undefeated *in gross*. The principle of rationality which demands that one always acts for some undefeated reason is therefore compatible, in the ordinary situation of an action with more pros than cons, with our acting on any one of the various reasons in favour of the action. This makes it a much more modest principle than at first sight seems to be needed to defend my promised strong conclusion that reasons in favour of an action are only justificatory if they are also the reasons for which one performed that action. And yet the modesty of this principle of rationality is also, in another way, its strength. For what this principle means is that it is quite pointless to cite, by way of justification, an undefeated reason for which one did not act, even though it would have been alright for one to act upon it if one had been minded to do so. Once one has attempted to make justificatory capital out of such a guiding but non-explanatory reason, one must still go on to identify some *other* undefeated reason which one *did* act upon in order to clinch the justification. For one must always act for some undefeated reason. But once one achieves this, the original non-explanatory reason one cited simply drops out of the picture. It adds nothing to one's case. The citation of the second reason was both necessary (it was acted upon) and sufficient (it was undefeated) to identify one's action as justified. Essentially, that is why justifications must have two matching parts: in the first place, an undefeated guiding reason, which is also, secondly, the explanatory reason for the justified action.

Notice that the reasons against one's action, which a full justification is needed to defeat, are not similarly two-pronged. It is enough that they were guiding reasons against one's action. For as I already said, there is no such thing as an explanatory reason against an action, so there can be no demand, concerning the reasons against an action, that in order to be counted against that action's performance, they must also play some explanatory role in that performance. What this means, in the everyday terms most familiar to lawyers, is that undesirable side-effects as well as undesirable intended results can count against an action, while only desirable intended results can ever count in its favour.[22] This is the basic all-pervading asymmetry between pros and cons, between reasons in favour and reasons against, between the pursuit of positive value and the avoidance of negative, that comprehensively carves up our lives as rational beings.

3. Fortifying the asymmetry

This basic asymmetry makes its presence felt in many ways. Most obviously and famously, it structures the distinction between people's virtues and their failings, and the related distinction between credit and blame. Ironically, this may be one of the factors which leads some to suppose that the asymmetry can have no impact on the logic of justification.[23] Their thinking goes something like this. It is one thing to say that an action is fully justified, so that blame can be eliminated. But it is a long way from there to the conclusion that the action is positively creditable. It is only when we take this further evaluative step that the claimed asymmetry between pros and cons can have a real impact. For there can be little doubt that whether an action is creditable turns primarily on the reasons for which it is performed. By making these very same explanatory reasons the key to justification, one wrongly eliminates the logical

---

[22] cf A Simester, 'Intention, Recklessness, and Morality' in *Harm and Culpability*, above n 3. My position in this essay directly confronts Simester's view that there are two alternative bases of blame, one connected with 'motive' and the other with 'reasonableness'. Reasonableness in action depends straightforwardly on the reasons for which one acts. Simester's examples do not contraindicate. In what he calls the 'Experiment Case', a great deal turns on the fact that (as Simester confesses, ibid, at 88, n 67) the 'neutral end' is not in fact neutral, but is a reason in favour of administering the drug. On my account, *if* this reason in favour is undefeated, which on the information given by Simester it might indeed be, *then* the administration of the drug can indeed be justified. It matters not that the motive is not good, so that the action is not creditable. As I explain in the next section ('3. Fortifying the asymmetry'), the question of whether a reason for acting is good, worthy, etc. is not the same as the question of whether it is undefeated.

[23] Thus G Williams, *Criminal Law: The General Part* (2nd edn, 1961), criticizing the decision in *Dadson*, above n 7, complains that 'the law of consummated crimes … governs conduct, not purity of intention'.

gap between justified and creditable action. One makes the earning of credit an automatic corollary of the mere elimination of blame.

The mistake here lies in the failure to bear in mind that reasons for action may vary in quality as well as strength. As I have already explained, other things being equal it is alright to act for any undefeated reason in favour of one's action. But sometimes it is *more* than alright to act for a particular undefeated reason. Sometimes there is also an undefeated second-order reason to act for that particular reason, e.g. a reason to support one's friends out of affection for them, to refuse conscription out of a sense of humanitarian duty, to tell the truth because it is the truth, etc. It does not mean that the other reasons for doing what one does automatically become unacceptable, so that acting on them can provide no justification. It means only that a particular reason is privileged, so that acting for that reason lends special value to one's action, value going beyond what is needed for mere justification. Often, indeed, there are several privileged reasons, and there arises a question of which of these one should act for. At this level, incomparability of value often precludes a straight answer. By acting in the same way for different privileged reasons people normally exhibit their incomparably different virtues. But whether or not one actually exhibits a virtue in the process, it is creditable to act for such privileged reasons in any case in which both they and the second-order reasons to act for them remain undefeated. This is not, I hasten to add, the only way in which one may earn credit. One's actions may be creditable because of *how* they are performed rather than why, in which case one should look to the value of skill rather than the value of virtue to supply the explanation. But either way, more is required for credit than is required for mere justification. An action may still be justified even though performed without any technical proficiency and for a most banal, trivial, and unimpressive reason. But the key point still stands that, to be justified, it must nevertheless have been performed for an *undefeated* reason.[24]

Does it follow that second-order reasons are irrelevant to justification? If only things were that simple. In many contexts, and notably in the law, the scope of justification is pervasively determined by the operation of second-order reasons. But these are not reasons to act for reasons, of the kind which allow for creditable action. These are reasons *not* to act for reasons. Such negative second-order reasons are in

---

[24] In some extreme cases, if one cannot act for particular reasons, or at a certain level of technical proficiency, then that strips out so much value from one's act that it would be better not to perform it at all. In such cases, the gap narrows between the point at which blame ends and the point at which credit begins.

operation whenever an action is required or forbidden. They are therefore the reasons at the heart of *wrongdoing*. This claim should be interpreted with care. We describe actions as 'wrong' in several senses. I already distinguished prima facie wrongness from the all things considered wrongness. At the same time one should be aware of a cross-cutting distinction between *advisory* wrongness and *mandatory* wrongness. Actions which are all things considered wrong in either the mandatory or the advisory sense can, in appropriate cases, be equally a source of blame. But the distinction between mandatory and advisory wrongness is nevertheless one of great importance. One does the wrong thing in the advisory sense if one does not do what one has reason to do. One does the wrong thing in the mandatory sense—for which we normally reserve more emphatic terms like 'wrongdoing', 'wrongdoer', and 'wrongful'—if one does not do what one has, in Joseph Raz's terms, a *protected* reason to do.[25] A protected reason differs from what I earlier labelled a 'privileged' reason. A privileged reason is a reason which one has reason to act for. A protected reason, on the other hand, is a reason for an action combined with a reason not to act for some or all of the reasons against that action. What happens when a reason is protected is that certain countervailing considerations are defeated in advance of any practical conflict. Because these reasons are pre-emptively defeated, action for these reasons does not meet the demands of the basic principle of rationality that one should always act for some undefeated reason. It may be asked how a reason can be defeated in advance of a conflict. Surely whether it is defeated depends on its relative strength when pitted against another reason, and therefore must await the conflict? This ignores the role of *rules* in practical reasoning. Rules are devices which improve our prospects of doing what reason demands by settling certain conflicts of reasons before they arise. They obviate the need for reliance on some of the raw pros and cons. It does not mean, as some have thought, that all rules are merely 'rules of thumb', or 'indicator rules', which provide a prima facie reason to believe that the action ought to be performed, without affecting whether the action ought to be performed.[26] On the contrary, real rules

---

[25] J Raz, *The Authority of Law* (1979), 17–19.

[26] i.e. that they are prima facie in the lawyer's evidential sense. Some of WD Ross's remarks in *The Right and the Good* (1930) may lead one to think that all sound mandatory rules are prima facie in this sense. See also JJC Smart, 'An Outline of a System of Utilitarian Ethics' in JJC Smart and B Williams (eds), *Utilitarianism: For and Against* (1973), at 42ff. On rules of thumb and indicator rules, see F Schauer, *Playing by the Rules* (1991), 104ff (and especially the note at 105).

are capable of affecting what really ought to be done. In rough outline, they do so because some guiding reasons in favour of certain actions are less likely to be properly followed, or more likely to corrupt the following of other reasons, if one tries to follow them. They are guiding reasons which had better not become explanatory reasons. Since, by the time they are explanatory reasons, it is too late to avoid their distorting effect, they are ruled out of being explanatory in advance by the operation of the rule. Consequently, of course, the price of following the rule is sometimes that one does not act as the underlying reasons apart from the rule would have one act. That in such cases one should nevertheless follow the rule is the small price that rationality pays for avoiding the risk that, by trying to act for some of the raw underlying reasons, one will otherwise very often act against reason. That explains why there are reasons not to act for certain reasons, and why some actions are as a result not merely advisable or inadvisable, but are actually required or prohibited.

In fulfilling its primary functions, the law rarely classifies actions as merely advisable or inadvisable.[27] But it often classifies them as required or prohibited. That is particularly apparent in the criminal law. The very idea of a 'criminal offence' is the idea of an action which is in the eyes of the law not merely wrong but wrongful, i.e. which there is, in the eyes of the law, not merely a reason but a protected reason not to perform. In fact the protected reason which the law creates is, by default, *absolutely* protected. So far as the criminal law is concerned, *all* reasons in favour of performing the criminalized action are defeated by virtue of the law's unquestionable and all-embracing authority. It means that one is left with no automatic access to any justificatory considerations, however powerful they might be apart from the law. What the law does, which nevertheless creates a role for some justificatory defences, is to provide us with *cancelling permissions* to perform, under certain specified conditions, the actions which it criminalizes. This may seem like a rather surprising proposition. After all, it was argued above that justificatory reasons do not *cancel* but rather *defeat* the reasons against an action or belief. Now,

---

[27] By 'primary functions' I mean non-self-regulatory functions. Among the law's functions are the governance of legislation and adjudication. In the fulfilment of these functions the law often avails itself of principles and values which provide merely advisory legal guidance to officials. But of course these functions are parasitic on others. The primary functions of law are its functions in affecting people's actions other than legislative and adjudicatory actions—if you like, outward-looking rather than inward-looking functions. Here, the law rarely makes do with mere advice, since it cannot normally count on automatic co-operation. On primary and secondary functions, see J Raz, *The Authority of Law*, above n 25, 163ff.

by contrast, the claim appears to be that justifications arise in the criminal law precisely when reasons are cancelled by permissions. But the air of paradox is dispelled as soon as one realizes that the law's cancelling permissions do not cancel the reasons not to perform the criminalized action, but merely cancel the second-order protective reasons not to act for certain countervailing reasons. Thus justificatory arguments which the law would otherwise disallow are specifically allowed. This means that the law does not only regulate the actions which one may perform, but also regulates the reasons for which one may perform those actions. It regulates the actions which one may perform by making some of them into criminal offences, which are prima facie wrongs. It regulates the reasons for which one may perform those actions by picking out certain reasons in favour of their performance as legally acceptable reasons. But, as ever, one benefits from the acceptable reasons in favour of one's action only if one actually acts for these reasons. For even legal rationality, with all of its second-order protection, is governed by the basic principle of practical rationality that one should always act for some undefeated reason. In the case of a criminal act, all reasons are defeated apart from those permitted by law. Thus to claim a justificatory defence, one must not only have, but act for, one of those permitted reasons.

The same is not true in a case to which the definition of the crime does not extend, i.e. in which 'an element of the offence is negated'. In such a case one need rely on no permission to act for specified reasons since the protected reason, which gives rise to the need for such permission, does not apply in the first place. So it does not matter why the defendant acted as he did, so long as that is how he acted. Here we see exactly what the English law student learns by reading *Deller* alongside *Dadson*: in some cases the defendant's motivation is beside the point, whereas in others it is decisive.[28] The real difficulty arises, however, when we try to draw the line in practice between the two types of case, between *Dadson* cases and *Deller* cases. Where we are dealing with raw pros and cons, it is easy to distinguish a justificatory argument from an argument to effect that there is nothing to justify. A justificatory argument is an argument which points to reasons in favour of the action performed rather than to the absence of reasons against it. But when protected reasons enter the equation, this test is no longer adequate to draw the distinction. That is because some of the reasons in favour of an action are already taken

---

[28] *R* v *Deller* (1952) 36 Cr App R 184; *R* v *Dadson*, above n 7. See the excellent discussion in JC Smith and B Hogan, *Criminal Law* (7th edn, 1992), 33–35.

into account in the structure of the protected reason. The rule has been shaped with an eye to many of the pros and cons of action in accordance with it. It means that sometimes, when one cites a reason in favour of one's action, one cites a consideration which should bear on the interpretation of the rule one is accused of violating rather than a consideration which bears on whether one is justified in violating it. Accordingly, the mere fact that one points to a reason in favour of one's action does not mean, in this context, that one asserts a justification as opposed to denying the application of the law to the case. Only if one asserts a justification, however, does it matter whether one actually acted for the reason in favour that one cites. It follows that in law one may sometimes benefit from a reason in favour of one's action which was not a reason for which one acted, even though in other cases one must have acted for the reason before one may benefit in law from its application. Unfortunately, there is no general test for telling the two kinds of case apart. It is a question of law, on which different legal systems may of course arrive at different answers, whether a given argument is to be regarded as justificatory rather than as bearing on the scope of the offence. In fact, for all I know, some legal systems may not bother to recognize justifications at all, so confident are they of the moral finesse of their offence definitions. This would tend to lumber them with a regrettable inflexibility, or force them to undesirable vagueness, or both. I will return to these possible moral objections below. But logically it is a perfectly possible solution. It has the pay-off that the legal system in question may take an interest in the reasons in favour of the action which the defendant performed without caring whether the defendant acted for those reasons. All I wish to stress is that this does not turn it into a legal system which endorses an 'objective' rather than a 'subjective' theory of justification, or into a legal system which allows justification to depend upon guiding reasons irrespective of explanatory reasons. It makes it into a legal system which, strictly speaking, does not care about justification at all.

4. The priority of justification over excuse

It is widely thought that excuses are more 'subjective' than justifications.[29] In one sense of 'subjective', as we will see, this is perfectly true. But it is

---

[29] K Greenawalt, 'The Perplexing Borders of Justification and Excuse', *Columbia Law Review* 84 (1984), 1897 at 1915–1918.

not true if we are using the labels 'subjective' and 'objective' to mark the contrast between explanatory and guiding reasons. Over a wide range of cases, excuses, just like justifications, depend on the union of explanatory and guiding reasons. Whenever excuses depend on the union of explanatory and guiding reasons, moreover, they do so precisely because justifications depend on the union of explanatory and guiding reasons. The structure of excuse derives, in other words, from the structure of justification, and thus shares in its combination of subjective (explanatory) and objective (guiding) rationality.

Some theorists have associated excuses with character traits.[30] They are mistaken if they think that every excuse is concerned with character. Many excuses are of a technical nature. They relate to levels of skill rather than degrees of virtue. Their gist is that the person claiming them does not possess the skills needed to do better, and should not be expected to possess those skills. Whether one should be expected to possess certain skills, or skills to a certain degree, depends, to some extent, on one's form of life. A doctor who tries to excuse her blundering treatment by claiming lack of diagnostic skill should not get far, whereas an amateur first-aider may be able to extinguish her blame, under similar conditions, by making exactly the same argument. But such excuses, even though they are of great legal importance, will not concern us here. Our concern will be with that major group of excuses which do indeed relate to character evaluation. These include excuses very familiar to criminal lawyers, such as excuses based on provocation and duress. Their gist is similar to that of technical excuses. It is that the person claiming them does not possess the virtues needed to do better, and should not be expected to possess those virtues. Again, which virtues one should be expected to possess, and to what extent, depends largely on one's form of life. A police officer is expected to exhibit more fortitude and courage than an ordinary member of the public, a friend is expected to be more considerate and attentive than a stranger, etc. What exactly does this mean? Essentially, it means that where there is a conflict of reasons, some people are expected to act for some reasons, whereas others are expected to act for other, often incompatible and incomparable, reasons. But obviously the need to claim an excuse from one's action arises only if one fails to establish a full justification. A fully justified action needs no excuse. So the point cannot be that

---

[30] See the useful bibliographical note in M Moore, 'Choice Character, and Excuse', *Social Philosophy and Policy* 7 (1990), 29 at 40–41. A subtle and sympathetic reconstruction of this approach to excuses is offered by B Sullivan in 'Making Excuses', in *Harm and Culpability*, above n 3.

those who act with excuse act for undefeated reasons, i.e. that it is alright
for them to act for those reasons. That would yield a full justification for
their actions. The point must be that there is something suspect about the
reasons for which they act. And indeed there is. They are not valid reasons.
They are what the person acting upon them takes to be valid reasons, *and
justifiably so*. Thus the structure of excuse derives from the structure of
justification. To excuse an action is not, of course, to justify that action.
Rather, one justifies one's belief that the action is justified.[31]

This explanation of non-technical excuses has to be modified and
extended somewhat to accommodate unjustified actions upon justified
emotions, attitudes, passions, desires, decisions, etc. as well as unjustified actions upon justified beliefs. Provocation, as Jeremy Horder has
explained, involves unjustified action out of justified anger.[32] Duress, or
a certain central kind of duress, can be similarly analysed as involving
unjustified action out of justified fear. But these are, in a sense, derivative cases. Emotions like anger and fear are mediating forces between
beliefs and actions. They enhance or constrain the motivating force of
certain motivating beliefs. Their justification therefore turns in part on
the justification of the beliefs which partly constitute them. Of course,
there is still a justificatory gap: an emotion is not fully justified merely by
the justification of its cognitive component. But justified emotion (and
in similar vein justified attitude or desire or decision) nevertheless entails
justified belief. Thus the most basic or rudimentary case of non-technical
excuse remains that of unjustified action upon justified belief. One must
therefore consider what is needed to make a belief justified. It is of course
one of the great problems of epistemology, and we cannot do justice to it
here. Suffice it to say that the general account of justification applicable to
action is also broadly applicable to belief. One must have an undefeated
reason for one's belief, and that must moreover be the reason why one
holds the belief. This explains the nature of epistemic faults, such as prejudice, gullibility, and superstition. One cannot understand these faults
unless one appreciates that a belief is justified, not only by the reasons

[31] cf S Uniake, *Permissible Killing: The Self-Defence Justification of Homicide* (1994),
15–25.
[32] J Horder, *Provocation and Responsibility* (1992), 158ff. This explains why women
who have killed after prolonged domestic violence and are denied provocation defences
on the ground that their reaction was not immediate do not much like the response that
they should instead claim 'diminished responsibility'. They want it to be acknowledged
that their anger was (at least partly) justified, and that *this* is why their admittedly unjustified action is (at least partly) excused. 'Diminished responsibility' is a claim which
suggests irrationality all the way down (meaning that it is not strictly an excuse: see n 35
below). It thus reduces the moral status of those who claim it.

there are for holding it, but also by the process of reasoning by which it came to be held, i.e. not only by guiding reasons but also by explanatory reasons. The same facts also explain why a requirement of *reasonableness* has traditionally been imposed upon excuses in the criminal law. It is not enough that one made a mistake as to justification, if it was not a reasonable mistake, it is not enough that one was angry to the point of losing self-control, if one's anger was not reasonable, etc.[33] By 'reasonable' here is meant, in my view, much the same as 'justified'. There must have been an undefeated reason for one's belief, emotion, etc. which also explains why one held the belief or experienced the emotion, etc. The fact that sometimes this element of reasonableness is dispensed with in the law does not show a drift towards a more purely 'subjective' account of excuses, i.e. one depending on explanatory reasons without regard for guiding reasons. It shows, rather, that some excuse-like arguments, in common with some justification-like arguments, may actually serve to negate an element of the offence rather than to excuse or justify its commission. Some mistakes, as the courts put it, may simply serve to negate the mens rea for the particular crime; and if, as may be, the mens rea required is, e.g. knowledge, then of course the reasonableness of one's mistake is neither here nor there.[34] The extent to which legal systems will tolerate such arguments depends on many contingencies about them, including the extent to which and way in which they implement the demand for mens rea. But this has nothing to do with excuses, in which an element of reasonableness, at some level, is conceptually necessitated whether the crime is one of full subjective mens rea or one of no mens rea at all.

Requirements of 'reasonableness' in criminal excuses also sometimes go beyond what the logic of excuses requires, and in that case they normally serve another role. They serve to orientate the law towards general application to people living many different forms of life, rather than

[33] See, among many examples, *Albert v Lavin* [1981] 1 All ER 628 (reasonable belief required for mistaken self-defence), *R v Graham* [1982] 1 All ER 801 ('fear for good cause' required for duress), *Phillips v R* [1969] 2 AC 130 9 (loss of self-control must be reasonable for provocation).

[34] That is the logic of the decisions in *R v Williams* [1987] 3 All ER 411 and *Beckford v R* [1987] 3 All ER 425, which should therefore not be understood as authorities on the mental element in excuses, let alone as authorities on the mental element in defences in general. At most, they show that self-defence is no longer regarded as a genuine defence in English criminal law. Instead, absence of self-defence is regarded as an implied element of every offence, and one to which an implied element of mens rea is automatically attached. It is an absurd rule, and one which should be overturned, but the reliance on *DPP v Morgan* [1975] 2 All ER 347 in both of the cases makes it the only viable interpretation of what they stand for. For excellent discussion, see A Simester, 'Mistakes in Defence', *Oxford Journal of Legal Studies* 12 (1992), 295.

tailoring it to suit the expected virtues of a certain kind of person lead-ing a certain kind of life. The debate about the extent to which the rea-sonable person should be 'individualized' to the characteristics of the defendant in the definition of criminal excuses is partly a debate about the extent to which the criminal law should aspire to this kind of gen-erality. Should the 'reasonable person' in provocation become the 'rea-sonable police officer' when the defendant is a police officer? Should the 'reasonable person' in cases of drunken mistake become the 'reasonable drunkard'? Once again there is no universal theoretical solution to this problem. Within broad limits, legal systems may quite properly vary in their willingness to individualize excuses and the general principles, if any, upon which they do so. But legal systems cannot, consistent with the logic of (non-technical) excuses, vary in the importance they attach to the combination of guiding and explanatory reasons in the excusa-tory scheme of things. Thus they cannot altogether eliminate the essen-tial 'objective' dimension of excusatory claims. They cannot ignore the important point that excuses rely on reason, not on the absence of it. That is, they rely on the ability of the person who claims to be excused to believe and feel as reason demands, and because reason demands it. Those people who cannot meet this condition do not need to bother making excuses. Such people are not responsible for their actions, and are free from blame as well as being improper targets for criminal liability, irrespective of both justification and excuse.[35] Justification and excuse both belong to the realm of responsible agency, and that is pre-cisely because both depend, to put it crudely, on the ability to live within reason.

---

[35] Notice that the effect of this claim is to deny the status of excuses to, e.g. insan-ity, infancy, and 'diminished responsibility'. I do not shrink from this pay-off. Excuses have a built-in precariousness. 'Don't make excuses' is sometimes a legitimate stricture. For many actions are inexcusable in some situations thanks to the fact that everyone is expected to have the virtues and skills necessary to perform them in those situations. But even in connection with these actions in these situations we should not blame the very young or (often enough) those suffering from serious mental illness. Notice that this does not commit me to the view that very seriously mentally ill people should get away with everything they do. I share Anthony Kenny's view that most mental illness is selective in its impairment of rationality, and should only preclude blame by extinguishing responsi-bility where relevantly operative. See A Kenny, *Freewill and Responsibility* (1978), 80–84. Even so, that is not enough to make an argument based on mental illness into an excusa-tory argument, since whether mental illness affects blame depends not on the nature of the action but on the relevance of the illness to its performance. Illustrated crudely: even if cannibalism were inexcusable, some mad cannibals would not be to blame for eating people. The blameless mad cannibals would be those mad cannibals, roughly speaking, who were cannibals because mad.

The logical relationship between justification and (non-technical) excuse helps to explain the so-called 'quasi-justificatory drift' of many familiar excuses.[36] In English law this is compounded by the law's cautious insistence on having a belt as well as braces: in general no excuse is accepted into the criminal law which is not also a partial justification, and no justification is accepted which is not also a partial excuse.[37] The drift of the excuse is not so much quasi-justificatory as truly justificatory. But neither of these facts should obscure the crucial conceptual distinction between justification and excuse. Nor should one be distracted by the paradoxical sound of the claim that an action which is justifiably believed to be justified is excused rather than justified. It only goes to show that, as between the concepts of justification and excuse, justification is the more fundamental. The same proposition also brings out the true sense in which excuses may be regarded as more 'subjective' than justifications. For by their nature excuses take the world as the defendant justifiably sees it rather than as it is. They look to what the defendant believes to be applicable reasons for action, so long as she does so on the basis of genuinely applicable reasons for belief. Justifications, meanwhile, look directly to the genuinely applicable reasons for action, without stopping to look for applicable reasons for belief. But in this whole contrast the talk of 'reasons' is talk of guiding reasons. It leaves on one side the fact that, in both justification and excuse, explanatory reasons also play a key role, and that, in this sense and to this extent, each is just as subjective as the other.

5. Institutional objections

Many of the arguments which lawyers give for dividing up justification and excuse along different lines from these are of a broadly institutional character. They are based, not on general considerations of rationality and value, but on views about the limitations which are imposed upon the logic of the criminal law by its legitimate social functions and roles.

---

[36] I borrow the label from S Gardner, 'Instrumentalism and Necessity', *Oxford Journal of Legal Studies* 6 (1986), 431 at 433.

[37] Hence the Law Commission's difficulties in *Legislating the Criminal Code: Offences Against the Person and General Principles* (Law Com No 218, 1993), 63–64. The Commission finds excusatory as well as justificatory strands in the cases on 'necessity' and jumps to the conclusion that there must be two defences rather than one. Not so: one defence, compound rationale.

Such arguments often lead to the conclusion that, while the general spirit of justification and excuse as I have explained them may remain broadly visible and important in the law, the distinction is not one to which the law can or should give exact doctrinal expression. Translation into the legal context means dispensing with some of the finer points. I will briefly mention two arguments which may be thought to point in this direction.

(a) The rule of law One alluring line of argument goes something like this. The question of whether an action is justified is, on any view, a question of whether it ought all things considered to be performed. If they are to have a role in the criminal law, justifications must therefore serve as guidance to potential offenders as to what, in law, they ought to be doing. Justification doctrines must belong to the law's 'conduct rules'.[38] But if it is to be possible to rely upon the law's justificatory doctrines in one's reasoning about what to do, it must be permissible in law to do as the justificatory doctrines require *for the very reason that they are part of the law.* Accordingly, the law cannot consistently demand, in the guidance it gives to potential offenders, that the action be performed instead for some *other* reason. It means that the law must introduce a schism between guiding and explanatory reasons in its institutional adaptation of the justificatory framework. The relevant guiding reasons are, of course, those which the law mentions as justificatory: the fact that one is under attack and self-defence is called for, the fact that crimes are being committed and need to be prevented, and so forth. But the law cannot demand that these also be the explanatory reasons for one's act of self-defence or crime prevention. The best it can demand by way of explanatory reason is that one acted thus because that is how the law would have one act. Thus even if there is a pros/cons asymmetry which lies at the heart of rationality, it cannot in principle be directly replicated in the institutional context of the criminal law. When justifications are being

---

[38] The contrast between 'conduct rules' and 'adjudication rules' which I introduce here is drawn from P Robinson, 'Rules of Conduct and Principles of Adjudication', *University of Chicago Law Review* 57 (1990), 729. Similar contrasts have been drawn by P Alldridge in 'Rules for Courts and Rules for Citizens', *Oxford Journal of Legal Studies* 10 (1990), 487 and by M Dan-Cohen, 'Decision Rules and Conduct Rules: On Acoustic Separation in Criminal Law', *Harvard Law Review* 97 (1984), 625. All three authors make interesting remarks on where justificatory defences might fit into such a scheme, and how the rule of law requirements might apply to them. I should stress that none of the three is seduced by the argument being outlined here, although none of them is entirely immune to its charms either. Dan-Cohen makes the best job of resisting it.

framed, the law can only state the guiding reasons, and leave the explanatory reasons to look after themselves. Explanatory reasons, however, can readily be counted on the excusatory axis instead. For excuses do not, on any view, bear on what all things considered one ought to be doing. Legal excuses therefore do not belong to the law's 'conduct rules' which are there to guide potential offenders, but rather to the 'adjudication rules' which are there to guide judges in dealing with potential offenders. They can thus remain sensitive to considerations which cannot in principle be the subject of guidance directed to potential offenders. It means that, while justifications become more 'objective' in their adaptation to the law's demands, excuses end up taking all the more 'subjective' elements under their wing.

This argument, which I have made as good as I can make it, nevertheless harbours many errors. At its heart lies the idea that justifications, as I analyse them, cannot play a role in the criminal law without violating the rule of law, which requires that the law's conduct rules should be capable of guiding those who are subject to them. But this complaint betrays a false assumption about the sense in which legal justifications are there to provide guidance to potential offenders in the first place. When the law grants a justification, as I explained above, it provides a *cancelling permission* to act for certain reasons which would otherwise be automatically defeated by the prohibition. But a permission to do something is, by itself, no reason to do it. Thus the law does not provide any reasons for one to do what the law holds to be justified. It simply allows that one may have such reasons and act on them. To say that justificatory rules belong to the 'conduct rules' of the law, and must serve to 'guide' potential offenders, is to give the impression that the law gives people positive reasons to do what the justificatory rules allow. But the law does no such thing. Thus the idea of someone who tries to follow a justificatory rule of criminal law, in the sense of acting because of the rule, is the idea of someone who mistakes it for something quite different from what it is. Anyone who sees a justificatory legal rule for what it really is will know that it cannot in itself motivate action in accordance with it since it gives no reasons for action but only cancels the law's otherwise pre-emptive reasons for not acting on certain independent reasons for the justified action, the latter being the reasons which account for its being justified. So there is no point in a law which attempts to turn its justificatory rules into rules which can be followed directly by potential offenders. In the process all that the law does is to defeat its own object, which is that people should act for the reasons which the law permits them to act for, and not for other reasons which the legal prohibition pre-empts.

That being so, perhaps justificatory rules of law are not best labelled as 'conduct rules' at all. Of course it is true that sometimes the law *combines* them with what are more perspicuously thought of as 'conduct rules'. Sometimes a police officer may be required by law to arrest using reasonable force, as well as being justified in using such force, which would otherwise be criminal, in effecting a legally required arrest. Such cases may be thought of as self-referential, since they look within the law rather than beyond it for the justifying reasons. But again they create no schism between explanatory and guiding reasons which could conceivably affect the conditions of legal justification. For the legally recognized and protected guiding reason for the arrest must also be, in such cases, among the reasons why the arrest was made if it is to count as fully justified in law. In other words, a police officer who does not act upon the legal rule requiring arrest in such a situation also does not benefit from it.[39]

These remarks show that a stark distinction between 'conduct rules' and 'adjudication rules' is inadequate to capture the complex inner logic of the criminal law. But they also show, for our purposes more importantly, that the rule of law does not militate against a role in the criminal law for justifications as I analyse them. On the contrary, it tends to count in favour of allowing them a significant role. I said earlier that legal systems may differ in the way in which they deal with particular rational conflicts in the structure of criminal liability. Some may incorporate into the very definition of the offence the same considerations which others treat as going purely to justification. But I also added that legal

---

[39] Opponents will no doubt respond by pointing out that, in English law at least, arrests may be made lawful *either* by the fact that they were made on reasonable suspicion of the commission of an offence *or* by the fact that, although the arrest was not made on reasonable suspicion, it turned out that a real offence was committed: Police and Criminal Evidence Act 1984, s 24. The second option is a special case of justification, normally known as *vindication*. It is the case in which one is justified in taking a chance that one will turn out to be right. It is not a counterexample to my account of justification nor to my remarks on arrest, since the law still requires, in the vindication cases in s 24, that the action be an *arrest*, which is *by its nature* an action performed for certain legal reasons. See JC Smith, *Justification and Excuse in the Criminal Law* (1989), 33–34. Tony Honoré has suggested to me, however, that there is a more general issue here. Cases of vindication, he believes, point to the need for me to make certain modifications to my analysis of justification. In these cases, one only has a hunch that undefeated guiding reasons exist, and one acts on this hunch. This, in Honoré's words, represents 'a tertium quid between acting for the guiding reason and acting as the guiding reason requires but not for it'. I am not convinced. In vindication cases one does not act because of one's hunch, but because, if I may put it this way, of what it is one hunches. What one hunches is the guiding reason. It is the fact that one acts for this reason, always assuming it is undefeated, that justifies one's taking the chance that one's hunch is right. That one hunches the reason rather than, e.g. knowing of it, does not diminish its explanatory role.

systems which try to follow the former route exclusively are apt to suffer from moral shortcomings, either being excessively rigid or excessively vague. Why do these dangers come of failure to recognize justificatory defences? The answer relates, predictably, to the demands of the rule of law.[40] In a legal system which adheres conscientiously to the rule of law, offence definitions will be so far as possible clear, accessible and certain in their application, so that they can be used for guidance by potential offenders as well as by courts and officials.[41] This means that actions which will fall outside the law must be largely decided upon in advance, and closure rules provided for any unexpected cases. But defences in general, and justifications in particular, are largely exempt from these tough demands which the rule of law places upon the definition and drafting of offences. I have just explained why. Legal justifications are not there to be directly followed by potential offenders. They merely permit one to follow reasons which would otherwise have been pre-emptively defeated. So there is no need for them to aspire to standards which apply to legal rules when they *are* there to be directly followed. It follows that justifications can introduce an element of flexibility into the law which often cannot be provided, consistently with the exacting standards of the rule of law, in the very definition of the offence. A legal system which tries to do without justifications in its criminal law is thus likely either to violate the rule of law by allowing its offence definitions to remain vague enough to accommodate judicial deliberations in novel and difficult cases, or else to conform to the rule of law in its offence definitions but at the high price that the novel and difficult cases will be decided without adequate scope for judicial deliberation. Justificatory defences provide a way out of the dilemma. It is not true that the same can be achieved by granting purely excusatory defences. For, as defenders of the 'conduct rules'/'adjudication rules' view of the justification/excuse distinction will be the first to point out, only actions which are all things considered wrong need to be excused. What a sophisticated system of criminal law has to have space to do is to grant that some actions covered by a legal prohibition, but not properly taken into account or accommodated by the formulators of that prohibition, are not all things considered wrong in the eyes of the law. By and large that can only be achieved, in

---

[40] The answer is suggested in G Fletcher, 'The Nature of Justification' in S Shute, J Gardner and J Horder (eds), *Action and Value in Criminal Law*, above n 4, 175.

[41] I have explored some aspects of these demands, and in particular the 'so far as possible' proviso, in 'Rationality and the Rule of Law in Offences Against the Person', *Cambridge Law Journal* 53 (1994), 502 (Chapter 2 in this volume).

conformity with the rule of law, by the continuing judicial development of genuinely justificatory defences.[42]

(b) The harm principle A related but distinct objection to the full legal implementation of the justification/excuse contrast, as I have explained, points to the limited moral resources of the criminal law. My analysis depended at more than one point on the invocation of what may be called 'perfectionist' categories, such as those of virtue and skill. I also relied upon the importance of basic principles of rationality. But it may be objected that it is not a proper function of the criminal law in a modern society to reflect judgments of virtue and skill, nor even to enforce norms of rationality. The criminal law in a well-ordered modern society is restricted to the task of harm prevention. The famous 'harm principle', first defended by JS Mill, sets the law's legitimate agenda, and constrains the law's perfectionist ambitions. Some have thought that this prevents legal defences, and in particular legal justifications, from carrying all the baggage of their moral counterparts. Notably, the demand that one acted for the justificatory reason to which the law gave recognition strikes some people as being quite out of place in a legal regime directed exclusively towards harm prevention. In such a legal regime, acceptable action is action which prevents, or on some versions is expected to prevent, more harm than it brings about. So long as this condition is met there is no further harm prevention advantage to be gained out of legal inquiry into whether the defendant did or did not have the prevention or avoidance of harm close to her heart at the time when she acted. That did not in any way affect the amount of harm she did or was expected to do. Nor will it affect the amount of harm done by others who, for whatever reason, follow her lead in performing analogous actions in similar situations. Thus her reasons for doing as she does are not the law's proper concern.[43]

Again, errors abound in this argument. The most striking is a far-fetched misinterpretation of the harm principle. The harm principle is a principle which exists to protect people from having to surrender their worthwhile pursuits and ways of life merely because those pursuits and ways of life are morally imperfect. Now, owing to the diversity of ultimate moral values, every valuable pursuit and way of life is morally imperfect. To possess the virtues and skills needed for one way

[42] Contrast S Gardner, 'Instrumentalism and Necessity', above n 36, at 436–437.
[43] This seems to be the key to understanding Robinson's position in 'A Theory of Justification', above n 12, at 273 and 292.

of life one must forego the virtues and skills needed for another. One effect, particularly in a complex and highly mobile modern society in which people are widely exposed to strangers, is that intolerance is widespread. We all find it hard to appreciate and respect fully the different virtues and skills exhibited by those many people that we encounter daily whose ways of life and pursuits are so markedly different from our own. We correspondingly inflate the importance of their limitations, and are continually tempted by the path of suppression. The harm principle, when conscientiously followed, provides some protection against the institutionalization of such temptations in cases in which certain ways of life and pursuits are unpopular with those who hold, whether through democratic or undemocratic channels, the power of suppression. The harm principle, thus defended, is the principle that harmless immoralities should not be officially prohibited or punished, and that harmful immoralities should not be officially prohibited or punished disproportionately to the harm they do.⁴⁴ But it is a long way from this to the proposition that official prohibitions and punishments should be tailored solely to the single overarching aim of harm prevention. What is lost in the transition to this proposition is the important point that, within the boundaries set by the harm principle, the law may be tailored to reflect countless considerations which have nothing much to do with harm. Compatibly with the harm principle, a legal system may limit its prohibition and punishment of harmful activities to those which are also, e.g., dishonest or malicious or inconsiderate. To put it another way, it does not follow from the premiss that the law should not institutionalize intolerance of any harmless immoralities that the law should not institutionalize the tolerance of some harmful ones. On the contrary, there are many harmful immoralities which should arguably be tolerated by law for the sake of other values, including perfectionist values. This is a matter of particular salience where the scope of criminal law defences is concerned. For, as I explained earlier, when the law grants a defence it tolerates, perhaps regretfully, a prima facie wrong. Assuming that the law is otherwise in conformity with the harm principle, this makes the granting of defences into an act of tolerance rather than an act of intolerance. Thus the harm principle has nothing significant to add beyond what it already contributed to the construction of the offence. Of course, that is not to say that the law should ignore considerations

---

⁴⁴ I have based my remarks on J Raz, 'Autonomy, Toleration and the Harm Principle' in R Gavison (ed), *Issues in Contemporary Legal Philosophy* (1987).

of harmfulness in constructing defences. On the contrary, other things being equal it should always give such considerations whatever rational weight they have, be it great or small. Nor is it to say that there cannot sometimes be positive moral principles requiring that particular harms no longer be officially tolerated. There is certainly no general principle of toleration which would allow the authorities to wash their hands of every problem and dispense with legal regulation altogether. The point is only that intolerance, not tolerance, is the problem which the harm principle, in particular, exists to counter. It is therefore not a general constraint on the legal perfectionism, but a constraint on perfectionist considerations invoked by themselves as if they provided a sufficient ground for official prohibition and punishment.

So, even if it is true that my analysis of justifications and excuses makes them necessarily sensitive to perfectionist considerations, that presents no automatic obstacle to their legal implementation. But, so far as justifications are concerned, I am not even sure that the sensitivity to perfectionist considerations is inevitable. My main argument for the combined subjective/objective (or explanatory/guiding) account of justifications was based on the fundamental principle of rationality that one should always act for some undefeated reason. That principle, I explained, has a broadly instrumental grounding: by acting for an undefeated reason one is more likely to do what one ought, all things considered, to do. That claim, it seems to me, is no less applicable where (let us suppose) what one ought to do, all things considered, is minimize the harm one does. And the claim is therefore no less applicable in some strange legal context to which a reductive harm-prevention objective has (myopically) been applied. Assuming that, e.g., actions in self-defensive situations are generally harm preventing, one will prevent harm more reliably by acting out of self-defence than by acting in such situations out of, e.g., spite or fear of the legal consequences. One should thus look for and react to the self-defensive aspects of one's situation, not to some other aspects. That is no less true in subsequent cases in which others follow one's example than it is in one's own case. Thus the fictitious, narrow-minded legal system we are considering does well, even by its own excessively parsimonious harm-prevention standards, to reflect the importance of explanatory reasons as well as guiding reasons in the law relating to self-defence. Justificatory defences as I analyse them are accordingly no less at home in a legal system intent on harm prevention and nothing else than they are in a legal system, like our own, with a less monomaniacal outlook.

6

The Gist of Excuses

It is often said that the criminal law judges actions, not character. That is true, but misleading. It is true that, barring certain exceptional and troubling examples, crimes are actions, and being a crime is therefore a property of actions.[1] Nevertheless, the criminality of an action frequently falls to be determined, in part, according to *standards of character*—according to standards of courage, carefulness, honesty, self-discipline, diligence, humanity, good will, and so forth. Nobody can be a thief in English law, for instance, unless she acts dishonestly.[2] There is, to be sure, a difference between asking whether the accused acted dishonestly, and asking whether she is dishonest. She is dishonest if and only if she tends to act dishonestly. In other words, judging a person dishonest has a diachronic aspect which judging an action dishonest lacks. But apart from this diachronic aspect, the standard by which we judge a person dishonest is exactly the same standard as that by which we judge an action dishonest. It is a standard of character, a standard which bears not only on what is done, but also on the spirit in which and reason for which it is done. The mere fact that I did something that a dishonest person might do—for example, pocketed someone else's cash without asking—does not entail that I am dishonest, and nor, by the same token, does it entail that I acted dishonestly. If I pocketed the cash to save the owner from an embarrassing revelation, or as part of a complex practical joke, or in the belief that the cash was left out for me, or even just absent-mindedly, then pocketing the cash was, other things

---

[1] The exceptional and troubling examples I have in mind are examples of status crimes such as those in *R* v *Larsonneur* (1933) 24 Cr App Rep 74 and *Robinson* v *California* 370 US 660, 82 S Ct 1417, 8 L Ed 758 (1966). Crimes of possession are on the borderline between action crimes and status crimes, and present some but not all of the same problems. Michael Moore thinks that crimes of omission are also troubling exceptions: MS Moore, *Act and Crime* (1994), 22–34. I do not share this view and when I speak of actions in the text I always mean to include omissions.
[2] Theft Act 1968, s 1.

being equal,[3] not a dishonest action any more than it was the action of a dishonest person. It may have been meddlesome, or puerile, or presumptuous, or thoughtless. But those judgments invoke quite different standards of character, depending on quite different configurations of reason and spirit, from the dishonesty standard specified for the identification of a thief in English law.

This example shows that, sometimes, standards of character figure in the criminal law because they are built into the definitions of particular criminal offences, i.e. they are part of what makes an action wrongful in the eyes of the criminal law. They also figure separately, however, in many of the criminal law's *excusatory* doctrines. Now a link between character and excuse has often been forged by those interested in the philosophical foundations of the criminal law. On one familiar view, sometimes called the 'Humean' view, we should grant an excuse to somebody in respect of what he did if and only if what he did was no manifestation of his character.[4] This view proceeds from the sound thought that excuses matter because a person's excused actions do not reflect badly on him—do not show him, personally, in a bad light. That being so, the thinking goes, an excuse must be something that blocks the path from an adverse judgment about an action to a correspondingly adverse judgment about the person whose action it is. The action is cowardly, say, but since this person does not otherwise tend towards cowardly actions, she herself is no coward. Her cowardly action is 'out of character'. And that, according to the Humean view, is the gist of excuses. But there is a good deal of confusion in this line of thought. For there is no such thing as a cowardly action which does not show its agent in a cowardly light. It is true that a cowardly light may be a rather unflattering light; as I accepted already, one cowardly action does not make a coward. But an unflattering light is not the same as a false light. In my cowardly action, by definition, I manifest at least the *beginnings* of a cowardly tendency, the *stirrings* of cowardice. By 'manifest' here I do not mean that my cowardly action is mere evidence of some condition called cowardice hidden within me, evidence which may ultimately be discounted for want of

---

[3] I say 'other things being equal' only to anticipate the objections: (1) that many people have mixed motives; and (2) that even without mixed motives pocketing cash to save someone from embarrassment might be dishonest under another description, e.g. as a concealment of the truth.

[4] P Helm, 'Hume on Exculpation', *Philosophy* 42 (1967), 268; MD Bayles, 'Character, Purpose, and Criminal Responsibility', *Law and Philosophy* 1 (1982), 5. That Hume is truly committed to this view is doubted by J Bricke in 'Hume, Freedom to Act, and Personal Evaluation', *History of Philosophy Quarterly* 5 (1988), 141.

corroboration. Cowards are no more and no less than people who tend
to perform cowardly actions. Their cowardly actions add up to *constitute*,
not to evidence, their cowardice.[5] Thus even if this cowardly action is
my first, and is quite unprecedented, it necessarily counts constitutively
and not merely evidentially against me whenever, thereafter, the question arises of whether I am a coward. And that is exactly what it means
to say that my cowardly actions show me in a cowardly light. It follows
that the Humean view unravels. If my excused actions do not show me
in a cowardly light, they cannot, after all, be cowardly actions. That
they are excused cannot therefore block the path from the judgment
that I did something cowardly to the judgment that I am a coward. The
excuse must intervene earlier to forestall the original judgment that this
was a cowardly action. Supporters of the Humean view may object that
this makes no sense, since if my action was not cowardly after all then
I scarcely need to make an excuse for it. What have I left to excuse? But
that question betrays another confusion. I need to make an excuse for
my action because it is wrongful. As criminal lawyers are usually the first
to point out, the wrongfulness of an action is not comprehensively or
invariably dictated by character standards. That point holds both in the
law and outside the law. Even morally speaking, it is perfectly possible for
actions to be admirable at the same time as wrongful, i.e. to be things that
should not have been done, whether prima facie or all things considered,
but which cast the person who did them in a favourable light.[6] *A fortiori*
there can be things that should not have been done, whether prima facie
or all things considered, but which do not cast the person who did them
in an *un*favourable light, but at worst an indifferent light. And that is
precisely the equilibrium which a valid excuse, whether inside or outside
the law, establishes.

So the gist of an excuse is not that the action was 'out of character', in
the sense of being a departure from what we have come to expect from

---

[5] Michael Moore rejects this 'dispositional' conception of character on the ground
that it 'doesn't say much about the person whose character it is': MS Moore, 'Choice,
Character, and Excuse', *Social Philosophy and Policy* 7 (1990), 29 at 42. But that is no
objection. By definition, whatever view of character is sound says as much about the person, in the dimension of character, as there is to be said. Moore's worry cannot be that the
dispositional conception doesn't say enough about the person, but rather that it portrays
the person to be, in at least one dimension, a less substantial entity than he imagined it
to be. And that is not surprising, since the person is a less substantial entity than most
people imagine it to be.

[6] For argument, see M Slote, *Goods and Virtues* (1983), 77–107; D Parfit, *Reasons and
Persons* (1984), 31–35; M Stocker, *Plural and Conflicting Values* (1990), 37–50.

the person whose action it is.[7] Quite the contrary, in fact. The gist of an excuse, as I will try to explain, is precisely that the person with the excuse lived up to our expectations. On first encounter, this claim may give the misleading impression that people's wrongful actions are excused so long as they continue to live up to the character standards that they have always lived up to, however appalling. One may have an image of someone excusing themselves by saying: 'I've always been spiteful and malicious, so how did you expect me to behave?' Being spiteful and malicious is, of course, no excuse for anything. Pointing to the spite and malice in one's wrongful actions is asserting, not denying, that these actions cast one in a bad light. So the question, for excusatory purposes, is obviously not whether the person claiming the excuse lived up to expectations in the predictive sense of being true to form or true to type or even true to our disappointing experience of human beings in general. The question is whether that person lived up to expectations in the *normative* sense. Did she manifest as much resilience, or loyalty, or thoroughness, or presence of mind as a person in her situation should have manifested? In the face of terrible threats, for example, did this person show as much fortitude as someone in his situation could properly be asked to show? In the face of constant taunts, did this person exhibit as much self-restraint as we have a right to demand of someone in her situation? The character standards which are relevant to these and other excuses are not the standards of our own characters, nor even the standards of most people's characters, but rather the standards to which our characters should, minimally, conform.

This word 'minimally' here may lead one to suppose that we are talking of uniform normative expectations—that the same basic standard of self-restraint or fortitude is the excusatory standard for all of us. But that is not so. Different people are subject to different normative expectations when their excuses are assessed. Imagine, for example, a young and inexperienced soldier operating a checkpoint in some troubled frontier zone, who has been warned that the intelligence services expect such a checkpoint to come under terrorist attack today. Already on edge, he misinterprets some motorist's actions—he thinks she was going for a

---

[7] That a person acted 'out of character' may, if accompanied by the appropriate sense of guilt or remorse, be a reason for forgiving her or showing her mercy, things which criminal courts often do at the sentencing stage of the criminal trial. But those whose actions are excused do not need any forgiveness or mercy, so this issue need not be explored here. For exploration of this and several related issues, see JG Murphy and J Hampton, *Forgiveness and Mercy* (1988).

gun, say, when she was only reaching for her car documents—and kills her with one panic-stricken shot.[8] There are various aspects of this situation which may attract our attention when we think about the soldier's possible excuses for this (as we will assume) wrongful killing. One is that he is young and inexperienced. There is a view of excuses, sometimes (mistakenly) labelled 'Kantian', according to which the standards of character applicable to an excuse are relativized to the *capacities* of the person claiming the excuse.[9] The soldier in our example does not react with the kind of level-headedness which some soldiers might have exhibited. But being young and inexperienced, the thinking goes, he may not have been *capable* of that more mature degree of level-headedness. One has to imagine how working in this troubled frontier zone, under constant tension and at constant risk, might have affected one so young and new to the job, and how his capacity for keeping a level head might have been affected by this. This is not the same, adherents of the 'Kantian' view would stress, as relying on mere predictions of how our soldier will stand up under pressure. Our soldier's excuse is not validated by the standards of level-headedness which he tends to live up to, so that he can excuse himself by saying: 'I've always been a bit of a panicker, so what did you expect?' Rather, the assumption in the so-called 'Kantian' view is that people may have in principle the capacity—the inner resources, if you like—to live up to standards of character higher than those which they do live up to. It is that capacity, thought to vary from person to person and indeed possibly within one person from one phase of her life to the next, which places a cap on our normative expectations of people when we come to consider their excuses. Thus whether the terrorist threat which was imagined to be posed by the motorist in our example excuses

---

[8] The scenario is loosely based on that in *R* v *Clegg* [1995] 1 All ER 334, where the legal issue was the availability of an excusatory defence to murder for those, particularly soldiers, who kill in mistaken or excessive self-defence. In that case, the victim of the shooting was complicitous in venal wrongdoing. This, together with the political context (the sectarian conflict in Northern Ireland), created distractions which I have stripped out of my own example.

[9] MD Bayles, 'Character, Purpose, and Criminal Responsibility', above n 4; N Lacey, *State Punishment: Political Principles and Community Values* (1988), 63. That Kant did not and could not have subscribed to any such view is apparent from the following passage in *The Doctrine of Virtue* (trans Gregor, (1964) at 66: 'We must not determine ethical duties according to our estimate of man's power to fulfil the [moral] law; on the contrary we must estimate man's power by the standard of the law, which commands categorically. Hence we must appraise this power on the basis of our rational knowledge of what men should be in keeping with the Idea of Humanity, not on the basis of our empirical knowledge of men as they are.'

what our soldier did depends, among other things, on whether, in shooting her dead, he showed as much level-headedness as he was capable of showing in the circumstances.

The supposed relationship between a virtue and the capacity for it needs a good deal of explanation if this view is to make sense. True, just because we are human beings, every one of us has the capacity to *develop* new virtues by learning to recognize different rationally-significant features of situations and respond to them in our actions by acting, in a suitably positive spirit, on the reasons they give. But that is not the capacity that the so-called 'Kantian' view is concerned with. It is not concerned with a capacity I might have at time (*t*) to develop virtues by time (*t*+1), but with a capacity I might have at time (*t*) to act more virtuously at time (*t*) than I do in fact act at time (*t*). Could there be any such capacity? That people *do* act 'out of character', and sometimes for better rather than for worse, cannot be doubted. Someone who never showed any heroic tendency in her life may, in some extreme situation, perform an act of great courage. And if she does do so, then necessarily she *can*. The real question is what sense it makes to think of this 'can' as the 'can' of capacity rather than merely the 'can' of possibility. Given the march of technology, I may one day enjoy the possibility of flying to the moon. But I will never enjoy the *capacity* to fly to the moon, because the fact that I can fly to the moon will never be owed to anything *about me*. Instead, my flying to the moon will exploit the capacities of others, e.g. engineers and spaceship commanders. They are the ones with the array of qualities—in this case, skills as well as virtues—that will get me to the moon.[10] Now courage is undoubtedly one of those qualities. Being courageous means that one has capacities that one would not otherwise have, such as the capacity to be a spaceship commander. That is because courage gives one the capacity to act courageously, and spaceship commanders, among others, need that capacity to be fit for their job. The question we are facing here is whether someone who is *not* courageous may nonetheless have that same capacity to act courageously. I must admit to finding the whole idea baffling. The reason is that I cannot see how someone with that capacity could fail to have the corresponding tendency. Someone may say that he understands the world just as the

---

[10] This is perhaps a suitable place to make clear, for the sake of completeness, that some excuses invoke technical standards rather than standards of character. Although these excuses differ in certain ways from those under discussion here, their gist mirrors that of the excuses under discussion here: that the person who has them lived up to expectations in respect of her skill.

courageous person understands it, and yet somehow does not manage, by and large, to put this understanding into practice. His inclination towards self-preservation often gets the better of him. To which my reply would be that in that case he is kidding himself if he thinks he understands the world just as the courageous person understands it. For a person who sees the world through genuinely courageous eyes, there is nothing to 'manage', no question of putting anything 'into practice', no room for any motivational obstruction between understanding why a situation calls for courage and acting courageously. If one sees the world through genuinely courageous eyes one does not see danger to oneself the way that more cowardly people see it, as a threat, but rather as a challenge, something which, up to a point, one inclines towards rather than away from. Up to that point, one therefore has no inclination to overcome, no will-power to exercise. One looks with bewilderment upon those who hold back and say they're too scared to act. How, one asks oneself, can they so comprehensively miss the point? And how, to return our question, can such people ever be thought to have a *capacity* for courage when, in their actions, they manifest nothing at all of the courageous mentality—when they admittedly do not share in the spirit of the courageous person, and therefore cannot be seeing the world as the courageous person sees it? Perhaps, like most people, they have the capacity to learn to be more courageous by being faced with fearful situations which put the trivial fears of their lives to date in perspective. Or perhaps one day they will simply act courageously, quite out of character—we human beings have an unpredictable side to us. But the idea that right now, as they shrink back, some of these people might already have the capacity for courage—that idea makes no sense. Right now, these people have no relationship to courage except a palpable lack of it. It follows that the standard of courage which they must show if they are to benefit from an excuse cannot be the standard of their own extant capacity for it. Because, in spite of what adherents of the so-called 'Kantian' view say, that standard does reduce straightforwardly to the standard of purely predictive expectation, the standard of character which those making the excuse already meet. That is because the extent of someone's capacity for courageous action at time (t) is no more and no less than the extent of her courage at time (t). Apart from that courage, there is no further something about her, at time (t), which can intelligibly be described as a capacity for acting courageously at that time. There is, in respect of truly courageous action, no further variety of 'inner resources' anyone could ever intelligibly be said to have.

Now it may be said that level-headedness, the virtue which is at stake in the case of our young soldier, differs from courage in precisely this respect. It may be said that it belongs, alongside self-discipline and self-restraint, to a family of virtues characterized by motivational conflict. On this view the spirit of level-headedness is not the positive I-can-cope-with-this, I-just-look-danger-in-the-eye spirit of the courageous, but an unstable teeth-gritted, whatever-I-do-I-must-stay-calm sense of apprehension and self-doubt. The level-headed person has a strong inclination to act in a panicky way, the story goes, which he controls only by sheer will-power. Therefore, apart from the question of whether our soldier is sufficiently level-headed, there is also the question of whether he has sufficient will-power, i.e. a sufficient capacity, to be any more level-headed than he is in such a situation. Personally, I doubt whether the virtue of level-headedness belongs to any such family of virtues or comprises any of these features, which strike me as the features of someone who is very far from level-headed. In fact, I think this is the non-level-headed person's stilted view of what life as a level-headed person might be like. But even if level-headedness were like this, those who rely on this fact when defending the so-called 'Kantian' view of excuses merely expose that view to deeper doubts in the process. They may rely on the fact that our soldier had limited will-power to suggest that our expectations of him in the dimension of level-headedness should be limited. But then they instantly face the question of why our expectations of him *in the dimension of will-power itself* should not exceed the standards which he currently meets in that dimension. Why, having been denied the excuse 'I've always been a bit of a panicker, so what did you expect?' should he nevertheless be granted the excuse 'I've always had a bit of a problem with will-power, so what did you expect?' Is there something about lack of will-power such that it doesn't show people in a bad light in the way that lack of courage or lack of level-headedness does?

Not for the real Kant, and not for the rest of us. If it makes any sense to say that our soldier was as level-headed as he was capable of being, as distinct from merely being as level-headed as he was, then it is always a possible answer to his purported excuse that *he simply should have had a greater capacity for level-headedness*. And when we ask 'by what standards should his capacity have been greater?', our excusatory focus naturally switches from the fact that he was young and inexperienced to the fact that he was a soldier in a troubled frontier zone. Why, of course—he should have had the capacity that a soldier in a troubled frontier zone should have had. His excuse, when he wrongly shoots the motorist, should be structured by normative expectations which are in turn structured by his role as a soldier. A soldier should be more level-headed than most (and therefore, if that really is something different, needs a greater capacity for level-headedness than most), because coping with tension and threats and emergencies is the soldier's stock-in-trade. A soldier who tends to panic is unfit to be a soldier. It is true, of course, that a junior soldier may not properly be expected to meet quite the same standards of level-headedness as, say, his platoon sergeant, and a rookie junior soldier perhaps *a fortiori*. But this has nothing to do with any capacity or incapacity the rookie soldier may have, at this early stage, to meet the higher standards of level-headedness which will later be expected of him. It has to do with the fact that the role of a soldier changes with rank and with training. The process of learning to be a soldier is partly the process of learning to be more level-headed that one might otherwise have been, of learning to see how the world looks without out the clouding presence of panic. Thus not even all soldiers, let alone all people, are subject to exactly the same normative expectations so far as their level-headedness is concerned. But, nevertheless, for each soldier and for each person the relevant normative expectations, *including expectations of capacity itself*, vary not according to capacity but according to role. Someone who tries to excuse her betrayals of her friends in the face of threats or other pressures to betray has his excuses judged by the standards of loyalty applicable to friendship, and if she is incapable of such loyalty (or, in my plainer terms, if she is not loyal enough) then that only goes to show that she is unfit for friendship, unfit to call herself a friend. A mountaineer who tries to excuse his cutting of the ropes between himself and his colleague when the link puts him in danger, even though the cutting of it may put his colleague in comparable danger, has his excuses judged by the standards of dependability befitting mountaineers, and if there is something about him which means that he cannot be that dependable (or, in my plainer terms, if he is not dependable enough) then that confirms, rather than denies, that he is unfit to join a mountaineering expedition.

Those still in the thrall of the supposedly 'Kantian' view of excuses are bound to balk at the implication, in this alternative and broadly Aristotelian view of mine, of an automatic correlation between being unfit for the role one occupies and being shown in a bad light. Doesn't this depend, they are sure to ask, on the soundness of the earlier claim that we all have the capacity to *develop* virtues and skills which would make us fit for the lives we lead, so that those who do not are being caught by some fallback doctrine of prior fault?[11] If it turned out that somebody could *never have become* fit to be a soldier, or a friend, or a mountaineer, then would it still be true that her unfitness to be one reflects badly upon her now that she is one? These questions comprehensively—I would say almost wilfully—miss the point. That our actions exhibit our unfitness for the role we are occupying, or more broadly the life we are leading, is just what it *means* for our actions to reflect badly on us. As I have just been trying to convey, there is no further question of whether our unfitness, in turn, reflects badly on us. There are, fundamentally, two closely related things that matter about our relationship with the life we lead, and the roles which go to make it up. The first is that we do not fail in those roles, that we do not do things which people in those roles should not do—that we do not betray our friends, trip up our fellow athletes, misdiagnose our patients' ailments. The second is that we are fit for those roles, that we have the qualities (the virtues, skills, and tastes, as well as the physical and mental constitution) which people in those roles should have—that we are loyal friends, fair minded (as well as powerful) athletes, thorough (as well as expert) doctors. As my list of examples brings out, our fitness regulates, up to a point, our prospect of failure. That we have the right qualities for our role contributes to our not doing the wrong thing, either constitutively (where the wrong thing is partly defined in terms of standards of character, skill, etc.) or at any rate instrumentally (where meeting a relevant standard of character, skill, etc. makes our doing the wrong thing less likely). Nevertheless, fitness and the avoidance of failure do not inevitably go hand-in-hand. I already mentioned the possibility of admirable wrongdoing—of actions which should not have been done but which reflect favourably on the person who did them. Such actions—the thoughtful act which back-fires and causes offence, the act of solicitousness for one's children which only brings out the worst in them—yield examples of failure in spite of fitness. Conversely, there are examples of unfitness without failure—police officers who treat suspects properly but are grudging about it, athletes who never cheat but only

---

[11] Many people describe the Aristotelian view as depending on this, which shows only that they have preoccupations quite different from Aristotle's own. See e.g. EL Pincoffs, 'Legal Responsibility and Moral Character', *Wayne Law Review* 19 (1973), 905; MS Moore, 'Choice, Character, and Excuse', above n 5, at 45–46. Aristotle did hold that all people have the capacity to develop virtues and skills, but the importance of the point was not, in his mind, that if it were the case that they never had this capacity they would be excused, or in some other way exonnerated, in respect of their later vicious actions. That these are vicious actions is enough *automatically* to pre-empt any such excuse, however the viciousness may have arisen: Aristotle, *Nicomachean Ethics*, 1113^b3–22.

because they fear disqualification. But in all this the question of whether and how one's actions reflect upon one *just is* the question of whether they point to one's fitness or unfitness for whatever role one is occupying, for whatever life one is leading. So valid excuses, which prevent one's wrong actions from reflecting badly upon one, cannot conceivably invoke standards of character (or for that matter standards of skill or taste or physical or intellectual fitness) which fall short of the standards of fitness for the role in which, by doing the wrong thing, one failed. In particular, those standards cannot be capped according to the capacities (be they past, present, or even future) of the person to whom the excuse is supposed to apply. For such incapacity, far from militating against unfitness, is a mode of unfitness in its own right.

Now of course there are some people whose incapacity goes very deep—taking them, in some or all of what they do, beyond the realm in which talk of the occupation of roles and the application of the standards of fitness for those roles makes any sense. Of these people we say that they are not responsible for their actions. One of the biggest sources of confusion in the study of excuses lies in the thought that those who make excuses are thereby denying their responsibility for their actions.[12] This thought is nourished by one of the many ambiguities of the word 'responsible'.[13] In one sense, being responsible for what was done means bearing the adverse normative consequences of its having been done. Many people who make excuses, for example those who make them in a criminal court, are denying that they should bear responsibility in this sense. But they are not denying their responsibility in a second sense, which is normally, and certainly in any legitimate criminal court, a precondition of responsibility in the first sense. By making excuses people are, on the contrary, *asserting* their responsibility in this second sense. For being responsible in this sense—being responsible for our actions—is none other than being in that condition in which our actions are amenable, in principle, to justification and excuse.[14] Justifications and excuses are available only to those whose

---

[12] Among many examples: JL Austin, 'A Plea for Excuses' in Austin, *Philosophical Papers* (1961), 123 at 124; E D'Arcy, *Human Acts* (1965), 85; George Fletcher, *Basic Concepts of Legal Thought* (1996), 104–105.

[13] The classic taxonomy of different senses of this word is HLA Hart, 'Varieties of Responsibility', *Law Quarterly Review* 83 (1967), 346. The two senses I am about to distinguish correspond, respectively, to Hart's 'liability responsibility' and his 'capacity responsibility', although his definitions depart from mine at certain points.

[14] And in which, I should add for the sake of completeness, we are also in a fit state to *offer* justification or excuse. When the question arises of whether we are responsible for our actions, attention must be paid to our condition at two separate stages—first at the

actions have intelligible rational explanations, i.e. whose actions properly reflected reasons for action that they took themselves to have, and this is the basic condition of our responsibility for our actions.[15] It is met by our young soldier, who, even in his panic, took himself to be facing a terrorist who was going for a gun, and who shot her in what he incorrectly took to be an act of self-defence. It is similarly met by those who commit wrongs under duress or provocation. They believe the threats or taunts they are facing to be reasons for them to do as they do, and they intelligibly, even if quite mistakenly, do what they do for those reasons. It is sometimes hinted that this element of rational intelligibility is all that it takes to ground an excuse. If only we can *make sense of* what someone did in the light of the reasons she took herself to have for doing it, then can't we by that token excuse her for doing it? The answer is that, of course, we can't, because even when we have made sense of the reasons on which someone acted, on any credible view we still have to *assess* her reasons, as well as the spirit in which she acted, according to the applicable standards of character. But the focus on making sense of people's actions in the light of their reasons rightly brings to the surface the important point that those whose reasoning *can't* be made sense of in this way, whether because of profound mental illness or infancy or sleepwalking or (on some interpretations of it) post-hypnotic suggestion, are not responsible for their actions and therefore need no excuses for what they do. And of course this means that there is a sense in which one very specific and deep-seated incapacity—namely the incapacity to reason intelligibly through to action—can place a cap on the standards of character by which one is judged when one makes an excuse. It places that cap by extinguishing the need for one to rely on excuses altogether. But it does not follow that when one does need to rely on excuses, one can enjoy an analogous cap based on one's *other* incapacities. For the analogy is false, since now one is not denying one's responsibility for one's actions, but asserting it instead.

Even once one has understood this contrast between denials of responsibility and excuses, it is easy to underestimate its importance. Criminal lawyers, in particular, tend to be fixated with responsibility in the first

---

time of the action which is under scrutiny, and secondly at the time of its evaluation, e.g. when the case comes to court. The basic idea of responsibility (also known as account-ability) is the etymologically undemanding one of an ability to respond to accusations, being in a position to account for one's actions: JR Lucas, *Responsibility* (1993), 5–12.

[15] I have tried to explain justifications, and their relationship to excuses, in J Gardner, 'Justifications and Reasons' in ATH Smith and AP Simester (eds), *Harm and Culpability* (1996) (reprinted as Chapter 5 in this volume).

sense I mentioned, and tend to take it for granted that any doctrine that serves to acquit the accused, and therefore to avert the adverse normative consequences of her action, is as good as any other so far as the accused is concerned. I have always found this an astonishing assumption, which implies that nobody who is tried in the criminal courts has, or even deserves to have, any self-respect. Self-respect is an attitude which everyone ought to have if they deserve it, and which, moreover, everyone ought to deserve. The self-respecting person aspires to live up to the proper standards for success in and fitness for the life she leads, and holds herself out to be judged by those standards. It follows that it is part of the nature of self-respect that a self-respecting person wants to be able to give an intelligible rational account of herself, to be able to show that her actions were the actions of someone who aspired to live up to the proper standards for success in her life and fitness to lead it.[16] She wants it to be the case that her actions were not truly wrongful, or if they were wrongful, that they were at any rate justified, or if they were not justified, that they were at any rate excused. A denial of responsibility rules all of this out, and that is, accordingly, the line of defence which counts as an admission of defeat for any self-respecting person.

The point can be nicely illustrated by comparing the defences of provocation and diminished responsibility which are found side-by-side in the modern English legislation on homicide, and both of which, if successfully pleaded, have the effect of substituting a manslaughter conviction for a murder conviction.[17] To those who have complained of deficiencies in the provocation defence, which is quite tightly circumscribed, it is sometimes said that they could always rely on the more loosely drawn diminished responsibility defence instead. If your long history as a victim of domestic violence was not allowed to affect the assessment of how gravely you had been provoked by your violent partner when you killed him, well why not say instead that your 'battered woman syndrome' left you with diminished responsibility for your actions?[18] After all, it surely comes to the same thing in the end. But it does not come to the same thing at all.[19] The whole point of the diminished responsibility defence

[16] In this explanation, I have been influenced by S Darwall, 'Two Kinds of Respect', *Ethics* 88 (1977), 36 and J Raz, 'Liberating Duties', *Law and Philosophy* 8 (1989), 3.

[17] Homicide Act 1957, ss 2 and 3.

[18] See e.g. *R v Thornton* [1992] 1 All ER 306 at 315–316, *per* Beldam LJ. The label 'battered woman syndrome' was coined in L Walker, *The Battered Woman Syndrome* (1984) and is now frequently used in English-speaking courts.

[19] The following point has been made many times before although its broader implications for the relationship between excuses and responsibility have rarely been

is that it depends on the *unreasonableness* of the defendant's reactions,
i.e. their unamenability to intelligible rational explanation. 'Why would
anyone have done that? It makes no sense. It must be some pathological
condition, some kind of "battered woman syndrome".' The whole point
of the provocation defence, on the other hand, is that it depends on the
reasonableness of the provoked person's reaction to the provocation. 'I can
see why she did it; she did it because she could see no other escape.' 'I can
see why she did it; she did it because she needed to save some vestige of her
dignity before he destroyed it utterly.' 'I can see why she did it; she did it
for the sake of the children, whom she thought would be the next target.'
Of course, intelligible rational explanations like this will not automatically be *sufficient* to make the provocation plea successful—that depends
on whether they also meet the relevant normative expectations—but they
are certainly *necessary*. Nobody can have a provocation defence without
them, but, equally, they cannot have a diminished responsibility defence
with them. Faced with the choice, any self-respecting defendant would
rather be able to give a intelligible account of herself in rational terms.
She would also rather be judged, in the light of that account, by the
proper standards of character, skill, taste, etc. for the life she leads, not by
some standard manipulated to take account of some claimed weakness
in her, which only brands her constitutionally unfit for the life she leads,
an incapable and pathetic specimen. Any self-respecting person would
rather have a provocation defence, in other words, that properly takes
account of the scale of the provocation she was subjected to but judges
her reactions to that provocation by the proper standards of character
applicable to all, as opposed to falling back on a diminished responsibility defence and conceding that those standards of character do not apply
to her in the first place.

I said 'applicable to all'; but surely, if I am true to my own Aristotelian
account of excuses, I must mean 'applicable to people in her role'? And
what, for these purposes, *is* her role? By exactly which standards of character should the law of provocation, through its reasonableness test, be
judging her? Certainly not by the standards of character which determine
fitness for being a victim of domestic violence. Since nobody should be
a victim of domestic violence, there is no self-respect in living up to any
standards of fitness for this role. Nor in living up to standards of fitness

appreciated. See e.g. P Crocker, 'The Meaning of Equality for Battered Women Who
Kill Men in Self-Defense', *Harvard Women's Law Journal* 8 (1985), 121 or A Norrie,
Crime Reason and History (1993), 254.

for being a killer, by the same token. The standards of fitness for being a parent? A partner? An airline pilot or gas installer (if that is what she also happens to be)? A citizen? The problem seems to be that the broadly Aristotelian view of excuses is role-based, but the modern criminal law is not. Surely we come before the modern criminal law, or if we take all this talk of 'equality before the law' seriously we are at any rate supposed to come before it, stripped of our roles, and so subject to the same rules and principles irrespective of the particular kind of life we lead?[20] Actually that is far from true when we look at the criminal law as a whole. A large and ever growing body of criminal law today is what academic commentators call 'regulatory' criminal law, criminal law that applies to us only in our roles as shopkeepers, householders, social security claimants, witnesses, motorists, parents, waste-disposal contractors, and so forth, and purports to judge our actions, *inter alia*, by standards of character specifically befitting these roles.[21] But the law of homicide is not part of the regulatory criminal law in this sense. Like the law of theft and the law of assault, it applies to us all, whatever furrows we may plough in life. So shouldn't the standards of character applicable to it, including those which govern the availability of excuses in it, be uniform? And if so, the question remains, what exactly should they be? My own view is that there is no fundamental objection to making excusatory standards vary, even in the law of homicide, according to the standards applicable to roles which the defendant occupies when he kills. If he kills while on duty and armed as a police officer, then there is no fundamental objection to judging him by the standards of courage, level-headedness and self-restraint applicable specifically to police officers. But I agree that the problem is more difficult when we are dealing with people who kill while occupying a role (such as that of robber or slave), the internal standards of which should not be supported by law because the role should not exist, or a role (such as that of lover or friend), the internal standards of which should be supported by law but do not include any relevant standards (e.g. have nothing specifically to say about level-headedness or courage). The criminal law then seems to have only two options. One is the *lowest common denominator* option. It holds people only to the minimum standards of character needed to lead *any* kind of worthwhile life. The

[20] See e.g. M Sandel, 'The Political Theory of the Procedural Republic' in AC Hutchinson and Patrick Monahan (eds), *The Rule of Law: Ideal or Ideology?* (1987), 85.
[21] Some textbook writers confuse 'regulatory' crime in this sense with *less serious* crime. For a welcome corrective, see N Lacey, C Wells and D Meure, *Reconstructing Criminal Law* (1990), especially at 233–256.

other is the *overarching role* option. It holds that, whatever other roles we may have in life, we also have the distinct role of being human beings, which itself sets basic standards of character. The former option, however, turns out to be a non-starter as soon as one realizes that there can be no common denominator across the various roles we occupy, except to the extent that there is an overarching role of being a human being. Every virtue, every skill, every taste is such that some roles make no specific demand for it, unless, as it turns out, they must incidentally make that demand just by virtue of being human roles. It follows that the lowest common denominator option collapses into the overarching role option. And that leaves the criminal law with the problem of setting distinctive standards of character (and other standards of fitness) for that overarching role, reopening that age-old intractable question of what it means to be human.

Of course this is not the place to tackle this question. Suffice it to say that it need not remain quite as intractable for the criminal law as it does for moral philosophers. For the law has a function not only in supporting but also in *establishing* the proper standards of character (as well as the other standards) for the roles it governs. That the regulatory criminal law does this is neither open to doubt nor, in general, a source of much moral anxiety. The measure of attentiveness required of drivers, the measure of probity required of company directors, the measure of truthfulness required of witnesses; these and many other standards of character are settled directly by doctrines of the regulatory criminal law. In some cases the roles themselves are creations of law, so that the law has no alternative but to set the applicable standards until the roles start to take on a life of their own. But even when roles do acquire a life of their own, and also when they are not creations of law in the first place, the law often has a role in settling which of various competing applicable standards will be the appropriate standard for the role. There comes a point at which, as between these competing standards, it matters less which of them becomes the standard for the role than that the standard for the role is authoritatively settled to allow us to have uniform expectations of each other when we are in that role. This is, of course, the classic 'co-ordination' argument for legal regulation.[22] It applies no less to standards of character than to other standards supported and enforced by law. And, if it is true that the non-regulatory criminal law is concerned with us in our overarching role as human beings, it applies no less to the

---

[22] See J Finnis, 'Law as Co-ordination', *Ratio Juris* 2 (1989), 97.

non-regulatory criminal law than to the regulatory criminal law. There is no reason to assume that the standards for this overarching role of ours are more determinately settled in advance of the law's intervention than they are for the less overarching roles of electrician or spouse or lawyer. Again, there may be a variety of competing defensible standards for failure and fitness as a human being *simpliciter*, and at a certain point in the competition it may be less important which one of them wins than that we have a clear winner to rely upon in forging our expectations of each other. The basic standard of honesty which people should show is not merely captured but *set* by the law of fraud and theft, and the setting of that basic standard by law rather than by, say, the person whose honesty is at issue is justified by the co-ordinating power of the law. Likewise, the law on duress and provocation, which settles which of a variety of possible and otherwise defensible minimum standards for courage and self-control we have a right to expect of each other, making that the true applicable minimum standard thanks to the extra value which comes of co-ordinating our expectations of each other to a uniform standard. To the extent that there is any real force in demands for 'equality before the law', that force comes of this consideration coupled with the consideration I adduced in the previous paragraph.[23] It comes of the instrumental value of uniform standards in resolving co-ordination problems coupled with the intrinsic value of granting self-respecting people what, as self-respecting people, they want—namely to be judged by the proper standards which apply to their role, be that their role as golfers or parents or guests or engineers or merely as people. And both of these considerations militate strongly against placing a capacity-based cap on the level at which the standards of character applicable to particular defendant's excuses are set.

It may be objected that the fact that this is the authoritative voice of the law speaking also introduces a major countervailing consideration. Surely, under the doctrine of the rule of law, it is crucial that people who are subject to the law's authority can be guided by the law, so that they can deliberately steer their lives round it and avoid the disruption

---

[23] I should say that I find the label 'equality' misleading in this setting, as in so many others. I find it more perspicuous to frame the demand as a demand that courts be faithful to their role as administrators of justice. I have explored some of the other implications of this role in J Gardner, 'The Purity and Priority of Private Law', *University of Toronto Law Journal* 46 (1996), 459 and in J Gardner, 'Crime: in Proportion and in Perspective' in AJ Ashworth and M Wasik (eds), *Fundamentals of Sentencing Theory* (1998) (reprinted as Chapter 11 in this volume).

of the law's adverse normative consequences? Doesn't it follow that a law which sets standards to which self-respecting people may well aspire but which they have no capacity to reach is in violation of the rule of law?[24] Yes and no. The consideration is a powerful one so far as the definitions of criminal offences are concerned. These should be such that everyone can be guided by them, and therefore should be such that everyone has the capacity to avoid violating them.[25] Although it can often be achieved in other ways, it is possible that this can sometimes be achieved only by individuating the standards of the offence definition, including its character standards, to the reduced capacities of the accused. If my Aristotelian understanding of character is correct, this solution comes to much the same thing as eliminating character standards from that offence definition altogether. So this rule of law argument may help to explain the Anglo-American criminal lawyer's traditional reluctance to employ character standards in the definitions of criminal offences.[26] But the same consideration does not apply to the definitions of criminal *excuses*, which are not supposed to provide any guidance to those whose actions may fall foul of the criminal law.[27] To attempt to benefit from a legal excuse by being guided by it is to forfeit that excuse. One is under duress, from the legal point of view, only if one's fear of the threats one is subject to was rationally adequate, in one's own eyes as well as according to the applicable standards of character, for one to commit the wrong one committed. Accordingly, if in evaluating those threats one also takes account of the likelihood that one will benefit from the legal excuse of duress when one gives into them, one's excuse is thereby lost. It is thus

---

[24] This was the essence of HLA Hart's famous defence of a capacity-capped doctrine of excuse in the criminal law: Hart, 'Legal Responsibility and Excuses' in Hart, *Punishment and Responsibility* (1968), 28 at 46–47. It is unclear whether Hart had a view about the gist of excuses outside the criminal law context, and if so how that view was related to his rule of law argument for the recognition of capacity-capped excuses in that context.

[25] I have considered some aspects of this requirement in more detail in J Gardner, 'Rationality and the Rule of Law in Offences Against the Person', *Cambridge Law Journal* 53 (1994), 502 (Chapter 2 in this volume).

[26] Consider the furore among the major academic textbook writers in England after the decision in *R v Caldwell* [1981] 1 All ER 961, which held an accused to capacity-independent standards in respect of recklessness. JC Smith and B Hogan, *Criminal Law* (5th edn, 1983), 52–58; G Williams, 'Recklessness Redefined', *Cambridge Law Journal* 40 (1981), 252.

[27] This distinction provides the key to answering Alan Norrie's important question: 'If doing justice to individuals involves recognising their motives in acting in the duress situation, why does the law not recognise their motives in all those other contexts in which crimes are committed?' (A Norrie, *Crime Reason and History*, above n 19, 166).

no objection to the law's definition of the excuse of duress that there are some people, their capacity for courage lacking, who cannot be guided by that definition. The same is necessarily true for everyone, irrespective of their capacity for courage; those with the lower capacity labour under no special disadvantage so far as the guiding power of the law is concerned. It follows that a capacity-based cap on the standards of character used in legal excuses cannot be justified along the rule of law lines, any more than it can be justified along any of the other lines we have been considering. Contrary to popular myth, the gist of an excuse, even in the criminal law, is not that one had no capacity to conform, in one's actions, to the standards of character which were demanded of one. On the contrary, as I have tried to explain, the gist of an excuse is that one lived up to those standards.

7

Fletcher on Offences and Defences

1. Fletcher's puzzle

Sometimes criminal lawyers use the word 'defence' in what Paul Robinson calls a 'casual' sense to designate any part of the defendant's case that, advanced successfully, would suffice to warrant an acquittal.[1] In this casual sense, imaginable defences to a criminal charge include such diverse lines of argument as alibi, denial of mens rea, denial of causation, *autrefois acquit*, self-defence, duress, and diplomatic or executive immunity. Private lawyers also use the word 'defence' in this sense: a defence, for private lawyers, is simply the defendant's reply to the plaintiff's claim. But in criminal law, unlike private law, there is also a stricter use of the word 'defence'. The word in its strict sense designates only those defences in the casual sense that are compatible with the defendant's conceding that the offence charged was indeed committed. Alibi and denial of mens rea or causation do not count as defences in this strict sense, because to offer these arguments is simply to deny the commission of the offence. On the other hand, self-defence, duress, *autrefois acquit* and immunity from prosecution do count as defences in the strict sense. To plead self-defence, duress, *autrefois acquit* or immunity from prosecution is to argue like this: 'Suppose I did commit the offence charged—I should still be acquitted.'

Using the word 'defence' in this strict sense, as I will use it from now on, yields a neat contrast between offences and defences. Every issue relevant to criminal liability is relevant either under the heading of 'offence' or under the heading of 'defence'. Criminal lawyers are prone to thinking that the allocation of issues as between these two headings is inconsequential, or at most a matter of classificatory convenience for textbook

---

[1] PH Robinson, 'Criminal Law Defenses: A Systematic Analysis', *Columbia Law Review* 82 (1982), 199.

writers.[2] Others think that the allocation of issues as between the two headings matters procedurally, when we come to discuss the shifting of probative or evidence-adducing burdens as between prosecutor and defendant.[3] In *Rethinking Criminal Law*, George Fletcher famously, and in my view rightly, rejects both of these views. The contrast between offences and defences has little to do with the shifting of any burdens, and nor should it have. On the other hand, the contrast between offences and defences is far from inconsequential, and its consequences extend not only to the organization of textbooks but also to the moral quality of the criminal law. According to Fletcher:

[t]here are at least four areas of legal dispute where recognizing the distinction could have concrete consequences. First, it is of critical importance in deciding when external facts, standing alone, should have an exculpatory effect. Secondly, it might bear on the analysis of permissible vagueness in legal norms. Thirdly, it might bear on the allocation of power between the legislature and judiciary in the continuing development of the criminal law. And fourthly, it might be of importance in analyzing the exculpatory effect of mistakes.[4]

When he makes these brilliant and original suggestions in *Rethinking*, with which I broadly concur, Fletcher is focusing on just one class of defences, namely justificatory defences. But it seems to me that his suggestions can and should be extended beyond justifications to take in excuses as well. Indeed, his fourth suggestion, as I read it, introduces us to the distinctively excusatory role of reasonable mistakes. Unfortunately, Fletcher and I have different views about which defences count as excuses and why.[5] So while I will have something to say about excuses later on, to begin with I will follow Fletcher in focusing largely on justifications. For completeness I should stress that there are various defences known to the criminal law that are neither justifications nor excuses. There are what Robinson calls 'non-exculpatory' defences (such as *autrefois acquit* and diplomatic and executive immunity) which bear on the standing of the court to try the case.[6] And there are some defences (infancy, insanity) which are genuinely exculpatory but which bear on the capacity and necessity to answer for what one did, whether by way of justification or excuse. I doubt whether any of Fletcher's four suggestions applies these

[2] See e.g. G Williams, 'Offences and Defences', *Legal Studies* 2 (1982), 233.
[3] See e.g. MS Moore, *Act and Crime: The Philosophy of Action and its Implications for Criminal Law* (1993), 179.
[4] GP Fletcher, *Rethinking Criminal Law* (1978), 555.
[5] See n 25 below and accompanying text.
[6] 'Criminal Law Defenses: A Systematic Analysis', above n 1, 229–232.

two types of defences. But be that as it may: moral consequences attach to the distinction between offences and defences so long as moral consequences *sometimes* attach to it. Among Fletcher's finest triumphs in *Rethinking* is the case he makes for thinking that sometimes they do indeed attach (namely, when the defences in question are justificatory).

What makes this even more of a triumph is that Fletcher manages convincingly to attach his four moral consequences to the distinction without ever quite getting to the bottom of the distinction itself. To be sure, he finds many helpful ways of *restating* the distinction ('these are cases in which the inculpatory dimension is overridden by criteria of exculpation',[7] 'grounds of justification represent licenses or permissions to violate the prohibitory norm',[8] etc.), but these restatements do not yet explain exactly what is being distinguished and how. What makes the difference between an 'offence' issue and a 'defence' issue, or an 'inculpation' issue and an 'exculpation' issue? What determines which issues should be allocated to which category? Fletcher understandably resists the idea that the answer depends on accidents of statutory drafting or judicial whim. He naturally suspects that a distinction on which so much of moral moment turns must itself turn on something of moral moment. But what does it turn on? After much fine-grained deliberation, Fletcher's answer still seems unsatisfying:

The minimal demand on the definition of an offence is that it reflect a morally coherent norm in a given society at a given time. It is only when the definition corresponds to a norm of this social force that satisfying the definition inculpates the actor. There is nothing inculpatory about driving. Nor is anything incriminating or inculpatory in carrying an object. Adding the element that the object belongs to another makes the act more incriminating; including the element of the owner's nonconsent brings us closer to a prima facie case of wrongdoing.... This discussion...illustrates the general methodology for distinguishing between the prohibitory norm and the countervailing criteria of privilege. The norm must contain a sufficient number of elements to state a coherent moral imperative.[9]

The reference to the mores of a 'given society at a given time' must surely be left on one side as a distraction. Social mores may bear on where the line ends up being drawn in a particular legal system, but the question remains: what line is it that social mores, and hence legal systems, are

---

[7] *Rethinking Criminal Law*, above n 4, 562.
[8] ibid, 563.
[9] ibid, 567–568.

trying to draw? In what way is an inculpation issue really different from an exculpation issue, in social or legal life? In this passage, and throughout his discussion, Fletcher's seems to get stuck at this answer: we have to ask when we have arrived at sufficient inculpation and then the rest will be exculpation. But this helps little when our original question was: what does the distinction between inculpation and exculpation—also known as the distinction between offence and defence—turn on?

2. Rational conflicts and remainders

In an important, but too-rarely-cited article, Kenneth Campbell argues that the distinction between offences and (justificatory) defences is ultimately based on the distinction between reasons against doing something and reasons in favour.[10] When someone pleads a justification, she is claiming that the reasons in favour of doing as she did stand undefeated by the reasons against. The reasons against are those that make what she did an offence. They have not gone away. They still make it an offence. But the reasons in favour prevail and make it a justified offence (and hence one of which she should be acquitted).

Think about this example, adapted from Campbell's discussion. Consent is sometimes a defence in the criminal law. The offence of assault occasioning actual bodily harm, for example, is committed even when there is consent. Consent merely serves to justify its commission. But sometimes—for example, in the law of rape—absence of consent is instead an element of the offence. The offence of rape is not committed, and hence does not need to be justified, if the sexual intercourse is consented to. Why the difference? Because, says Campbell, there is no general reason not to have sexual intercourse. Whereas there is a general reason not to occasion actual bodily harm. Actual bodily harm is *per se* an unwelcome turn of events, even when consensual; sexual intercourse is not *per se* an unwelcome turn of events, but becomes one by virtue of being non-consensual. This contrast is captured in the law's treatment of consent under the 'defence' heading in assault occasioning actual bodily harm, but under the 'offence' heading in rape.

Of course, it is possible for people to disagree about whether there is a general reason not to have sexual intercourse or a general reason not to

---

[10] K Campbell, 'Offence and Defence' in I Dennis (ed), *Criminal Law and Justice* (1987), 73.

occasion actual bodily harm. That is not denied. Campbell's only point is that if one has such a disagreement, one is apt also to disagree about whether the issue of consent should be handled under the 'offence' or the 'defence' heading. Those who think that, in the law of rape, sexual intercourse *tout court* should be regarded as the real offence and consent as a defence had best be able to identify a general reason not to have sexual intercourse, such that one needs a defeating reason in favour before one should engage in it. And likewise, those who think that there is no reason not to occasion actual bodily harm, such that one needs no defeating reason to occasion it, had better stand up for the view that consent, in cases of assault occasioning actual bodily harm, belongs not under the 'defence' heading but under the 'offence' heading.[11]

Central to Campbell's modest proposal is the idea that cases of justified offending are not cases of innocuous action: the offence is still committed and is still, *qua* offence, unwelcome. Its commission, albeit justified, remains regrettable. It would have been better still had there been no occasion to commit it, and hence no need to ask whether its commission was justified or not. This we can call the 'remainders thesis': justified action still leaves a remainder of conflicting reasons that were, regrettably, not conformed to. As Campbell spells the thesis out:

> The reasons may have been overwhelmingly in favour of performing the action, but as long as the law takes the view that some harm has nevertheless been done it recognises the continuing existence, even in those circumstances, of a *prima facie* reason against. Suppose someone kills a terrorist who is about to detonate a bomb which will certainly kill dozens of people. His action is certainly permissible, and probably more than just that. So long, however, as the law takes the view that the life, even of that terrorist, was something of value then it recognises the existence of some reason against the action, albeit one which was clearly overridden.... [But] it can be different in a society with different values. Take the case of outlawry. Someone who kills an outlaw in those societies which recognise such an absence of status requires no defence in the sense in which this is opposed to an offence. His act is simply not within the defining terms of the relevant form of homicide, since these do not extend to victims who are beyond the protection of the law. From the legal point of view there was not even *prima facie* reason against this killing for, from that point of view, this life simply has no value.[12]

The remainders thesis is captured in Campbell's claim that the law 'recognises the *continuing* existence', in the terrorist case, of a prima facie

---

[11] Which was indeed the line taken by the minority (Lords Mustill and Slynn) in the famous British sado-masochism case *Brown* [1994] AC 212.
[12] 'Offence and Defence', above n 10, at 83.

reason against killing. To call the reason 'prima facie' is not to claim that it appears to be there but is exposed as illusory when the terrorist's nefarious plot is exposed. Rather the reason not to kill the terrorist is really there and continues to be there and to exert its force throughout, such that killing the terrorist is regrettable—even though this is a case with a stronger conflicting reason such that killing him is justified.

To see whether Fletcher might help himself to Campbell's modest proposal as a way of explaining the distinction between offences and defences, we need to know: does Fletcher endorse the remainders thesis? In *Rethinking* there is much to suggest that he does. I already quoted, for example, his reference to justified offences as 'prima facie cases of wrongdoing'. Maybe he uses the expression 'prima facie' as Campbell does, to refer to a real and continuing reason that is regrettably defeated? I also already quoted Fletcher's remark that 'grounds of justification represent licenses or permissions to violate the prohibitory norm'. So the prohibitory norm *is* violated and this, one may think, must surely be regrettable. And yet, continues Fletcher: 'A justification is not a conflicting norm imposing a countervailing duty to act.'[13] Does he mean only that there is no legal duty to perform justified actions, even to stop Campbell's terrorist? Or does he mean that there is no conflict to be resolved (and hence no remainder)? To add to our doubts, he goes on to label cases of justified action as falling under 'exceptions' to norms,[14] and he talks of justified offences as only 'nominally' violations.[15] Both of these formulations suggest a rejection of the remainders thesis. They suggest that when one is justified in committing an offence, one has no more cause for regret than when one commits no offence at all. There is no real reason against doing as one does. In which case, we must read Fletcher as rejecting the remainders thesis and hence as having no use for Campbell's modest proposal.

3. From reasons to norms

How are we to interpret Fletcher on the subject of remainders? One thing to notice is that, while Campbell is talking about conflicts of reasons (and rational remainders), Fletcher is talking about conflicts of norms

---

[13] *Rethinking Criminal Law*, above n 4, 563–564.
[14] ibid, 565.
[15] ibid, 561.

(and normative remainders). A norm is not simply a reason. It is a reason with a special structure. The structure depends on what kind of norm it is. For simplicity's sake, I will focus on *mandatory* norms, the norms according to which a certain action is required or prohibited. In the helpful terminology devised by Joseph Raz, mandatory norms are 'protected' reasons.[16] They are reasons to perform the required act (or not to perform the prohibited act) that also serve as reasons not to act on some or all of the conflicting reasons. Thus, for example, the norm of Italian cooking that prohibits the use of metal implements to chop basil (assuming it is a sound norm) is a reason not to use metal implements to chop basil and also a reason not to act for the reason that a metal implement is the one closest to hand. And the moral norm that prohibits promise-breaking (assuming it is a sound norm) is a reason not to break promises and also a reason not to act for the reason that doing so would be cheap and convenient. The structure of the reason means that it punches above its weight. Of course, it still has weight as an ordinary reason for action, but it also has a second dimension of force, which Raz dubs its 'exclusionary' force.[17] A mandatory norm is a reason that defeats some conflicting reasons by weight, but defeats others by exclusion. Irrespective of their weight, the excluded reasons are not to be relied upon as reasons for action (and in that sense no longer register as reasons).[18]

When the law requires or prohibits a certain action—for example, by creating a new criminal offence—it purports to exclude all conflicting reasons. Legally, upon the creation of a new criminal offence, one has reason not to act on any reason that militates against conformity with the norm (i.e. that militates in favour of committing the offence). It should be stressed that the law is perfectly happy for one to act on any reason at all *in favour of* conformity with the norm. One need not do so because of the legal norm. All the law cares about is conformity, never mind *why* one conforms. But by the same token the law is not interested in why one didn't conform. Any reason one gives for non-conformity with the norm falls on deaf ears. At least, this is the position if all the law does is to create a criminal offence. Everything changes, however, if the law offers, in addition, a justificatory defence. When it does so, the law selectively opens its ears to some reasons that some defendants may have had for non-conformity with the law's norms. It allows the fact that one was

---

[16] J Raz, *Practical Reasons and Norms* (2nd edn, 1990), 191.
[17] ibid.
[18] Of course, exclusionary reasons may themselves sometimes be defeated in what Raz calls 'second-order' conflicts. ibid, 47.

provoked, or threatened, or attacked, for example, to count as a legally admissible reason in favour of non-conformity with the norm. In short, when the law grants a justificatory defence it *unexcludes* some otherwise excluded reasons, and allows them once again to punch their weight in an ordinary rational conflict with the law's ordinary (now unprotected) reasons for not offending. At this point, everything depends on the comparative weight of the reasons.

Elsewhere I have tried to capture this complex structure by describing justification defences in the criminal law as 'cancelling permissions'.[19] Some permissions (sometimes known as 'strong permissions') are norms in their own right.[20] But a cancelling permission is not. When the law grants a cancelling permission by creating a justification defence it does not set up a second (permissive) norm that conflicts with the (mandatory) norm created by the law's specification of the offence. Rather, it creates a gap in the mandatory force of the mandatory norm, a gap through which certain conflicting reasons are readmitted as legally acceptable reasons for acting. Across a certain range of cases, the mandatory force of the norm is cancelled. And yet it would be misleading to say that the norm itself is cancelled. For it still exerts its ordinary rational pull as a reason not to commit the offence. All it loses is its secondary protective layer. In this sense, the case of a justification defence in criminal law falls somewhere between the case of an ordinary justification and an exception to the norm. It is like an ordinary justification in that there is still a rational conflict exactly as Campbell describes, with a rational remainder. There is still something to regret in the fact that one commits the offence; the violation is not just nominal. On the other hand, a justification defence in criminal law is like an exception to the norm in that the mandatory force of the norm is strictly speaking in abeyance where the defence applies. So there is a normative remainder in one sense, and not in another. The law does not simply cancel (or create an exception to) the norm. But the law does cancel (or create an exception to) the mandatory part of the norm's normative force.

Here we have a possible explanation for Fletcher's apparent equivocations about the remainders thesis. Fletcher is half-right to call justification defences 'exceptions', but also half-right to think that actions falling under them 'violate the prohibitory norm'. The truth, as we have seen,

---

[19] J Gardner, 'Justifications and Reasons' in AP Simester and ATH Smith (eds), *Harm and Culpability* (1996), 103 at 117 (Chapter 5 in this volume).
[20] e.g. GH von Wright, *Norm and Action* (1963), 85–89.

is somewhere between the two. And Fletcher is certainly right to think that '[a] justification is not a conflicting norm imposing a countervailing duty to act'. Not only is there no countervailing duty to act; there is no conflicting norm full stop. A justification defence is conferred not by another norm but by the carving out (from the original norm that creates the offence) of permissive space for people to act on certain conflicting reasons. So while there is no conflict of norms, there is a conflict of reasons. If Fletcher agrees, then he can after all help himself to Campbell's modest proposal for the explanation of the offence/defence contrast: if there is no conflict of reasons, and hence no rational remainder, then what we are looking at is not a defence but a denial of the offence.

In sketching the 'cancelling permissions' view of justificatory defences, I tried to bring out not only how it harmonizes with Campbell's proposal, but also what it has to recommend itself to Fletcher. Recall Fletcher's first suggested consequence of the offence/defence contrast: 'it is of critical importance in deciding when external facts, standing alone, should have an exculpatory effect'. What Fletcher means is that the state of the world alone, quite apart from the defendant's responsiveness to it, can suffice to negate an offence. But a justificatory defence is available only where the defendant is responsive to the state of the world.[21] The 'cancelling permissions' view of justificatory defences explains why this should be so. As I mentioned, when it comes to the legal norm that creates an offence, all the law cares about is conformity, never mind *why* one conforms. It is no skin off the law's nose whether one acts for legal, moral or prudential reasons, or indeed no reasons at all, so long as one does not break the law. But when it comes to the conferring of a justificatory defence, things are different. What the conferring of the defence does is to unexclude certain conflicting reasons for action, such that these reasons (unlike others) are now available to be relied upon as reasons in favour of violating the norm. To avail oneself of the defence, one relies upon the reasons. It is no good merely to act in the way that someone relying upon the reason would act. Excluding a reason makes it a defeated reason, i.e. a reason for which one should not act. Unexcluding it merely reverses the process. It changes what one should do, on balance, only by changing what reasons one has available to act on. If one does not act on them, then one has no justification.[22]

[21] To see the difference at work in English law, cf *Dadson* (1850) 4 Cox CC 358 with *Deller* (1952) 36 Cr App R 184.
[22] I have explored the point in much greater detail in 'Justifications and Reasons', above n 19.

4. Wrongs and faults

Fletcher offers one further reflection on the possible import of the offence/ defence contrast, which I have not yet mentioned:

> [L]et us think of inculpatory conduct as the violation of a prohibitory norm. For examples we need only think of the basic commandments of Western society. Thou shalt not kill, thou shalt not steal – these are the basic prohibitions on which there is consensus even in morally relativistic, post-religious societies. Yet these simple imperatives that we invoke in blaming others point merely to paradigmatic instances of wrongdoing. In order to make out a complete case of responsible wrongdoing, whether in law or in moral discourse, the simple imperatives must be supplemented in exceptional cases. The supplementary criteria are grounds of justification and excuse.[23]

There is more than one way to interpret this passage. On the interpretation I will favour and discuss, Fletcher is saying that prima facie wrongs are by default 'strict' wrongs, i.e. do not include a requirement of fault. It is only when we come to assess justifications and excuses that we are assessing fault. In suggesting this interpretation, I don't mean to attribute to Fletcher the view that prima facie wrongs are by default wrongs without mens rea. Clearly, that is not his view. One of Fletcher's examples ('thou shalt not kill') is of a prohibitory norm that can be violated entirely accidentally, but the other ('thou shalt not steal') is of a prohibitory norm that can only be violated intentionally (i.e. with mens rea). That, however, is irrelevant to the interpretation of Fletcher's passage that I am advancing. The point I am emphasizing is that either of these prohibitory norms can be violated without fault on the part of the violator. That is because neither norm makes space, as it stands, for any assessment of the violator's reasons for doing as she does. And that, Fletcher may be interpreted as saying, is where justifications and excuses come into play: they invite us to assess the violator's reasons for violating the norm, to see whether she is at fault.

If this is Fletcher's view, I agree with it completely. I have argued at length elsewhere that the ordinary or basic kind of wrongdoing is 'strict' wrongdoing, e.g. hurting people, upsetting people (for whatever reason).[24] I have also argued that excuses, like justifications, are defences

---

[23] *Rethinking Criminal Law*, above n 4, 562.
[24] J Gardner, 'Obligations and Outcomes in the Law of Tort' in P Cane and J Gardner (eds), *Relating to Responsibility: Essays for Tony Honoré on his 80th Birthday* (2001).

to wrongdoing that call for an assessment of the wrongdoer's reasons.[25] And I also believe, although I have never argued, that someone is at fault in committing a wrong if and only if he commits it without justification or excuse. But all of this adds up to yield a puzzle, which is also a puzzle for Fletcher as I have just interpreted him.

Fletcher has it that only 'paradigmatic' wrongs are captured in such 'simple imperatives' as 'thou shalt not kill'. I say similarly that such simple wrongs are just the 'ordinary' or 'basic' type of wrongs. On both views, however, there can be more complex and less ordinary wrongs that are partly constituted by the fault of the wrongdoer. Classic examples in the law include wrongs partly constituted by the recklessness or negligence of the wrongdoer. These can be called 'fault-anticipating' wrongs. The fault of the wrongdoer—that she lacks (certain) justifications and excuses—is a necessary condition of her violating the prohibitory norm. At least some justifications and excuses are anticipated in the prohibitory norm. But how can this be? For surely the whole point about justifications and excuses, the point that Fletcher emphasizes time and again and I have endorsed from the outset of this discussion, is that justifications and excuses are defences in the strict sense. To offer one is not to deny that one violated the norm. It is to say: 'I may have committed the wrong but...'. With fault-anticipating wrongs, however, this logic seems to be defied. Where these wrongs are concerned, a justification or excuse seems also to be a denial of the wrong; a defence seems also to be denial of the offence. How is this possible? How can there possibly be any fault-anticipating wrongs?

To answer this question, it is not enough to draw attention to the complications that I added to Campbell's story in the previous section ('3. From reasons to norms'). True, mandatory norms often take the shape they do to reflect not only the reasons in favour of doing what they make mandatory, but also at least some of the reasons against. That is the most obvious explanation of why some or all of the reasons against doing what the norm makes mandatory are excluded from consideration by the norm. They have already been taken into account and given their full weight in the original specification of the norm, and to let them in again as defences would mean counting them twice. Sometimes, of course, they were given their full weight in the specification of the norm without

[25] J Gardner, 'The Gist of Excuses', *Buffalo Criminal Law Journal* 1 (1997), 575 (Chapter 6 in this volume). This is where Fletcher and I disagree about excuses. My explanation of excuses excludes insanity whereas his (hesitantly) includes it. See *Rethinking Criminal Law*, above n 4, 835–846.

showing up in the norm's final shape (e.g. because they were not weighty enough). On other occasions, they show up in the norm's final shape as simple exceptions. At common law, for example, murder can be committed only under 'the Queen's peace'. Those who kill enemy combatants in wartime need not argue that they did so for the defence of the realm (or for other lawful reasons) because the offence of murder does not extend to their actions in the first place. Their argument has already been anticipated in the shape of the prohibitory norm, by way of ordinary exception. There being no violation, no defence is needed. There is no logical puzzle about this.

Fault-anticipating wrongs are different. They are logically puzzling. This is because they do not merely obviate the need for a defence, or otherwise take account of its force, in the shape they give to the offence. Rather they make the commission of the offence depend on whether the defendant actually has, or lacks, the relevant defence. To deny having committed the offence, one must assert the acceptability of one's reasons for having done as one did, either by justifying it or excusing it. The logical puzzle can be brought out more vividly, perhaps, by putting it in these terms. If the prohibitory norm has not been violated, what is there to justify or excuse? But if there is nothing to justify or excuse, how can the absence of a justification or excuse bear on whether the norm has been violated?

The correct way to dissolve the puzzle is to recognize that these fault-anticipating wrongs are in a way parasitic or secondary wrongs. One commits them only if one lacks a justification or excuse for something *else* one does as part and parcel of committing them. In some cases, the 'something else' is not the violation of a mandatory norm at all, but merely the failure to conform to an ordinary reason. One has a weighty reason not to take one's children mountaineering, for instance, but one's only duty is not to do so recklessly, or not to do so negligently. What is prohibited by the prohibitory norm is not conforming to the reason without (certain) justifications or excuses. In other cases, the 'something else' is the commission of another, simpler wrong. One commits a wrong by spreading gossip, say, but a different and further wrong by spreading gossip maliciously or dishonestly. What is prohibited by the prohibitory norm is violation of another prohibitory norm for which one lacks (certain) justifications or excuses.

In cases of both of these types—which frequently arise in the law as well as in morality—one can agree that a certain argument is a defence while insisting that it is also a denial of the offence. That is because it is a defence to a *different* offence from the one that is denied. The offence that is denied is the one that is constituted by an indefensible or inadequately defended commission of the offence that is not denied. This shows why it is natural to think (as I think, and I like to think Fletcher thinks) that wrongs of the ordinary or basic type are strict wrongs, wrongs of the type captured in 'thou shalt not kill'. Wrongs that are committed only by those who are at fault are parasitic on such simple wrongs as these. They are further wrongs that one commits by committing simpler 'strict' wrongs without (certain) justifications or excuses.

Those who think that wrongs committed with fault are the ordinary or basic type, and that 'strict' wrongs are special or odd, need to think again. They need to learn from *Rethinking Criminal Law*. They need to grasp, in particular, the full significance of the distinction between offence and defence. For that distinction, technical and legalistic though it may sound, turns out to be the key to understanding the relationship between wrongdoing and fault—not only in law, but in morality as well.

8

Provocation and Pluralism

Until the House of Lords decision in *R v Smith*,[1] English criminal law harboured two competing views of the moral structure of its provocation defence. On one view, favoured in a line of Court of Appeal decisions beginning in the early 1990s,[2] the provocation defence is conceived as a close relative, morally speaking, of the diminished responsibility defence that appears next to it in the Homicide Act 1957 ('the 1957 Act'). To be provoked to a murderous rage is to suffer a temporary diminution of one's responsibility, a moment of madness. On the rival view endorsed by the Privy Council in 1996,[3] the provocation defence is rather to be *contrasted* with the diminished responsibility defence. The diminished responsibility defence created by section 2 of the 1957 Act exists to make allowances for conditions of pathological unreasonableness. By contrast, the provocation defence referred to in section 3 of the 1957 Act is a defence available only in respect of *reasonable* losses of temper. It is reserved for cases in which (in the words of the section) 'the provocation was enough to make a reasonable man do as [the defendant] did'.

Rather than decide cleanly between these two views, the House of Lords in *Smith* helped itself to one of its favourite pseudo-solutions: when in doubt, pass the buck to the jury.[4] The moral structure of the provocation defence, said the three Law Lords in the majority, was itself a matter for the jury to determine under the 1957 Act. Deciding which allowances to make to which angry defendants is not the business of the trial judge, and nor, accordingly, is it the business of the House of Lords. This self-denying ordinance on the part of the majority was not really as self-denying as it looked, however, for their Lordships gave as their main reason for passing

---

[1] [2001] 1 AC 146.
[2] *R v Ahluwalia* [1992] 4 All ER 889, *R v Dryden* [1995] 4 All ER 987, *R v Humphreys* [1995] 4 All ER 1008, *R v Campbell* [1997] 1 Cr App Rep 199.
[3] *Luc Thiet Thuan v R* [1997] AC 131.
[4] For similar acts of buck-passing by the House in the recent history of criminal law, see *R v Reid* [1992] 1 WLR 793 and *R v Woollin* [1999] AC 82.

the buck to the jury the need for the defence to be interpreted with sufficient sensitivity to differences between individual defendants. They rejected the view of the Privy Council as being too restrictive on this front, and (in effect) preferred the line of Court of Appeal authorities. The standard of 'reasonableness' in the provocation defence is not to be taken literally, said the House of Lords, for taking it literally would mean holding everyone to a uniform standard, rather than allowing the standard to be tailored, as the jury would naturally tailor it, to suit the special (sympathetic) features of each defendant and his or her predicament.[5]

The decision in *Smith* has been criticized in some detail, and on various grounds, elsewhere.[6] The aim of this paper is not to reiterate the same criticisms. Rather, our concern here is with a philosophical problem that formed the backdrop to the decision in *Smith*. For although *Smith* was nominally a case about the adaptability of the provocation defence in the face of certain mental illnesses and personality disorders, there lurked behind it a broader set of worries about the suitability of the provocation defence, as traditionally understood, to today's cosmopolitan social conditions. It is one thing to insist on the uniform standard of the reasonable person when it can safely be assumed that people in the same physical space share the same social and cultural space. But an increasingly mobile populace creates increasingly fragmented social and cultural space, with a corresponding fragmentation of the standards that are expected of people and regarded as proper. How can the criminal law continue to uphold a uniform standard of character in this more cosmopolitan environment? Specifically, is there any longer a defensible role for a standardized 'reasonable person', the quality of whose temper is a suitable measure for all of us? Once this cosmopolitan worry takes hold in respect of *cultural* difference, it readily extends itself to the many other dimensions in which people differ as well. Supposed differences of temperament as between men and women, as between the gay and the straight, as between the educated and the uneducated, etc., also become sources of disquiet. It is not long before one is worrying about the potential unfairness of ignoring any personal idiosyncrasy that may have been a factor in explaining the defendant's

---

[5] cf the US Model Penal Code §210.3 and accompanying comment 5(a) by the drafters: 'In the end, the question is whether the actor's self-control can be understood in terms that arouse sympathy in the ordinary citizen.'

[6] In J Gardner and T Macklem, 'Compassion without Respect? Nine Fallacies in *R v Smith*', *Criminal Law Review* [2001], 623.

reactions.[7] Against this backdrop, one can sympathize with the anxiety of the House of Lords that the Privy Council's uncompromising reaffirmation of the 'reasonable person' standard was not only lacking in compassion towards those suffering from some mental illnesses and personality disorders—the narrow legal issue at stake—but was also insufficiently astute, more broadly, to the moral consequences of human diversity.

One can sympathize with this anxiety, but should one share it? No. The moral consequences of human diversity are accommodated quite adequately within the moral structure of the provocation defence as conceived by the Privy Council. The reasonableness standard should remain unqualified as the proper standard for judging the defendant's loss of self-control. In defending this view, this paper proceeds by disaggregating the various legal questions that dictate the availability of the provocation defence, questions which were distinct at common law and which were left distinct in the 1957 Act, but which the House of Lords in *Smith* preferred to run together. It turns out that there are no fewer than three distinct elements of standardization built into the defence of provocation, each of which has its own pluralistic space already built into it. And it turns out that this pluralistic space is enough.

1. The need for a provocation

Neglected in *Smith* and in many other cases, is the following very obvious point: that to have a defence of provocation one needs to have been provoked. It may be thought that to cross this initial threshold it is enough simply to point to things that were done or said that were the cause of one's anger. Section 3 of the 1957 Act, however, does not merely (or even) require that the defendant have been *caused* to lose her self-control by the things done or said; preserving the common law on this point, it requires that she have been *provoked* to lose her self-control by the things done or said. Since 1957, the courts have increasingly suppressed the difference.[8]

---

[7] To see how easily one may slide from worrying about cultural differences between people to worrying about *all* differences between them, see the classic discussion in A Ashworth, 'The Doctrine of Provocation', *Cambridge Law Journal* 35(1976), 292 at 300.

[8] See *R* v *Doughty* (1986) 83 Cr App Rep 319: 'It is accepted by [the Crown] that there was evidence which linked causally the crying of the baby with the response of the appellant. Accordingly ... the section is mandatory.' The remarks that follow cast doubt on both the legal and the moral soundness of this well-known and so far still authoritative decision.

But should they have done so? What exactly *is* the difference that they have suppressed?

To grasp the difference, one needs to begin by understanding what it is to provoke somebody. This is because the passive category 'being provoked' is parasitic on the active category 'provoking'. Of course this does not mean that one can only ever be provoked by someone's provoking one. There are cases of error of judgment in which one is provoked by what one mistakenly regards or treats as someone's provoking one. But even in those cases it is clear that to be provoked to lose one's self-control is not merely to be *caused* to lose one's self-control by things that someone did or said. In order to explain how it came to pass that one mistakenly regarded or treated something as provoking, one must invoke the concept of a provocation. One must make the things said or done that caused one to lose one's self-control intelligible as examples of possible provocations. To put the point tersely: one can't make something a provocation by thinking it so except by understanding what could possibly make that same something a provocation *apart from* one's thinking it so. Accordingly, one always needs to know what it is to provoke somebody (active) in order to know what it is to be provoked (passive), even in cases in which one was (so to speak, mistakenly) provoked without anybody having provoked one. Not all possible causes of anger are provocations to anger, in short, for not all involve a provoker or someone mistakenly but intelligibly taken to be a provoker.

These remarks tell against a view according to which what counts as provocative lies simply in the apprehension of the provoked person. But they also tell, by the same token, against a view according to which it lies in the apprehension of the provoker, for he too cannot make something a provocation merely by thinking it so. So where should we look for the all-important threshold element of provocation? The answer is that we cannot but look to the social forms invoked in the transaction between the provoker and the provoked. This is true across all the possible ways of provoking people, which include goading them, nagging them, and hassling them, as well as insulting them. For simplicity's sake, the point will be illustrated solely in relation to insult, but the conclusions can be applied equally to the other modes of provocation just mentioned. So how is the possibility of insult structured by social forms? Although it is always possible to develop new ways of insulting people, all of them necessarily trade on ways of insulting people that are already socially established. One implication of this is that in each different social milieu there is a different menu of possible insults, and more broadly of possible provocations. The reference is to 'possible' insults here partly to leave open the question of whether everything that is socially regarded as insulting really is insulting. Some things widely regarded as insults (for example, 'liberal' or 'academic' or 'gay') might well be compliments, and this will bear on how provocative the law should hold them to be, a question to which we will come in the next section ('2. Evaluating the provocation'). In this section the question is different. It is the prior threshold question of whether it is intelligible for the defendant to have claimed that what caused him to be so angry was something that provoked him, whether he was right to have been provoked by it or not.

What are the implications for the law of this way of thinking about the threshold question? The first point to note is that the courts have clearly been right to warn juries in provocation cases that different words and deeds have different significance for different defendants. It is true that jurors should not ask themselves, for example, what the alleged insult would have meant to *them* or to *the man on the Clapham omnibus*. But this is not because the defendant might have personal idiosyncrasies that set him apart from others. It is because he might inhabit a different social milieu from the jury or from the man on the Clapham omnibus, and so might participate in a different menu of possible slights and put-downs. In deciding whether the defendant was provoked, the jurors need to adjust their horizons to accommodate different social milieux, with their different indigenous forms of insult. The fact that the defendant is a Muslim, say, can be pertinent to the question of whether there was a provocation only if there is a Muslim social milieu in which there is a distinctive menu of possible insults, some of which are unknown or not available as insults to non-Muslims.[9] Unless there is a similar social milieu of schizophrenics, say, the same argument does not apply to make the fact that a defendant was a schizophrenic relevant to the threshold question of whether she was provoked.

This shows that there was method in the madness of the common law's traditional assertion that only certain legally recognized insults were capable of constituting provocation in law.[10] The common law was warranted in this claim if and to the extent that these were the only

---

[9] For excellent illustrations of this principle in action, see *R v Uddin*, The Times, 14 September 1929 and the original trial judgment (regrettably overturned on appeal) in *R v Parnerkar* [1974] SCR 449.

[10] See Holt CJ's important exposition of the categories in *R v Mawgridge* (1707) Kel 119. Notice that all the provocations known to the common law were insults. One could not be provoked by non-insulting annoyances inflicted on one by others, however serious. For excellent explanation of why, see J Horder, *Provocation and Responsibility* (1992), 23ff.

(sufficiently grave) forms of insult that were possible in the locally available social milieux of the day. This concession to the common law's approach sheds new light, in turn, on the reforms to the common law that were made by section 3 of the 1957 Act. The reforms evidently reflected the fact that the locally available forms of insult, and hence of provocation, were multiplying, and in some cases being displaced, with the fragmentation, and in some cases eradication, of social milieux. Since judges must look to precedent where juries need not do so, section 3's solution of leaving it to the jury to devise for themselves the menu of possible provocations was one way to remove certain conservative restrictions from that menu. But it did not imply that the menu had been abolished and replaced with a free-for-all in which anything at all could in principle amount to a provocation if the defendant lost his temper in the face of it. The jury still needed to ask itself, and still needs to ask itself today, much the same question that judges used to ask at common law: were these deeds or words that caused the defendant to lose her self-control *capable of amounting to provocation,* such that she was not just caused but *provoked* to lose her self-control?

It might be protested, at this point, that the requirement that the defendant have been provoked and not merely caused to lose self-control is but a legal technicality without moral substance. By common consent, provocation is a (partial) excuse for murderous actions. Surely what matters from the excusatory point of view is the defendant's turbulent state of mind, her loss of reason or will, not how it was triggered?[11] Things might be different if provocation were a (partial) justification, and the question were whether there was someone, a provoker, who was part author of his own misfortune, or who deserved to die, etc. Then it would clearly be important to distinguish the provoking of anger from the mere causing of anger. But when we think about excusing someone, what we care about is his state of mind and how it *inhibited* his acting justifiably, and from that point of view, surely, it doesn't matter whether the anger was triggered by a person or an animal or an electrical storm, so long as the effect on the defendant was the same in every case?

[11] HLA Hart, *Punishment and Responsibility* (1968) 153, adopting a view of excuses made prominent by JL Austin in 'A Plea for Excuses', in his *Philosophical Papers* (1961), 124. cf the Law Commission's argument for extending the duress defence to take in cases of so-called 'duress of circumstances': 'the effect of the situation on the actor's freedom to choose his course of action ought equally to provide him with an excuse for acting as he does.' (*Legislating the Criminal Code: Offences against the Person and General Principles* (Law Com No 122, 1992), 60).

However, this protest mischaracterizes the distinction between excuses and justifications. True, excused actions are unjustified ones. Nevertheless, in making an excuse one relies on the fact that one's unjustified action was taken on the strength of a justified belief or attitude or emotion, etc. An excuse for an angry action, *qua* angry, depends on the justification of the anger itself. Even in the realm of excuse, therefore, the analysis is moral and not merely causal, for the question of the justification of the anger (and hence the excuse of the angry action) is a moral question.[12] Those who take the opposite view fall into the trap of confusing excuses with denials of responsibility. People who are not responsible for their actions admittedly face no justificatory questions. But by the same token they face no excusatory questions either. They are beyond justification and excuse. Their actions do not call for justification, but neither do the emotions or attitudes or beliefs, etc. on the strength of which they acted, and the justification of which would amount to an excuse for their actions.

Now anger is a fundamentally interpersonal emotion. At the heart of its cognitive component (for all emotions have a cognitive component) lies the idea that one has been wronged by another person.[13] This includes the vicarious case in which someone else has been wronged, and one feels angry on his or her behalf by putting oneself in his or her shoes. Either way, it is of the essence of anger that there is a (supposed) wrongdoer against whom the anger is directed. True, there are forms of incompletely directed anger, such as anger 'against the world', or an anger-like belligerent frustration at the way one's life is heading. But to make sense of these reactions, at least as kinds of anger, one cannot but regard them as anthropomorphic 'as if' reactions. It is *as if* one has been wronged by the world. The fates, as we may put it, are against one. Such metaphorical personifications are necessary to make any sense of the anger as anger, for they conjure up the idea of a wrongdoer, an idea that lies at the heart of

---

[12] For a more detailed explanation, see J Gardner, 'The Gist of Excuses', *Buffalo Criminal Law Review* 1 (1998), 575 (Chapter 6 in this volume). Strictly speaking, this explanation only covers excuses based on standards of character. Others are based on standards of skill, and are not relevant to the present context. Similar views of the logic of excuse emerge from J Horder, *Provocation and Responsibility*, above n 10, at 127ff, and from DM Kahan and MC Nussbaum, 'Two Conceptions of Emotion in Criminal Law', *Columbia Law Review* 96 (1996), 269 (although the latter prefer to avoid the word 'excuse', precisely because of the risk that it will be understood in the way that is being warned against here: ibid, 318–319).

[13] For a good discussion of this dimension of anger, see P Greenspan, *Emotions and Reasons* (1988), 48–55.

the emotion of anger. And just as this 'as if' feature needs to be brought out to make sense of incompletely directed anger, so it needs to be justified to justify that anger, and hence to excuse actions performed on the strength of that anger.

Defending the metaphorical deployment of a moral principle is, however, a tall order. It is not surprising, then, if we come to regard the persistent crying of babies, or the sudden good luck of one's neighbour set against one's own bad luck, as at best morally marginal cases of provocation, well outside the paradigm. If (in the thrall of a confused view of the logic of excuses) the courts have nevertheless been persuaded since 1957 to treat such cases as being on all fours with the paradigm of a provocative insult, then it is time the courts took a less jaundiced look at what animated the old common law on this front.[14] Of course it would be a moral mistake, as well as a violation of the letter and the spirit of the 1957 Act, to return to the era of a finite list of affronts which are capable in law of counting as provocations. But it would be both a moral insight and in accordance with the letter and the spirit of the 1957 Act to insist that, as a condition of a successful provocation plea, there must at least have been something intelligible as a provocation.

2. Evaluating the provocation

The preceding remarks dealt with the threshold question: was the defendant provoked? To answer this question in the affirmative the defendant need only show that what caused her to get angry to the point of losing her self-control (and hence to do as she did) was intelligible as an instance of a provocation in her cultural milieu. This leaves open, however, the question of whether she really *should* have been provoked by it as she was. This second question has come to be known in law as the *gravity* question. But in fact it conceals two subsidiary issues, only the second of which is aptly described in terms of gravity.

The first subsidiary issue is the issue of whether the things that are intelligible as insults in a particular cultural milieu really are insulting.

---

[14] To be fair, the law since 1957 has not gone as far as to regard as potentially provocative the sudden good luck of one's neighbour set against one's own bad luck. The question, however, is why it should not go this far now that it has recognized the persistent crying of a baby as potentially provocative in *Doughty*, n 8 above. The technical legal answer is that in the misfortune case, unlike the baby case, nothing was 'done or said' to provoke. As Smith and Hogan observe in *Criminal Law* (9th edn, 1999) 355, 'this distinction begins to look a little thin' once we have provocative babies.

(Again let's focus on the case of insult for simplicity's sake, but analogous questions arise concerning other modes of provocation, such as goading.) Calling someone 'queer' is *intelligible* as an insult in many cultures. That it is *used* as an insult in many cultures proves this. But the question remains as to whether it really is insulting to be called 'queer' when there is absolutely nothing wrong with being queer and (apart from the prejudice one must endure at the hands of those who wrongly think it wrong) it does not blemish one's life. This is not a question of whether being called 'queer' is a particularly grave insult but a question of whether it really is an insult at all. In other words, it is not a question of whether the defendant should have been angered as much as she was by it, but the question of whether she should have been angered by it at all.

The other subsidiary issue is the issue of how serious (or grave) an insult a certain insult is. We reach this subsidiary question of degree only when we have agreed that what we are dealing with really is an insult. Even if, in some contexts, it really is an insult to call someone 'queer', quite possibly it is not as much of an insult as, in those contexts, it is widely taken to be. These two subsidiary issues may be dealt with under the same heading because, as far as making space for differences among defendants is concerned—as far as the problem of social pluralism is concerned—they raise variants of exactly the same puzzle. The first issue raises in a dramatic form the puzzle raised in a more muted (and sometimes almost imperceptible) form in the second.

The puzzle is structurally identical to a puzzle that is also found in the law of defamation: under what circumstances would 'a right-thinking person' reduce his opinion of another thanks to the association of that other with a quality that is not truly obnoxious but is widely thought to be so? In the law of defamation there has been much doublespeak on this subject. In that context the courts are under some pressure to concede popular prejudices to the plaintiff who claims to have been defamed by their invocation, and the pressure is that those very prejudices may subsequently have been the immediate occasion of her special damage.[15] One may doubt the wisdom of succumbing to this pressure, but let's concede that it may possibly be justified by the special focus on damage in the law of tort. No similar pressure exists in the law of provocation. So the

---

[15] *Yousoupoff* v *Metro-Goldwyn-Mayer Pictures Ltd* (1934) 50 TLR 581. *Per* Slesser LJ: 'It is to shut one's eyes to reality to make these nice distinctions.' For interesting discussion of the way in which growing cosmopolitanism should impact upon the use of the 'right-thinking person' test in defamation, see JG Fleming, *The Law of Torts* (8th edn, 1992), 526–527.

puzzle should be approached with a more open mind. Granted that the justification of anger is a moral matter, one's first instinct is to say that the provocation should be judged for the provocation it really was, for its true moral import, quite irrespective of the provocation it was commonly thought to be. It is one thing to factor cultural milieu into the question of what is *intelligible* as an insult, but quite another—and one is tempted to say, a mistake—to factor cultural milieu into its evaluation.

Possibly the mistake is sometimes just that simple—the mere question 'are you gay?' normally justifies no anger at all, and would not excuse a venomous verbal response, let alone an enraged killing. But typically the situation is more complex. It is widely regarded in some sub-cultures as the gravest of insults, for example, to call somebody 'a grass' (meaning a police informer, or even, in some particularly degenerate milieux, someone who merely calls the police). Clearly the law cannot regard calling the police, in itself, as obnoxious. So can it regard the taunt 'grass' as justifying any anger? Strictly speaking, shouldn't one be proud to be a grass and react with pleasure? Or at least shouldn't that be the law's position on how one should react?

The solution is not so simple. To call someone a grass is, in the cultural milieu in question, *a specific way of calling him or her a traitor*. It is (let us concede) genuinely obnoxious to be a traitor, and the law need have no problem in conceding this. The problem in the interpretation of the insult arises from the fact that there is nothing truly treacherous about calling the police, or at least such must be the view of the law. The accusation of betrayal is false, therefore, yet it remains an accusation of betrayal, and (true or false) an accusation of betrayal really is an insult. It is this insult, the accusation of betrayal (and not the non-insult of being reminded that one has called the police), the gravity of which the law needs to assess for the purpose of assessing the justifiability of the defendant's anger. How, after all, could one assess the gravity of a non-insult?

The same is true in a multitude of other cases. There is nothing wrong with homosexuality. Yet calling someone a 'pansy' as a code word for 'homosexual' wrongly associates homosexuals, and the person being addressed, with an unprepossessing kind of fey weakness. Therein lies its potential to be a real insult.[16] When the law comes to assess the gravity *qua* insult of calling someone a pansy, it is this—the allegation of fey

---

[16] Likewise, publicizing someone's homosexuality (i.e. 'outing') is sometimes a way of accusing him or her of hypocrisy or cowardice, and that accusation can certainly be an insult. Notice that this insult has often been wielded by gay activists who presumably agree that there is nothing wrong with being gay.

weakness—that is the insult the gravity of which the law must assess. This is plainly true when the insult is addressed to a homosexual (who may rightly bristle not only at the innuendo that he is fey and weak, but also at the further stereotyping innuendo that gay men generally are fey and weak—in other words, that he is fey and weak because he is gay). But notice that it is also true when it is addressed to a heterosexual (who may still rightly bristle at the innuendo that he is fey and weak even though he does not suffer the further insult of being stereotyped). The only difference is that in the first case the insult is necessarily graver, thanks to the extra innuendo, than it is in the second.

So to return to the question: can one be insulted by an allegation of some quality that is widely but wrongly taken to be obnoxious? The answer is yes and no. No, if that is the end of the story. But yes if the allegation is of something wrongly taken to be an instance of what is rightly regarded as a wider kind of obnoxiousness. Then the real insult, and the one which must be tested for gravity, is not the superficial, pseudo-insult, which is not in fact genuinely insulting, but the under-lying insult, which is. It is possible for one to make a mistake here in either direction. One may become so absorbed in the certainty that there is nothing wrong with being homosexual that one fails to see the hidden insults imported into the language used by homophobes. On the other hand, one may become so committed to putting people into their social context that one correctly sees the presence of an insult but wrongly iden-tifies the insult as that which it is locally, but wrongly, thought to be.

These remarks expose the limited way in which a defendant's personal idiosyncrasies can bear on the gravity of the provocation. It is not that he has his own judgment of what is insulting, and to what extent it is insulting, a judgment that needs somehow to be respected or accommo-dated by the law. His judgment in these matters is no more authoritative than that of his or any other community: he and all his peers might wrongly think that homosexuality is obnoxious and so might become quite unjustifiably enraged, or at any rate much too enraged, at being (say) on the receiving end of a homosexual advance. In that case his provocation plea ought to be in serious trouble. Notice further that the question of whether he is or is not a homosexual does not affect how seriously his view of the insult is to be taken: merely as a view, this too is irrelevant. What his being or not being a homosexual does affect, or may affect, is how grave a certain insult *really is*, never mind how he feels about it. We saw this in the case of the 'pansy' taunt: it was double the insult to the homosexual, who was insulted both by being labelled fey and weak, and by having his sexuality stereotyped. So the gravity of this insult is greater for the homosexual addressee, whatever he himself may think.

Notice here that the sensitivity to personal idiosyncrasies that we are introducing turns conventional assumptions on their heads. It is, in our example, more grave for a homosexual to be called a pansy than for the same taunt, all else being equal, to be hurled at a straight man. Perhaps, of course, all else will not be equal: perhaps in some gay sub-cultures the word 'pansy' will have taken on an amusing nuance so that its ironic meaning predominates. Or perhaps there is a longer story to be told about the implications that this particular taunt carries within a certain relationship, in which it has been used before as a code word. Or perhaps 'pansy' is a word that can be used to convey more than one insult, and we need to know who exactly the addressee of the insult is to work out which insult it was. None of these special circumstances (which may be thought of as special idiosyncrasies of the defendant, if you like) is necessarily ruled out as a factor in the assessment of what counts as a genuine insult and to what extent. But notice *how* such factors might be relevant to that assessment. They are relevant because they reveal whether the words or deeds in question really *were* insulting in some hidden way, or more or less insulting than at first they might seem to someone not *au fait* with the full circumstances. The mere fact that the parties or their peers or indeed all the inhabitants of their social milieu *think* the words or deeds insulting, or more gravely insulting that others might suppose, does not even begin to make them so.

This explanation admittedly glosses over a range of special difficulties which might be thought of as difficulties of cross-purposes as between the provoker and the person provoked. Sometimes the provoker means something different by what he says from what he is understood by the person provoked to be saying. Sometimes, on the other hand, he has a further intention (such as the intention to provoke) to which the person provoked is oblivious. The above remarks do not point to any particular account of what should be done in such special cases. They do point to some possible significance in the speaker's intention, for often one expresses a different or additional insult if one intends something by what one says than if one does not. But still unresolved are the further questions about what to do about mistakes on the defendant's side regarding such matters. Since we are in excusatory territory here the answer may be to extend the excusatory logic, and to allow the defendant the benefit of her reasonably mistaken beliefs about meaning.

But this takes us beyond the core issue, which is the issue of how to assess the gravity of a provocation where no cross-purposes are involved. Here the main principle is clear: an insult is only as insulting as it really is, when addressed to this defendant in these circumstances. No amount of thinking it more insulting, on the part of the defendant or his peers or society at large, can make it more insulting.

3. The standard of self-control

Having settled the issue of the gravity of the provocation, and identified the variables that can affect the gravity of the provocation to different people, one might expect there to be no further variables when we come to the question of whether the reasonable person would have lost self-control to the point of killing. To the question 'would a reasonable person have lost self-control to that point in the face of this insult?', one might expect the answer to turn entirely on the gravity of the insult. Naturally, there may be some built-in latitude in the standard of the reasonable person. It is true that reasonable people vary somewhat in their reactions.[17] But for the purposes of the provocation defence we are presumably interested only in the lowest possible level of self-control that any reasonable person would have. Once we locate that constant, and we know the gravity of the insult, don't we also automatically know whether the reasonable person would have lost self-control to the point of killing?

Not quite. It is conceded in the *Smith* case, as in all the other cases, that the standard of self-control should not be lowered merely to meet the bad temper of the bad-tempered person.[18] This is trivially necessary to maintain the idea that there is such a thing as a standard of temper, without which the statutory reference to the reasonable person, as a standard of temper, would be unintelligible. Of course much else is also necessary in order to settle the question of which standard that standard is going to be, the gravity of the insult having been established. We need to know more positively whether there are any relevant variables beyond

---

[17] Some people think of 'reasonableness' as a standard that is distinctive for the extra latitude it gives. Various reactions or judgments would be reasonable where only one would be right, rational, justified, etc. This contrast is attacked in J Gardner and T Macklem, 'Reasons' in J Coleman and S Shapiro (eds), *The Oxford Handbook of Jurisprudence and Philosophy of Law* (2002).

[18] *R v Smith*, n 1 above, 173 *per* Lord Hoffman, and 180 *per* Lord Clyde.

the excluded variable of mere bad temper, or whether the reasonable person is, as seemed at first sight, constant in respect of temper. What of other special characteristics and predicaments that people might seek to rely upon that are not mere bad temper but are nevertheless offered as explanations of variations in temper? This is the category of characteristics and predicaments that the law has been struggling with since *Camplin*.[19] What about age? What about a history of abuse? What about a mental illness? What about being a harassed parent?

It seems that a subtle misunderstanding often creeps into responses to this question. The question at this stage is not one of mere explanation. The question here is one of justification—that is, justification of one's becoming so angry as to lose self-control and kill, thereby excusing one's killing. It is not a matter of *why* one lost one's temper, but a matter of why one *should* have lost it. That 'should' is built into the very idea of having a standard, and hence built into the very idea of the reasonable person as a standard. So the question is, are there different standards of temper *that are properly applicable* to different people in respect of the same insult (that is, where the insult is equally grave to each)? Whatever those standards are, it must be possible to fail to live up to them. That is part of the very idea of a standard. If the standard were to be so personalized as to accommodate every feature of a person, other than the mere fact that they were bad-tempered, then it would effectively accommodate the fact that they were bad-tempered as well, for it would allow them to benefit from any explanation they might care to offer of why it was that they were bad-tempered. It would follow that they could not fail to meet the standard, except inexplicably,[20] and so strictly speaking would not be held to any standard at all.

So are there different standards of temper that are properly applicable to different people in respect of the same insult? When the question is put that way it seems obvious that there are. A recruitment advertisement for the Metropolitan Police recently challenged readers on the question of whether their self-control in the face of grave provocation would be up to the standard reasonably expected of a police officer. The reason for asking the question was that the standard is higher than that applicable to people generally. Notice that this is not because police officers

---

[19] *DPP* v *Camplin* [1978] AC 705.
[20] Are there any cases falling within this exception? Probably not. People sometimes use the word 'inexplicably' to mean 'unpredictably', or 'irrationally'. But in this context 'inexplicably' must mean literally 'without explanation'. Probably no failure to meet a standard is without explanation.

necessarily have more self-control; it is because as police officers they ought to have. A police officer challenged by a superior on the question of why she lost her temper on a particular occasion would and should get nowhere by pointing out that she was no more temperamental than an ordinary member of the public. The point is that as a police officer she has no business being even ordinarily temperamental. Her business is to exhibit special coolness under pressure. If she is not up to that then plainly she should not be a police officer. Her loss of temper, if ordinarily temperamental, falls below the applicable professional standard and so gives her no excuse in disciplinary proceedings.

Should it nevertheless give her an excuse in criminal proceedings, if she lost her temper to the point at which she killed? No doubt there are arguments to be had about the extent to which special professional standards should be carried over into the general criminal law. But the very fact that these arguments are intelligible shows that variations in the standard of self-control are possible. These must be variations of a certain kind. To be precise, they must be variations in *roles*. The reason is that to meet a standard is a matter of being up to scratch at something, whether by being good at it or merely adequate, and the question always arises of what the something is that one should be up to scratch at. That something is a role. The two roles in play in the present example are the role of police officer and that of ordinary member of the public.[21]

If in principle standards of self-control can be higher than the one applicable to people in their capacity as ordinary members of the public, they can surely also be lower. Of course, in lowering the standard one

---

[21] Sometimes in legal treatments of provocation, 'ordinary' is offered as a more perspicuous replacement for the statutory term 'reasonable', e.g. by Lord Goff in *R* v *Morhall* [1996] 1 AC 90. But as the discussion here shows, the relevant ideas of ordinariness and reasonableness are distinct. When the standard of self-control in provocation is said to be the standard of the merely 'ordinary' person, this must be interpreted to mean the *ordinarily reasonable* person. The reasonableness standard is not evaded but is implied: cf Neil MacCormick, 'Reasonableness and Objectivity', *Notre Dame LR* 74 (1999), 1575 at 1580–1581. The standard of 'ordinary' reasonableness is always the standard of reasonableness applicable to a role which is non-specialist relative to some more specialist one that people may have in mind. Thus relative to the specialist role of a police officer, the role of being an ordinary member of the public sets the 'ordinary' reasonableness standard. It may be more natural not to call being 'an ordinary member of the public' a 'role' at all. The word 'role' may more naturally be reserved for something relatively specialist. But notice that being an ordinary member of the public can itself become relatively specialist, and hence more naturally be described as a role, when contrasted with (say) simply being a human being. The semi-technical use of the term 'role' ignores these nuances and treats every dimension of one's life in which one may come up to scratch, or fail to do so, as a role.

faces the same kinds of moral and policy debates that one encounters in raising the standards. Those debates are debates about the desirability of institutionalizing in the law standards that belong to roles that are out of the ordinary in calling for or permitting a more temperamental disposition. We all know, for example, that young people are typically more temperamental than adults. Perhaps one aspect of that is that they are less self-controlled. Yet one may and should ask whether and to what extent they should be like that. Arguably there is a role of being a teenager, in which being more temperamental than an adult is a good or fitting thing to be. Arguably, that is how a teenager should be: impulsive, passionate, heedless. At the very least to be so seems morally acceptable in a teenager to an extent that it would not be in an adult. Again, there is a question of whether it is a good idea to embody this different standard in the excuses available in the criminal law, as we presumably should embody it in the excusatory practices of good parenting. If a teenager is provoked to lose his self-control to the point at which he kills, when a reasonable adult would not have been so provoked, should he be held to the adult standard or the teenage standard? Notice that the answer is not a function of the self-control that he actually has, nor of the self-control that people of his age generally have, but rather of the self-control that he and they ought to have if they are to be fit to call themselves proper, self-respecting teenagers.[22]

Is it possible to extend this point to the predicament, say, of battered women, whether their predicament is expressed as a syndrome or simply as a terrible history? The answer depends on whether there is such a thing as a set of special standards for being a good or adequate battered woman, such that this adds up to a role in the sense in which we have been using the term. Even if there are such special standards, is this a role that the criminal law should institutionalize? Both of these subsidiary questions are hard to answer. Probably, if there is a distinct role of being a battered woman, with its own distinctively lowered standards of self-control, it should not be institutionalized. This is not simply because the standards are lower, for lower standards should sometimes be upheld, when they are constitutive of worthwhile roles. It is because the role of a battered woman should not exist and its unwarranted existence in our society should not be given the stamp of legal approval. To draw a dramatic

---

[22] cf the remark of Bridge LJ in the Court of Appeal in *Camplin*, n 19 above, 261: 'youth, and the immaturity which naturally accompanies youth, are not deviations from the norm; they are norms through which we must all of us have passed before attaining adulthood and maturity.'

parallel, it is possible for people to be good slaves, not just in the sense of being good at performing the tasks of slaves, but also in the sense of being temperamentally and dispositionally well suited to slavery. In an attenuated sense such people can be 'self-respecting slaves', for they live up to the standards of the role that they are forced to play. Nevertheless, the role is foul and its standards should not be institutionalized in law. If a slave is provoked to the point of killing someone, be it his master or some other person, in circumstances where a freeman would not be so provoked, the slave's response should be judged by the standard appropriate to freemen, not the lesser standard of a lesser being.[23] That is where real self-respect lies.

Of course this—the lowering of standards to fit the role—is not the argument that many campaigners make or wish to make with respect to battered women. The argument that many wish to make is an argument that abandons standards altogether. For them there is no question of *judging* the reactions of battered women, of seeing whether they are up to scratch, of assessing them as reasonable. It is just a matter of making the space to 'excuse' them, by accommodating the reactions that they have been reduced to by their batterers. This is, of course, quite literally to diminish their responsibility by abandoning any claim that they are people who can be judged by standards, in this case by standards of self-control. This makes the whole exercise of accommodation self-defeating, however, since the whole point of pleading provocation rather than diminished responsibility is to garner the respect and self-respect that flows from being judged by the proper standards. The plea of provocation then becomes merely euphemistic: it is really a defence of diminished responsibility by another name, with a more positive public relations spin. Nor should one imagine that the spin is *all* positive. Those who use violence in domestic settings are often systematic torturers. Part of the evil of what they do lies in its tendency gradually to brutalize and

---

[23] By the same logic, the abhorrent standards which define being a good slavemaster have no place in a civilized criminal law. This is because even when they are by chance good standards, they are good standards packaged in a bad role. Charged with excessively bad-tempered killing of a slave, the criminal law should have little room for the argument that such bad temper is fitting in a slavemaster and marks him out as a good one. Responding to an earlier version of this argument Nicola Lacey presents it as resting on the idea that the criminal law should not recognize the internal character-standards of roles where those roles are in turn defined in terms of criminal conduct. But that is not the idea. The idea is that criminal law should not recognize the internal character-standards of morally disgraceful or degrading roles. See N Lacey, 'Partial Defences to Homicide' in A Ashworth and B Mitchell (eds), *Rethinking English Homicide Law* (2000), 125.

dehumanize its victims. It is one thing for the law to admire the resilience of those who survive this torture and manage to maintain their reasonableness. It is quite another for the law to pretend that the torture is never successful, that it never does brutalize and dehumanize its victims to the point at which they no longer react reasonably so that their responsibility is diminished. To pretend that such torture is never successful by rebranding genuine diminished responsibility cases as provocation cases is to understate the evil of the torturer.

4. The question of fact for the jury

We have identified three objective (that is, impersonal) questions that the jury needs to confront in deciding whether 'the provocation was enough to make a reasonable man do as [the defendant] did' under section 3 of the 1957 Act. First, there is the question of whether the words or deeds identified by the defendant as provocative were capable of being provocative. Is it intelligible to claim to have been provoked by them? Second, there is the question of how provocative those words or deeds really were (to which the answer may still be not at all). Not everything that is intelligible as a provocation is the grave provocation that it was taken to be. Finally, there is the question of whether loss of self-control to the point of killing was justified by the provocation as it has been identified at the second step, so as to (partially) excuse the killing. These three questions are objective in the sense that they all hold the defendant up to standards, which necessarily he or she may fail to meet.

It is true that none of these objective questions can be asked entirely in the abstract, without knowing anything about the defendant and his background. To work out what is intelligible as a provocation one needs to know something about the defendant's cultural milieu, for different words and deeds are intelligible as insults in different cultural milieux. To work out how provocative the words or deeds really were to the defendant one sometimes needs to know whether the defendant possessed or was merely accused of possessing the supposedly distasteful feature that was the subject-matter of the provocation, for sometimes extra insults are built into already insulting remarks when those remarks are addressed to people with particular features. Finally, to work out what standard of self-control the defendant should be held to, we may need to know in what role he reacted as he did, for different roles are constituted by different standards. These are three different dimensions in which facts about the particular defendant may be relevant to the objective aspects of the provocation defence, but these aspects of the provocation defence remain objective despite their sensitivity to facts about the particular defendant because the standards are not being adjusted merely to make them easier for a defendant who tells a morally sympathetic story to meet. They are all variations relevant in one way or another to the reasonableness of someone's anger, and hence do not require any suspension or qualification of the requirement of reasonableness itself.

Naturally, with all these standards in mind and correctly applied, the jury have not quite finished their task. They must also ask whether the defendant actually did lose her self-control to the point at which she killed. It is not enough that it would have been reasonable for her to do so if in fact she did not do so. This is sometimes known as the 'subjective' element in provocation, but that terminology is misleading. It is better described as the *narrative* element of the defence—that is to say, the story of the defendant's actual reactions, to which the objective standards are applied. The defendant is judged by standards of self-control in response to provocation only because she claims to have lost her self-control. If she did not lose her self-control, the standards do not apply to her. So there is no getting away from the question of whether she really did lose self-control.

In answering this question, the jury naturally needs to hear about anything that makes it more or less likely, evidentially speaking, that the defendant did indeed lose her self-control. Every idiosyncrasy of the defendant, extending even to an hysterical or obnoxious temperament, is relevant to this question. In tackling the earlier three questions, the courts have often spoken of them as raising problems of the admissibility of evidence. But there are no such problems. All information about the defendant's idiosyncrasies is admissible on the normal relevance condition, that is, if it helps to establish that he or she did indeed lose self-control to the point of killing. There is no question of the law keeping such information from the jury. The question is only what the jurors should do with it when they get it. The proposal here is that they can and should consider *all* of it as evidence of whether the defendant really did lose self-control to the point at which she killed. But they should not consider *any* of it—at least not at face value—in determining the standards to which her reactions will thereafter be subject. In determining those standards, some but not all of the evidence adduced to show that she really did lose self-control may be collaterally or back-handedly relevant. That is to say, it is not relevant merely because it helps us to understand the defendant's reactions, to see things as she saw them. It is relevant because it helps us to work out how she *ought* to have seen them.

It is fair to add that in practice there are very limited prospects of a jury finding that a defendant who killed did not in fact lose self-control to the point at which she killed, even though a reasonable person would have done so in the same circumstances. For this possibility to arise, the defendant has to be an unreasonably calm or thick-skinned person and yet to have killed for some other reason in the very circumstances in which a reasonable person (less calm, less thick-skinned) would have lost self-control to the point of killing. How might one set about establishing, in the prosecution's shoes, that the defendant is unreasonably calm or thick-skinned? Showing that she is calm or thick-skinned on other occasions is of limited value to the prosecution in view of the possibility of people acting out of character (to say nothing of the admissibility problem relating to character evidence). So what they need is evidence that she was unreasonably calm or thick-skinned on this occasion.

Sometimes, the manner of the killing, or the delay between the supposedly provocative conduct and the killing, may constitute such evidence. The reasonable person would have struck out blindly and/or at once, whereas the defendant attacked only methodically or after a delay. But notice that it is open to the jury, under section 3 of the 1957 Act, to hold that the reasonable person would also have had a methodical or delayed loss of self-control. Loss of self-control is not necessarily incompatible with such responses.[24] If the jury holds that the reasonable person would have shared these responses, then the evidence of the method and/ or delay on the part of the defendant no longer helps to show that she was unreasonably calm or thick-skinned. If, on the other hand, the jury holds that the reasonable person would not have shared these responses, then the provocation defence is doomed to fail on the objective standards and the question of whether the defendant really did lose self-control becomes moot. Either way, the evidence of method and/or delay in the defendant's reactions does not help the prosecution to win on the narrative element of the defence. Again, the issue is solved in the way that the jury approaches the objective standards. That is why in practice it is unlikely that a case will arise in which a defendant passes the objective standards but fails to establish the narrative element. In particular, it is no more likely in cases of delay than in cases of sudden response.

[24] As correctly recognized in *R* v *Thornton* [1992] 1 All ER 306 and—for all its other flaws—*R* v *Ahluwalia*, n 2 above.

5. Conclusion

The majority of the House of Lords in *Smith* contradicted the traditional interpretation of Lord Diplock's judgment in *Camplin*. Many have thought that Lord Diplock meant to attribute different 'characteristics' to the reasonable person for the purposes of different 'objective' issues arising under section 3 of the 1957 Act.[25] If, for example, the defendant was taunted about his bad temper, then (in a sense) the jury were to consider the effect of this on someone who was both bad-tempered and yet not bad-tempered—bad-tempered for the purposes of assessing the gravity of the provocation (after all, bad-tempered people may well be taunted about the fact, and the taunts may mean something different to them because the taunts are true)—not bad-tempered, on the other hand, for the purposes of assessing the proper measure of self-control (to understand that somebody is bad-tempered is to understand that they ought to be better tempered and hence judged by higher standards of temper than they actually live up to).

The majority of the House of Lords in *Smith* denied that Lord Diplock meant to draw any such distinction, the application of which they thought would require excessive mental gymnastics of the jury.[26] But it seems more natural to think, on the contrary, that Lord Diplock intended to draw exactly this distinction. For it is a brave but oversimplified stab at the truth.[27] In fact, there are not two but *three* different issues in respect of which section 3 requires the jury to set standards by which the defendant is to be judged, and in respect of each of these issues different facts about the defendant and his background may bear on what counts as his meeting those standards. In respect of whether the words or deeds that are claimed to have amounted to provocation are capable of amounting to provocation, the defendant's cultural milieu may be relevant. In respect of how grave the provocation really was it may be relevant (as Lord Diplock saw) whether the defendant actually possessed the characteristic about which he was taunted. And in respect of whether he should have

---

[25] No doubt under the influence of Andrew Ashworth's famous article 'The Doctrine of Provocation', n 7 above.

[26] *Smith*, n 1 above, 167–168 *per* Lord Hoffmann, and 184 *per* Lord Clyde.

[27] Contrast Yeo's hasty remark (cited with approval by Lord Hoffmann in *Smith*, n 1 above, 167) that the distinction 'bears no conceivable relationship with the underlying rationales of the defence of provocation': S Yeo, *Unrestrained Killings and the Law* (1998), 61.

lost self-control to the point at which he killed, we may need to know what role he or she was occupying at the time. In each case, facts about the defendant and his background are needed, not to make the objective standard of reasonableness any the less objective, but to identify exactly what would count as meeting the objective standard of reasonableness in the defendant's case. For the excusatory logic of the provocation defence is not the logic of lowering standards but the logic of upholding them.

True, Lord Diplock's attempt to capture this logic in his well-known model jury direction left something to be desired. The direction is a truncated and garbled rendition of the position that Lord Diplock advances, and making any sense of it at all takes very great powers of concentration. You may say that it would take even greater powers of concentration to grasp the pluralistic position spelled out above. But it does not follow that the exercise is a difficult one for the jury. What is spelled out above is merely what tolerably morally sensitive people inarticulately do when confronted with the question of whether a reasonable person would have done as the defendant did—unless, of course, they are misled by lawyers and judges who persist in attempting to impose alien (technical) ways of thinking about the problem. There is a case for the judge, in directing the jury, to say nothing that goes beyond the language of section 3. The question of whether the reasonable person would have reacted as the defendant did became invested with regrettable technicality at common law. The reform in section 3 was designed to overcome the tendency of judges to add their own further glosses to the question of how the reasonable person would have reacted. But judges have been unwilling to surrender their privilege to do so. The majority of the House of Lords in *Smith* may think that they have finally overcome the problem of judicial gloss in the law of provocation, but in fact they have taken it to a new nadir. Their raising the question of what the standard is by which the defendant ought to be judged, only to allow that it can be just about any condescending standard that one may care to mention, is not the end of the taste for judicial gloss, but its *reductio ad absurdam*.

9

The Mark of Responsibility

I

We all want our wrongs and mistakes to have been justified. Failing that we want them to have been excused. No sooner have we noticed that we did something wrong or mistaken than we start rolling out our justifications and excuses. Why is this? You may say the answer is obvious. By justifying or at least excusing our wrongs and mistakes we may be able to avoid shouldering some or all of the nasty moral or legal consequences of committing them. We may be able to avoid a liability to be punished or admonished, or a duty of reparation or apology, or the loss of a right to be rescued or compensated, or various other unwelcome changes in our moral or legal positions. In short, we may be able to avoid being held *responsible* for what has gone amiss. Ronald Dworkin usefully calls responsibility in this sense 'consequential responsibility'.[1] I am consequentially responsible if some or all of the unwelcome moral or legal consequences of some wrong or mistake (whether mine or someone else's) are mine to bear. Responsibility in this consequential sense is by its very nature an unwelcome thing to have descend upon one, and hence something that, all else being equal, any rational being would rather avoid. So, all else being equal, a rational being will resort to any argument she can lay her hands on that might possibly help her to avoid it. Which arguments will succeed in eliminating her responsibility will vary depending on what wrong or mistake has been committed and what unwelcome moral or legal consequence is stored up for her. But valid excuses will help to get her off the hook at least in some cases, and valid justifications more often. That's why it's as well for her to have her justifications, and failing that her excuses, at the ready.

This is hunky dory as far as it goes. But I don't think it goes very deep. There is another deeper story that also helps us to see why, as rational

---

[1] R Dworkin, *Sovereign Virtue: the Theory and Practice of Equality* (2000), 287.

beings, we might want our wrongs and mistakes to be justified, or failing that excused. It is what we could call the Aristotelian story. As rational beings we cannot but aim at excellence in rationality. The only way we have to question that aim—by asking 'What reason do I have to excel at rationality?'—already concedes the aim by demanding a reason, by demanding that the case for rationality be made rationally. And of course at that point rationality makes it own case: what else could we have reason to do, or think, or feel, but whatever reason would have us do, or think, or feel? So as rational beings—beings who are able to follow reasons—we cannot but *want* to follow reasons—to excel in rationality.[2] One implication of this, among many, is that as rational beings we cannot but want our lives to have made rational sense, to add up to a story not only of whats but of *whys*. We cannot but want there to have been adequate reasons why we did (or thought or felt) what we did (or thought or felt).

You will not be surprised to hear that, at least where our actions are concerned, these rational explanations come in two different flavours, namely the justificatory flavour and the excusatory flavour.[3] The case of justification is the case of direct rational explanation. Under the heading of justification we claim to have done what we did for adequate reasons. More exactly, we claim that the reasons in favour of what we did were not all of them defeated by conflicting reasons, and that our action was performed on the strength of some or all of the undefeated reasons in its favour. The case of excuse, meanwhile, is the more complex case of indirect rational explanation. We concede that we did not act as we did for adequate reasons, but we did act on the strength of beliefs or emotions or desires that were themselves adequately supported by reasons. Suppose that we injured someone in what we thought was an act of self-defence, because we strayed accidentally onto the set of an action movie and found ourselves caught up in the action. Maybe we did act excessively in the thrall of fear or confusion, but the fear or confusion itself was not excessive. We were not being hysterical or gullible

---

[2] Aristotle's own argument for this conclusion is both more complex and more fragmented than the simple one offered here. But his key point remains that rationality is a capacity that makes the case for its own realization. The most important fragments of the argument are found at *Nicomachean Ethics*, 1097ᵇ24–1098ᵃ17, 1103ᵃ23–25, 1168ᵃ5–9.

[3] For more detailed study of the two flavours, see, respectively, J Gardner, 'Justifications and Reasons' in AP Simester and ATH Smith (eds), *Harm and Culpability* (1996) (reprinted as Chapter 5 in this volume) and 'The Gist of Excuses', *Buffalo Criminal Law Review* 1 (1997), 575 (reprinted as Chapter 6 in this volume).

in reacting as we did. Here the justification of the fear or confusion does not transmit itself onwards to justify the action that was taken *in* fear or confusion. Nevertheless, it does excuse that action. Such an indirect rational explanation is obviously second best. It includes an admission of rational defeat: one was not justified in what one did. But it is better than nothing. It explains why one did what one did in terms of reasons, albeit not exactly reasons for doing it. And explanation in terms of reasons is what a rational being aspires to. That is why, as rational beings, we cannot but want our wrongs and mistakes to have been justified, or failing that at least to have been excused. This makes it part of our *nature* (in Aristotle's sense of *ergon*, purpose, destiny) to hunt for justifications and excuses as soon as we spot that we have done something wrong or mistaken—never mind what unpleasant moral or legal consequences we can or can't avoid thereby.

In my experience even the most thoughtful of lawyers tends to find this second story academic, in the pejorative sense, especially when I end the story with those words 'never mind what unpleasant moral or legal consequences we can or can't avoid thereby'. Even as morally sensitive lawyers, we are prone to embrace and promote a largely Hobbesian view of human nature, according to which the only natural aim of rational beings is to stop nasty consequences, including nasty moral and legal consequences, from descending upon their own heads. The job of lawyers, on this same view, is mainly to make sure that the nasty consequences do not descend on the heads of their clients, or in the case of more crusading lawyers, on the heads of a certain supposedly deserving class of potential clients. Either way, everything comes down to who wins and who loses, who gets off the hook and who stays on it. To be fair, lawyers do often have to deal with people whose predicaments are towards the Hobbesian end of the spectrum: desperate people faced with the threat of prison or deportation or bankruptcy, destructively bitter people who have been betrayed and deserted by their spouses and partners, and of course corporations (to whom the Aristotelian considerations arguably do not apply). I am not encouraging lawyers to treat such clients to disquisitions on the deeper implications of their rational natures. But nor, on the other hand, should lawyers regard themselves as being professionally unaffected by these implications.

My favourite illustration of the importance of the Aristotelian story is an illustration from the criminal law. During the early 1990s there was in England a string of legally problematic and politically controversial cases concerning the scope of the provocation defence as it was available to women victims of domestic abuse who killed their abusers.[4] Various judge-made restrictions on the provocation defence (some of them hard to fathom) made it foreseeably difficult for these defendants to plead it successfully. At least some of them, however, could alternatively or additionally[5] have mounted a successful defence of diminished responsibility, based on psychiatric evidence that their long exposure to domestic abuse had reduced them to a condition of 'learned helplessness' or had inflicted a similar personality disorder. The effect of a successful diminished responsibility plea, like that of a successful provocation plea, would have been to substitute a manslaughter verdict for a murder verdict. Purely from the point of view of consequential responsibility—getting off the murder hook—the diminished responsibility defence seemed to be just what some of these defendants needed. The sophisticated campaign on their behalf proceeded, however, on the footing that a diminished responsibility verdict, however easily secured, was not at all what these defendants needed. What they needed, even if it was bound to be trickier to argue, was a provocation defence.

Now why would that be? You may say that a finding of provocation sounds better, does more to rescue the defendant's reputation and perhaps the reputation of abused women in general, than one of diminished responsibility. But that just returns us to the question. Why would *that* be? The answer, it seems to me, lies in the moral and legal structure of the provocation defence. To successfully argue provocation, one need not argue that one had valid, let alone adequate, reasons to kill. One need not present one's actions as even partly justified. One certainly does need, however, to make an excusatory case. One needs to argue that, even if one had inadequate reasons to kill, one had adequate reasons to get angry to the point at which one killed. In the term favoured by law, one needs to argue that getting angry to a murderous extent was *reasonable*. No such reasonableness test applies in the defence of diminished responsibility. This is the main reason why diminished responsibility is less complicated to plead. But at the same time the absence of any reasonableness test is also the main reason why any rational being would resist making use of the diminished responsibility defence if the provocation defence were

---

[4] The *causes célèbres* were those of Kiranjit Ahluwalia, Emma Humphreys, Carol Peters, Amelia Rossiter, Pamela Sainsbury, June Scotland, and Sara Thornton. The reported appellate decisions: *R v Thornton* [1992] 1 All ER 306, *R v Ahluwalia* [1992] 4 All ER 859, *R v Humphreys* [1995] 4 All ER 1008, and *R v Thornton* (No 2) [1996] 2 All ER 1023.

[5] On the logic of pleading both defences together, see RD Mackay, 'Pleading Provocation and Diminished Responsibility Together', *Criminal Law Review* [1988], 411.

available to her instead, all else being equal. By making use of the diminished responsibility defence she demeans herself as a rational being. She opts for a non-rational explanation of what she did, one that makes do with attributing the fact that she killed to her disturbed emotional condition. By making use of the provocation defence, by contrast, she defends herself against the same charge with her head held high as a rational being. She relies not simply on her disturbed emotional condition, but on the *rational defensibility* of her disturbed emotional condition. There were *reasons* for her to get angry or aggrieved to a murderous extent, and she got angry or aggrieved *for* those reasons, and as a rational being she wants the law to recognize this rational explanation. She doesn't want to be dismissed as someone who can't explain herself rationally, someone whose responsibility, and hence whose participation in the human good, was diminished. She wants to give an account of herself as a fully responsible adult, sane, human being.[6]

I may have used this illustration too often but for present purposes it does have a special claim to be mentioned. By introducing us to the legal defence of diminished responsibility, the tale of the provoked victims of domestic abuse introduces us to a second notion of responsibility, distinct from the notion of consequential responsibility with which we started. I will call it responsibility in the basic sense, or 'basic responsibility' for short. Like any rational being, the defendants in the cases just mentioned wanted to avoid responsibility in the consequential sense; they wanted to avoid facing the unwelcome moral or legal consequences of their wrongs. But they didn't want to do so by denying, or casting doubt on, their responsibility in the basic sense, at least not if they could avoid it. On the contrary, they wanted to *assert* their responsibility in this basic sense. They wanted to assert that, in spite of all they had been through, they were fully responsible adults. And they asserted this precisely by arguing that, although unjustified, their actions were excused. You may ask: how can offering an excuse serve as an assertion, rather than a denial, of responsibility? The answer is breathtakingly simple. Only those who are responsible in the basic sense *can* offer excuses. That's because

---

[6] Sadly, some campaigners thought that the way forward would be to allow such defendants the provocation defence, but with the applicable standard of self-control lowered to take account of their 'learned helplessness'. This proposal later prevailed (in a mealy-mouthed form) in the House of Lords: *Smith (Morgan)* [2000] 4 All ER 289. For criticism of the development, see D Nicolson and R Sangvi, 'Battered Women and Provocation: the Implications of *R v Ahluwalia*', *Criminal Law Review* [1993], 728, and J Gardner and T Macklem, 'Compassion without Respect: Nine Fallacies in *R v Smith*', *Criminal Law Review* [2001], 623.

responsibility in the basic sense is none other than an ability to offer justifications and excuses. In the idioms we more often use, it is the ability to explain oneself, to give an intelligible account of oneself, to answer for oneself, as a rational being. In short, it is exactly what it sounds like: response-ability, an ability to respond.

II

I just said that only those who are responsible in the basic sense can *offer* excuses. You may think 'offer' was a strange choice of word. Rather than focusing our attention on the time when the wrong or mistake was committed, this fast-forwards us to a later time when the person who committed it is in the dock, literally or figuratively. At the earlier time we might say that the wrongdoer *has* an excuse; only at the later time can she *offer* it. Which time do I have in mind as the time when her responsibility is settled?

We are used to thinking that responsibility is settled at the earlier time, at the time of the wrong or mistake. Nothing that happens later can make a difference. When we come to the trial—or the nasty scene or the difficult telephone call—everything is in principle retrospective, including the question of responsibility. But I think this is a mistake. I think it is one of the many symptoms of a common tendency to confuse excuses with denials of responsibility in the basic sense. To assess people's excuses, as well as their justifications, we have to stop the tape at the moment at which the wrong or mistake was completed. That's because excuses and justifications are putative rational explanations of the wrong or mistake, and rational explanation is explanation in terms of the reasons that the agent had, and acted on, at that time. But a denial of responsibility, not being a putative rational explanation of what one did, is not subject to the same freeze-frame restriction. On the contrary, one's responsibility, in the basic sense, has a diachronic (cross-temporal) aspect. I don't mean that the determinants of basic responsibility are status conditions, such that they necessarily eliminate one's responsibility for everything one does over a certain period. Some factors bearing on basic responsibility—such as infancy—do set status conditions in this sense. But others do not. One may be responsible for one thing one is doing and not for another thing one is doing at exactly the same time. For instance, if I am suffering from a delusional mental illness, my responsibility is only absent in respect of the actions which are explained by the delusions.[7] And maybe even the delusions are occasional. So I don't mean to suggest that one's basic responsibility, or lack of it, is necessarily an ongoing condition. What I mean when I say that basic responsibility has a diachronic aspect is that in respect of any one action relative to which one's responsibility is in question, the question of whether one is responsible straddles the gap between the time at which the action was performed, and the time at which the question itself arises. It straddles the gap between the time of the crime and the time of the trial. The simplest instance of such straddling in the law is the argument of rational incomprehension that applies at the time of the crime under the name of insanity, and then again at the time of the trial under the name of unfitness to plead. One of these we tend to think of as a doctrine of substantive law affecting criminal guilt. The other we think of as a doctrine of procedure affecting the right to proceed with the trial. But in respect of rationale both are part of the same diachronic standard, which is a legal standard of basic responsibility.

So when I said that responsibility in the basic sense is an ability to *offer* justifications and excuses—or alternatively the ability to explain oneself, to offer an account of oneself, to answer for oneself—I did mean what I said. I meant to refer to an ability that the responsible person has at the time of the confrontation with her accusers, at the trial or the public inquiry or the family inquisition or the exchange of angry letters, a time when her wrong or mistake is already in the past. But I also meant, of course, to build into my expression a reference to the time of the wrong or mistake itself. An ability to offer justifications and excuses, in the sense I had in mind, implies an ability to *have* a justification or excuse. If you prefer to spell this out, you could say that basic responsibility is an ability to give a rational explanation for one's actions without giving one's actions any rational explanation that they didn't actually have, i.e. without inventing reasons for what one did. Naturally we should expect some people to fib or self-deceive or misremember, to *rationalize* their actions ex post facto. You may say, indeed, that everyone has a tendency to rationalize. They present their reasons as better than they were, or they present themselves as having reasons when they had none. But I reply: no wonder they do. After all, as the Aristotelian story showed, any rational being wants to be responsible. The fact that people sometimes try to make themselves seem to be responsible for their actions by rationalizing what they did ex post facto is a sign of how badly they want to be responsible.

---

[7] For discussion, see A Kenny, *Freewill and Responsibility* (1978), 82–83.

They make themselves seem to be responsible agents by making themselves seem to have had a rational explanation, which they now present as if it were real, maybe even convincing themselves. Perhaps we should sometimes, for practical purposes, give these people the responsibility they want. Perhaps we should treat them as if they were the responsible agents that they claim to be. Perhaps they should still bear some of the consequential responsibility that they might bear if they were indeed responsible in the basic sense. But that is another question. The key point for present purposes is that the ability that constitutes one as responsible, in the basic sense, is a *composite* ability. It is an ability which straddles the temporal gap between the wrong or mistake and the trial or recrimination, and which also straddles the conceptual gap between the ability to respond to reasons in what one originally does or thinks or feels, etc., and the ability to use those same reasons in explaining what one did or thought or felt.

Aristotle had a single word to straddle the conceptual gap. He spoke of *logos*, and the word captured for him, and presumably for his contemporary readers, a single concept. But translators find it hard to capture in English. In the *Ethics* they generally render it as 'reason',[8] but in the *Rhetoric* and *Politics* as 'speech'.[9] Maybe the closest equivalent we have in English is the word 'argument'. An argument is an inference from premises to a conclusion, and all rational thought is in that sense argumentative even when it is only the inference from 'man-eating tiger' to 'run'. But an argument is also something that we have with each other, a kind of dialogue in which inferences are used to make progress. Unfortunately, the word 'argument' has distracting overtones on both sides, making one think, on the one hand, of a rather intellectualized kind of thought, and on the other, of a rather aggressive kind of dialogue. *Logos* had neither overtone, so far as one can tell from the contexts in which it is used in the classics. The problem for us seems to be that a millennium of empiricist overindulgence has dulled the Anglophone conceptual palate. We have come to think, when we think about it at all, of the human abilities of reason and communication as two distinct abilities only contingently related. But that is a mistake. To have the distinctively human form of each is not, as Hobbes imagined, just to be able to do a better job than other creatures of anticipating and avoiding nasty consequences descending upon us, or even a better job of warning each other about those consequences by making a wider range of

---

[8] See e.g. Aristotle, *Nicomachean Ethics*, 1139^{a}4–5; *Eudemian Ethics*, 1219^{b}29ff.
[9] See e.g. Aristotle, *Rhetoric*, 1355^{b}1; *Politics*, 1253^{a}10.

noises. It is not just to have a more developed form of reason and a more developed form of communication than other creatures. It is to have the reason of a communicator, and the communication of a reasoner. The distinctively human form of reason is one which grasps the meaning of things as well as their instrumentality, and hence which depends on the ability to conceptualize and interpret that is part of being a human communicator.[10] Meanwhile, the distinctively human form of communication is one which offers reasons or challenges them or purports to create them and hence which requires on both sides (speaker and hearer) a developed ability to use reasons.[11] In short, to grasp our natures as human beings, we need to think of ourselves in terms of a composite speech-and-reason ability of the kind that Aristotle called *logos*. If I am right, one central component of this ability is our basic responsibility: which is a compound—*not a mixture but a compound*—of our ability to use reasons in acting, thinking, choosing, wanting, etc. and our ability to use those reasons *again* in giving an account of whatever it was we did, thought, chose, wanted, etc., and in that sense, as rational beings, giving an account of ourselves.

III

In these remarks, some may see the beginnings of a philosophical basis for the currently fashionable idea that responsibility must be understood *relationally*. Roughly the idea—we find it made explicit by Rorty, and regularly gestured towards by Rawls—is that responsibility, in the basic sense, is always responsibility *to* someone.[12] If asserting one's responsibility means not only having a rational account of oneself but also giving such an account, as I have claimed, then surely there must be someone to whom this rational account is owed, someone with whom one is supposed to enter into the Aristotelian dialogue. We need to begin by

---

[10] cf Aristotle, *Nicomachean Ethics*, 1147^b1ff: '[I]t turns out that a man behaves incontinently under the influence (in a sense) of reason and opinion ... [T]his is the reason why the lower animals are not incontinent, viz because they have no universal [conceptual] beliefs but only imagination and memory of particulars.'

[11] cf Aristotle, *Politics*, 1253^a10ff: 'And whereas mere voice is but an indication of pleasure and pain, and is therefore found in other animals..., the power of speech is intended to set forth the expedient and inexpedient, and therefore likewise the just and the unjust.'

[12] R Rorty, 'Is Truth a Goal of Enquiry? Davidson vs Wright', *Phil Q* 45 (1995), 281 at 283 ('justification is relative to an audience'); J Rawls, *A Theory of Justice* (1971), 580–581.

finding out who. We need to begin there because who is to receive the explanation, in turn, affects what suffices as a rational explanation. One must justify oneself or excuse oneself *to* that person. So justifications and excuses are also relational things. When people speak of justification or excuse *tout court*, they are suppressing a crucial variable. They always need to ask: 'To whom am I justifying or excusing myself?'

I agree that this last question has its moments. There is often a strong case for framing or editing one's justifications and excuses to suit particular audiences, or more generally to make them engage with the interests of particular people. Those charged with serious offences are heading for big trouble, for example, if they didn't take professional advice on how to explain in court the reasons for which they acted. Should they conceptualize the attack that they fought back against as having been a reason for self-defence, or a reason for anger under the heading of provocation, or a reason for emergency steps to be taken under the heading of necessity? It can make all the difference to their chances of conviction or acquittal. Meanwhile, those who are threatened with a duty of reparation rather than a liability to punishment had better take account of the fact that not all the justifications and excuses that may help them to avoid the latter are equally relevant to the former: morally as well as legally, a duty of reparation arises in respect of many wrongs that are justified or excused, where the justification or excuse in question is not related to the interests of the very person to whom the reparation would be paid. These are two different types of cases in which we might like to speak of someone justifying or excusing herself *to* someone. But these types of cases provide no comfort to believers in the relational view. Remember the contrast I drew at the outset between the two explanations of why we all hunt around for justifications and excuses whenever we perpetrate wrongs and mistakes. One—the shallower, Hobbesian explanation— was that as rational beings we all want to avoid consequential responsibility. The other—the deeper, Aristotelian explanation—was that as rational beings we all want to assert basic responsibility. In cases of the types just mentioned one certainly needs to tailor one's justifications and excuses to make them serve the Hobbesian objective better. But this assumes that one already has non-tailored justifications and excuses that one can tailor to suit the occasion. In other words, it assumes that if one were pursuing one's Aristotelian objective free from the pressures of one's Hobbesian objective, one would be able to offer a different justification or excuse, less narrowly conceptualized or less focused on the interests of a particular person. What believers in the relational view need to explain is why *that* justification or excuse—the one that would be made in pursuit of the Aristotelian objective and free from the Hobbesian objective—would necessarily also be relational.

I suspect that some supporters of the relational view fail to keep the two concepts of responsibility as sharply distinct as they should, and the appeal of their views rests to some extent on that lack of sharpness. At any rate, as soon as one brackets the Hobbesian factors—if I could call them that for short—it becomes much harder to see where the relational view gets its appeal. That asserting ourselves as responsible beings requires some interlocutor, someone to talk to, is not in doubt. But why does it need a *particular* interlocutor? In respect of the same wrong or mistake, couldn't I assert my basic responsibility by offering the same account of myself to everyone I come across, from judges in the Old Bailey to friends in the pub to strangers on the bus? Remember that, by hypothesis, I am no longer interested in whether my account of myself makes my interlocutors sympathetic, rebuilds my friendship with them, persuades them to let me off punishment, or anything like that. Those are just more of the same Hobbesian factors: more unwelcome consequences that I might want to avoid and that we have, for the sake of argument, bracketed out. What I care about, under the Aristotelian heading, is giving, so far as I am able, a *good* account of myself. If it really is a good account and other people can't see how good it is then, relative to the Aristotelian story of basic responsibility, that's *their* problem. Naturally, not every account I give of myself that is rationally intelligible will be a good one, and not every justification or excuse I offer as a responsible agent will be a successful one. But that is not the point. The point is that the *test* of its success, within the Aristotelian story, is whether it succeeds in providing good reasons why the wrong or mistake was perpetrated, or at least why the agent was driven or drawn to perpetrate it. Whether it succeeds in persuading its audience of the quality of those reasons is another matter altogether.

Probably some extreme supporters of the relational view don't regard this as another matter altogether. They regard the quality of reasons as simply reducible to their ability to persuade some actual person or constituency of people. But if they think that, then rather than regarding them as champions of the classical idea of *logos*—reason as a dialogical activity—we should regard them as solipsists who have lost touch with the commonality of purpose that unites us all as rational beings and brings us into dialogical engagement with each other. As if to reaffirm his belief in commonality of purpose, Rorty says he prizes 'solidarity' over 'objectivity'.[13] But in the only senses of 'solidarity' and 'objectivity' that matter one cannot have one without the other.[14] It is central to the classical idea of *logos*, and central to our nature as rational beings, even in these dark post-Hobbesian days, that all involved in the dialogue are aiming at successful understanding of the world around them, and not at mere mutual persuasion. Persuading someone to accept inadequate rational explanations is, for rational beings, the epitome of a pyrrhic victory, even if it means—no, *especially* if it means—that we get away with murder by doing so.

IV

I gave particular attention to the relational view because I think it holds special temptations for lawyers, especially common lawyers, and perhaps my last remarks on the subject helped to show why. Did my claim that we are 'aiming at successful understanding of the world around [us], and not at mere mutual persuasion' ring any bells? I think it might well be interpreted by some common lawyers as a coded warning of an imminent attack. It may seem to herald yet another in a long line of criticisms of the common law's adversarial process. But I am not heading towards any such criticisms now. On the contrary, I am heading for a guarded commendation. For all its vulnerability to abuse by crafty and sometimes unscrupulous lawyers excessively preoccupied with getting people on or off the hook, I think we should mostly try and take a prouder attitude towards the legal process. We should not think of it as mainly an instrumental appendage to substantive law. In fact we should think of its value as first and foremost intrinsic rather than instrumental.

The intrinsic value I have in mind is, of course, the value of basic responsibility itself. It is the value of being able to offer an account of oneself as a rational being. Naturally not all those who are accused of legal wrongs or mistakes offer personal accounts of themselves in court. Yet all who get as far as trial have the opportunity to do so. Those who choose not to nevertheless typically offer their self-explanations via their legal representatives. In the common law, these explanations tend

[13] R Rorty, 'Solidarity or Objectivity?' in his collection *Objectivity, Relativism, and Truth* (1991), 21.

[14] Much the same point is made (in the context of epistemology rather than ethics) in J McDowell, 'Towards Rehabilitating Objectivity' in R Brandom (ed), *Rorty and his Critics* (2000), 109.

to take the form of long, stilted conversations, involving statements of claim and defences, counterclaims and counterdefences, and then (in the courtroom) opening speeches and replies, examinations-in-chief and cross-examinations, and summings up on both sides. In comparing these stilted conversational devices with rival mechanisms—for instance, with civilian inquisitorial processes or with less formal dispute resolution models such as mediation—we all tend to assume in our usual Hobbesian way that they are to be compared first and foremost in terms of their effects on getting people on or off the hook—where that includes reaching agreed solutions about who pays for the window and who says sorry and who has to feel remorse, etc. (which are also allocations of consequential responsibility). Even those who like to evaluate rival legal procedures in terms of their fairness—and they often like to say that this is a *non*-instrumental way of evaluating it—tend to default to thinking of fairness, in this procedural context, in terms of the relative ability of the two sides to get on or off the hook. Does someone hold disproportionate sway over the way the case turns out? But it seems to me that if we are thinking in this way then we are missing the most fundamental point of all this legal rigmarole, all these pleas and committals and verdicts and even the physical layout of the courtroom with the dock and the stand and the bench. The fundamental point is to have structured explanatory dialogues in public, in which the object of explanation is ourselves. This point is not a point relative to which the procedure is instrumental; rather the point is *in* the procedure.

I just threw in, as if it were somehow integral to the value I am identifying, the fact that the explanatory dialogues of the law are held in public. What's the sudden significance of this? Well of course like everything under discussion here, it has more than one significance. But the pertinent significance right now seems to me to be this. The public character of self-explanation in court constitutes the law's most forthright rejection of the relational view. The law admits that some people—the plaintiff in a civil suit, and the prosecution in a criminal case—have the right to bring people to account. It insists on its own right to do the same. But the account they bring people to is not, at the deepest level, an account addressed specifically to them. It is addressed to the world at large, to be assessed on its merits as a rational explanation. If it's to be assessed on its merits, you may say, the law has a strange way of showing it. It forces the explanation into conceptual strait-jackets and ties us all in procedural knots. But that is an easy caricature. Certainly the law is a highly technical pursuit. But the self-explanations that people give of themselves when they take the stand are rarely highly technical in the same way. True, if their lawyers present the case then things may be different. But even then the *facts* must first be explained by non-lawyers and merely squeezed into the legal categories by the lawyers. Moreover, the legal categories themselves are typically left more elastic in respect of justifications and excuses than in respect of the definitions of the wrongs themselves, precisely to allow for accommodation of (at least some) meritorious but unanticipated self-explanations.[15] And in a criminal case, before a jury or lay magistrate, even the lawyer's technical handling of these already more elastic categories is controlled by the need to convey the gist of the defence case to lay people. I am inclined to think that this fact provides the beginnings of a case for jury trial. But more importantly, for present purposes, it helps us to defuse the myth that legal fora make people's self-explanations arcane.

I should stress that these remarks are not, at least I hope not, the signs of an early onset of common law chauvinism. I tend to think that, thanks to the pervasive collision of incommensurable values, there is no one best way to run a legal system. My remarks were only intended to draw attention to one of the several incommensurable values that is often neglected in legal debate and commentary, as well as in some legal and moral philosophy, namely the value of basic responsibility which is instantiated in, rather than instrumentally served by, the legal process. My point was the (I thought) rather intriguing one that although this value is neglected in anglophone legal debate and commentary, and is completely at odds with the still studiously Hobbesian thinking of most common lawyers, it is not neglected in the common law itself. Possibly the opposite: possibly it is overindulged and/or captured in an exaggerated way by the common law. Possibly, some or all of the common law systems have come to embrace the pursuit of 'argument' complete with its extra overtones of intellectualization, on the one hand, and aggression on the other. Possibly, some other legal systems in rival traditions have all this in healthier perspective. All of that is beyond my ken.

So, in short, the point I am making is not really about the common law, or its adversarial processes, in particular. It is simply that these processes bring out my broader point in a vivid way. And my point is that we should think of the courtroom struggle as a site of intrinsic as well as instrumental value. So even if for some reason we abolished the whole apparatus of

[15] For further discussion, see G Fletcher, 'The Nature of Justification' in S Shute, J Gardner and J Horder (eds), *Action and Value in Criminal Law* (1993).

criminal sentences and civil remedies, we should still think twice about abolishing the trials themselves. In fact one important (although not sufficient) reason for *having* the apparatus of criminal sentences and civil remedies is to *motivate* the trials themselves. It is to put people under extra instrumental pressure to give decent public accounts of themselves, in the knowledge that doing this will normally help them to eliminate or reduce the burden of consequential responsibility that they might otherwise bear.[16] To that extent, the importance of basic responsibility isn't derivative of the importance of consequential responsibility. The reverse is true. The importance of consequential responsibility derives from that of basic responsibility. To this extent, consequential responsibility is justified as the *mark* of basic responsibility.

V

This is just one of several ways in which the importance of consequential responsibility derives from that of basic responsibility. As I have admitted all along, there are also ways in which, conversely, the importance of basic responsibility derives from that of consequential responsibility. It is a two-way street. The only reason I have for thinking that basic responsibility is the more basic of the two is this. To the extent that the importance of basic responsibility derives from that of consequential responsibility, the derivation is entirely instrumental. It all rests on the fact that basic responsibility has consequential responsibility among its consequences. But to the extent that the importance of consequential responsibility derives from that of basic responsibility, the derivation is not only instrumental. I just mentioned the important argument that having a regime of consequential responsibility dependent on basic responsibility encourages people to give proper accounts of themselves, and hence serves the value of basic responsibility instrumentally. But

[16] Of course, the same apparatus can also motivate defendants to deny their basic responsibility. One of the most important arguments against resort to severe penalties and remedies is that the threat of them tends to coerce people into demeaning themselves in court. Defendants are put in a position in which it would be unreasonable for them to face up to their wrongs. So it is a mistake to assume that enthusiasts for the value of basic responsibility ought equally to be enthusiasts for harsher implementations of consequential responsibility. Perhaps the most insightful *exposé* of this mistake is R A Duff, *Trials and Punishments* (1986). The position I have sketched in this section has some notable features in common with Duff's 1986 position, although the differences are no less striking.

beyond that, being held consequentially responsible can also, in at least some of its forms, be important as a way of *expressing* one's basic responsibility. Since the reverse is not true, basic responsibility is more basic than consequential responsibility. In the mutual exchange of value between the two, basic responsibility is the only one that pays its way in intrinsic value.

The exact way in which being held consequentially responsible can express one's basic responsibility requires careful handling. There are many modes of consequential responsibility (a liability to be punished, a duty to atone, the loss of a right to be compensated, etc.) and there is probably no single thing that subjection to each of them expresses in common with all the others. In particular, the expressive relationship to basic responsibility probably varies from mode to mode. But the core idea that consequential responsibility can express basic responsibility is clear enough. It underlies the much maligned proposal (usually associated with Hegel) that all wrongdoers have a right to be punished.[17] I think the way this proposal is usually formulated is unfortunate, and the widespread maligning of it is consequently mistaken. It would be better to say less melodramatically that, if they are basically responsible, all wrongdoers have an *interest* in being punished. Since all rational beings want to assert their basic responsibility, all else being equal they cannot but welcome whatever contributes to that assertion. Punishment contributes to that assertion if it expresses their basic responsibility—if that is the public meaning of a punitive action. So all else being equal rational beings do have an interest in being punished whenever they are basically responsible for their actions. The problem is that as soon as we look at that proposition we realize that all else is *not* equal, because punishment is always at the same time, in its Hobbesian way, an *un*welcome consequence which every rational being would wish to avoid. There is a necessary conflict here between the conflicting demands of the assertion of one's basic responsibility and the avoidance of one's own suffering.

Cases like this led Kant down the road to his radical split of morality from prudence, via the distinction between the noumenal and the phenomenal. He was inclined to say that noumenally we welcome our own punishment, whereas phenomenally we do what we can to escape it.[18] That way of putting the point has its merits. It reminds us of the distinction with which I started, the distinction between the two stories, the

<hr>

[17] See Hegel, *Philosophy of Right* (trans Knox, 1942), 70.
[18] Kant, *The Metaphysics of Morals* (trans Gregor, 1996), 108.

Aristotelian story and the one that I later dubbed the Hobbesian story. Kant saw the force of the Aristotelian story very clearly. He saw that there are some abilities that are such that any being that has them necessarily aims to excel in them. And he agreed with Aristotle that our rational ability is such an ability.[19]

But whereas Aristotle meant to *include* our Hobbesian ability to avoid nasty consequences descending upon us under the heading of our rational ability,[20] Kant thought that this aspect of our rationality, belonging to the part that we share with less developed rational creatures, couldn't be embraced within our rational ability in the sense that mattered for the Aristotelian story. It had to be relegated to a distinct domain of lesser 'prudential' reason. This was a fallacious move. Alas, Kant then compounded the fallacy. In building up the rival 'moral' domain, he mistakenly focused not on our sophisticated communicative powers as human beings, but on the power of our *wills* to defy our reason, and hence optionally to follow it. He built this up as the special ingredient *x* that distinguished our rational ability from that of other, lesser rational creatures. By this route he arrived at an account of our basic responsibility in which the acid test was freedom of the will. Corroborating some earlier Christian myths, this account disastrously set the tone of our secular folk theory of responsibility, and indeed our secular folk theory of morality, for the intervening 200 years—even though throughout this time our lives were still lived exactly as if the folk theories were as false as they really are.

In saying this, I am not allying myself with those post-Kantians who doubt whether we have this famous power to confront reasons as options. I agree that we have it. In the face of incommensurable values we cannot but exercise it. And those of us who are lucky enough to live our lives above the desperate Hobbesian threshold of a struggle for survival, and who inhabit certain propitious cultural conditions, are able to live our lives largely as we choose. Our freedom is not, as some post-Kantians argue, a fiction or a myth. On the other hand, contrary to what many post-Kantians assume, our freedom is totally irrelevant to our responsibility. What our responsibility depends on is our ability to explain ourselves rationally, and that is totally unaffected by whether we confronted or engaged with our actions and thoughts and feelings as optional, as things that we could opt to have or not to have by sheer force of will. You

[19] Kant, *Groundwork of the Metaphysic of Morals* (trans Paton, 1964), 64.
[20] See e.g. Aristotle, *Nicomachean Ethics*, 1140ª24–28.

can work back from this bold assertion to certain of my detailed views about the conditions under which we are responsible. You can work out, for example, that I for one don't think coercion generally eliminates or even diminishes our responsibility for our actions. I think it furnishes us with a justification, or failing that an excuse. It can do this only if our responsibility survives it intact, for only those who are responsible can have, and make, justifications and excuses.

You may be surprised that I have managed to get this far without saying more about this kind of problem—more about exactly which circumstances eliminate or diminish our basic responsibility, and which circumstances, on the other hand, serve to justify or excuse us. I have even managed to avoid explaining even in outline how to distinguish a rational explanation from a non-rational one. And obviously I'm not about to do it now. You may have thought that a paper about the 'mark of responsibility' would be about these problems. But first things first. The most elementary problem of what we inherited from Kant has been that it has distracted us altogether from the reason-communication interface at which our responsibility resides, and focused our attention on the red herring of the reason-will interface instead. In the process we lost sight, or should I say lost folk-theoretical sight, of the important corollary of the Aristotelian story that our basic responsibility depends not only on the conditions that obtain when we commit our wrongs and mistakes, but also on the conditions that obtain later when we are confronted with those wrongs or mistakes. It depends not only on our ability to *have* a certain kind of explanation for what we do or think or feel, but also our ability to *offer* that explanation. And it depends not on our ability to offer that explanation to a particular audience, but on our ability to offer it *tout court*—at the bar, if you like, of reason itself.

VI

In many contexts, the words 'responsibility' and 'accountability' are interchangeable.[21] But contemporary political discourse has also carved out a special niche for the word 'accountability'. One is accountable, to contemporary ears, only if there is someone to whom one is responsible. Accountability therefore has a relational aspect that responsibility lacks.

[21] As in J Bennett, 'Accountability' in Z van Straaten (ed), *Philosophical Subjects* (1980).

It is not enough to make one accountable that one is apt to (and hence reasonably expected to) justify or excuse one's actions. There must also be a person or body of people to whom one owes the justification or excuse. This is the person or body that *holds one to account.*

One currently fashionable mode of accountability is public accountability, meaning accountability to the electorate, or the taxpayers, or the citizenry, either directly or through their representatives. Some seem to think that this is the default mode of accountability—that the electorate, or some similar popular body, is the natural body to hold one to account. You may say that I already gave succour to this idea in section IV above. I pointed to the public character of proceedings in court—an accounting that is offered to the whole world—as a way of expressing a defendant's basic responsibility, the raw non-relational condition on which all relational modes of responsibility are based. Isn't accountability to the electorate, through Parliament or the media, just the same kind of thing? Doesn't that give public accountability a certain special priority as a mode of accountability? No. An electorate, or a taxpayer population, or a citizenry, is not the world at large. It is a special constituency with its own sectional interests, apt to extract correspondingly distorted justifications and excuses from those who are accountable to it. Besides, accountability *in* public is not the same as accountability *to* the public. Defendants in court are (luckily) not accountable to the public. They are accountable to the court. The court merely puts their account in the public domain—gives it a public audience—to convey that the defendant is before the court *qua* person, and not *qua* occupant of some specialized social role with some specialized line of accountability. Public accountability, accountability to the electorate or the taxpayers or the citizenry, is by contrast a specialized line of accountability, a relational mode of responsibility that is an incident of only some specialized social roles. It belongs first and foremost, although perhaps not only, to certain public officials who wield executive authority.

The case of the courts highlights some interesting questions about what accountability is *for*. It is currently fashionable to deride judges as 'unaccountable', usually as shorthand for 'publicly unaccountable'. And yet judges are bound to, and normally do, give much more detailed accounts of themselves than do many other public officials. They give reasoned judgments in open court to justify most of the actions they take. And their reasons are apt to be scrutinized closely on appeal, more closely than the reasons of most other public officials, who are subject only to the lighter touch of judicial review. Judges are, in short, the public servants who are already bound to give, and already give, the fullest account of themselves in public. So what is the supposed problem to which greater public accountability would be a solution? Of course we all know the depressing answer. The real gripe of those who deride judges as 'unaccountable' is that judges can't be ejected from office by the electorate, or by their elected representatives, when their very full justifications for acting as they do are disliked. There are no electoral sanctions or remedies for bad self-explanations.

Since judges exist mainly to provide a check on the inevitable populist excesses of the elected branches of government, thoughtful people must regard this lack of electoral accountability on the part of judges as at least partly a blessing. But that is not the theme I want to explore here. The theme I want to explore here is connected with a point I made at the end of section IV above. As I said there, one important (although not sufficient) reason for having a regime of sanctions and remedies is to motivate those subject to those sanctions and remedies to give a decent account of themselves. The puzzle is this. When people are inclined to give such an account anyway, as judges generally are, one important reason for subjecting them to a regime of sanctions and remedies is missing. What is the residual case for having a regime of sanctions and remedies in such circumstances? Is there a suspicion that the justifications and excuses would tend to be better—such that the actions being justified or excused would also be better—if there were sanctions and remedies to concentrate the minds of those who offer them? Or is it that that the justifications and excuses being given are somehow not the real ones, so that one needs to have some way of applying pressure for a more frank self-explanation?

It seems to me that, whatever case may be made for the availability of sanctions and remedies in such cases, it cannot but rely on the suspicion of wrongdoing. To challenge someone to justify or excuse herself, with a threat of punishment in the event that her justification or excuse is unsatisfactory, is to accuse her of committing a wrong. This accusation is part of the public meaning of such an action of challenging and threatening even if the person doing the challenging and threatening tries to repudiate it. He can't escape it by saying: 'I'm not accusing you of wrongdoing, but you'd better have a good explanation of why you did that, or else.' This is crude doublespeak. True, wrongs are not the only things that call for justification or excuse. A justification or excuse—an answer to the question 'Why did you do that?'—is called for whenever anyone does anything that she has any reason not to do, and this condition is met by virtually everything we do. But only some of the things that we do that we have a reason not to do are things that we have an *obligation* not to do, such that doing them is wrongful. And only when we do something wrongful, and lack justification or excuse for doing it, are we aptly punished for doing it. Punishment is an apt response only to unjustified and unexcused wrongdoing. Accordingly, threatening punishment for an action already done is accusing the agent of having committed an unjustified and unexcused wrong. When coupled with an opportunity to offer a satisfactory justification or excuse and thereby to avoid the punishment, threatening the punishment is accusing the agent of wrongdoing, albeit may be not unjustified and unexcused. There is no morally acceptable case for making such an accusation unless one makes it sincerely, i.e. unless one reasonably suspects that the accusation is true. So anyone who threateningly asks 'Why did you do that?' is claiming to have a reasonable suspicion that the person she is addressing is a wrongdoer.

You may object that not every sanction or remedy, not every adverse consequence that might ensue in the event of an unsatisfactory justification or excuse, is a punitive one. People may lose their jobs simply because they are no good at them, and this need not be a punishment for anything. This is true, but irrelevant to the argument just set out. By *threatening* any adverse consequence in the event of inadequate justification or excuse, one turns the threatened adverse consequence into a threatened punishment. How so? One reacts punitively to what someone did whenever one reacts with the intention that she should suffer for having done it. By threatening adverse consequences in the event of an inadequate justification or excuse, one evinces this intention in advance.[22] That is because one cannot use the threat as the incentive one intends it to be unless, were it carried out, the person to whom it is addressed would suffer. This makes the suffering part of one's intention. It follows that whatever adverse consequences one threatens are rendered punitive by one's act of threatening them, wherever the threat is also designed to be an incentive. Thus, for example, reparative damages in tort law are not in their nature punitive. They can and should be exacted without the intention that the defendant should suffer. That is why it is consistent with the principles of tort law that the defendant be fully indemnified by an insurance company. But anyone who threatens

---

[22] On threats and intentions, see J Finnis, J Boyle, and G Grisez, *Nuclear Deterrence, Morality and Realism* (1988).

to exact reparative damages in the event that the person threatened does not settle the case or give in to some other demand turns the threatened exacting of damages into a threatened punishment for non-co-operation. Likewise, dismissing an employee in the event of underperformance need not be punitive. But using the threat of dismissal to secure better performance from the employee turns the threatened dismissal into a threatened punishment. If exacted, it would now be a punishment for underperformance—which entails an accusation of wrongdoing—not only a way of replacing an underperforming employee. For the suffering involved in being dismissed would no longer be a side-effect but rather an intended effect of the dismissal. That is why securing self-explanation by threats is necessarily accusatory, however it is dressed up.[23]

I am not saying that one cannot have a culture of accountability that is not a culture of suspicion and accusation. A culture in which people routinely explain themselves without fear or favour is such a culture. But the culture of accountability that we now seem to have—in which requests for self-explanation are routinely coupled with threats of loss of office, loss of promotion, loss of funding, loss of contracts, and so on—is unavoidably a culture of suspicion and accusation. Most of the time, it seems to me, such suspicion and accusation is unwarranted. There is usually no reason to suspect a breach of any obligation by anybody. For example, it is part of the job of most public officials to spend public money. Some of them may spend it badly, and among those who do there may be a further sub-group who spend it wrongfully (e.g. feather-bedding their friends, failing to keep an eye on where it is going). To demand that every spender of public money be 'held to account for every penny spent'—where this carries with it an implicit threat of adverse consequences in the event that it was not spent wisely—is to accuse every spender of public money, even those who spend public money impeccably, of spending it wrongfully. In this regime, everyone is always a suspect. If politicians wonder why trust in politicians has declined when the trustworthiness of politicians (let's concede) has not, they need look no further for an explanation. The system of accountability on which politicians themselves have come to insist as part and parcel of 'New Public Management' is an ideology of

---

[23] Often, in the patronizing environment of contemporary 'appraisal' and 'audit', the threats are dressed up as warnings or advice, and the punishments are dressed up as rewards foregone. 'To guarantee your annual bonus, you'll need to reprioritize' usually means 'work harder or we'll dock your pay'. The warning or advice is a threat if the person giving it has control over (or is representing those who have control over) whether and why the reward will be lost; the loss of the reward is punitive if it is intended that the person shall suffer by its loss (and irrespective of whether she is otherwise entitled to it).

total suspicion (or, to put the same idea in other words, total mistrust).[24] It should come as no surprise that the more this system comes to be taken for granted as the way to run the country (and indeed the way to run everything else), the more suspicious everyone is of those whose upstandingness the system is meant to secure.[25] These people must be up to something, observers conclude, because the system constantly accuses them of being up to something.

No doubt this line of thought can be developed further. There are reasons to think (although empirical work would be needed to establish) that there is an element of self-fulfilling prophesy in the ideology of total suspicion. Probably, as people are routinely accused of wrongdoing, they become dispirited and less inclined to co-operate in the activity in respect of which they are accused. Possibly they also become more inclined to conceal and dissemble and react defensively for fear of what will become of them if they reveal their ordinary human limitations. If these hunches are true, then the threat-based mode of accountability to which people are now routinely subject in their working lives is doubly counterproductive. In the first place—a trite point—inasmuch as organizations depend for the quality of their work on the spirit of those who work in them, this mode of accountability is apt to reduce organizational performance. In the public sector, in particular, the 'New Public Management' may make public services cheaper but also worse value (by eroding the surplus of unpaid co-operation that was once called the 'public service ethos'). In the second place, the same threat-based mode of accountability may be counterproductive even from the point of view of accountability itself. That is to say, people may be disinclined to explain themselves honestly and openly for fear that every little slip they make will be punished.

Of course, the fear of exposing oneself to terrible consequences by telling the truth can equally be a distorting force in the criminal justice system. But at least in the criminal justice system the accusation of wrongdoing must be based on a reasonable suspicion and those who are accused are therefore, within limits, reasonably put in peril of exposing themselves. There is no similar excuse for today's systems of bureaucratic accountability to have driven ordinary innocent people into the fearful Hobbesian defensiveness and evasiveness that now often seems to

[24] For a thoughtful explanation and assessment of 'New Public Management', see J Martin, 'Changing Accountability Relations: Politics, Consumers and the Market', available at: http://www.oecd.org/dataoecd/10/58/1902695.pdf.
[25] This theme, and those that follow, were nicely explored by O O'Neill in *A Question of Trust* (2002), ch 3. I have also been influenced by M Power, *The Audit Society: Rituals of Verification* (1999).

dog their working lives. Yet—and here is the element of self-fulfilling prophesy—to the extent that ordinary innocent people are indeed driven into Hobbesian defensiveness and evasiveness, the culture of suspicion has, perversely, helped to create the very conditions that are supposed to necessitate it. The ideology of total suspicion makes people more worthy of suspicion by constantly suspecting them. It helps to dig the hole from which it is supposed to extract us, and thereby prolongs its own miserable life. That, at any rate, is my hypothesis.

10

The Functions and Justifications of Criminal Law and Punishment

I

According to a classificatory scheme familiar to German criminal lawyers, the criminal justice system contributes to 'Negative General Prevention' by deterring a population from norm-violation (aka wrongdoing). It contributes to 'Positive General Prevention' when it helps to instil in a population respect for norms, thereby reducing the need to deter violations.

In Andrew Ashworth's view, Positive General Prevention represents an important function of both criminal law and criminal punishment. Yet it does not play an important role in the justification of either criminal law or criminal punishment.[1] How can this be? What else could justify a social practice but its functions? What further justificatory presence could serve to reduce an important function to justificatory unimportance? What indeed could count as 'importance' in the realm of functioning if not justificatory importance? True, some social scientists give an excessively instrumentalist reading to the word 'function', with the result that those ideals and practices which are not justified in largely instrumental terms may be classed as not having a 'functional' justification.[2] This means that their most important functions will not necessarily show up as important elements of their justification. But Ashworth does not seem to share in this rather technical and *recherché* use of the word 'function'. He gives no hint of departing from the ordinary sense in which it may be said that social practices have, e.g., expressive and constitutive functions as well as instrumental ones. So I will assume here that Ashworth means to drive some different wedge between functional importance and justificatory importance.

---

[1] A Ashworth, 'Was ist positive Generalprävention? Eine Kurze Antwort' in B Schünemann, A von Hirsch and N Jareborg (eds), *Positive Generalprävention: Kritische Analysen im deutsch-englischen Dialog* (1998), 68–69.

[2] For an example of this usage, see J Gray, *Mill On Liberty: A Defence* (2nd edn, 1996), 151ff.

One possibility is that Ashworth is thinking primarily of what we may call the 'subjective' dimension of justification. Justification has both objective and subjective dimensions, in the sense that whether an action (or belief) is justified depends both on whether there are undefeated reasons for performing it (or holding it) and on whether the agent acts (or believes) for one or other of those reasons.[3] In the case of social practices, which are complexes of actions, the functions of each practice supply the reasons for that practice to be nurtured and maintained, as well as the reasons for particular people to join in with it by performing actions recognizably forming part of its complex. But the fact that *some* of these practice-supporting reasons may be undefeated, so that joining in with the practice can in principle be justified, does not mean that all the reasons in favour of joining in are undefeated. Some may be defeated by being excluded from consideration, so that while one should still do as they recommend, one should not do so because they recommend it.[4]

For example, most employers in Europe today should employ more black staff than they do, but (barring special circumstances) they should not employ them because they are black. Similarly, that it helps one to get over a bereavement is a strong reason in favour of starting a new relationship, but one should not start the new relationship in order to get over the bereavement. These are cases where certain people should not act on certain reasons even though they are reasons for their doing as they do. Likewise, there are many reasons in favour of criminalization and criminal punishment on which certain officials in the criminal justice process should not act. Legislators, justice ministers, trial judges, jurors, appeal judges, probation officers, prison governors, and so on all have their own role to play in the social practices of criminal law and criminal punishment and these roles are demarcated not only by a repertoire of actions which incumbents may in principle be justified in performing, but also by a repertoire of reasons on which incumbents must act if their actions are to be justified.

So it is possible that what Ashworth wants to say is this: that the function of Positive General Prevention, important though it may be in making a case for criminal law and criminal punishment, should not figure, or should not figure centrally, in the case which certain officials themselves make for the invocations of those social practices which lie within their

---

[3] See J Gardner, 'Justifications and Reasons' in ATH Smith and A Simester (eds), *Harm and Culpability* (1996), 103 (Chapter 5 in this volume).

[4] The idea of an 'exclusionary reason', i.e. a reason not to act on a reason in favour of what one does, comes from J Raz, *Practical Reasons and Norms* (2nd edn, 1990), 35ff.

official powers. If that is what he means, I cannot dissent. It may be that, for example, sentencing judges should give relatively little weight, or even no weight at all, to Positive General Prevention factors. I suppose one might try to convey this point by saying that Positive General Prevention is important as a function of sentencing but unimportant as an element of its justification. But of course in saying that, one is obscuring the crucial possibility that, were it not for the important function of Positive General Prevention, the sentencing of criminals by judges, rightly remaining blind to considerations of Positive General Prevention, might be impossible to justify. The justification for judges doing as they do may depend on considerations with which the judges themselves can have no truck, and so the justificatory importance of Positive General Prevention need not equate to the justificatory importance which certain officials, for example judges or legislators, may properly give it in their work.

Some of Ashworth's remarks support this interpretation of what he is saying.[5] Others point to a somewhat different interpretation according to which Positive General Prevention factors are justificatorily unimportant because they are justificatorily *insufficient*.[6] Of course, Ashworth is quite right to think that, by themselves, Positive General Prevention factors do not add up to a complete case for criminalizing or punishing anyone. In that sense they do not 'justify' criminal law and punishment. But, in that sense, does *anything* justify criminal law and punishment? I very much doubt it. Given that criminalizing and criminally punishing people commits the State to the prima facie barbarity of deliberately damaging those people's lives, I cannot see that any one of the multifarious lines of argument that exist for doing such things could ever provide one with sufficient justification by itself. One needs to pray in aid all of the valuable functions of criminalizing and punishing people in order even to get close to an adequate justification.

Some people have resisted such cumulative justification on the ground that it tends to lead to persistent conflict among the multifarious considerations. How can one live with an arrangement in which (for example) both deterrence and retribution form part of the justification for criminalizing and punishing people, since deterrence plainly points to criminalizing

---

[5] For instance, Ashworth's issue 'How much punishment?' is an issue which arises centrally for judges, and his concern here may be that judges will give Positive General Prevention weight, or too much weight, when it is not their business, or not their primary business, to do so. See 'Was ist positive Generalprävention?', above n 1, at 67.

[6] For instance, ibid at 68: Positive General Prevention 'fails to supply a sufficiently weighty justification for such a system'.

certain actions where retribution points the other way, deterrence advises long sentences of imprisonment in some cases in which retribution points to short ones, and so forth? The answer to this challenge has already been outlined. The fact that all the arguments in favour of punishing must be marshalled on the objective side of the justification does not entail that all must figure on the subjective side as well. Judges need never face some of the underlying conflicts since some of the conflicting considerations are not considerations on which they, as judges, should act. But it does not mean that these considerations are justificatorily unimportant. On the contrary, since criminalization and criminal punishment are prima facie such abhorrent practices, they need all the justificatory support they can get, and any valuable function they may have, however modest, may under some conditions make all the difference between the justifiability and the unjustifiability of the practices. It is particularly hard to see how what is admitted by Ashworth to be an *important* function of criminalization and criminal punishment could even become, by this route, justificatorily unimportant. Defenders of these practices may have a little room for jutsificatory manoeuvre, so that genuinely trivial functions of criminal law and punishment can be disregarded, but they certainly do not have so much room for manoeuvre that they can put admittedly important functions on one side as surplus to justificatory requirements, even if they can manage to find logical space for a notion of importance which is not itself cashed out in purely justificatory terms.[7]

II

It is hinted by Ashworth[8] and stressed by some others[9] that the insufficiency of Positive General Prevention as a justification for criminalization

[7] For completeness, I should just mention that there is a third possible interpretation of what Ashworth is saying, which is also supported by some of his remarks in ibid, 66 and 68. He may be saying that while criminal law and punishment do much to serve Positive General Prevention, Positive General Prevention can equally or better be served by other, less abominable, means than criminal law and punishment. I agree but believe this to be irrelevant to the importance of Positive General Prevention in justifying criminal law and punishment. We do not, as Ashworth's remarks on this point presuppose, have *pro tanto* reason to do whatever will be necessary to do whatever we have reason to do. Rather, we have *pro tanto* reason to do whatever will be sufficient to do whatever we have reason to do. See Kenny, 'Practical Inference', *Analysis* 26 (1966), 65.

[8] Positive General Prevention 'rid[es] on the coat-tails of negative general prevention or of desert': Ashworth, 'Was ist positive Generalprävention?', above n 1, at 67.

[9] For example, Schünemann, 'Zur Kritik an der Theorie der positiven Generalprävention', in *Positive Generalprävention*, above n 1, citing Hörnle and von Hirsch,

and criminal punishment is insufficiency of a peculiar, and allegedly peculiarly damaging, sort. It is insufficiency which comes of the fact that Positive General Prevention arguments are *logically parasitic*. The problem is not merely that a full justification for criminalization and criminal punishment requires Positive General Prevention to be supplemented with other considerations—for that, surely, is no problem at all. The problem, rather, is that Positive General Prevention itself, by its own logic, requires Positive General Prevention to be supplemented with other considerations. The thought is that instilling in people the disposition to respect or obey norms, the project which lies at the heart of the Positive General Prevention argument, is warranted only if those norms are sound. Logically speaking, then, the norms of the criminal law have to be sound before considerations of Positive General Prevention can even begin to bite in defence of criminalization and criminal punishment. It follows, according to this line of thought, that Positive General Prevention can only be a logically secondary aspect of the arguments for criminalization and criminal punishment. It can never sit, so to speak, in the logical driving seat.

This line of thought is fallacious in several respects. Most obviously, it is true of all arguments for punishment, criminal or otherwise, that punishment is warranted under those arguments only on condition that the norm violated is, on other grounds, a sound one. Those who believe otherwise betray a lingering affection for the long-since discredited 'sanction theory of duty', according to which whether one is under a duty to do such-and-such depends on whether one can rightfully be punished for doing such-and-such.[10] In fact the question of whether one is under a duty is logically prior to the question of whether one can rightfully be punished for its breach, because the fact that one was under a duty which one breached is a reason for the punishment, and what is more a reason which must be present and acted upon as a condition of one's punishment being rightful. Thus no theory of punishment can affect whether murder is wrong. It affects only whether, given that murder is wrong, murderers or certain murderers ought to be punished. The same is true, incidentally, of a theory of criminalization. A theory of criminalization does not (and should not aspire to) tell us whether murder is wrong. It can only tell us whether, given that murder is wrong, it is also a candidate for criminalization. So being logically parasitic in the sense just encountered doesn't seem to be

'Positive Generalprävention und Tadel', *Goltdammer's Archiv für Strafrecht* 142 (1995), 267.

[10] Hacker, 'Sanction Theories of Duty' in AWB Simpson (ed), *Oxford Essays in Jurisprudence, Second Series* (1971), 60.

a characteristic of Positive General Prevention alone, but equally of deterrence, retribution, rehabilitation and all other penological lines of argument. It should also be pointed out that countless sound arguments are logically parasitic in the relevant sense, with no obvious resulting lack of credibility or justificatory importance. If I promise to do x, my duty to keep my promise turns partly on whether x is something I should ever have promised to do in the first place. But it does not follow that, when promising to do x is alright, my having promised to do it was not a condition of my having the duty to do x now. Nor does it make the arguments for keeping one's promises any the less significant or pivotal. The view that *pacta sunt servanda* is not even slightly weakened by the discovery that its application and force depends to some extent upon an independent evaluation of the actions which the promisor promised to perform. This is a closely analogous case to the case of Positive General Prevention, in which the value of instilling in people the disposition to obey norms obviously depends to some extent upon an independent evaluation of the norms which, as a consequence of this process of instilling, people are meant to be disposed to obey.

But all of this is in any case beside the point, because the so-called 'objection' that Positive General Prevention is logically parasitic only applies to what Michael Baurmann calls 'narrow' Positive General Prevention,[11] which is the doctrine that criminalization and criminal punishment should serve to instil in people a disposition to obey or respect *the norms of the criminal law*, i.e. to be law-abiding people. Under this doctrine the norms which one is supposed to become more disposed to obey are the very same norms of the criminal law to the justification of which considerations of Positive General Prevention are supposed to contribute. But as Baurmann says, there is a broader (and to my way of thinking infinitely more attractive[12]) version of the Positive General Prevention doctrine according to which criminalization and criminal punishment should serve to instil in people a disposition to avoid wrongdoing. One may have a disposition to avoid wrongdoing without having any disposition to be obedient or faithful to law, or even to avoid the particular actions which the criminal law picks out as wrongful. The conscientious anarchist does not necessarily commit more wrongs merely because he or she has no disposition to accede

---

[11] Baurmann, 'Theorien der Generalprävention' in *Positive Generalprävention*, above n 1.

[12] More attractive because the stricter version has moral appeal only if people in general have a prima facie moral obligation to obey the law, which, in my opinion, they do not have.

to the law's authority. And there is no reason to believe that the Positive General Prevention argument could not apply in the case of the conscientious anarchist, i.e. that her disposition to avoid wrongdoing could not be reinforced by the message sent out by some or all criminal trials and punishments, even as she doubts the legitimacy of those very trials and punishments. Couldn't that message, for example, make her ever more disposed to affirm her (*arguendo* sound) anarchist convictions, and ever more inclined to avoid the wrongs of complicity with an (*arguendo* illegitimate) system? In that case we would have an admittedly unusual (because somewhat convoluted) example of Positive General Prevention in action. But Positive General Prevention in the broader sense this would certainly be, and so far as I can see there is no vestige here of the logical parasitism which was supposed to be a pitfall of Positive General Prevention. So even if I could understand, as I fear I cannot, what kind of weakness or disability is supposed to be inflicted on Positive General Prevention by its supposed logical parasitism, I cannot see how the broader and more plausible version of Positive General Prevention suffers from that weakness.

III

In its broader version, as far as I can make out, the Positive General Prevention argument contains just three major, or normative, premises. These are:

1. *Ceteris paribus*, it's a good thing if people do no wrong;
2. *Ceteris paribus*, it's a better thing still if people have no disposition to do wrong;
3. *Ceteris paribus*, prevention is better than cure.

These three major premises combine with a minor, or informational, premiss, namely:

4. Criminalization and criminal punishment can both help to prevent people from forming or maintaining the disposition to do wrong.

All of which leads to the conclusion:

5. *Ceteris paribus*, criminalization and criminal punishment are good things.

And there we have the whole Positive General Prevention argument, in plain and simple terms. Of course the minor or informational premiss (4) may be questioned by people with empirical research at their fingertips.[13] That is not my domain; as a theorist I can speak at best to the soundness of the major or normative premisses (1–3) and the logic leading to conclusion (5). But so far as these matters are concerned, I am at a loss to see what could possibly be wrong with them. Premiss (1) is analytically true, i.e. it is part of the very concept of a wrong that it is a good thing if people do not commit wrongs; the '*ceteris paribus*' in this premiss is needed simply to remind us that the avoidance of wrongdoing is not the only good thing in the world. Premiss (2) strikes me as impeccable in view of two considerations. Firstly, because having no disposition to do wrong makes doing no wrong less painful for those who do no wrong, since they do not have to struggle with themselves whenever opportunities to do wrong arise. Secondly, because people with dispositions to do wrong are (again, analytically) less admirable in point of character than those with no such dispositions, and the world is (analytically) a better place if inhabited by admirable beings. Premiss (3), meanwhile, is convincing on the simple ground that what is cured has already been suffered, whereas what is prevented has not. From these three premisses it follows straightforwardly that in its broad version Positive General Prevention is worth attaining through the criminal law and criminal punishment.

What is more the argument gives Positive General Prevention the prima facie moral edge over Negative General Prevention (or deterrence), which rests on premisses (1) and (3) but has no truck with premiss (2). It also gives Positive General Prevention the prima facie moral edge over Positive Special Prevention (or rehabilitation) which rests on premisses (1) and (2) but makes no allowances for (3). Of course it does not follow from this that we should invest more energy in arranging our criminal justice system to serve the ends of Positive General Prevention than the ends of Negative General Prevention or Positive Special Prevention. By (2) and (3), that would only be true *ceteris paribus*, i.e. on the assumption (*inter alia*) that there are no differences of feasibility as between these ends. Again, empirical studies may show us that, for example, Negative General Prevention is easier to achieve than Positive, in which case the *ceteris paribus* moral advantages of Positive General Prevention are diluted, perhaps to a very large degree, by the difficulties of making it work. The strength

---

[13] For consideration of premiss (4), see Schumann, 'Empirische Beweisbarkeit der Grundannahmen von positiver Generalprävention', in *Positive Generalprävention*, above n 1.

of any argument is, of course, a function of the combined strength of its major and minor premisses, and not of its major premisses alone.

But the qualification '*ceteris paribus*' which recurs throughout the Positive General Prevention argument does not only serve to remind us that the argument as a whole may be weakened by difficulties of achieving the results advertised in (4). It also alerts us to the possibility that the individual premisses (1–3) are open to collateral moral challenge, i.e. that in spite of their strong prima facie moral appeal, there might be independent moral objections to reliance upon these premisses as part of the case for criminalization and criminal punishment. Of course there are many fearsome moral attacks to be made on criminalization and criminal punishment *tout court*. I already conceded a prima facie abhorrence of these practices, and I am not about to go over that point again. At this stage, rather, I want to mention moral objections which are specific to the premisses of the Positive General Prevention argument. I will mention two of them which seem to me to underlie much of the hostility which is felt, in some quarters, towards this argument.

In the first place, it may be objected that premiss (2) tends to license State manipulation. It is one thing to coerce us into changing our behaviour, as, for example, the Negative General Preventionists want the State to do. That is surely bad enough. But it may be thought that, on the part of a liberal government, manipulation is worse still because it is a condition of its success that it is opaque to those who are subjected to it. Manipulation does not confront but bypasses our rationality; it does not override what we want to do with something we want very much to avoid but rather makes us believe that we wanted to do something different in the first place. That kind of surreptitious approach to its people, the liberal State should prefer to avoid. It may even be suggested that it is a condition of legitimacy of the liberal State, captured in the famous Rawlsian requirement of 'free public reason',[14] that the State should not bypass our rationality. For myself I think there may well be some truth in this suggestion. But it does not, so far as I can see, affect premiss (2) of the Positive General Prevention argument one jot. The mistake in thinking that it does comes of the assumption that the only way to affect people's dispositions is to manipulate people. But that is simply not true. Even though there are many borderline and difficult cases, it is palpably not true of *all* encouragement, discouragement, praise, criticism, advice, warning, explanation, education, advertising, argument, and persuasion

---

[14] See Rawls, *Political Liberalism* (1993), 212ff.

that it is manipulative. And yet all of these things may have an effect, intended or unintended, on our dispositions. Our dispositions listen to reason too; our reason need not be side-stepped in order to get them to change. And thus the criminal justice system may alter our dispositions without manipulating us. Antony Duff's argument that the criminal trial is a communicative process, which speaks to defendants as rational beings, is but one memorable example of an argument which relies on the non-manipulative but also non-coercive power of the criminal law, its ability to speak to us in a way which changes how we think about things and how we are inclined to react to them.[15] Again, there may be empirical doubts about the feasibility of Duff's project, but as far as its moral acceptability is concerned there is surely no reason to doubt it, and no reason, moreover, to doubt the possibility of its extension beyond the defence of Positive Special Prevention (getting the defendant to recognize the error of her ways by reasoning with her) to the larger aim of Positive General Prevention (getting people in general to think of certain ways as erroneous by reasoning with them). For as I said already, Positive Special Prevention and Positive General Prevention share their reliance on premiss (2).

But even as we come to grant premiss (2), our critical attention shifts to premiss (3). Isn't this subject to a separate objection, to which the same premiss in the classic Negative General Prevention argument has also been subjected, namely that it seems to allow people to be used as means rather than ends? After all, for all its innocent charm, premiss (3) is already envisaging that the prevention of wrongdoing will take place by criminalization and criminal punishment, i.e. that some people will be criminalized and criminally punished in order to send out a generally preventative message to others which will affect their dispositions. We are not merely talking about public information films or citizen education classes here, but about deliberately inflicted violence and deprivation *pour encourager les autres*. Given this fact, is it still true that prevention is better than cure? Or isn't it the case (as many retributivists argue) that cure (meaning in this context *ex post facto* intervention in wrongdoing) is the only morally acceptable option for punishers given that people should be treated as ends rather than means? Again, we may be distracted here by thought of a manipulative paradigm, a paradigm of 'using' people by circumventing their rationality. But once that distraction is stripped out—as it should be, since the objection to using people as means is

---

[15]   RA Duff, *Trials and Punishments* (1986), 233ff.

quite different from the objection to manipulating them—we are left with the question of whether and if so in what sense it is wrong to treat people as means. Given the depth and difficulty of this problem, here I confine myself to a couple of brief remarks. First, much of the force of the claim that people should not be treated as means comes of the more plausible (and more authentically Kantian) maxim that people shouldn't be treated *merely* as means, i.e. as means and nothing else.[16] These two maxims come to the same thing in the present context for anyone who thinks that we need a singular sufficient justification for criminalization and punishment. But for those of us who believe that criminalization and criminal punishment call for cumulative justification, in which the Positive General Prevention argument is just one of several that build up to provide the justification of these practices, the two maxims have quite different implications. The maxim that people shouldn't be treated as means rules out premiss (3) of our argument, whereas the maxim that people shouldn't be used merely as means is compatible with premiss (3) so long as we only hold punishment and criminalization to be justified where supported by other arguments which do not contain this premiss, i.e. which do not treat the trial and sentencing of criminal offenders as means to crime prevention. Secondly, the question arises of who is going to be doing the treating. If, as I argued before, the subjective dimension of justification need not completely mirror its objective dimension, then premiss (3) need not figure in the reasoning of anybody who is actually criminalizing or punishing criminals, but only the reasoning of people like us (i.e. theorists) who are bound to step back and consider the whole rational picture. The maxims 'do not treat people as means' and 'do not treat people *merely* as means' differ not in the actions which they forbid (both, for example, forbid criminal conviction and punishment of the innocent if either of them does) but in the reasons on which they permit people to act. It follows that there is only an objection to their inclusion in an argument for criminalizing or punishing if the argument in question is going to be relied upon by some criminalizing or punishing official. But the mere fact that Positive General Prevention does its fair share in justifying criminalization and criminal punishment does not mean that any official should rely on it, i.e. that it should form part of that official's reasoning. Thus the objection to premiss (3) turns out to be chimerical, whether we read 'merely' into its maxim or not.

---

[16] Kant, *Groundwork of the Metaphysic of Morals* (trans Paton, 1964), 96.

11

Crime: In Proportion and in Perspective

1. The displacement function

What is the criminal law for? Most explanations nowadays focus exclusively on the activities of criminal offenders. The criminal law exists to deter or incapacitate potential criminal offenders, say, or to give actual criminal offenders their just deserts. In all this we seem to have lost sight of the origins of the criminal law as a response to the activities of *victims*, together with their families, associates, and supporters. The blood feud, the vendetta, the duel, the revenge, the lynching: for the elimination of these modes of retaliation, more than anything else, the criminal law as we know it today came into existence.[1] It is important to bring this point back into focus, not least because one common assumption of contemporary writing about punishment, including criminal punishment, is that its justifiability is closely connected with the justifiability of our retaliating (tit-for-tat, or otherwise) against those who wrong us.[2] The spirit of the criminal law is, on this assumption, fundamentally in continuity with the spirit of the vendetta. To my mind, however, the opposite relation holds with much greater force. The justifiability of criminal punishment, and criminal law in general, is closely connected to the *un*justifiability of our retaliating against those who wrong us. That people are inclined to retaliate against those who wrong them, often with good excuse but rarely with adequate justification, creates a rational

---

[1] For those who accept that ancient criminal law had this *raison d'être* but who doubt whether it has done much to shape criminal law 'as we know it today', I commend J Horder, 'The Duel and the English Law of Homicide', *Oxford Journal of Legal Studies* 12 (1992), 419.

[2] For instance, PF Strawson, 'Freedom and Resentment', *Proceedings of the British Academy* 48 (1962), 187; JM Finnis, 'Punishment and Pedagogy', *The Oxford Review* 5 (1967), 83; JG Murphy and J Hampton, *Forgiveness and Mercy* (1988); MS Moore, 'The Moral Worth of Retribution' in F Schoeman (ed), *Responsibility, Character, and the Emotions* (1987).

pressure for social practices which tend to take the heat out of the situation and remove some of the temptation to retaliate, eliminating in the process some of the basis for excusing those who do so. In the modern world, the criminal law has become the most ubiquitous, sophisticated, and influential repository of such practices. Indeed, it seems to me, this displacement function of the criminal law always was and remains today one of the central pillars of its justification.

This is not to deny the justificatory importance of the criminal law's many other functions, several of which obviously do focus on the activities of offenders. As students of criminal law, we have all been brought up on the idea that the various arguments for having such an institution are rivals, each of which takes the wind out of the others' sails. We must therefore decide whether we are retributivists, or rehabilitationists, or preventionists, or reintegrationists, or whatever else may be the penological flavour of the month. If we insist on an intellectual pick-and-mix, we are told, we can maybe get away with allocating different arguments strictly to different stages of the justification, e.g. deterrence to the purpose of criminal law in general and retribution to the justification of its punitive responses in individual cases.[3] Still, we must make sure the rival arguments are kept strictly in their separate logical spaces, or else, according to received wisdom, they tend to use up their force in clashes with each other.[4] To my way of thinking, however, this supposed rivalry among justifications for criminal law and its punitive responses is illusory. The criminal law (even when its responses are non-punitive) habitually wreaks such havoc in people's lives, and its punitive side is such an extraordinary abomination, that it patently needs all the justificatory help it can get. If we believe it should remain a fixture in our legal

---

[3] The classic version of such a structured hybrid justification is HLA Hart, 'Prolegomenon to the Principles of Punishment' reprinted in his *Punishment and Responsibility* (1968). A different variation is to be found in A von Hirsch, *Censure and Sanctions* (1993).

[4] For more or less frank expressions of this anxiety, see N Lacey, *State Punishment: Political Principles and Community Values* (1988), 46ff, especially at 52; PH Robinson, 'Hybrid Principles for the Distribution of Criminal Sanctions', *Northwestern University Law Review* 82 (1987), 19, especially at 31–34; ND Walker, *Why Punish?* (1991), 135–136; RA Duff, 'Penal Communications: Recent Work in the Philosophy of Punishment', *Crime and Justice* 20 (1996), 1 at 8. More theoretically puritanical critics go further, and argue that mixing different arguments for the justification of punishment is doomed irrespective of attempts to keep them in separate logical spaces, e.g. J Morison, 'Hart's Excuses: Problems with a Compromise Theory of Punishment' in P Leith and P Ingram (eds), *The Jurisprudence of Orthodoxy* (1988); A Norrie, *Law, Ideology and Punishment* (1991), 125–135.

and political system, we cannot afford to dispense with or disdain any of the various things, however modest and localized, which can be said in its favour.[5] Each must be called upon to make whatever justificatory contribution it is capable of making. If and to the extent that the criminal law deters wrongdoing, that is one thing to be said in its favour. If and to the extent that it leads wrongdoers to confront and repent their wrongs, then that counts in its favour too. Likewise, the power of the criminal law, such as it is, to bring people with mental health problems into contact with those who can treat their conditions, to settle and maintain the internal standards of success for social practices such as marriage and share-dealing, and to stand up for those who cannot stand up for themselves. Even apparently trivial factors such as the role of the criminal law in validating and invalidating people's household insurance claims must be given their due weight. All of these considerations, and many others besides, add up to give the institution whatever justification it may have, and to the extent that any of them lapse or fail, the case for abolition of the criminal law comes a step closer to victory.

It is true, of course, that sometimes the considerations conflict, i.e. in some cases some of the considerations which support the criminal law's existence point to its reacting in one way while others point to its reacting in a dramatically different way, or not reacting at all. Sometimes it is even the case that considerations which partly support the criminal law's existence turn against it, and partly support its eradication. The only general thing that can be said of such conflict cases is that they reinforce still further the need for the criminal law to muster whatever considerations it can in its own defence, since by their nature these cases pit additional arguments against whatever course the law adopts for itself. So the existence of such cases strengthens, rather than weakens, my main point. It is also true that different arguments contribute to justifying different aspects or parts of the criminal law to greater or lesser extents. Considerations of deterrence do not support the criminalization of activities which cannot effectively be deterred by criminalization, and considerations of rehabilitation do not support the criminal conviction of people who cannot effectively be rehabilitated. In similar vein, the criminal law's function of displacing retaliation by or on behalf of victims does not support the criminalization of victimless wrongs, or of wrongs whose victims do not offer or inspire

---

[5] Contrast the position recommended by AGN Flew in 'The Justification of Punishment' in HB Acton (ed), *The Philosophy of Punishment* (1969), where the justification of punishment is held to be 'overdetermined' by the many reasons which count in favour of punishment.

retaliatory responses. Criminalizing these wrongs will fall to be justified on an accumulation of other grounds, or else not at all. That still leaves the displacement function, however, as a central pillar of the criminal law's justification. By describing it as a central pillar, I mean only that some core parts of the edifice of the modern criminal law cannot properly remain standing, in spite of the existence of other valid supporting arguments, in the absence of the law's continuing ability to pre-empt reprisals against wrongdoers. In this chapter, accordingly, I want to sketch some of the major and (I believe) escalating difficulties of principle and practice faced by the modern criminal law in attempting to fulfil this displacement function and keep the heart of its edifice intact.

2. Humanity and justice

To continue fulfilling its displacement function satisfactorily has always been a grave challenge for the criminal law, because by the nature of the endeavour there is very little margin for error. On the one hand, the criminal law's medicine must be strong enough to control the toxins of bitterness and resentment which course through the veins of those who are wronged, or else the urge to retaliate in kind will persist unchecked. On pain of losing a central pillar of its justification, therefore, the criminal law cannot afford to downplay too much its punitive ingredient, the suffering or deprivation which it can deliberately inflict on the offender in response to the wrong. In the end, particularly in the absence of genuine contrition from the offender, that deliberate infliction of suffering or deprivation may be all the law can deliver to bring the victim towards what the psychotherapists now call 'closure', the time when she can put the wrong behind her, finally laying to rest her retaliatory urge. On the other hand, the law's medicine against that same retaliatory urge cannot be allowed to become worse than the affliction it exists to control. It must stop short of institutionalizing the various forms of hastiness, cruelty, intemperance, impatience, vindictiveness, self-righteousness, fanaticism, fickleness, intolerance, prejudice and gullibility that the unchecked desire to retaliate tends to bring with it. On pain of sacrificing a central pillar of its justification, therefore, the criminal law cannot simply act as the proxy retaliator any more than it can simply dilute its punitive side to the point where it is incapable of pacifying would-be retaliators.

As if this perennial predicament were not difficult enough for the criminal law, two further rational constraints upon the modern State have only served to compound the problem as we face it today. The first is the modern State's powerful duty of humanity towards each of its subjects. To avoid surrendering the whole basis of its authority—as the servant of its people—the modern State in all of its manifestations is bound to treat each of those over whom it exercises that authority as a thinking, feeling human being rather than, for instance, an entry on a computer, a commodity to be traded, a beast to be tamed, a social problem, an evil spirit, a pariah, or an untouchable. The anonymous bureaucratic machinery of the modern State which came into existence to honour this duty is also, notoriously, the main contemporary cause of its violation. It is a depressingly short step from stopping thinking of someone as a serf to starting thinking of them as a statistic. But even if the pitfalls of bureaucratization are avoided, the practice of punishing criminal offenders inevitably calls the State's humane record into question, because of the element of deliberately inflicted suffering or deprivation which punishment by definition imports. Such an infliction of suffering or deprivation by the State cannot be justified solely on the ground that worse suffering or deprivation will be avoided as a result, even if the suffering which will be avoided as a result is suffering that would otherwise be deliberately inflicted on that very same person by other people's reprisals against her. The State's duty of humanity to each person has an agent-relative aspect, i.e. it emphasizes the State's own inhumanity towards a person and not just the sum total of inhumanity towards her which occurs within the State's jurisdiction or under its gaze.[6] This means that, other things being equal, the State's proper response to the fact that a wrongdoer is faced with the threat of retaliation is to protect the wrongdoer rather than to punish her, even if, thanks to the ruthlessness and cunning of the would-be retaliators, punishing her promises to be more effective in reducing her overall suffering.[7]

For punishment to be a morally acceptable alternative to protection, the State has to assure itself not only that the measure of punishment controls retaliation while stopping short of becoming a mere institutionalization

---

[6] I cannot offer a proper defence of this claim here. For those who are interested, the basis of such a defence lies in the fact that the moral duties under discussion in this section occupy the lower level of a two-level approach to moral reasoning. They summarize and organize certain ultimate moral considerations, but are not ultimate moral considerations themselves.

[7] That might include, e.g., providing a safe house, or taking criminal libel proceedings against those who make public accusations in a way which will incite reprisal. The demand for protection applies *a fortiori* to those who did wrong but who were acquitted at law, where reprisals not only threaten the wrongdoer but also challenge the law's own authority to deal with the wrong.

of the retaliator's excesses, but also that the act of punishment affirms, rather than denies, the punished person's status as a thinking, feeling human being. That is not impossible. Many familiar features of modern criminal law, including some important substantive doctrines of the general part as well as many procedural, evidential and sentencing standards, reflect the State's successive efforts to meet this condition. Together, these features are supposed to ensure that trial and punishment for a criminal offence affirms the moral agency and moral responsibility of the offender, and in the process (since moral agency and moral responsibility represent a significant part of what it is to be a human being) affirms the offender's humanity.[8] For the reasons just outlined, I regard the constancy of this affirmation as a *sine qua non* of the criminal law's legitimacy. In saying this I am not retreating from my earlier claim that the function of displacing reprisals against wrongdoers is a central pillar of the criminal law's justification. I am only adding the complication that, for better or worse, this function cannot always be legitimately performed by the criminal law.

That point is reinforced when we move from the State's duty of humanity to its parallel, and no less important, duty of justice. Questions of justice, unlike questions of humanity, are questions about how people are to be treated *relative to one another*. Some contemporary political philosophers imagine that all questions dealt with by the institutions of the modern State should be dealt with, first and foremost, as questions of justice. 'Justice,' as John Rawls put it, 'is the first virtue of social institutions.'[9] The basic thought behind this view is the sound liberal one that under modern conditions the State should keep its distance from its people, leaving them free to make their own mistakes. Casting all questions for the State in terms of justice is one possible way to ensure this distance because, as the old adage goes, justice is blind. To do its relativizing work, justice must isolate criteria (although not necessarily the same criteria in every context) for differentiating among those who come before it. And to give these criteria of differentiation some rational purchase, they must be implemented against a background of assumed, but often entirely

---

[8] I have discussed some aspects of the substantive criminal law which contribute to this aim in J Gardner, 'On the General Part of the Criminal Law' in RA Duff (ed), *Philosophy and the Criminal Law* (1998).

[9] J Rawls, *A Theory of Justice* (1971), 3. Rawls's slogan can bear various interpretations apart from the rather literal one I have adopted in the text. On one very different interpretation, Rawls was only saying that justice is the *last resort* of social institutions, i.e. when all else fails social institutions should at the very least be just. See J Waldron, 'When Justice Replaces Affection', *Harvard Journal of Law and Public Policy* 11 (1988), 625.

fictitious, uniformity. The just person, if you like, refuses to take sides in order to take sides; she artificially blinds herself to some qualities of people and aspects of their lives in order to be able to make something of the other differences between them. Rawls memorably conveyed the idea when he spoke of 'the veil of ignorance' behind which just policies are conceived.[10] Now, as many of Rawls's critics have demonstrated, it is very doubtful whether cultivating this kind of artificial blindness to some of our qualities and some aspects of our lives is the proper way for the modern State as a whole to keep its distance from us. It leads to the wrong kind of distance, a remote and sometimes callous disinterest in people's well-being, which the State cannot legitimately, or even (some say) intelligibly, maintain across the board.[11] On the other hand, there is very good reason to think that at least one set of institutions belonging to the modern State, viz the courts of law, should normally keep their distance from us in precisely this way. Courts are law-applying institutions, and it is in the nature of modern law, with its rule of law aspiration to apply more or less uniformly to all of those who are subject to it, that questions of how people are to be treated relative to one another always come to the fore at the point of its application. If we pursue this line of thinking, which of course calls for much more detailed elaboration, justice does turn out to be the first virtue of the courts even though not of other official bodies. The courts' primary business becomes, as the law itself puts it, 'the administration of justice'.

In the criminal law context, where (if the rule of law is being followed) the substantive law is relatively clear and certain, the most obvious everyday impact of the court's role as administrator of justice is in the procedural and evidential conduct of the trial—in determining, for example, the probative relevance and prejudicial effect of certain background information about offenders and witnesses, or the acceptability of certain modes of examination-in-chief and cross-examination. In these matters the court's first priority is to specify the density of its own veil of ignorance, the scope of its own blindness, the limits of forensic cognisance.[12] And it must do the very same thing once again at the

---

[10] *A Theory of Justice*, at n 9 above, 136ff.
[11] Both the conceptual and the moral objections are represented in M Sandel, *Liberalism and the Limits of Justice* (1982), 24–28 and 135–147. Likewise, with a strikingly different twist, in J Raz, *The Morality of Freedom* (1986), 110–133 and 369ff.
[12] Isn't there a basic problem with letting an institution decide what it shall take notice of? Doesn't it have to know what it should not know in order to know whether it should know it? True enough. That is why, in trial by indictment, the *voir dire* exists to separate the function of determining what will be hidden by the veil of ignorance from

sentencing stage of the trial where the law, rightly attempting to adjust for the inevitable rigidity and coarseness of its own relatively clear offence-definitions, typically leaves the court's options more open. Of course, in approaching these sentencing options, the court cannot ignore the State's duty of humanity, in the fulfilment of which the State's law-applying institutions must also do their bit. This is a duty which also has implications for sentencing. In the name of humanity, there must always be space for something like a plea in mitigation to bring out the offender's fuller range of qualities, the wider story of his life, some of which was necessarily hidden behind the 'veil of ignorance' during the earlier parts of the trial. But we may well ask: what is it, exactly, that falls to be mitigated when a plea in mitigation is presented to the court? If I am right so far, what falls to be mitigated is none other than the sentence which is, in the court's opinion, required by justice. Identifying a just sentence is thus the proper starting point. A court which begins from some other starting point, some other prima facie position, is a court which fails to observe its primary, and indeed one may be tempted to say definitive, duty.

Again, nothing in this proposal detracts from my original claim that the control of reprisal is a central pillar of the criminal law's justification. The proposal merely introduces a further troublesome complication. The complication is that, while the control of reprisal forms a key part of the argument for having criminal law and its punitive responses in the first place, those who must implement the criminal law and its punitive responses cannot legitimately make the control of reprisal part of *their* argument for doing so.[13] Displacement of retaliation is a reason for punishment which cannot be one of the judge's reasons for punishing. Judges cannot begin their reasoning at the sentencing stage by asking: what sentence would mollify the victim and his sympathizers? Instead they should always begin by asking: what sentence would be just? I should stress that I am not assuming at the outset that these two questions are unconnected. At this stage I mean

the function of deliberating about guilt and innocence behind the veil of ignorance. This double-insulation against unwitting prejudice provides a major part of the case for retaining a right to jury trial whenever serious criminal charges are laid. On the question of a criminal charge's seriousness, see sections 3 and 4 below.

[13] This helps us to see why as theorists we should not fear the multiplicity of considerations which add up to justify the practice of criminal punishment. As administrators of justice, judges are heavily restricted in their access to many of these considerations, and thus do not have to face all the conflicts among them in their raw form. I have discussed this in greater depth in J Gardner, 'The Purity and Priority of Private Law', *University of Toronto Law Journal* 46 (1996), 459.

to leave open the possibility that, for example, victims and their supporters might want nothing more than the very justice which it is the court's role to dispense, so that doing justice will reliably serve that ulterior purpose. My only point is that the courts should not share in this ulterior purpose themselves; they should insist on thinking in terms of justice irrespective of whether doing so serves the further purpose of pacifying retaliators. For the criminal court, justice is an end, and that remains true even if, for the criminal justice system as a whole, justice is at best a means. In this respect the criminal court in a modern State is a classic bureaucratic institution. It has certain *functions* which cannot figure in its *mission*, and which therefore cannot directly animate its actions.

It is not surprising that this distinctively bureaucratic aspect of courts, and especially criminal courts, has been a cause for much complaint, particularly among victims of crime and their sympathizers, who accuse the courts of leaving them out in the cold, being out of touch with their concerns, stealing their cases away from them, etc. I already mentioned the challenge of maintaining a humane bureaucracy, and maintaining humanity towards victims is an aspect of that challenge to which I will return at the very end of this chapter. But in the context of the criminal law, the pre-eminence of the court's duty of justice creates a prior difficulty, which this discussion was designed to highlight, and aspects of which will occupy our attention over the next few pages. As I explained before, in fulfilling its displacement function the criminal law must always walk a fine line between failing to pacify would-be retaliators and simply institutionalizing their excesses. What we have just added is that under modern conditions an extended section of this fine line, the section which passes through the domain of the courts, must be walked wearing justice's blindfold. What hope can we have for the criminal law's fulfilment of its displacement function under these conditions?

3. The proportionality principle

In exploring this question, I want to focus attention on one particular principle of justice which is of profound moral importance for the criminal courts in their sentencing decisions, namely the principle that the punishment, if any, should be in proportion to the crime. I choose this principle not only because of its moral importance (to the explanation of which I will return presently), but also because so many people apparently read it as a principle which focuses on how the offender is to be treated relative to her victim or victims, and thus see it as a straightforward way of having the retaliatory impulses of victims systematically reflected in the administration of justice. To my mind, this victim-oriented reading is a serious misreading of the proportionality principle. The State's duty of justice, like the State's duty of humanity, has an important agent-relative aspect. The relativities with which the modern courts must principally contend under the rubric of justice are relativities between the State's treatment of different people, not relativities between how the State treats someone and how that someone treated someone else.[14] Therefore the question of proportionality in sentencing which concerns a modern criminal court is primarily the question of whether this offender's sentence stands to his crime as other offenders' sentences stood to their crimes. This means that the proportionality principle does not in itself specify or even calibrate the scale of punishments which the State may implement, but simply indicates how different people's punishments (or to be exact their prima facie punishments before any mitigating factors are brought to bear) should stand *vis-à-vis* one another on that scale.[15]

It does not automatically follow from this, however, that the victim's predicament or perspective cannot properly be introduced into the court's deliberations under the heading of proportionality. According to the proportionality principle, the sentence in a criminal case should be proportionate to *the crime*. If the court can point to features of the crime committed in the case at hand which make it more or less grave than other comparable crimes that have been dealt with by the courts, then the proportionality principle plainly points to a corresponding adjustment of the prima facie sentence. It means that everything turns on the applicable conception of 'the crime' and the specification of its axes of gravity. Now it may be thought that the law itself sets these parameters, so that the matter is simply a technical legal one. Crime, some will say, is a purely legal category, and a crime is none other than an action or activity which meets the conditions set by law for criminal conviction.[16] Thus

---

[14] See n 6 above.

[15] Thus I am going to be writing about what von Hirsch calls 'ordinal proportionality' rather than 'cardinal proportionality': A von Hirsch, *Censure and Sanctions* (1993), 18–19. As it happens I also believe in a principle of cardinal proportionality, but it has a very different foundation and applies to the legislative business of setting sentencing maxima rather than to the sentencing stage of criminal trials. It is also worth mentioning that both cardinal and ordinal principles of proportionality need to be applied with the State's duty of humanity in mind, since this forbids cruel or brutalizing punishments even when these would be proportionate. None of this affects the substance of my argument.

[16] G Williams, 'The Definition of Crime', *Current Legal Problems* 8 (1995), 107.

'the crime' referred to in the principle of proportionality can be none other than the crime as legally defined. It would follow that whether the victim's predicament or perspective is relevant under the heading of proportionality would depend only on whether the legal definition of the crime made specific mention of it. A crime defined in terms of the suffering or loss inflicted upon its victim would leave space for, even perhaps require, the degree of that suffering or loss to be brought to bear on the sentence under the proportionality principle, thus giving some aspects of the victim's predicament or perspective a role in the court's deliberations under the heading of justice. But a crime without such a definitional feature would naturally leave no such space and offer no such role to victim-centred considerations.

In fact, the problem is much more complicated than this. It is true that crimes are, in one ('institutional') sense, just activities which meet the conditions for criminal conviction. But criminal conviction is an all-or-nothing business. Questions of gravity can certainly be a relevant factor, on occasions, in determining which of a number of related crimes the accused should be convicted of, e.g. whether he is a murderer or a manslaughterer, a robber or a thief, etc. But for any *single* criminal offence considered by the jury or magistrate, the ultimate answer can only be guilty or not guilty; gravity is neither here nor there.[17] What is more, where the rule of law is properly observed, criminal offences are defined so as to facilitate exactly this kind of all-or-nothing decision-making. Rape, in England, is sexual intercourse without consent undertaken in the knowledge of, or reckless as to, the lack of consent. Grey areas and borderline cases of consent, sexual intercourse, knowledge and recklessness have all been, so far as possible, defined out.[18] There is nothing in the definition of rape, apart perhaps from the difference between the knowing rapist and the reckless one,[19] that could conceivably afford a sentencing judge any significant axis of gravity.

---

[17] It is true that the Scots allow for 'not proven' as a *tertium quid*, but of course it still has nought to do with the gravity of the crime. The US solution of 'first degree' and 'second degree' crimes may look at first like another counterexample, but all it does in reality is multiply the number of separate crimes to which the all-or-nothing guilty/not guilty decision must be applied.

[18] *R v Olugboja* (1981) 73 Cr App Rep 344 and *R v Linekar* [1995] 2 Cr App Rep 49 illustrate the law's attempts to turn certain grey areas between consent and non-consent into brighter lines. *Kaitamaki v R* [1985] AC 147 does the same with respect to 'sexual intercourse'. The mens rea elements were hotly debated in the early 1980s, but the debate was simply between two different ways of artificially stripping grey areas from the concept of recklessness, the broader contrived definition in *R v Pigg* [1982] 2 All ER 591 giving way to the narrower one in *R v Satnam S* (1983) 78 Cr App Rep 149.

[19] cf *R v Bashir* (1982) 77 Cr App Rep 327.

So does the proportionality principle, by itself, prescribe the same sentence for all knowing rapists, irrespective of their brutality, treachery, bigotry, cowardliness, arrogance, and malice? This challenge cannot be avoided by observing that most crimes do harbour some residual questions of degree in their definitions—that grievous bodily harm is more grievous in some cases than in others, that some acts of dishonesty are more dishonest than others, etc. That is not the point. The point is that, where the rule of law is observed, individual criminal offences are not defined in law so as to retain a topography of gravity for the sentencing stage, but rather so as to flatten that topography, so far as possible, for the all-or-nothing purposes of conviction and acquittal. There is no reason to think that a definition crafted primarily for one purpose, viz that of flattening the rational variation between different cases of the same wrong, should be regarded as authoritatively determining the scope of the court's veil of ignorance when its job turns, at the sentencing stage, from eliminating such rational variation to highlighting it. There is no reason to assume that the court will find all, or any, of the relevant variables still inscribed on the face of the crime's definition.

It follows that, for the purpose of the principle that the sentence should be in proportion to the crime, we need to go beyond a purely institutional conception of the crime. I do not mean to write off all institutional circumscriptions. It seems to me to be a sound rule of thumb, for example, that evidence which was inadmissible in the trial on grounds of its irrelevance to the charge before the court should not be taken into account when the gravity of the crime is being assessed for the purposes of proportionate sentencing. That an act of dangerous driving caused death should be treated as irrelevant to the gravity of the crime if the crime charged is dangerous driving rather than causing death by dangerous driving. No doubt this is bound to frustrate victims of crime and their sympathizers who may have little patience with the due process principle that people should only be tried for the crimes with which they are charged and sentenced for the crimes which were proved against them at trial—recall that the predictability of such impatience was among the factors which justified the State in monopolizing retaliatory force to begin with. But be that as it may, the due process principle *itself* requires that we go beyond a merely institutional conception of the crime. To implement the principle of due process, just as to implement the principle of proportionality in sentencing, we need some grasp not only of the crime's legal definition but equally of what counts as the *substance* or the *gist* or the *point* of the crime as legally defined—and that is an unavoidably evaluative, non-positivistic issue.[20]

Here, for example, are a couple of classic due process questions. Apart from the charge spelt out in the indictment or summons, were there other lesser offences with which the accused was also implicitly being charged, which did not need to be spelt out? And when does the defendant's previous wrongdoing pass the 'similar fact' test, so that evidence of it is relevant for the purposes of proving the offence charged on the present indictment? Lawyers have often struggled to answer these questions in institutional terms, by pointing to features of crimes which figure in the positive legal definitions.[21] But that, as we should all have realized by now, was always a false hope. One cannot apply or even adequately understand these questions without developing what we may like to call the moral map of the crime, highlighting evaluative significances which may be missing from the law's pared down definition. Thus even if, as I suggested, the principle of proportionality in sentencing does usefully borrow some institutional circumscriptions from the due process principle, that ultimately just reiterates rather than eliminates the fundamentally evaluative, non-positivistic question of what counts as 'the crime' for the purposes of assessing the proportionate prima facie sentence. One still needs a moral map of the crime, and the question remains, after all this, of whether the predicament or perspective of the victim can figure anywhere on that map.

4. Perspectives on crime

One significant strand of the literature on criminal law and criminal justice proceeds from the thought that many, if not all, crimes are covered by one and the same moral map. This is the map of the offender's *blameworthiness* or *culpability*. Following this map leads to a specific interpretation of the principle of proportionality, according to which making the sentence proportionate to the crime means making the sentence

---

[20] This is not a criticism of legal positivism. Legal positivists hold that validity of a law turns on its sources rather than its merits. That does not prevent them from holding that legal reasoning reflects on the merits as well as the sources of laws, since there is no reason to suppose that legal reasoning is only reasoning about legal validity. See J Raz, 'On the Autonomy of Legal Reasoning', *Ratio Juris* 6 (1993), 1.

[21] See *R v Novac* (1977) 65 Cr App Rep 107 and *R v Barrington* [1981] 1 All ER 1132 to see how the issue arises in relation to the similar fact doctrine; concerning counts in an indictment, the issue is well-illustrated in the leading case of *R v Wilson* [1984] 1 AC 242.

proportionate to the offender's blameworthiness or culpability in committing the crime.[22] Let's call this the 'blameworthiness interpretation' of the proportionality principle. In the minds of many adherents as well as many critics, the proportionality principle in its blameworthiness interpretation systematically excludes victim-centred considerations from the proper scope of the court's prima facie sentencing deliberations. The pivotal thought behind this is that a person's blameworthiness in acting as she did is a function of how things seemed to her at the time of her action.[23] It may of course be a more or less complex function. On some accounts of the function, blameworthiness increases or decreases according to how much of the evil of her action the agent appreciated. For others, it is a question of how much the agent should have appreciated, given the various other things she knew at the time. Either way, the crucial manoeuvre so far as blameworthiness is concerned is supposedly to look at the situation *ex ante*, from the perspective of the perpetrator. But that perspective, it is often claimed or assumed, is fundamentally at odds with the perspective of the victim, who looks at the wrong *ex post* and is interested not so much in how things may have seemed to the perpetrator, but rather in how things actually occurred or turned out.[24] On this view, the victim and those who sympathize with him are aggrieved first and foremost because of what he suffered or lost at the

[22] A random selection: H Gross, 'Culpability and Desert' in RA Duff and N Simmonds (ed), *Philosophy and the Criminal Law* (ARSP Beiheft 19, 1984), 59; CL Ten, *Crime, Guilt, and Punishment* (1987), 155ff; A Ashworth, 'Taking the Consequences' in S Shute, J Gardner and J Horder (eds), *Action and Value in Criminal Law* (1994), 107 at 116–120. Von Hirsch also makes culpability the only axis of crime-seriousness when he introduces the proportionality principle on p 15 of *Censure and Sanctions* (1993). But contrast the more complex 'harm-plus-culpability' standard used for proportionality on p 29 of the same volume, and elsewhere in von Hirsch's work, e.g. in his *Past or Future Crimes* (1985), 64ff. See further n 30 below.

[23] Among diverse writers who allocate blameworthiness on these terms, we find D Parfit, *Reasons and Persons* (1986), 24–25; S Sverdlik, 'Crime and Moral Luck', *American Philosophical Quarterly* 25 (1988), 79; R Swinburne, *Responsibility and Atonement* (1989), 34–35; D Husak and A von Hirsch, 'Culpability and Mistake of Law' in *Action and Value in Criminal Law*, at n 22 above; A Ashworth, 'Belief, Intent and Criminal Liability' in J Eekelaar and J Bell (eds), *Oxford Essays in Jurisprudence: Third Series* (1987), 1 at 7.

[24] Talk of the 'victim perspective' and the 'perpetrator perspective' on wrongdoing will be familiar to those conversant with the literature on anti-discrimination law. See AD Freeman, 'Legitimizing Racial Discrimination through Antidiscrimination Law: A Critical Review of Supreme Court Doctrine', *Minnesota Law Review* 62 (1978), 1049. The version of the distinction relied upon here is slightly less ambitious than Freeman's, although the two are closely related. The distinction I am speaking of figures prominently in Sverdlik, 'Crime and Moral Luck' and in A Ashworth, 'Punishment and Compensation: Victims, Offenders and the State', *Oxford Journal of Legal Studies* 6 (1986), 86 at 96. cf also J Coleman, 'Crimes, Kickers and Transaction Structures' in

perpetrator's hands, whether or not the perpetrator appreciated or could have appreciated the full extent of this loss or suffering at the time of acting. If that is so, then the conception of the crime which lies at the heart of the proportionality principle on its blameworthiness interpretation is not the victim's conception. In fact it is diametrically opposed to the victim's conception. If anything, the proportionality principle in this interpretation seems to oblige courts systematically to *compound* the frustration of victims and their sympathizers, and hence to *aggravate* their retaliatory instinct, by insisting on seeing things the offender's way and hence (through the already aggrieved eyes of victims and their sympathizers) doggedly taking the offender's side in the whole conflict. Thus, on this view of the matter, fidelity to the proportionality principle scarcely militates in favour of the sentencing process making a systematic positive contribution to the fulfilment of the criminal law's displacement function.

There is, however, a great deal of confusion in this line of thinking. I can only scratch the surface of a few of the problems here. The problems start with a failure to spell out what blameworthiness or culpability *is*, which leads to an oversimplification of the principles on which it is incurred. Blameworthiness has a four-part formula. To be blameworthy, one must: (a) have done something wrong and (b) have been responsible for doing it, while lacking (c) justification and (d) excuse for having done it. Each of elements (a), (b), (c) and (d) can undoubtedly be sensitive, to some extent and in some respects and on some occasions, to how things seemed to the blameworthy person at the time of her action. Elements (c) and (d) in fact incorporate an across-the-board partial sensitivity to the *ex ante* perspective of the perpetrator. Take element (c) first. An action is *justifiable* if the reasons in favour of it are not defeated by the reasons against; but it is *justified* only if the agent acts for one or more of those undefeated reasons.[25] It follows that a purported justification based on considerations unknown to and unsuspected by the agent at the time of the action is no justification at all. Thus justification always does depend, in part, on how things seemed to the agent at the time of the action. Conversely, justification also depends, in part, on how things actually were. No matter how things seemed to the agent, if the reason

JR Pennock and JW Chapman (eds), *Nomos XXVII: Criminal Justice* (1985), 313 on the contrasting 'economic' and 'moral' perspectives of tort law and criminal law.
    [25] I have defended this account of justification in J Gardner, 'Justifications and Reasons' in AP Simester and ATH Smith (eds), *Harm and Culpability* (1996), 103 (Chapter 5 in this volume).

for which she acted was not in fact an undefeated one then she can has no justification. If she fails the test of justification on this score, the agent must retreat to element (d), the excuse element, to resist the allegation of blameworthiness. Here we find an additional sensitivity to the *ex ante* perspective of the perpetrator: here the agent can rely on what she mistakenly *took* to be undefeated reasons for her action, provided only that she was justified in her mistake. But again this last proviso shows that even excuses are not entirely insensitive to how things actually were; for whether the agent was excused by her mistakes depends on whether her mistakes were justified, and that in turn depends, like any justification, on whether there really were undefeated reasons for her to see the world as she did.[26] So in both elements (c) and (d) we have questions which focus on how things seemed to the agent *as well as* questions which focus on how things really were. Justification and excuse have some across-the-board agent-perspectival dimensions, but are neither of them a pure function of how things seemed to the agent at the time of the action.

Things get more complicated still when we add elements (a) and (b) to the stew. It is tempting to think that wrong action is the mirror image of right or justified action, so that, adapting from the account of right or justified action just outlined, whether one's action is wrong depends on whether the reasons in favour of performing it were defeated by the reasons against and whether one acted for one of the latter reasons. Thus obviously no action could be wrong if the agent had no inkling of anything that made it wrong. But right and wrong are in fact dramatically asymmetrical. There are many more ways of doing the wrong thing than there are of doing the right thing. In particular, there is no general sensitivity of wrongdoing to the reasons for which one acted. It is perfectly true that some wrongs, e.g. deceit and betrayal, cannot be committed without certain knowledge or belief on the part of the person who commits them, and others, such as torture and extortion, require a certain intention. But this is not true of all wrongs. One may do wrong by breaking a promise or neglecting one's children quite irrespective of what one knew or had reason to know, and *a fortiori* quite irrespective of why one did it. The same holds true, I believe, of killing people or wounding them, damaging their property, poisoning them, and countless other wrongs which are of enduring importance for the criminal law. It is wrong to kill people or wound them, and one may kill someone or wound them by playing with intriguing buttons or switches which were none of one's proper concern, quite irrespective of whether one

[26]   ibid, at 118–122.

knew or had grounds to know the true awfulness of what one was doing. If one's *ex ante* perspective is to be relevant to one's blameworthiness in respect of such killings or woundings, on this view, it must be relevant by virtue of some other element of blameworthiness, such as the justification or excuse element. To be sure, it may also be relevant to one's responsibility, element (b) of the blameworthiness equation. But again its relevance here can only be occasional and limited. To deny that one was a responsible agent one must not only deny that one knew what one was doing, but also point to some underlying explanation such as psychotic delusion, infancy, or (on some views of the phenomenon) hypnosis which puts one temporarily or permanently out of reach of reason so that normal rational standards of justification and excuse do not apply to one. This is a very limited (and decidedly bottom-of-the-barrel) opening for one's ignorance to affect one's blameworthiness. So again, there is nothing here to make blameworthiness, in general, into a function of how things seemed to the agent at the time of his or her action. In fact, the influence of elements (a) and (b) in the blameworthiness equation fragments and complicates the conditions of blameworthiness even further, so that very few things can be said, in general, about the balance of agent-perspectival and non-agent-perspectival factors which will bear on the net blameworthiness of the agent.

Whatever one may think about the details of this elaboration of the conditions of blameworthiness, it draws attention to one crucial point which is far too easily overlooked. The crucial point is that there is no such thing as blameworthiness at large, or blameworthiness *tout court*. Our blameworthiness is necessarily our blameworthiness in respect of some specific action or activity we engaged in, such as killing, wounding, deceiving, betraying, torturing, or breaking a promise.[27] And whether

---

[27] While we are blameworthy only in respect of actions, we are *to blame* in respect of consequences. To be to blame for a given consequence, we must be *responsible for* that consequence. Doesn't this complicate element (b) of my blameworthiness equation, which spoke only of responsibility for *actions* and therefore (you may say) swept under the carpet the further agent-perspectival conditions of responsibility for consequences? The answer is no. Whether we are responsible for consequences is already taken into account in element (a) of the blameworthiness equation. In the relevant sense, we are responsible for those consequences which contribute constitutively to the wrongness of our doing as we do. We are *to blame* for those consequences, accordingly, when that condition is met and elements (b), (c) and (d) of blameworthiness are also present. There is thus no further question, on top of those already anticipated in my blameworthiness equation, of whether our responsibility or blame extends to a particular unforeseen or unforeseeable consequence of our actions. Much effort in moral and legal philosophy has been wasted thanks to the mistaken assumption that one has two bites at the cherry: first one can deny that one was blameworthy in respect of the action and then one can deny,

and to what extent our blameworthiness is a function of how things seemed to us at the time of our action depends in very large measure on *which* action or activity we are supposed to be blameworthy in respect of, since different agent-perspectival conditions for blameworthiness evidently come into play for different actions and activities. Now there are those who try to make the determination of which action or activity we engaged in *itself* a function of the way things seemed to us at the time when we acted. Their response to my example of the person who kills unwittingly by playing with intriguing buttons and switches is to deny that it involves a killing, not because killing in particular is held to be, like deceit, an action with some definitive knowledge requirement, but rather because the scope of agency is always, so to speak, in the eyes of the agent. Fundamentally, we do only whatever we take ourselves to be doing.[28] Personally, I find this a deeply counterintuitive account of human agency.[29] But more importantly for present purposes, if this account of human agency is accepted, it makes a mockery of the process of determining blameworthiness which I outlined in the previous paragraph. We cannot ask, as I asked in the last paragraph, whether the killer was a responsible agent when he killed, or whether he had any justifications or excuses for doing it. For on this account of human agency *there was no killing*. The most the agent did was press buttons, or fiddle with things that didn't concern him. Having no possible inkling of the death-dealing aspect of what he was doing, he didn't kill anyone. All the hard work which the piecemeal doses of subjectivity in the separate elements of blameworthiness were supposed to do is thus pre-empted by a massive and all-consuming injection of subjectivity in the doctrine of human agency to which it is applied. We are not deprived of our (admittedly controversial and seriously under-specified) answer to the question of whether the button-presser was a blameworthy killer. *We are summarily deprived of the question itself.*

If we rescue the question, as I am sure we should, by jettisoning the extremely restrictive account of human agency which put it out of

separately, that the blameworthiness extended to a given consequence of the action. In fact the correct answer to the first question necessarily settles the second.

[28] cf Elizabeth Anscombe's misleading remark in *Intention* (2nd edn, 1963), 53: 'What happens must be given by observation; but ... my knowledge of what I do is not by observation.' A Ashworth's 'Taking the Consequences', above n 22, is an example of a work which rigorously implements the highly subjectivized account of agency which this remark may be taken to support.

[29] I also believe it is incoherent: see 'On the General Part of the Criminal Law', above n 8.

bounds, we can instantly see that the juxtaposition with which this section began was grievously exaggerated. There is no automatic and comprehensive opposition between assessing the gravity of a crime in terms of the offender's blameworthiness and assessing the gravity of a crime according to the way it impacts upon its victim. That is because, to assess the offender's blameworthiness we must begin by asking 'blameworthiness in respect of which action?' and this requires us to interrogate our account of human agency. Since on any plausible account of human agency there can be actions which are, like killing and wounding, defined at least partly in terms of their actual impact upon other people independently of the way things seemed *ex ante* to the perpetrator, it follows that an inquiry into the perpetrator's blameworthiness cannot be made independent of this impact. In fact, if we were to examine more thoroughly the so-called 'victim perspective' with which we started, I think we would find that the link between the blameworthiness of an offender and what irks the victim or her sympathizers is even more intimate than this last remark suggests. I believe it is the action of killing or wounding, complete with (but not limited to) the death or wound it involves, that normally aggrieves victims and their sympathizers and sparks their retaliation. Thus the starting point of the blameworthiness inquiry—the action which was wrongful—is also the normal trigger for retaliatory responses on behalf of the victim. Of course there may be differences of perception and emphasis. It is true, for example, that *excuses* tend to be looked upon less generously by victims and their supporters than their importance for blameworthiness would indicate. Victims and their supporters may also have trouble with some justifications where their interests were not among the main reasons in favour of the justified action, and they may be more doubtful than the court might be, especially under the influence of psychiatric testimony, about a wrongdoer's supposed lack of responsibility. This means that the blameworthiness inquiry could certainly drive some wedges between the court's proportionality-driven thinking on matters of prima facie sentencing and the demands of victims and their supporters. But one only drives wedges between surfaces which are in their original tendency attached to one another. On my account, that is exactly the situation with the offender's blameworthiness and the victim's grievance. It follows that there is no fundamental opposition of perspectives, no chasm of understanding, dividing the blameworthiness interpretation of the proportionality principle from the demands of those whose retaliation must be displaced if the criminal law is to fulfil its displacement function.

Here I am talking as if the blameworthiness interpretation of the proportionality principle came out basically unscathed from the process of correcting the analysis of blameworthiness which went into it. But of course it did not.

What we have discovered in the process of explaining the concept and conditions of blameworthiness is that it makes no sense to prescribe, simply, that the sentence in a criminal trial should be in proportion to the offender's blameworthiness in committing the crime. For that prescription falls into the trap of presenting blameworthiness as an independent quantity, something that one can have more or less of *tout court*. Now that we have brought to mind the important point that blameworthiness is always blameworthiness in respect of some action, the blameworthiness interpretation in its original form should be replaced by a sharper ('modified blameworthiness') interpretation of the proportionality principle according to which the sentence should be in proportion to the offender's wrongful action, adjusted for his blameworthiness in respect of it.[30] This reinterpretation, with the slightly more complex moral map of a crime it implies, makes several important advances over the simpler blameworthiness interpretation it replaces. Let me mention just two of them here.

First, the modified blameworthiness interpretation helps to bring out what *justifies* the proportionality principle, and lends it the moral importance in the courtroom that I so confidently spoke of earlier. Although a principle of justice, the proportionality principle also contributes directly and powerfully to the court's compliance with the State's duty of humanity, and it takes much of its moral force from that contribution. As already mentioned, the State's duty of humanity requires it to affirm the moral agency and moral responsibility of those whom it punishes. The proportionality principle in its modified blameworthiness interpretation puts both the offender's agency and her responsibility centre stage. To ask about the offender's blameworthiness is to emphasize her responsibility. That is not only because element (b) of the blameworthiness equation is the element of responsibility. It is also because questions of justification

[30] Compare this with von Hirsch's more complex version of the proportionality principle, mentioned in n 22 above, which requires the crime to be in proportion to blameworthiness-plus-harm. Von Hirsch's principle comes close to mine in several ways, but still seems to leave blameworthiness as a free-floating quantity. It may be said that it does not float free because it is now attached to a harm. But harms cannot be blameworthy. Only *doing* harm can be blameworthy. If von Hirsch's principle is that the sentence should be in proportion to the harmdoing adjusted for the harmdoer's blameworthiness in respect of it, then the only thing which divides us is that I refuse to reduce all wrongdoing to harmdoing. This has consequences: see n 32 below.

and excuse—elements (c) and (d)—are applicable only to responsible agents, so that applying standards of justification and excuse to people is an assertion of their responsibility. But on top of that, the modified blameworthiness interpretation brings out the importance of questions about the offender's agency which are not highlighted in the simple blameworthiness interpretation. It reminds us that treating someone as an agent is of importance quite apart from treating them as responsible. Even someone who is not responsible for their actions is an agent, and should still be treated as one. True, the duty of humanity as I expressed it goes further, and demands that offenders be treated as *moral* agents and as *morally* responsible. This arguably introduces further complications which point to a need for some further modification of the modified blameworthiness interpretation. Nevertheless, the complications do not alter the main point, which is that by punishing people in proportion to their crimes, where those crimes are mapped according to the action which made them wrongful adjusted for the offender's blameworthiness in respect of them, the court contributes decisively to the affirmation of the offender's humanity which is a *sine qua non* of the legitimacy of any modern State punishment. But remember that this is a function of the modern State's special duty of humanity towards its people, which comes of its claim to authority and its associated role as servant of its people. Those of us who stake no similar claim to authority and have no similar role in other people's lives are not covered by the same strict humanitarian duty towards them.[31] Thus the strictness of the court's attention to questions of moral agency and moral responsibility need not, rationally, be mirrored in all interpersonal transactions between wrongdoers and people they wronged, or supporters, or even onlookers. That is one important reason why the victim of a crime and his or her sympathizers may sometimes *quite properly* (i.e. independently of their various impatiences, hastinesses, prejudices, etc.) have less time for the niceties of blameworthiness than the court is morally required to have.

Second, the modified blameworthiness interpretation has the advantage that it alerts us to the *limitations* of the proportionality principle as a principle of justice for scaling criminal sentences. The principle's usefulness depends first on the court's ability to discern what is supposed to be the wrongful action in the crime, and then the court's ability

---

[31] Although, as I have assumed throughout this paper, we all have various more limited duties of humanity towards each other. Extra-judicial punishers such as teachers and parents are covered by the State's stricter duty to the extent that they echo the State's claim to authority and its basis.

to compare this action with other actions, before it can even start to settle degrees of blameworthiness as between them. This may not always be possible. Some pairs of wrongful actions are incommensurable. It means that the proportionality scale will not always be perfectly transitive.[32] The adjustments for differential blameworthiness required by the modified blameworthiness interpretation of the proportionality principle can only take effect within the transitive parts of the scale. It may be possible to compare a less blameworthy robbery with a more blameworthy theft. But it will not necessarily be possible, even in principle, to assess a more blameworthy theft alongside, say, a more blameworthy assault. Here, sentencing practice may have to move in relatively independent grooves, with guidelines that do not add up to a comprehensive code. The axes of gravity that operate at the sentencing stage will not necessarily, or even typically, allow the gravity of each crime to be plotted relative to that of every other crime. That, in my view, is no violation of the proportionality principle, nor on the other hand, an indictment of it, but rather one of its welcome implications. The idea that all crimes are covered by a single moral map has, on closer inspection, very little to recommend it.[33]

5. Filling the displacement gap

The foregoing does something to explain how the courts, as blindfolded administrators of justice, can in spite of their blindfolds systematically help to fulfil the criminal law's displacement function. Even though the justice that victims and their sympathizers want (which is primarily justice

---

[32] In their classic article 'Gauging Criminal Harm: A Living-Standard Analysis', *Oxford Journal of Legal Studies* 11 (1991), 1, A von Hirsch and N Jareborg argued that all harms with which the criminal law should be concerned are commensurable, allowing a transitive sentencing scale under the proportionality principle. I think they are wrong about the commensurability of harms, and about the commensurability of living-standards on which their argument was based. But even if they are right, it is a long way from the doctrine that all harms are commensurable to the doctrine that all *wrongs* are commensurable, since a wrong is an action, and even when it is an action defined in terms of the harm done, the harm done is only one constituent of the wrong. This means that von Hirsch and Jareborg still have some way to go to show that the proportionality scale is transitive. And here I am granting the generous assumption that elements (b), (c) and (d) of the blameworthiness equation do not introduce yet further incommensurabilities. On the proliferation of incommensurability in an action-centred view of morality, see J Raz, *The Morality of Freedom* (1986), 321ff.

[33] See J Gardner, 'On the General Part of the Criminal Law', above n 8, for a much closer inspection.

between offender and victim) is not the justice that courts are licensed and required to provide by the proportionality principle (which is primarily justice between offender and offender), the proportionality principle, correctly interpreted, nevertheless shares some of its basic moral geography with the retaliatory logic of victims and their sympathizers. For some distance, courts and retaliators travel on the same path even though the former cannot, consistent with their mission, deliberately track the latter. But as I have also attempted to show, the two paths do diverge at certain obvious points. First, as I started section 2 ('Humanity and justice') by explaining, to preserve the legitimacy of the criminal law's monopolization of retaliation, the courts must stop short of institutionalizing the excusable but unjustifiable retaliatory excesses of victims and their sympathizers. Second, as I explained in section 3 ('The proportionality principle'), the principle of due process means that the wrongful action at the heart of the offender's crime cannot always, in the eyes of the law, and notably for the purposes of sentencing, be the same wrongful action which inspires retaliation by or on behalf of victims. The need to restrict the trial to the substance of the charges with which it began may lead to some differences between the victim's perception and the law's rendition of what the offender has done, even when the victim is not driven to retaliatory excess. Finally, the requirement to adjust the sentence for the offender's blameworthiness may, as I just explained in section 4 ('Perspectives on crime'), drive some extra wedges between the court's sense of proportionality and the victim's retaliatory inclinations, even where those inclinations are not excessive and there are no due process impediments to their reflection in law. The court, as an agent of the State, owes a duty of humanity to all which may often exceed the duty each of us owes to other people, and which therefore requires the court to affirm each offender's moral agency and moral responsibility more conscientiously than need be the case in many of our ordinary interpersonal transactions, including transactions with those who wrong us. These three factors add up to constitute what I will call the 'displacement gap' in criminal sentencing: the gap between what retaliators want and what the courts can, in good conscience, deliver.

Traditionally, this displacement gap has been filled by the law's own wealth of symbolic significances. What was confiscated from victims and their sympathizers in point of retaliatory force has traditionally been compensated by the ritual and majesty of the law, and by the message of public vindication which this ritual and majesty served to convey. At one time it was the ritual of the punishment itself which made the greatest contribution. The pillory, the stocks, the carting, the public execution and various other modes of punishment involving public display allowed the State to close the displacement gap by exhibiting the offender in all his shame and humiliation, in all his remorse and regret, while the proceedings remained under some measure of official control to limit retaliatory excess.[34] But of course a new penal age dawned in the nineteenth century which put the offender out of reach and out of sight in the prison, where measured punishment and control of retaliation could be more successfully combined, both with each other and with the new disciplinary ambitions of supervision and rehabilitation.[35] From then on, the burden of providing ritual and majesty to fill the displacement gap was to a large extent shifted off the shoulders of the punishment system (which was now practically invisible to the general public except in the gloomy expanse of the prison walls) and onto the shoulders of the trial system instead. The courts themselves now had to offer the would-be retaliator the kind of public vindication which would once have been provided by the act of punishment, and the ritual and majesty of the courtroom had to substitute for the ritual and majesty of the recantation at the gallows. Of course the pressure to get this substitution exactly right was eased by the fact that the prison would to some extent protect the offender against the retaliator even if the displacement gap had not been successfully filled by the court. But it was still crucial that the trial itself should offer the victim and his sympathizers some symbolic significances which would divert them from taking the matter into their own hands, e.g. if the offender was acquitted, or if a custodial sentence was not used, or once the custodial sentence had expired. For this purpose the court could only rely on continuing respect, indeed deference, for its own heavily ceremonial processes and practices. If the court's processes and practices were to fall into disrepute, if they came to be seen as just distracting frippery, then the vindicatory symbolism of the trial would be lost and the displacement gap would open wide for all to see. We would then face a major legitimation crisis in the system of criminal justice.

My view is that we now face this crisis in Britain, and for the very reason I have just given. During the 1980s and 1990, the steady creep of

---

[34] How could the death penalty ever have been consistent with limiting retaliatory excess? Surely nothing could ever have exceeded death? Wrong. That one died with one's soul cleansed by confession or recantation was one mercy. That one died after judicial proceedings in which one was able to put one's defence, and therefore treated as a responsible agent, was another. On the mistaken assumption that the widespread availability and use of the death penalty in early-modern England was a sign of *sheer* brutality in criminal justice policy, see JA Sharpe, *Judicial Punishment in England* (1990), 27ff.

[35] The line of thinking in this paragraph obviously owes something to M Foucault's *Discipline and Punish: The Birth of the Prison* (1977). I hesitate to specify exactly what.

the ideology of consumerism has led people to regard the courts, along with many other key public institutions, as mere 'service providers' to be judged by their instrumental achievements. League tables, customer charters, satisfaction surveys, outcome audits and efficiency scrutiny became the depressing norm. Respect for valuable public institutions declined at the same time as expectations of them increased. Even among those who took themselves to be anti-individualistic, the demand that institutions should become more 'transparent' and 'accountable' came to be regarded as orthodoxy, and euphemistic talk of 'cost-effectiveness' became acceptable. All this was, essentially, a corruption of a sound idea, which I mentioned at the outset—the idea that modern government is the servant of its people. It was mistakenly assumed that since public bureaucracies existed to serve social functions, ultimately serving people, they ought to be judged by the purely instrumental contribution they could make to those social functions, and hence their instrumental value for people. But it was forgotten that many social functions were not purely instrumental functions, i.e. many institutions made an intrinsic or constitutive contribution to their own social functions. The mission of such institutions, to return to my earlier expression, was partly integral to their function. The National Health Service and other organs of Beveridge's Welfare State are the most familiar examples in Britain; people who regard themselves as collectivists should rue the day they ever tried to defend these in purely instrumental terms, which was the day they surrendered to the creeping individualism of the consumer society. But the criminal courts exemplify the point even more perfectly. Historically, they filled the displacement gap in criminal justice by their own (to the public eye) bizarre and almost incomprehensible processes, their own special black magic if you like, which lent profound symbolic importance to their work. But armed with new consumerist ideas people came to see all these processes as mere frippery. They came to ask what the courts were *achieving* by their black magic, and whether it was giving them the *product* they wanted, whether this was the *service* they were looking for, and of course those questions quickly broke the spell. The courts could no longer fill the displacement gap from their own symbolic resources, since their own symbolic resources had been confiscated by the popular expectation of raw retaliatory results.

The consequence of this rapid social change is that the displacement gap is now an open and suppurating social wound, and the threat of retaliation by or on behalf of aggrieved victims of crime looms ever larger. The courts themselves sometimes feel the pressure and feel constrained to penetrate their own veil of ignorance, abandoning their mission to do justice where, as increasingly often, it parts company with their function to displace retaliation. That seriously violates their duty as courts, which is above all the duty of justice, and which positively requires them to stay 'out of touch with public opinion' on matters of sentencing policy. Meanwhile, populist politicians pander to retaliatory instincts by threatening to publish names and addresses of ex-offenders, to force ex-offenders to reveal old criminal records, even to license vigilantes in the form of private security guards— all in order 'to hand justice back to the people'. What they do not appear to appreciate is that all of this makes the justification for the criminal law less stable, not more so. For if the criminal law cannot successfully displace retaliation against wrongdoers, but instead collaborates with it, then a central pillar of its justification has collapsed.

I do not mean to suggest that the courts' recent well-documented waking up to the existence of victims is in every way a bad thing. There has been for as long as anyone can remember a tendency for criminal courts, with typical bureaucratic abandon, to pretend that nobody was concerned in their processes but themselves. Victims of crime, in particular, were kept badly informed and given no quarter at all in the operation of the system. Except insofar as they were witnesses, they were expected to find out for themselves where and when the trial would take place, to queue for the public gallery, to sit with the accused in the cafeteria, etc. In their capacity as witnesses, meanwhile, no concessions were made for the special difficulty of confronting those who had wronged them. Much of this amounted to a violation of the State's duty of humanity towards the victims of crime, and to the extent that it still goes on it still does.[36] The courts should remember that victims, as well as offenders, are thinking, feeling human beings. But this has absolutely no connection with the far more sinister contemporary campaigns to turn victims into parties to the criminal trial or administrators of criminal punishments, or in some other way to hand their grievances back to them.[37] That victims do not try, convict sentence or punish criminal offenders, and have no official part in the trial, conviction, sentencing and punishment of criminal offenders, is not an accident of procedural history. It is, on the contrary, one of the main objects of the whole exercise.

---

[36] On which, see H Fenwick, 'Rights of Victims in the Criminal Justice System: Rhetoric or Reality?', *Criminal Law Review* [1995], 843.

[37] A prescient manifesto for criminological consumerism was N Christie, 'Conflicts as Property', *British Journal of Criminology* 27 (1977), 1, which spoke of conflicts being 'stolen' by criminal law and needing to be 'returned' to the parties through procedures which were 'victim-oriented' as well as 'lay-person-oriented'.

12

Reply to Critics

1. The rule of law and the harm principle

The criminal law is concerned with wrongdoing. Of course, not all wrongs recognized by the law are crimes. There are also torts, breaches of contract, equitable wrongs, etc. On the other hand, all crimes are wrongs recognized by the law. The word 'recognized' here is deliberately ambiguous. It covers two different scenarios. In scenarios of the one type—*malum in se*—the wrong in question is a wrong anyway, quite apart from the law's recognition of it as a wrong. In scenarios of the other type—*malum prohibitum*—it is the law's recognition of the wrong that makes it into a wrong. The distinction is simple, but its application is far from clear-cut. Even murder and rape, paradigmatic *mala in se*, are sharpened up by the law near their borderlines. The law, and especially the criminal law, needs more determinacy in the demarcation of wrongs than is needed, or possible, in ordinary life apart from the law. This means that we should have modest expectations when debating the merits of different ways of demarcating particular wrongs. We should not, for example, expect there to be an independent answer to the question of which kinds of fraud, used to induce a sexual encounter, suffice to turn the inducer into a rapist. This is a line that the law itself has to draw. Within limits, it can reasonably be drawn by different legal systems in different places.

The need for added (and up to a point arbitrary) determinacy in the demarcation of criminal wrongs principally reflects the demands of the ideal known as the rule of law. Under the rule of law, *inter alia*, we must all be given adequate warning of what the law requires of us, be informed of any charge against us and given an opportunity to answer it, and be judged in court in accordance with the law that we were charged under. In short, we must not be ambushed by the law. Towards the end of 'Rationality and the Rule of Law in Offences Against the Person' (Chapter 2),

I outlined one way in which the criminal law can improve its conformity with the rule of law, one way in which it can give us better warning
before we blunder into committing a crime. It can do this, I said, by
making crimes more 'action-specific'. A more action-specific crime is one
that is more specific concerning the possible means of its commission.
A crime of causing death by dangerous driving, for example, is more
action-specific than a crime of causing death *simpliciter*.

Alan Bogg and John Stanton-Ife protest that the connection I am
trying to make between action-specificity and the rule of law is unclear.
It is unclear, they write:

> ... why exactly the rule of law's warnings, where they succeed in demanding
> advertence, should also require great specificity of action-description. It is
> not clear that is how this extra requirement would serve the rule of law values
> of avoiding arbitrariness and human indignity or promoting freedom or
> autonomy.[1]

I am not sure that I agree with the list of 'rule of law values' here.
Sometimes, as we just saw, the rule of law positively requires an element
of arbitrariness. To meet the demands of the rule of law, a criminal wrong
sometimes needs to be sharply demarcated by arbitrary legal fiat. So
perhaps there is a difference of opinion here over how to interpret the
ideal of the rule of law.

Bogg's and Stanton-Ife's main challenge, however, lies in their
suggestion that action-specificity does not aid conformity with the rule
of law even as I interpret it. Action-specificity, they say, adds nothing to
the law's ability to warn us of our impending violations. My contrary
line of thought goes like this. In countless everyday activities (switching
on a light, opening a door, riding a bike, cooking a meal ...), one may
cause another's death. So an offence of causing death *simpliciter* gives
one no simple and reliable way of avoiding its commission. Whereas one
has a simple and reliable way of avoiding the commission of an offence
of causing death by dangerous driving. One may simply give up driving.
Bogg and Stanton-Ife counter, not implausibly, that the same protection against ambush by the law could equally be provided by adding an
element of mens rea into the crime of causing death *simpliciter*. If it is
turned into an offence of knowingly causing death (if, in their words, it
is a crime that 'demands advertence'), one also has a simple and reliable

---

[1] A Bogg and J Stanton-Ife, 'Protecting the Vulnerable: Legality, Harm and Theft',
Legal Studies 23 (2003), 402.

way of avoiding its commission. One can stop whatever one is doing as soon as one knows that one will thereby cause death. If the mens rea element is already in place, what extra protection against ambush is added by the action-specificity?

The answer is that the action-specificity adds a second and different protection against ambush. It enables one to organize one's life so as to avoid even having to worry about committing certain criminal offences, viz those that can only be committed while driving. The same goes for criminal offences that can only be committed by threatening, trading, using a telephone, etc. Of course, the argument only applies where the action in question is one that cannot be performed without noticing that one is performing it. But so long as that condition is met, the specific action's inclusion in the definition of the offence makes a distinct contribution to one's freedom. It means that one need not have the existence of the offence in the back of one's mind whenever one does anything at all. One need only have it in the back of one's mind when one is performing the specific action of driving, betting, publishing, trading, etc. The offence of theft under the Theft Act 1968, on which Bogg and Stanton-Ife focus, is a good example. There are many reasons to regret the way in which the element of 'appropriation' in the definition of theft was gradually emptied of content by the English courts after 1968. But one is that this has gradually deprived each of us of one reliable and simple way we would otherwise have had of steering clear of the law of theft, viz by not appropriating anything belonging to another. It is some comfort, but not complete comfort, to discover that we can still avoid the law of theft by not being dishonest in anything we do, whether we appropriate anything or not. From the point of view of the rule of law, it is better to have the belt as well as the braces. *Pace* Bogg and Stanton-Ife, neither is superfluous.

The ideal of the rule of law regulates the way in which wrongs can be recognized by the criminal law. Some wrongs, such as betraying a friend, cannot be criminalized consistently with the rule of law. Others, such as interrupting or talking over other people in a conversation, cannot be criminalized consistently with the harm principle. The role of the harm principle in thinking about the criminal law is often exaggerated. Some people think that, thanks to the harm principle, they need to explain the wrongfulness of every criminal wrong in terms of its harmfulness. If there is no harm, there can be no wrong. This is a mistake. Many actions, such as rape and blackmail, are wrongful quite independently of their harmfulness. The role of the harm principle comes later, in regulating whether and how such wrongs are properly recognized by law. This is one theme of 'The Wrongness of Rape' (Chapter 1). Arthur Ripstein misrepresents the theme somewhat when he accuses the paper of trying:

... to explain the wrongness of such acts by appeal to the harm they do to the 'practice' of sexual autonomy, as if rape would not be wrongful in a society that had not 'adopted' such a practice.[2]

In fact 'The Wrongness of Rape' does not try to explain the wrongness of rape by an appeal to this harm, or to any other harm. It tries to explain the wrongness of rape by pointing to the rapist's sheer use of another person, a use which may be entirely harmless. The puzzle explored towards the end of the paper was this: how, if at all, can the criminalization of such wrongful but harmless rape be reconciled with the harm principle? The answer suggested in the paper is that the harm principle does not require of each legal prohibition that it (proportionately) prohibits harmful wrongdoing. Rather, it requires of each legal prohibition that it (proportionately) serves to prevent harm. The law may prevent harm by prohibiting a harmless wrong where the non-prohibition of such a harmless wrong would itself be harmful. If harmless rape were not prohibited, that would probably increase the incidence of harmful rape (because it would license men to regard women as less sexually autonomous, and hence encourage their use as sex objects). So far as the harm principle is concerned, such an indirect connection to harm is all that is required to justify a (proportionate) legal intervention. But it is not what makes rape wrongful. Rape is *malum in se* and remains wrong irrespective of the case for legal intervention.

Ripstein misrepresents this line of thought in a second way when he associates it with the view that the harm principle authorizes the use of the law to protect social practices. It is true that the harm principle authorizes the use of the law to protect social practices, where the loss of the practice in question would be harmful. This is how the crime of bigamy passes the test of the harm principle. It protects the social practice of marriage, on the footing that having this practice gives many people an option without which they would be worse off. If there were no such practice, then there should be no such crime. But the crime of rape is different. It attempts to protect sexual autonomy, especially that of women, irrespective of whether there is already a social practice of respecting their

---

[2] A Ripstein, 'Beyond the Harm Principle', *Philosophy and Public Affairs* 34 (2006), 215 at 227.

sexual autonomy. If there is no such practice there should be, for people are harmed by its absence, and one task of the law of rape is to help bring it into existence. That is the position represented by 'The Wrongness of Rape'. Nowhere in the paper is it suggested that the practice must already exist for the harmfulness, let alone the wrongfulness, of rape to be established. Rape, the essay makes clear, is wrongful at all times and in all places. Barring times and places where the law is counterproductive, it ought also to be a crime in all times and in all places. At any rate, the harm principle yields no credible objection to its criminalization.

Peter Cane complains that this way of reading the harm principle strips it of its motivation and its power:

> We might say (as Gardner and Shute say in relation to rape) that a society in which the creation of certain risks was not a crime, or in which attempting and contemplating crimes were not themselves crimes, would be (in some sense) a worse society to live in than one in which they were. A worry about this sort of argument, however, is that it depends on the aggregate effect of many such acts, and does not seem to justify coercion of any individual agent. At the same time, classifying such 'diffuse effects' as harm 'seem[s] to reduce the significance of Mill's principle to vanishing point.'[3]

Cane is here forgetting, I think, that the would-be rapist is a would-be wrongdoer. This already picks him out as a suitable person to be threatened with punishment (coerced). It is not the job of the harm principle to pick him out again. The job of the harm principle is to regulate the wider purposes of the law that does the threatening. This law, and indeed every coercive law, must have and fulfil a harm-prevention purpose. The prevention of offence, distress, pain, vice, or indeed further wrongdoing is not sufficient warrant for coercion by law unless by such coercion the law also prevents harm. The law's threats, moreover, must be in proportion to the harm thereby prevented.

Even as interpreted in 'The Wrongness of Rape', this is a principle of much more than vanishing significance. True, it includes diffuse effects among those that can warrant proportionate coercive interventions. But the effects in question must be harmful, not just bad. A law might be proposed, for example, to criminalize the possession of material that contains photographic depictions of (simulated) torture or rape designed

---

[3] P Cane, 'Taking Law Seriously: Starting Points of the Hart/Devlin Debate', *Journal of Ethics* 10 (2006), 21 at 33–34. The words quoted by Cane at the end of the passage are from NE Simmonds, 'Law and Morality' in E Craig (ed), *Routledge Encyclopedia of Philosophy* (2004).

for the sexual arousal of its viewers. Such material is intrinsically abhorrent. All else being equal, the world is a better place if none of it exists,
and thus if nobody possesses it. Perhaps a ban on possession can take
us a long way towards that result. In which case the ban has a lot to be
said in its favour. Nevertheless, the ban is warranted, according to the
harm principle, only to the extent that it also serves to prevent harm. Not
everything that makes the world a better place prevents harm. To prevent
harm is to improve someone's prospects in life. Without further inquiry,
we cannot tell whether anyone's prospects are going to be improved, let
alone proportionately improved, by a ban on possession of this kind of
material. We need to know who is supposed to benefit, and by how much,
and at what cost, and so on. It is no answer to say that we all benefit just
by the bare fact that such material no longer exists. Such material exists
right now and many people's prospects are unaffected either way by it.
Sure, they are offended or upset to encounter the material or to hear of
its existence. But afterwards their lives go on as before; the encounter is
upsetting but harmless. To justify a ban on possession under the harm
principle we need to find the people who are not so lucky, the ones whose
life-prospects are being affected adversely by the non-existence of the
ban. Probably there are such people. Probably the ban does indeed pass
the test of the harm principle. Probably, for example, it makes a diffuse contribution to improving the way in which women generally are
regarded, and hence treated, by men. Possibly it also makes a less diffuse
contribution to protecting some women somewhere from some men who
are tempted to act out fantasies that they have seen depicted in pornography. All of this requires detailed empirical study. And that is the
point. The point is that the government does not adequately defend the
proposed ban until it explains which harms the ban is intended to prevent and why the ban is a proportionate measure to prevent them.

So the harm principle is far from redundant. Yet it cannot do all the
work sometimes assigned to it. Satisfying the harm principle is a necessary but not a sufficient condition for the law to use coercion against
would-be wrongdoers. The law must also respect the right to freedom of
expression, the right to freedom of conscience, the right to sexual freedom, the right to political participation, the right to privacy, etc., each of
which restricts the law in the kinds of harms it can legitimately prevent
and the ways in which it can legitimately prevent them. Quite possibly—
this also requires detailed thought—the mooted law against possession of
violent pornography falls at the hurdle of the right to freedom of expression or the right to sexual freedom even if it passes the hurdle of the harm

principle. In addition, as already outlined, it has to overcome the obstacles created by the ideal of the rule of law, which regulates the way in which laws are created, promulgated, and maintained. And on top of all that there is the basic principle of rationality by which nobody, not even the law, should take futile or counterproductive actions. If one expected all the work that is done by these various principles to be done by the harm principle, then inevitably one is disappointed by the principle's more humble contribution to settling the limits of legitimate law.

2. Differentiating wrongs

According to 'The Wrongness of Rape', those who are raped and know it tend to be traumatized by the rape because rape is wrong quite apart from the trauma of it. The pure case of rape, on this view, is the case of rape that goes undetected and hence unexperienced by its victim. Victor Tadros wonders whether the point is supposed to extend beyond rape:

> Similarly, we might seek to identify what is wrong with domestic abuse in the absence of the psychological trauma that is suffered by victims. Perhaps it will be claimed that the 'pure' case of domestic abuse is the case in which the victim is not traumatized by the abuse ... But I think that would be a mistake. The fact that there may be cases of this sort ought not to incline us to think that psychological trauma is not central to what is wrong with domestic abuse.[4]

I do not share Tadros's confidence that we should think of domestic abuse (or recognize it in the criminal law) as a distinct wrong. I think it is better thought of as an insidious pattern of behaviour in which various different wrongs—they may include wrongs of manipulation, coercion, intimidation, exploitation, theft, harassment, humiliation, neglect, assault, battery, torture, rape and ultimately murder—are repeated episodically. Yet one characteristically wrongful aspect of domestic abuse that gives it some unity is the abuser's use of terror (the terror of episodic repetition) with a view to breaking the will of the abused person.[5] Now obviously one cannot use terror against a person without terrifying her. So I agree with Tadros that, in the case of domestic abuse, some of the wrongs of the

---

[4] V Tadros, 'The Distinctiveness of Domestic Abuse' in RA Duff and S Green (eds), *Defining Crimes: Essays on the Special Part of the Criminal Law* (2005), 119 at 136.

[5] To be more exact, it is a regime of alternating terror and false hope that is designed by the abuser (albeit perhaps only subconsciously) to induce a condition of severe dependency, and hence a radical loss of personal autonomy, in the person abused.

wrongdoer are partly constituted, even in the purest case, by the reaction of the person who is wronged. The reaction in question, the terror, is a reaction to other actual and threatened wrongs that also form part of the pattern of abuse. Rape is different because in the case of rape the reaction under discussion is a reaction to the rape itself, not to some other actual or threatened wrong. This illustrates the point, also made in 'The Wrongness of Rape', that different wrongs are wrong in different ways, by virtue of different lines of argument, and each therefore calls for study in its own right. There is no general formula of wrongdoing.

Terrorizing, unlike rape, is a wrong partly constituted by its result, viz the terror of the person terrorized. If recognized in criminal law this wrong would count, in criminal lawyer's terms, as a 'result crime'. 'Result crimes' are those that are committed by making a certain causal contribution to a certain outcome. Andrew Ashworth, who has some lingering doubts about result crimes in general, focuses his criticisms of my work on just one sub-category of result crimes. These are constructive crimes: result crimes that one commits by committing another (lesser) crime and thereby contributing to a certain outcome (which may or may not have been foreseen or foreseeable). In 'Rationality and the Rule of Law in Offences Against the Person', I suggested a possible way of thinking about constructive crimes. I said that by committing the lesser crime one 'changes one's normative position' such that a certain outcome that would not otherwise have counted against one now counts against one, and adds to one's crime. Ashworth complains that I do too little to explain this remark. It strikes him as cryptic. What he does manage to glean by way of explanation he finds unsatisfying:

> Gardner sets great store by the fact that people have been 'put on notice' by the law's clear statement ... that this higher liability may be imposed if the outcome is more serious than D anticipated. Fair warning and notice are important components of the rule of law, but they are not capable of supplying substantive moral justification for a particular head of liability. Giving fair warning of an unfair rule does not turn it into a fair rule.[6]

I agree. I regret that my remark about 'changing one's normative position' was taken (and not only by Ashworth) to be an attempt at offering a 'substantive moral justification' for any constructive criminal liability. When I wrote the words I didn't really mean to justify anything. I only meant to analyse the law's own moral outlook. I meant, in other words, to set out

---

[6] A Ashworth, 'A Change of Normative Position: Determining the Contours of Culpability in Criminal Law', forthcoming in *New Criminal Law Review* 11 (2008).

the thing that needs to be justified rather than the justification. I meant to present the law as morally intelligible but not necessarily as morally acceptable. But I can see that I muddied the waters by casually mixing in some alien notes of approval and disapproval.

My 'fair warning' remarks, on the other hand, were meant to have some justificatory importance. They were meant to meet an important objection to constructive criminal liability, viz that it breaches the rule of law. This struck me and still strikes me as an important objection to constructive criminal liability because the principle *actus non facit reum nisi mens sit rea* is itself a constituent principle of the rule of law. It should be interpreted accordingly. If constructive liability does not breach the rule of law then equally it does not breach the *actus non facit reum* principle, as correctly interpreted. So I thought it worth showing that constructive liability does not breach the rule of law.

But this, of course, is a mainly negative project. If successful it shows that constructive criminal liability does not fall foul of one particular moral objection. It does not provide anything resembling a positive moral case for constructive criminal liability. Indeed nothing in 'Rationality and the Rule of Law' provides or attempts to provide such a positive moral case. Inasmuch as I have tried to provide a positive moral case, I have set it out elsewhere. Elsewhere, to be more exact, I have argued (against Kant) that acting with bad results (and irrespective of fault) is the basic or elementary type of moral wrongdoing. Some of the relevant considerations are sketched in 'Justifications and Reasons' (Chapter 5) and in 'Crime: in Proportion and in Perspective' (Chapter 11). However, my main work on this topic is not included in this volume because it is not focused principally on the criminal law but rather on the law of torts.[7] It therefore requires some adaptation to fit the criminal law context. I am inclined to think that two main adaptations are required. First, unlike tort liability, criminal liability should not descend on those who commit moral wrongs of the basic kind unless they do it culpably. Justifications and excuses, in other words, should always be available to those who commit criminal wrongs (or else should be anticipated in the very definitions of those criminal wrongs). Second, the rule of law makes stricter demands of the criminal law than it does of the law of torts. This is where the *actus not facit reum* principle, and other requirements of fair

---

[7] J Gardner, 'Obligations and Outcomes in the Law of Torts' in P Cane and J Gardner (eds), *Relating to Responsibility* (2001); J Gardner, 'The Wrongdoing that Gets Results', *Philosophical Perspectives* 18 (2004), 53.

warning, come in. I see nothing in these two adaptations that would cast suspicion on constructive criminal liability as such.

One can see in these remarks the explanation for a certain ambivalence that Ashworth detects in my attitude to constructive crimes. Sometimes I talk as if the basic moral wrong of a constructive ('unlawful act') manslaughterer is his unlawful act, the fatal consequence of that act being an aggravating factor. Sometimes, on the other hand, I talk as if the basic moral wrong is the killing, the unlawful act being a precondition for attaching criminal liability to the killing. Ashworth protests:

> [I]t is unclear whether Gardner is able properly to claim that his starting point is that D killed V, when the change of normative position on which he places such weight is surely an assault, and nothing more. This, after all, is how he explains other examples – [on Gardner's analysis of a section 47 crime] the assault changes D's normative position so as to render him properly liable for the more serious offence of assault occasioning actual bodily harm.[8]

The answer is that there are two competing criteria of basicness. Morally, the killing is the basic wrong and the prior unlawful act is a precondition for its criminalization. However, in the criminal law's own perspective— with everything seen through the distorting lens of the rule of law—the unlawful act is the basic wrong which changes the defendant's normative position in such a way that its fatal consequences can be counted against him. That, at any rate, is how I see the matter.

Result crimes, as I said, are those that are committed by making a certain causal contribution to a certain outcome. We have just been scratching the surface of the question of whether result crimes should exist. But if result crimes should exist, what causal contribution must one make to the result before one commits them? Many courts and textbook writers seem to expect the answer to this question to belong to the general part of the criminal law, and hence to remain constant across all result crimes. In 'Rationality and the Rule of Law in Offences Against the Person', I challenged this expectation. I suggested that we can draw rational distinctions between wrongdoers not only according to the outcomes of what they do (death, grievous bodily harm, actual bodily harm, etc.) but also according to the causal contribution that they make to those outcomes (occasioning, causing, inflicting, etc.). In 'Complicity and Causality' (Chapter 3), I developed this idea, and fortified it in the process. I argued that such causal distinctions among wrongs not only

---

[8] A Ashworth, 'A Change of Normative Position', above n 6.

can be drawn in rationally defensible ways, but to some extent *must* be: as rational beings, responsible for our actions, we cannot live without them. The distinction between principals and accomplices, in particular, is a causal distinction central to moral life, which is part of rational life. Of course, it does not follow that the distinction need be institutionalized in the criminal law. But it is so institutionalized, and part of the aim of 'Complicity and Causality' was to show that this part of the criminal law has a moral foundation.

One possible reaction to this line of thought is to deny that a crime of complicity is a result crime—in other words to deny that it is a wrong committed by making a causal contribution to something. Responding to 'Complicity and Causality', Lindsay Farmer flirts with this possibility. But he ends up defending only the more modest thesis that a wrong of complicity is not *always* a wrong committed by making a causal contribution to something. He floats a number of possible counterexamples. One is the case in which I help to conceal the wrong of another, e.g. by hiding the body of a murder victim. He says that in this case 'while the action of the accessory does not cause the action of the principal (in Gardner's terms) it undoubtedly "contributes" to it'.[9] I am not sure what to make of the quotation marks around 'contributes' here. More importantly, I am not sure which action Farmer means by 'the action of the principal'. If he means the action of escaping detection or arrest, then concealing the body may certainly contribute, and in a straightforwardly causal way, to the action of the principal. But if he means the original action of killing, then I do not see how the concealer contributes to it at all. Unless, of course, there is something we are not being told. Did the concealer offer to conceal the body beforehand? In that case, she may have made a contribution to the killing (as an encourager). In that situation, as I explained in the penultimate section of 'Complicity and Causality', the contribution is still causal. So I see nothing here to suggest that the contributions made by some accomplices are of a non-causal type.

Another case that strikes Farmer as a counterexample to my thesis is the case in which one is morally complicit in wrongs committed by one's country. For countries, he says,

… do not act through [their citizens] but act (in different ways) in the name of their citizens. The forms of representation and collective action always already

---

[9] L Farmer, 'Complicity beyond Causality: a Comment', *Criminal Law and Philosophy* 1 (2007), 151 at 153.

imply a notion of political and legal complicity that goes beyond the causal forms discussed by Gardner.[10]

This is the kind of case I mentioned in the final section of 'Complicity and Causality'. Thanks to the work of Christopher Kutz, I was astute to the difficulties of explaining how those human agents who are also constituent members of a collective agent come to be responsible for the actions of that agent.[11] I did not offer a general answer, because it seems to me that there is no general answer. Rather, there are two possibilities. The first is that an individual member of the collectivity is personally responsible as an accomplice because she failed to prevent the collectivity's wrong, failed to impede it, or made some other wrongful causal contribution to its commission. The second is that she is vicariously responsible, meaning that, just because she is a member of the collectivity, she is responsible for what the collectivity does irrespective of whether she made any causal contribution to its being done. It seems to me that between them these possibilities exhaust the possible modes of responsibility for the wrongs of another. That my country represents me and thereby 'acts in my name' is clearly not a *tertium quid*, for it leaves open precisely the question at issue, namely: what is the *basis* of my responsibility, if any, for the acts of those who represent me? Is it a personal responsibility as an accomplice, based on something I do to contribute to their wrongdoing, or is it a vicarious responsibility based on my membership alone?

Farmer doubts whether this distinction between personal and vicarious responsibility can be sustained. His doubts centre, not on the joint exhaustiveness of the two modes of responsibility, but on their mutual exclusivity. He mentions two sources of doubt. One is that the law might choose a regime of vicarious responsibility as a way of giving legal effect to what is really (i.e. apart from the law) a kind of personal accomplice responsibility. Thus possibly the vicarious responsibility of an employer for his employee's torts is a 'way of institutionalizing in law the fact that [employers are] *always* participating in the wrongs of their subordinates because of their position'.[12] The second is that there seem to be some cases at the borderline that are indeterminate as between personal accomplice responsibility and vicarious responsibility. The position of being vicariously responsible 'can[not] always be distinguished from the position of

---

[10] ibid, 154–155.
[11] C Kutz, *Complicity: Law and Ethics for a Collective Age* (2000).
[12] 'Complicity beyond Causality', above n 9, 153.

failing to prevent wrongdoing'.[13] I agree with Farmer on both points. Some of the law's policy goals, in extending liability out beyond principal wrongdoers, can be served either by a regime of personal accomplice responsibility or by a regime of vicarious responsibility. The law therefore has, within limits, a choice of regimes, and different legal systems can reasonably choose differently. But a choice presupposes a distinction. So, for that matter, does a borderline. It is true that, in some cases there is no telling whether one's responsibility for the wrongs of another is personal or vicarious; it could plausibly be analysed either way. But this does not mean that there is anything amiss with the distinction. Every distinction yields indeterminate cases at the borderline. Lawyers, driven by the ideal of the rule of law, are paid to get such cases decided one way or the other, to force them off the borderline. Philosophers have no such duty. Their job is to understand the world, not to change it.

Like Farmer, Tatjana Hörnle doubts whether causality can do the work that I expect of it in explaining the nature of complicity. But her doubts are less far-reaching than Farmer's. In particular, unlike Farmer, she agrees with me that making a causal contribution to the wrong of a principal is a necessary but insufficient condition for being an accomplice. Where she thinks I err is in trying to draw a causal *distinction* between principals and accomplices. She writes:

Not much is gained by invoking causality to decide whether someone is to be punished as principal or as an accomplice. Causation is a necessary condition for both, but different criteria are needed to discriminate between principals and accomplices.[14]

Hörnle's words 'punished as' draw attention to one respect in which she misreads me. She attributes to me the view, which she thinks a good rule of thumb, 'that accomplices should receive lighter sentences than principals'.[15] This is not my view and I can see nothing in 'Complicity and Causality' that supports it. Often the biggest fish, the one who deserves the most punishment, is an accomplice. I am not thinking about those unusual cases, mentioned by Hörnle, in which an infant or a mentally ill person is used as a tool to carry out a crime. Here, as Hörnle rightly points out, the user is a principal rather than an accomplice, because the infant or mentally ill person is not responsible for her actions. I am

[13] ibid.
[14] T Hörnle, 'Commentary to "Complicity and Causality"', *Criminal Law and Philosophy* 1 (2007), 143 at 147.
[15] ibid, 146.

thinking, rather, of the everyday situation in which a gangster 'persuades' some petty criminal to carry out a 'hit' in lieu of repaying a debt. Here the gangster, although the prime mover, is an accomplice, while the debtor, although a pawn, is the principal. It seems to me that in this story, all else being equal, the accomplice is the one who should be punished more severely by the criminal law. With this in mind I tend to favour the doctrine in the Accessories and Abettors Act 1861, under which the maximum sentence for the accomplice is identical to that for the principal, leaving the court free to determine which, in any given case, is the more egregious offender. This clearly sets me against Hörnle's rival proposal that principals should be distinguished from accomplices by their supposedly greater degree of control over the commission of the offence. For in the case I just sketched the accomplice, the one who makes the indirect causal contribution to the death through the principal, is the one who exercises greater control over the killing.

In 'Complicity and Causality', I focused on cases of killing, which I treated (for the sake of argument) as a wrong *per se*. I needed to illustrate the contrast between principalship and complicity using a simple wrong that is constituted by making a direct causal contribution to an outcome. I did not mean to suggest that the principalship/complicity distinction is always and only a contrast between direct causal contribution and indirect causal contribution. Some wrongs—such as rape and attempted murder—are not constituted by making a causal contribution to anything. Other wrongs—such as assault occasioning actual bodily harm or permitting premises to be used for the purposes of prostitution—are constituted by making a causal contribution that need not be direct. In the latter cases, some or all of the domain of complicity is inevitably absorbed into the domain of principalship. We have seen this development very starkly in the law of torts, especially in connection with the tort of negligence. As well as making extensive use of vicarious liability, the courts have overcome the absence of complicity liability in tort law by extending the class of principal wrongs to include many indirect causal contributions to damage. This tendency has been less marked in the criminal law, although the criminal courts are so bewildered by causal questions that it is often hard to tell. Perhaps this is what encourages Farmer to say that often 'the distinction [between principals and accomplices] confuses the issue and might usefully be discarded'.[16]

---

[16] L Farmer, 'Complicity beyond Causality', above n 9, 154.

But the importance of a distinction is not a function of its ease of use. The distinction between principals and accomplices might perhaps be excised from the law (e.g. for rule of law reasons), but, as 'Complicity and Causality' tries to show, it cannot be excised from life.

3. Justifying wrongdoing

Is there such a thing as justified complicity? The question I have in mind is not a moral or legal one. It is a conceptual one. As I framed the question in 'Complicity and Causality': is complicity the unjustified thing or the thing that calls for justification? The papers 'In Defence of Defences' (Chapter 4) and 'Justifications and Reasons' (Chapter 5) tackle the master question of which this question about complicity is one instance. Is there such a thing as justified wrongdoing? Is wrongdoing the unjustified thing or the thing that calls for justification? A convergence of Benthamite and Kantian influences has privileged the former view. How so? Wrongdoing is action in breach of duty. According to Bentham, one has a duty to perform that action which, on the balance of reasons, one ought to perform. According to Kant, reasons of duty defeat all other reasons and cannot be defeated even by other duties, for duties by their nature cannot conflict. So according to Kant and Bentham alike, once wrongdoing is established, there can be no further question of justification. The question is already closed. In 'In Defence of Defences' this is labelled the 'closure' view of wrongdoing. I argued that the closure view is mistaken. There is nothing contradictory (or even puzzling) in the proposal that, although I acted wrongfully (in breach of my duty), I was amply justified in doing so.

Mitchell Berman professes to be agnostic about the closure view. Even so, he has doubts about my case for rejecting it. My case includes the thought that wrongs, even justified ones, leave trails of unfulfilled duty behind them. Justified wrongs are hence suitable occasions for such remedial actions as (depending on the circumstances) reparation, apology, and regret. Berman objects:

[A]lthough Gardner is surely right that some duties – most especially the duty to show regret – arise from justified actions, ... this is not, I think, because the justified action remains *wrongful*. Rather, it's because the justified action has produced some unfortunate state of affairs (such as injury to another person) about which it is a mark of decency, and perhaps a duty of empathy, to feel regret. Tellingly, this duty to express regret arises even from conduct that (on most accounts) is not wrongful at all – such as nonnegligently causing injury to a negligent victim.[17]

Non-negligently causing injury to a negligent victim can indeed be wrongful, so its regrettability does not help to make Berman's point. Yet he has a good point. Remorse, on the one hand, is apposite only in respect of unjustified and unexcused wrongs. Regret, on the other hand, is an apt reaction to many things that are not wrongs at all (including some things that are not actions at all, but mere happenings). So where in between these attitudes, we may wonder, is the distinctive attitudinal trail that is appropriately left behind by justified wrongs?

An answer was famously offered by Bernard Williams. Williams identified a distinctive attitude: agent-regret, something more than regret, but less than remorse.[18] It is regret about an action that one had a reason, sometimes a duty, not to perform, regret that is not extinguished by the recognition that one's non-performance was not one's fault. Does this help? The problem is not that no such attitude exists. Clearly it does. The problem is that agent-regret is phenomenologically distinct from simple regret only inasmuch as it adds a judgment on the part of the regretter that (albeit faultlessly) she failed in some respect as an agent. In experiencing agent-regret as a distinct attitude, in other words, the regretter presupposes that the closure view is false. One therefore needs to rely on the falsity of the closure view in order to defend the regretter's experience of agent-regret as a distinct attitude. One cannot at the same time rely on the regretter's experience of agent-regret as a distinct attitude to defend the thesis that the closure view is false. This point can be generalized. In general, it is hard to make a positive case for the falsity of the closure view. The issues at stake are among the deepest in the philosophy of rationality. If one wishes to draw conclusions at this depth, it is hard to find any deeper truths that one can rely upon as premisses. The best one can do is bring out some ways in which the falsity of the closure view chimes with ordinary moral experience. One is therefore always vulnerable to the response—characteristic of tidy-minded Benthamites and Kantians—that ordinary moral experience is shot through with irrationality. This explains the sense that some may have, on reading 'In Defence of Defences' and 'Justifications and Reasons', that neither paper

---

[17] M Berman, 'Justification and Excuse, Law and Morality', *Duke Law Journal* 53 (2004), 1.

[18] B Williams, 'Moral Luck', *Proceedings of the Aristotelian Society Supplementary Volume* 50 (1976), 115 at 122–124.

offers much in the way of positive argument. Each proceeds mainly by setting out a view and showing how it hangs together with itself, as well as resonating with various aspects of ordinary moral experience (some of which are reflected in English criminal law).

Responding to 'Justifications and Reasons', Alan Norrie reasserts the closure view. My response to that view, he says,

> ... is to argue that the prima facie reason is not merely provisional or evidential in character, so that even if it is defeated it is not undermined or cancelled. Yet how can this be the case? If it is defeated then it is indeed undermined, and, more strongly, cancelled. In the relevant sense, the prima facie reason did not turn out to designate an actual wrong, but one that was only putative.[19]

'Justifications and Reasons' already showed how it *can* be the case that a prima facie reason is not cancelled, by showing that there is an intelligible sense of 'prima facie' other than the 'provisional or evidential' one preferred by Norrie. But is this intelligible sense the *relevant* sense when we come to explain the logic of justification? The question is complex. One thing that I attempted to do in 'Justifications and Reasons' and again in 'Fletcher on Offences and Defences' (Chapter 7) was to show how the closure view gets its false allure. Some of its allure, in my view, just comes of wishful thinking (if only life were simpler; if only there were no tragedy; if only there were never anything to rue in a justified action). But some of its allure comes of the fact that it contains a grain of truth. In the justificatory scenario there is indeed some cancellation of reasons going on. A justification for wrongdoing, as I explained it, is a cancelling permission. It does not cancel the reason not to commit the wrong—it only defeats that reason—but it does cancel the reason's mandatoriness. This proposal contradicts the closure view but preserves an important aspect of it, and this helps us to see why Norrie might be resistant to its abandonment. (Although, as I joked in a footnote to 'In Defence of Defences', it is curious to find Norrie's resistance to the abandonment of the Kantian closure view presented as part of his critique of Kantian thinking in criminal law theory!)

Norrie also has a lawyer's objection to my abandonment of the closure view. He objects to the 'contingency' or 'fluidity' of the resulting distinction between offences and defences, which means that the same legal doctrine (e.g. self-defence, consent, necessity) or the same case (e.g. that of a mercy killer or a soldier killing in battle) could be placed on opposite

---

[19] A Norrie, *Punishment, Responsibility, and Justice* (2000), 153.

sides of the line by different legal systems, or indeed by the same legal system at different times or for different purposes or in different contexts. This is similar to Farmer's objection to my use of the distinction between personal and vicarious responsibility. Both Norrie and Farmer exhibit the traditional lawyer's interest in how to classify particular doctrines and cases, and they seem to expect philosophical analysis to settle such matters in advance of the law. But I have more modest ambitions. It is true that I often reveal my views about which cases fall on which side of the line in morality apart from the law. Nevertheless the law, as I have always tried to emphasize, faces many constraints, but also many choices, in settling how morality is to be institutionalized. I regard it as a merit of 'Justifications and Reasons', not a failing, that it explains what the difference is between denying an offence and offering a (justificatory) defence, and what makes that difference salient for rational beings, without attempting to pre-empt the decisions of particular legal systems about whether and where to draw the line in particular legal contexts.

4. From justification to excuse

Although I have not made it my main mission to classify them, I have frequently used legal doctrines and cases from particular legal systems to exemplify the categories under investigation. This exposes me to an oft-repeated line of criticism. The criticism is that the doctrines and cases are not examples of what I take them to be examples of. Peter Westen, for instance, objects to my use of duress cases in 'The Gist of Excuses' (Chapter 6):

Gardner's problem with duress is this: Gardner argues that excuse comes into play only with respect to offenses that are unjustified; yet, given Gardner's definition of 'justification', offenses committed under duress – as opposed to offenses committed under mistaken duress – ought to be regarded as offenses that are *justified*.[20]

We should leave aside for a moment cases of mistaken duress, which raise classificatory problems of their own. Is Westen right to think that, where the threat is real and the person threatened does not misperceive it, a duress defence is always a justificatory defence? There is no doubt that

---

[20] P Westen, 'An Attitudinal Theory of Excuse', *Law and Philosophy* 25 (2006), 289 at 348.

sometimes it is. Sometimes the person threatened was right, all things considered, to commit the wrong that he committed in response to the threat. But sometimes he was not so lucky. His fear of the threat's being carried out, itself justified, drove him to commit an unjustified wrong. This is not a case of mistake. The person threatened did not misinterpret the threat or misjudge the likelihood of its being carried out. He merely overreacted; he let his fear get the better of him. Usually the overreaction was exactly what the threatener banked on. The threatener selected a vulnerability of the person threatened: his love of his children, his loathing of rats, or just his anxiety about his own fate (excessive preoccupation with which is a widespread human limitation and therefore the simplest one to exploit without special knowledge of the person one is threatening). The person threatened exhibited this limitation in his action of surrendering to the threat. Then the allowing of the duress defence is, as the courts sometimes put it, a 'concession to human frailty'. The fortitude exhibited is suboptimal but not below acceptable limits. In this case the force of the duress defence is excusatory rather than justificatory.

What leads Westen to deny the existence of this class of cases (cases of excusatory duress without mistake of fact)? He writes:

A person who is correct in thinking that A's threat is genuine is a person who acts both in his mind and in actuality upon a balance between self-interest and the interests of others that society regards as acceptable, all things considered – which is precisely the sort of person whom Gardner has said is 'justified'.[21]

The problem here is that 'act[ing] upon a balance ... that society regards as acceptable' is ambiguous, even when we restrict our attention to the actuality rather than A's perception. Even when she in no way misperceives her situation, it is possible for the way that A balances two considerations to live up to the relevant standard for thought without her action on the strength of that thought living up to the relevant standard for action. Of course there is something of the tragic about this possibility. That one thinks acceptably about how to act, and acts on the strength of that thinking, does not guarantee that one acts acceptably. What it does guarantee is that one is not at fault in acting unacceptably. For while one lacks a justification, one has a full excuse. Westen accepts this much in cases of misperception, and so classifies a reasonably mistaken belief in duress as excusatory, even though duress itself would be for him justificatory. His error lies in failing to see that misperceptions are not the only distortions in practical rationality that can drive a wedge between what one acceptably thinks about what to do, and what one acceptably does. Strong emotions too can supply the relevant distortion, for reasonable practical thought is characterized and constituted by reasonable affect as well as by reasonable cognition.

Hamish Stewart and Victor Tadros both take my account of excuses to task on the very point that Westen concedes. They both hold that a reasonable mistake as to an element of a justificatory defence preserves the justificatory character of the defence, rather than turning it into an excuse. I will come to Stewart's line of thought in section 7 ('The hierarchy of defences') below. Here let me focus on Tadros's criticism, which takes the form of a *reductio*:

> [On Gardner's view] it is difficult to see how one could ever be justified in taking a risk where things do not turn out as one hoped. If even reasonably held beliefs cannot ground a justification defence where the facts turn out unexpectedly to be different from those that D believes them to be, where are we to stop in our analysis of what the facts are? For it is always the case, where one takes a risk and things turn out badly, that there is some further fact about the world that one could have known that would make that risk not worth taking. This is true even if determinism is false: there are facts about what will happen in the future as well as facts about the world as it is now.[22]

Here, Tadros raises another of the most difficult problems in the theory of reasons. Reasons are facts. If I make a mistake of fact (e.g. if I think I am being attacked when I am not) then I do not have the reason to act that, in the grip of that mistake, I take myself to have (e.g. to defend myself). I may have ample reason to believe that I have that reason to act, but this can only furnish me with an excuse, not a justification, for so acting. This is the view advanced in 'Justifications and Reasons' and assumed in 'The Gist of Excuses'. Tadros challenges it by asking us to shift from the present tense to the future tense, thinking about cases where one acts on the strength of beliefs about what is yet to take place. Suppose D thinks that, in all likelihood, he is going to be attacked later. On one view, the probabilist view, the risk that D is going to be attacked later is a fact in its own right and is capable of counting as a reason for D to run away. There are risks in the world, and not only in our incomplete *ex ante* beliefs about the world. On another view, the actualist view, D is either going to be attacked or he is not. D has a reason to run away only if he is indeed going to be attacked. If D is not going to be attacked, then

---

[22] V Tadros, *Criminal Responsibility* (2005), 286.

the most D can possibly have is a reasonable *belief* that he has a reason to run away. Tadros thinks that my view of the present-tense cases commits me to taking an actualist view in the future-tense cases, such that all references to risks in practical argument should be read as references to epistemic uncertainties (i.e. as a shorthand reference to the existence of reasons to believe in the existence of reasons to act), and hence should be read as excusatory rather than justificatory. He takes this to be a *reductio* of my position on the present-tense cases.

To this objection I have various reactions. First, I am not convinced that my view on the present-tense cases commits me to the actualist view on the future-tense cases. I do not find the question of whether there are facts about what will happen in the future as easy to answer as Tadros seems to find it. Second, I do not find the advertised implication of the actualist view (viz that reasonably mistaken gambles on the future can only excuse, and not justify, actions taken on the strength of them) as unpalatable as Tadros seems to expect. To the extent that I am sympathetic to the actualist view,[23] this is partly because of this implication, not in spite of it. Third, thanks to the existence of what (in 'Fletcher on Offences and Defences') I called 'fault-anticipating wrongs', what would otherwise excuse one's action is sometimes sufficient to make it the case that one commits no wrong in the first place, so that one has nothing to excuse. Many wrongs are defined in terms of recklessness or negligence and hence build a sensitivity to risk into their very definitions. More generally, many rules exist to regulate risk-taking, providing more concrete practical guidance on how to cope with epistemic uncertainty. In this way the rationality of belief can be indirectly relevant to the rationality of action.

Finally, it is salutary to note how much trouble Tadros himself has in escaping from an epistemic conceptualization when talking about the present-tense cases. He returns to a case devised by Bernard Williams.[24] I have in front of me a glass of petrol. I have ample reason to believe it to be a glass of gin. Do I have any reason to drink it? Williams and I agree that the answer is no. There may be a complete and adequate rational explanation for my having drunk the contents of the glass if that is what I do. But the explanation includes (because there is) no reason for my

---

[23] In a paper called 'The Mysterious Case of the Reasonable Person', *University of Toronto Law Journal* 51 (2001), 273, I confessed to actualist sympathies. Tadros relies on this confession to corroborate his charges.
[24] B Williams, 'Internal and External Reasons' in R Harrison (ed), *Rational Action* (1979), 17 at 18.

having drunk the contents. It cites only the ample reasons for me to have *believed* that I had reason to drink the contents. Tadros says, by contrast, that there was also a reason for my having drunk the contents. His argument goes like this:

> I am still motivated by a fact about the world in this case: the fact that it appears [to be gin in my glass]. That appearance does not always correspond to reality does not deny the status of that latter as a fact about the world. It may be objected to this that ... talking of the fact of appearance collapses into talk of belief. But that is not the case. The fact of appearance is to be distinguished from belief by virtue of the fact that appearance is appearance to any believer, not just this [one].[25]

Tadros cannot literally mean that appearance is appearance to *any* believer. Believers with unreasonable beliefs are distinguished by their failure to see things as they appear to others to be. Who are these others? They are those with reasonable beliefs. So the standard of appearance is none other than the standard of reasonable belief, i.e. the standard of those with beliefs that are held for adequate reason. The relevant standard, in other words, remains epistemic. In a sense it is true, as Tadros adds, that 'appearance is objective whereas belief is subjective'. But the objective standard in question is an objective standard applicable to belief, viz the standard of being a belief held for adequate reasons. This being so, Tadros has not identified a way to escape from my conclusion about the present-tense cases, whatever we may want to say about the future-tense cases. Acting on what Tadros calls the appearances, is reasonable action not in the literal sense of being justified action but in the elliptical sense of being action on the strength of reasonable beliefs, which is excused.

At one point, Tadros seems to mount a more radical challenge to this thesis. He seems to deny that there is any difference between having adequate reason to believe that one has a reason to act and actually having that reason to act. 'It is difficult to see,' he says of Williams's petrol-drinking case, 'how to drive a wedge between having good reason to believe that the stuff is desirable to drink and having good reason to drink it.' This remark comes as a surprise. It seems to undermine many of Tadros's previous thoughts, which presuppose that there is logical space for people to make reasonable mistakes as to the existence of reasons for acting. If it turns out that there is no such logical space, because one always has all the reasons for acting that one reasonably believes oneself to have, then the question of whether reasonable mistakes regarding justificatory features of one's actions are excusatory does not arise, and there

[25] V Tadros, *Criminal Responsibility*, above n 22, 284.

is no point in Tadros debating the answer with me. It seems to me that Tadros does not really mean to pursue this nuclear option. Perhaps all that he is trying to say is that Williams and I have exaggerated the *importance* of the contrast, within the rational explanation of human action, between reasons to believe in reasons to act and reasons to act themselves. If that is what he means then my answer is that the importance of this contrast would be very hard to exaggerate. It is absolutely central to a proper understanding of our predicament as rational beings.

5. Excuses and incapacities

Tadros's critique of my account of excuses continues with an attempt to re-establish a relationship between excuses and incapacities. In 'The Gist of Excuses', I argued that an incapacity to act better than one does is no excuse, and does not constitute the gist of any excuse. Central to my argument was the thesis that courage and honesty and other moral virtues are none other than capacities to act in certain ways, viz in the ways that exhibit those virtues. This has two implications. First, nobody ever has the capacity to exhibit more courage (etc.) than they do exhibit. So one's capacity to exhibit courage cannot possibly be used as a standard against which to judge one's exhibitions of courage. Since it cannot be used as a standard, it obviously cannot be used as an excusatory standard. Second, anyone who lacks the capacity to exhibit courage also lacks courage. So the assertion of an incapacity to act more courageously than one did, inasmuch as we can make sense of it, is not exculpating but inculpating. In making this assertion one is confessing to one's inadequate moral character, confirming one's fault. Since an excuse is one kind of denial of fault, such an assertion cannot be excusatory.

Tadros resists both of these lines of thought. Against the first, he raises a complex and fascinating objection. At its heart lies the following supposed counterexample:

I am in the pub with a few friends. We have time for two drinks. . . . If I buy neither round of drinks, that may show that I am not generous, particularly if I am wealthier than my friends. But in not buying the first round of drinks I show nothing about my capacity for virtue. This shows that I may have the capacity for generosity but not exercise it. Although I have the inclination to be virtuous, I also allow other people to be virtuous by buying a round of drinks. In doing so I show that I possess a different virtue, sensitivity.[26]

[26] ibid, 312.

The lesson of the example, says Tadros, can be generalized across the moral virtues, including courage: 'in failing to manifest a virtue at an appropriate time, I do not necessarily show that I do not possess that virtue, or the capacity for [that] virtue'.[27]

This, however, cannot conceivably be the lesson of Tadros's example. Why not? Because, according to Tadros himself, the occasion of the first round of drinks was not 'an appropriate time' for me to exhibit generosity. Given that I was about to buy the second round of drinks, buying the first would have been, says Tadros, 'beyond the realm of generosity':

> Not only am I not required to buy both rounds of drinks, I would also not be generous in doing so. This is what Aristotle means when he says that in acting virtuously we must avoid both excess and deficiency: the doctrine of the mean.[28]

The Aristotelian doctrine is correct. Insensitive (indiscriminate) generosity is not virtuous generosity. Rather, it is generosity to a fault, a distinct moral vice. Possibly I have an unexercised capacity for generosity-to-a-fault when, in Tadros's example, I do not buy the first round of drinks but only the second. But I cannot have an unexercised capacity for *virtuous* generosity when I do not buy the first round of drinks but only the second. This is because a capacity counts as unexercised only if there is also an opportunity for its exercise. And *ex hypothesi* there is no such opportunity in Tadros's example. There was no occasion for me to do any better, from the point of view of virtuous generosity, than buy the one round of drinks that indeed I did buy. So Tadros fails to show, by this example, that anyone ever has the capacity to exhibit any moral virtue beyond the moral virtue that he does exhibit. He fails to show any gap between virtue and the capacity for it that would enable us to judge people's exhibitions of virtue relative to their capacity for such exhibitions.

Tadros resists my second line of thought in a very different way. He criticizes my failure to note that there are some moral vices with which the criminal law should not concern itself:

> [T]hose that show themselves only to have the vice of cowardice, as opposed to showing that they have an insufficient regard for the criminal law and the values that it enshrines, ought to be entitled to a defence of duress. Those who could not have resisted had they held the criminal law in sufficiently high regard have displayed none of the vices required for criminal liability.[29]

---

[27] ibid, 313.   [28] ibid, 312.   [29] ibid, 317.

I am taken aback by the suggestion that 'insufficient regard for the criminal law' ought to be thought of as a vice, even by the criminal law itself. It is one of the hallmarks of fascist law that it judges people not by their attitudes to authentically valuable things but by their attitudes to the law itself (which may or may not be valuable depending on its content, and which is already made distinctly less valuable by the very fact that it contains this narcissistic insistence on respect for itself). Perhaps Tadros means to emphasize not the criminal law as such, but only 'the values that it enshrines', as proper objects of regard; and perhaps he means to restrict attention to cases in which these values are valid (i.e. are not erroneously espoused). I certainly hope he does not mean to go further in making a false idol of the law.

But be all that as it may, I am not sure how Tadros's criticism in this passage is supposed to bite against my views. In 'The Gist of Excuses', I did not discuss the question of which failings of character should be recognized as such by the criminal law. I happen to think that the criminal law could legitimately take an interest in any of them, but that was not my point. My point was rather that once the criminal law has recognized that something is a failing of character (as it does with cowardice in the face of threats, intemperance in the face of taunts, inattentiveness in the face of risks, and various other shortcomings), it cannot allow people to argue that they lacked the capacity to avoid exhibiting that very same failing. For this lack of capacity *is* their failing. This applies as much to the failings to which Tadros would like to see the criminal law attend (cruelty, callousness, prejudice, etc.) as it does to those failings that I discussed.

Barry Mitchell shares Tadros's sense that there must be a logical gap between virtue and the capacity to exhibit it. He accuses me of harbouring 'a singularly simplistic view of capacity according to which a person who has the capacity to behave in a particular way in the circumstances will behave in that way'.[30] This view is indeed simplistic, but the simplification is Mitchell's, not mine. I advanced the much narrower proposition that *some* capacities—virtues of character—are capacities that one does not possess unless one possesses the matching propensities. They are capacities that exist only in their exercise. That proposition does not commit me to any more general 'view of capacity'. But it seems that Mitchell would be unhappy with it all the same. For he uses my illustration of

---

[30] B Mitchell, 'The Minimum Culpability for Criminal Homicide', *European Journal of Crime, Criminal Law and Criminal Justice* 9 (2001), 193 at 196.

the narrower proposition that I advanced to bring out what he holds to be simplistic about the broader proposition that I did not advance. I had written:

If one sees the world through genuinely courageous eyes one does not see the danger to oneself the way that more cowardly people see it, as a threat, but rather as a challenge, something which, up to a point, one inclines towards rather than away from.[31]

Mitchell has the following complaint:

The truth is that we simply do not fully understand why some people are braver than others. Moreover, people may behave courageously when faced with a particular set of circumstances simply because at the critical moment they focused more on the need to (seek to) prevent some other harm than on the danger to himself. We do not know how far they [their?] focus on the harm to others rather than themselves is a matter of chance rather than a manifestation of some aspect of their personality which enables them to be brave. Another person may, on that occasion have focused instead on the danger to himself, but on a subsequent occasion would have shown the same degree of fortitude as the courageous person. The second person does not necessarily have a lesser capacity for being courageous.[32]

This criticism seems to be at cross-purposes with the passage that it is supposed to criticize. I said nothing about why people are brave, or what brings it about that they react bravely today and without any bravery tomorrow, or similar questions of aetiology. I have no views on these matters which, as Mitchell points out, require empirical investigation.[33] I discussed only the conceptual question of *what counts as* bravery. This question must be answered first. One must always know what counts as an X before one can discuss any empirical questions about Xs.

Mitchell must have his own idea of what counts as courage, but I am not sure what it is. Inasmuch as I can work it out, it seems to have a starting point in common with my own. He seems to agree with me that the person who 'focused on the danger to himself' was not being courageous on the occasion on which he did so; only 'on a subsequent occasion' did he show 'the same degree of fortitude [=courage?] as the courageous person'. So a person is courageous only when he does not 'focus on the danger to himself'. One's courage (as I put it) depends on

[31] ibid, 173.
[32] ibid, 196.
[33] Mitchell complains (ibid, 196) that in my paper 'there is a conspicuous absence of any attempt to address the scientific data available'.

how one sees the world. But does Mitchell mean to add the extra qualification (against me) that such a focus does not show one to be courageous
if it is 'a matter of chance rather than a manifestation of some aspect of
[one's] personality'? Or is this extra variable relevant only to determining whether one had the 'capacity for being courageous' when one was
not? If the latter, which way does it cut? Does one have the capacity to be
courageous only if one's focus was or would have been a 'manifestation of
some aspect of [one's] personality' or only if it was or would have been a
matter of chance? If the former, then what aspect of one's personality are
we looking for other than the courage itself? For it must clearly be something other than the courage to save us from vicious circularity; it must be
a further trait that 'enables [one] to be' courageous rather than simply
constituting one's courage. But what could this further trait be? Could
this trait (unlike one's courage) be a capacity that exists only in its exercise? If not—if it could be a capacity without propensity—then in what
sense would it qualify as an 'aspect of one's personality'? And if this trait
is a capacity that exists only in its exercise, then what is so wrong with
the view that courage itself is also the same kind of capacity? All of these
are obscurities that prevent us from crystallizing, and hence evaluating,
Mitchell's rival account of courage (if rival it be).

Jeremy Horder is another critic who thinks that I underestimate the
significance of incapacity in setting excusatory standards in the criminal
law. At least he rejects my rival explanation for the variability of excusatory standards as between defendants. Some excusatory statements that
are commonly interpreted as capacity-invoking ('she's a kid', 'he's a
beginner') are better interpreted, in my view, as role-invoking. In a case
of provocation, for example, the excusatory salience of being an adolescent is not that adolescents *cannot* be as even-tempered as adults but that
they *should not* be. One should act one's age. Adult temperance would
not befit an adolescent. This view is sketched in 'The Gist of Excuses'
and elaborated, with more examples, in 'Provocation and Pluralism'
(Chapter 8). Horder objects:

The problem with this view is that the very fact that I need an excuse, because
I have engaged in wrongdoing, shows that I have failed in my role . . . [T]he more
serious the wrongdoing the more plausible it will be to say that one failed to meet
the preconditions for successful role-fulfilment, and so the normative expectations attached to one's role are no longer relevant.[34]

---

[34] J Horder, *Excusing Crime* (2004), 115.

Horder seems to be making two distinct objections here. The first is *ad hominem*. I (Gardner) am the one who holds that wrongdoing should be understood as failure in a role. Suppose this is true, says Horder. How, having failed in a role, and hence having fallen short of the expectations for that role, can one still meet the expectations of that role and hence enjoy a role-specific excuse? I explained how this can be so in 'The Gist of Excuses', in a passage that is earlier quoted by Horder. I pointed out that there are two sets of standards (and hence two sets of expectations) that go to define a role. There are standards of success/failure and standards of fitness/unfitness. One can fail in a role without being unfit for it. The role's excusatory standards are among its standards of fitness/unfitness. So one can meet these excusatory standards even though one has committed a wrong and hence failed in the role. Which is just as well, since one needs an excuse precisely because of one's failure.

Horder's second point is that (serious) wrongdoing should not, in any case, be understood as failure in a role. Instead, it should be understood as failure at an earlier hurdle, before one even gets to occupy, and hence be judged by the standards of, any role. What should we make of this idea? A wrong is no more and no less than a breach of duty. There are clearly many duties that are incidents of friendship, parenthood, citizenship, etc. One is subject to them only if one is in the role of friend, parent, citizen, etc. It follows that there are some wrongs that one commits only as an occupant of these roles. Perhaps, according to Horder, these are not *serious* wrongs? Horder does not seem to honour this 'seriousness' restriction in the rest of his argument. He goes on to say that 'avoid[ing] wrongdoing'—serious or not—is 'avoid[ing] violating the conditions in which we and others can securely and confidently set about right-doing', this in turn being the point at which we assume our various roles.[35]

To make sense of this proposal, as Horder points out, we need to be able to distinguish between 'doing ... what is right' and 'avoiding ... what is wrong'.[36] But this distinction is obscure and Horder's examples do not help us to unpack it.[37] Avoiding wrongdoing is the same as right-doing. The rightdoer fulfils her duty; the wrongdoer breaches it. There is

[35] ibid, 116.
[36] ibid, 116.
[37] He cites some remarks made by Joseph Raz in *The Authority of Law* (1979), at 224, as helping to unpack the distinction and show its import. But the cited passage from Raz deals with a different distinction, viz the distinction between avoiding evil and doing further good beyond avoiding evil. Raz's distinction is axiological, whereas Horder's is deontic.

no *tertium quid*. Of course there are many valuable things that one might do beyond the call of duty. Some of these may make one particularly successful in one's role. But one does not need to do any of these things to be an adequate occupant of one's role, i.e. to avoid failure in it. To avoid failure in one's role one need only perform its duties. So Horder gives us no credible reason to think that wrongdoing, serious or otherwise, is not failure in a role. Consequently he gives us no reason to think that excusatory standards cannot likewise be role-specific standards.

6. Adapting excuses to the criminal law

I already mentioned and doubted Tadros's view that the criminal law (in forging its excusatory doctrines) should not be concerned with deficiencies of character *tout court*, but should limit its attention to a subset of deficiencies which evince 'insufficient regard for the criminal law and the values that it enshrines'. William Wilson also argues that my view of excuses needs to be modified before it is suitable for use in the criminal law. Focusing on the example of duress, he writes:

[C]oercion may excuse in different ways. Sometimes . . . reasonableness of reaction clearly grounds the defence and in such cases the presence or absence of subversion of the 'will' must be of peripheral concern. . . . In other cases it is equally clear that the defence may be grounded not in the reasonableness of the reaction but simply in the unfairness of expecting conformity [to the criminal law]. Here the defendant may be acting upon fear alone where he just 'does it' regardless of the consequences because he is too terrified to do anything but obey. . . . His claim to be excused is that we cannot always be expected to live up even to the standards which we set for ourselves. The criminal law is in place to punish us for our self-interestedness and the lack of concern we show to others not the fortuitous falls from grace which attend our unpracticed responses to crisis.[38]

I have a few preliminary comments about this passage. First, I am not sure why Wilson puts 'will' in inverted commas in the second quoted sentence, but with the inverted commas excised there is no reason to think that a focus on reasonableness of reaction marginalizes questions about the subversion (or overbearing) of the will. One's will is overborne, in the relevant sense, when someone else, by issuing a conditional threat, intentionally creates a reason (or what one reasonably takes to be a reason)

---

[38] W Wilson, 'The Filtering Role of Crisis in the Constitution of Criminal Excuses', *Canadian Journal of Law and Jurisprudence* 17 (2004), 387 at 405–406.

for one to φ, and one φs for that reason, and one could not reasonably
have been expected to do otherwise than to φ for that reason. The reasonableness of one's reaction is, in short, a necessary condition of the
overbearing of one's will. Second, I am not sure what is supposed to be
the extra significance, in the penultimate quoted sentence, of our falling
short 'even [of] the standards which we set for ourselves'. Since it is part
of being human that one always aims to be justified in what one does,
the standards that we set for ourselves are always higher than excusatory
standards. They are justificatory standards. One cannot be expected
invariably to live up to these higher justificatory standards, but still one
is held to (and holds oneself to) standards of character and skill. This
is exactly what 'The Gist of Excuses' points out. So here Wilson seems
to echo, not challenge, my views. Third, the final quoted sentence can
be interpreted (and is presented by Wilson in his footnotes) as echoing
Tadros's view that only some and not all standards of character should be
institutionalized in the criminal law. But this point bears on what should
qualify as a reasonable reaction for the criminal law's purposes, not on
whether reasonableness of reaction is the right thing for the criminal law
to care about. So this remark seems orthogonal to Wilson's main complaint, which is that reasonableness of reaction is not the right thing for
the criminal law to care about, or rather not the only one.

So what is the other right thing for the criminal law to care about?
While in some cases it should admittedly care about the reasonableness
or otherwise of D's reaction, according to Wilson, in other cases the
criminal law should care about the fairness or otherwise of expecting
D to conform to its norms. This, for Wilson, is the gist of at least some
criminal law excuses. By way of example, he mentions automatism and
involuntary intoxication as well as duress. Now automatism is not an
excuse but a denial of responsibility. And involuntary intoxication is not
a defence at all (excusatory or otherwise) but merely a possible way of supporting one's denial of mens rea.[39] But never mind these quibbles about
particular legal doctrines. Whichever legal doctrines it is supposed to
apply to and illuminate, Wilson's proposal is unhelpful on different and
deeper grounds.

It is unfair to expect conformity to criminal law norms in a wide variety of circumstances and for a wide variety of reasons. It is unfair to

---

[39] Strictly speaking, the involuntary intoxication doctrine is merely an exception to
the general doctrine according to which evidence of intoxication cannot be used to support a denial of mens rea for crimes of 'basic intent' (and arguably may even be used to
help establish such a mens rea).

expect conformity to a criminal-law norm when, in violation of the rule of law, no fair warning of its potential application is given. It is unfair to expect conformity to a criminal-law norm when the defendant is not responsible for her actions (e.g. is an infant or severely mentally ill or is sleepwalking). It is also unfair to expect conformity with a criminal-law norm when breach of it is justified or excused. In each of these cases there is a different explanation of why it is unfair to expect conformity with the norm. In the last case, it is unfair to expect conformity with the norm because the breach of it is excused. So it cannot possibly be the case, *pace* Wilson, that the breach is excused because it is unfair to expect conformity with the norm. An explanation of the nature of criminal excuses must explain not only *that* it would be unfair of the criminal law to expect conformity with the norm when non-conformity is excused, but also *why*: what it is about an excuse that *makes* it unfair to expect such conformity. In all of the examples given by Wilson, the explanation is the same. It is that the defendant's reaction to the crisis before him was within the bounds of reason. In the example given in the passage—of someone who gives in to a threatener regardless of the consequences—the explanation is no different. Was it reasonable for D to be this terrified of the threatener, so terrified that he obeyed in blind panic and ended up doing an unjustified (unreasonable) thing? Was he justified in his terror, even though not in his terrified action?

7. The hierarchy of defences

As these remarks make clear, I subscribe to what Douglas Husak calls 'the logical priority thesis', according to which one needs to understand what a justification is in order to understand what an excuse is. Husak criticizes this thesis, and my reliance on it, by criticizing a thesis that he takes to be entailed by it:

All theorists who hold the [logical] priority thesis are committed to the claim that justifications and excuses are mutually exclusive. Excuses are defined so that if a defendant has an excuse, he cannot also have a justification. This definition, of course, entails (as its contrapositive) [that] if a defendant has a justification, he cannot also have an excuse.[40]

---

[40] D Husak, 'On the Supposed Priority of Justification to Excuse', *Law and Philosophy* 24 (2005), 557 at 560.

Husak offers three main objections to this claim of mutual exclusivity. The first is that one may, on one and the same occasion, act with both justification and excuse. One may act in self-defence, for example, even though one also acted under grave provocation. The second, which turns out to be a variant of the first, is that there may be partial justifications and partial excuses, which might in principle add up, on a particular occasion, to yield a more complete defence. Using excessive force in self-defence is always partially justified (because *ex hypothesi* one is justified in using *some* of the force that one uses) but beyond that point one needs to carve out an excuse (e.g. that one was reasonable in one's misjudgment of the amount of force that was called for). The third, well-illustrated by the same example, is that there could be hybrid defences, 'shar[ing] characteristics of both justification and excuse'.[41]

I agree with Husak on all three points and follow him in thinking that, for these reasons among others, justifications and excuses cannot be mutually exclusive in the sense of never being available in tandem in respect of one and the same wrong. What I do not understand is why my endorsement of the logical priority thesis is supposed to commit me to the opposite view. It is true that in 'Justifications and Reasons' I characterized excused actions as unjustified actions on the strength of justified beliefs, emotions, attitudes, etc. The reference to 'unjustified actions' suggests mutual exclusivity. The characterization is, however, a bit rough and ready. All I meant was that excuses are offered *on the footing* that the action is unjustified. The action may in reality be fully justified. Yet one concedes otherwise (at least for the sake of argument) when one offers an excuse.

Thus—to develop an example of Husak's—when A says 'excuse me' as he squeezes past B to exit the bus, A need not be denying that his action is justified. A may well believe that squeezing past is fully justified and this belief may well be true. Quite possibly B is blocking A's way, time to exit the bus is short, A has an urgent reason to exit, B's reaction time is slow, and squeezing past is therefore the right thing to do all things considered. Nevertheless, by asking B to excuse him, A is conceding *arguendo* that he is incompletely justified. Making this concession is a convention of good manners that, by promptly revealing one's willingness to admit error, helps to avoid triggering conflict. If B is a person of good manners he will promptly reciprocate by saying something like 'no, excuse *me*!' and then the incident will be over. This example bears out Husak's view

---

[41] ibid, 583.

about the mutual exclusivity of justifications and excuses. A may have a valid excuse to offer even though he also has a valid justification that he declines to offer. He may equally have a valid excuse to make up for any incompleteness in his justification. He may also have a hybrid defence that is part justification and part excuse. But none of this is inconsistent with my version of the logical priority thesis, according to which making an excuse is asserting that one's action, even if unjustified, was taken on the strength of justified beliefs, emotions, attitudes, etc. This 'even if' formulation makes clear that, as between justification and excuse, there is no mutual exclusivity of the kind that Husak objects to.

My analysis of the example of A and B does, however, presuppose another thesis to which Husak takes exception. This is the 'normative priority thesis' according to which it is better, all else being equal, to be justified than to be excused. Husak resists this thesis by counterexample:

> Smith and Jones deliberately inflict a fairly serious but not life-threatening injury on White. Imagine the story is embellished in either of two ways. In the first scenario, Smith's behaviour is barely tolerable, although no one would regard it as commendable. Suppose White is a deranged thief who is escaping with Smith's television set. Smith's act, I assume, is permissible and thereby justified. In the second scenario, Jones is well below the age of criminal responsibility, and injures White in a schoolyard brawl. Even if Jones has not acted in self-defence, I assume he is excused. ... I believe that the former scenario casts the agent in a worse moral light. Had I seriously injured a person at some point in my life I would prefer to have done so under the circumstances described in the second scenario.[42]

Unlike Husak, I do not see any reason to regard Jones as excused. His defence, if he has one, is that he is not responsible for his actions. But let's leave this point on one side for a moment. There are two other problems with the way that Husak sets out his challenge. First, we may wonder whether he honours the 'all else being equal' proviso in the normative priority thesis as I defend it. Isn't Husak perhaps tempting us to think of Smith as an intentional injurer and Jones as an accidental injurer? And aren't we perhaps distracted by sympathy for the deranged White in the first scenario, which does not extend to the brawling White in the second? Don't we tend to think that Jones's childish mistakes should be forgiven and forgotten more readily than Smith's adult ones, forgiveness being a quite separate matter from justification and excuse? And doesn't the description of Smith's action as 'barely tolerable' make his supposed justification seem

[42] ibid, 573.

dubious in a way that Jones's supposed excuse is not? Greater toleration, all else being equal, is normally called for in respect of unjustified actions. All of this makes me think that Husak is not setting a fair test for the normative priority thesis. He is subtly stacking the deck in favour of Jones and against Smith, and hence in favour of excuses and against justifications.

Secondly, Husak asks which of the two agents is 'cast[ ] ... in a worse moral light'. This is a misleading way to phrase the question. It suggests that, according to believers in the normative priority thesis, excused wrongdoers are more blameworthy or less creditworthy than their justified counterparts. But this cannot be the implication of the normative priority thesis. Most believers in the normative priority thesis, including me, hold that there can be complete excuses as well as complete justifications, and that what makes an excuse or justification complete is the fact that it renders the agent entirely blameless. And most believers in the normative priority thesis, including me, hold that justified wrongdoers need not be creditworthy at all, let alone more creditworthy than excused wrongdoers. So the respect in which it is better to be justified than excused, according to most believers in the normative priority thesis, cannot be that justification earns one less blame, or more credit, than excuse. The normative difference must lie elsewhere. On my version, the difference is that justification brings one closer than excuse does to perfect conformity with reasons, and hence closer to perfect success as a rational being. That one falls short of perfect success as a rational being need not be one's fault; nor need the degree to which one falls short reflect the degree of one's fault. Failure need not betoken unfitness. Yet failure is still a matter of regret, and it still leaves a blemish on one's life. Making an excuse, I claim, is admitting a failure (in conformity with reasons) that goes one step beyond the failure one already admits in offering a justification, and that remains true even though both equally constitute denials of one's fault. As I put the point in 'The Mark of Responsibility' (Chapter 9), excuses are 'second best' to justifications because they involve 'an admission of rational defeat'. This is all that there is to the normative priority thesis as I defend it. Inasmuch as Husak suggests otherwise by landing me with the view that excuses 'cast[ ] [one] in a worse moral light' than justifications, his objection does not hit home.

I have also expressed the normative priority thesis in terms of self-respect. I said this in 'The Gist of Excuses':

The self-respecting person aspires to live up to the proper standards for success in and fitness for the life she leads, and holds herself out to be judged by those

standards. ... She wants it to be the case that her actions were not truly wrongful, or if they were wrongful, that they were at any rate justified, or if they were
not justified, that they were at any rate excused.

This is where Hamish Stewart's criticisms come in. Recall that Stewart,
like Tadros, is interested in why I classify as excused, not as justified,
those who act on the strength of reasonable mistakes concerning the
existence of justificatory facts. Some of his objections to this classification parallel Tadros's. But Stewart also has an extra objection. He objects
to my classification because, in tandem with the claims I made about the
self-respecting person, it suggests to him:

> ... that the self-respecting individual ought to reproach himself or herself for
> acting on facts that he or she could not reasonably have known. ... In terms of
> the reasons that [a defendant] could reasonably have been expected to act upon
> ... there is no difference between [a case of self-defence and a case of reasonably
> mistaken self-defence], and [the defendant] ought therefore to respect himself
> equally in each case.[43]

Here Stewart makes a misinterpretation similar to Husak's. I am sorry
that I failed adequately to forestall it. It is not my view that someone who
has an excuse should reproach himself. To be fully excused (I repeat) is
to be faultless, and hence beyond reproach. But suppose Stewart were
to replace 'reproach himself or herself for acting' with 'be sad that he
acted'. This would correct the misinterpretation. But it wouldn't affect
the more important challenge in Stewart's second sentence. For Stewart's
main quarrel with me is this: whether or not there is any difference in
warranted self-reproach, there is no difference in warranted self-*respect* as
between D1 who defends himself against an actual attack and D2 who
similarly defends himself against what he reasonably imagines to be a
similar attack.

I can see now why my remarks were taken to suggest that the excused
D2 should respect himself less than the justified D1. But that is not
what I actually said. What I actually said, and certainly what I meant,
is that a self-respecting D2 would *want* to have been justified rather
than excused. He would wish that his situation had been D1's situation,
i.e. that he had not been wrong-footed by reason. That is because, as a
rational being, he cannot but aspire to conform maximally to reason,
and his self-respect is bound up, not with the conformity itself, but with

[43] H Stewart, 'The Role of Reasonableness in Self-Defence', *Canadian Journal of Law
and Jurisprudence* 14 (2003), 317 at 322–323.

the aspiration. His self-respect is threatened by his lowering his sights as a rational agent—by his being no less content to make an excuse than to claim a justification, or no less content to deny his responsibility for his actions than to do either of those things. It does not follow that he compromises his self-respect by the mere fact that he actually *is* excused rather than justified, or actually *does* lack responsibility rather than being excused or justified—so long as he is not indifferent to that being the case, so long as he does not approach with equanimity the question of which argument he is going to offer in his defence.

Ronnie Mackay and Barry Mitchell take exception to the claim, emphasized in 'Provocation and Pluralism' and in 'The Mark of Responsibility', that a denial of responsibility is, all else being equal, the least appetizing of all defences for a self-respecting person to offer. They focus on the negative attitude to mental illness which they find implicit in this view and in the examples that were used to illustrate and corroborate it:

Small wonder that defendants are reluctant to plead insanity when we encounter the type of stigma which is being promulgated here. In essence what Gardner and Macklem are telling us is that a diminished responsibility verdict, like insanity, is one to which stigma is attached. This not only perpetuates an unfortunate attitude towards the mentally disordered but also relegates the interest in avoiding a murder conviction as being less important than what is referred to as a defendant's 'interest in being accorded their status as fully-fledged human beings'.[44]

The final salvo in this passage (after the 'but also') ignores the 'all else being equal' proviso which is an important part of the claim to which Mackay and Mitchell are objecting. The claim is not that the interest in avoiding a murder conviction is less important than the interest in being treated as a fully responsible person. The claim is only that the latter is also an interest that the law (and lawyers) should protect. The more severe the penalties he faces, the more a defendant is under rational pressure to find a way to secure his own acquittal. The point may come at which using a demeaning argument to get off the hook is reasonable. If so, it is the law that is being unreasonable. Its penalties should not be so severe

---

[44] R Mackay and B Mitchell, 'Provoking Diminished Responsibility: Two Pleas Merging Into One?', *Criminal Law Review* [2003], 745 at 757. The quotation at the end of this passage is from J Gardner and T Macklem, 'Compassion without Respect? Nine Fallacies in *R* v *Smith*', *Criminal Law Review* [2001], 623, a paper that is not included in this publication.

that a defendant has no reasonable alternative but to demean himself in order to avoid incurring them.

But does a defendant really demean himself by relying on his mental illness for exoneration? I think that he does. No self-respecting person, in my view, would wish this line of defence upon himself. Mackay and Mitchell do not actually say that this view is mistaken. They seem to be more concerned about the way in which it might be used against mentally ill people, or the way that mentally ill people might feel about it. If so I share their concern. Mentally ill people have often been persecuted, neglected, patronized, and treated as objects of mirth. Their woes have often been compounded by quack treatments, pointless incarcerations, and brutal 'care' regimes. They have often fallen victim to bizarre superstitions and prejudices. But one should not conclude from the fact that mentally ill people have been on the receiving end of so much baseness and stupidity that their mental illness should be regarded with equanimity. Mental illness is not like homosexuality or left-handedness, unobjectionable traits that do not need any remedy. Mental illness really is a kind of illness and illnesses by definition call for treatments and cures. So long as it can be done without mistreating anyone, or committing other wrongs, the world would be a better place with all illnesses eradicated. Mental illnesses, in particular, make the following case for their own eradication. One cannot live a distinctively human life without a full range of rational faculties (cognitive, affective, deliberative, conative) in decent working order. Mental illnesses are illnesses that consist in the malfunction, partial or complete, of one or more of these rational faculties. In more severe cases they restrict, or even sometimes prevent, participation in a distinctively human life. And the ability to participate in a distinctively human life is one of the conditions for being a fully-fledged human being.

This suggestion rings alarm bells because it sounds like (and has often been taken for) an invitation to treat mentally ill people as if they were not people, to treat them like wild animals or even like plant life. But it is no such thing. We shouldn't want a wolf or a palm tree to be able to hold down a job or give a rationally intelligible account of itself, but we should want a mentally ill person to be able to do these things. Why? Because a mentally ill person meets the *other* conditions for being a human being (notably the genetic and physiognomic conditions) and this makes the aspirations and expectations of a successful human life applicable to her. We should therefore want to see her illness cured, and failing that, its symptoms alleviated. We should aspire that she lives the best human life that is possible for her, with the maximum possible participation in distinctively human value. And we should all want her to have rights and resources that will protect her from further injustices and inhumanities, including those that have characterized some past misguided models of treatment and cure for mental illness. We should want a mentally ill person, in short, to be as fully human as possible.

Being responsible for one's own wrongs is a distinctively human capacity and one that is central to all distinctively human lives. It is the capacity that makes self-respect possible, for self-respect is the attitude of one who can sincerely say, of anything she did wrong, that she was justified in doing it, or, failing that, excused. We should all wish mentally ill people to have the opportunity to lead self-respecting lives. 'All' here includes mentally ill people themselves. They should prefer to have justifications for their actions, or failing that excuses, and should prefer not to have to fall back on their illnesses to furnish them with a defence. Alas, some mentally ill people do have to fall back on their illnesses to furnish them with a defence on at least some occasions. Thanks to mental illness, their actions sometimes defy rational explanation and must be put down to pathology. To deny that this is regrettable, it seems to me, is to claim that mentally ill people have nothing wrong with them. Is this what Mackay and Mitchell are claiming? I hope not.

8. Responsibility, relations, and relativities

Antony Duff picks up another theme from 'The Mark of Responsibility'. I argued there that basic responsibility, unlike some other kinds of responsibility, is non-relational. One is not responsible to anyone in particular. Duff objects:

An Old Bailey judge or a stranger on the bus to whom I sought to answer for my unfeeling behaviour towards my aunt would naturally reply that I did not have to answer for such conduct to them. The more significant point is that they have no right to demand that I account to them for myself or my conduct in this respect: if they tried to call me to account for my unkindness towards my aunt, I could properly reply that it was none of their business (unless they were suitably connected to my aunt). . . . [F]or many moral wrongs, and for other non-moral matters, I am responsible only to some specifiable people, not to all.[45]

---

[45] RA Duff, 'Answering for Crime', *Proceedings of the Aristotelian Society* 106 (2006), 85 at 88–89.

I hope that my postscript on accountability, which was added to 'The Mark of Responsibility' after Duff wrote this passage, may now help to clear up the apparent disagreement between us. Being basically responsible, on the view I defended, is not a normative position that one occupies. It is not, for example, a duty or a power or a cluster of duties and powers. Rather, it is a capacity and a propensity to answer for oneself. It may figure in the justification of various duties and powers, including a duty on me to answer to some people as opposed to others, or a power in some people as opposed to others to impose a duty on me to answer to them. Such duties and powers may also be referred to as my responsibility (or, more fashionably, as my accountability). But they are not my *basic* responsibility because they are *based* on my basic responsibility: my basic responsibility, my capacity and propensity to answer for myself, forms part of the case for my being responsible (accountable) to someone in particular.

It is true, as I explained in 'The Mark of Responsibility', that those who are basically responsible always have a reason to explain themselves. Their propensity, in other words, is a rational one. But a reason is not a duty. One can owe a duty to somebody, but one cannot owe a reason to somebody. Of course one can have a reason to do something with or to someone. One can have, for example, a reason to give a gift to someone in particular. In that sense a reason can be relational. Yet it cannot be relational in the further sense in which a duty can be relational, viz in having another person, a rightholder, to whom it is owed. And it is this further relationality of duties, their oweability to rightholders, that Duff invokes in the passage quoted above. This shows that he is talking about a slightly different topic from the one I was talking about in the passage he criticizes. He is talking about the next topic along. After we have established that a given agent is basically responsible, capable of giving an account of herself, we may raise the further question of who, if anyone, is entitled (i.e. has a right) to call her to account. The position I took in 'The Mark of Responsibility' does not commit me to giving 'anyone and everyone' as the answer to this follow-up question. I agree with Duff that one needs to have some *locus standi* to be entitled to call another to account.

There is something misleading, however, about Duff's use of the phrase 'none of your business' to convey the absence of the required *locus standi*. In 'Complicity and Causality', I aligned myself with the agent-neutralist view according to which wrongdoing by anyone is fundamentally everyone's concern. We all have one and the same reason (the fact that the wrong is a wrong) to avoid the commission of any wrong by anyone. But it is a different matter to ask which of us has a *duty* or a *right* to avoid the commission of a particular wrong by another. The answer depends mainly on what would make for (as I called it) 'the efficient use of rational energy'. It depends mainly on how well a particular person is placed to secure the avoidance of the wrong in question, thereby conforming to the reason that he has, in common with everyone else, to avoid its commission. What does this have to do with the relationality of responsibility? The fact that everyone has a reason to avoid the wrongdoer's committing a wrong does not by itself entail that everyone has a reason to get the wrongdoer, having committed the wrong, to account for herself. Nevertheless, the agent-neutralist line of thought can readily be extended. Just as everyone's wrongdoing is everyone's concern, so everyone's responsibility is everyone's concern. We each have reason to see to it that people in general answer for their wrongs, and one way in which I can see to it that people answer for their wrongs is to have them answer to me. That is one way, of course, but is it the optimal way? Not always. What we face here is once again mainly a question of the efficient use of rational energy. It may not be my place (my role) to extract justifications and excuses. It may be the law's place, or the place of the person who was wronged, or the place of the wrongdoer's friends and family, etc. But where this is so, it is mainly (not only, but mainly) because and to the extent that this person with *locus standi* is the one who is best-placed to do the extracting, i.e. who will do the best job of conforming to the reason that we all have in common to see to it that the wrongdoer answers for her wrongs.

I did not mount a full defence of this agent-neutralist view in 'Complicity and Causality'. I only paused to indicate how, once the efficiency principle (as I will call it) is factored in, the agent-neutralist view is compatible with a great deal of superficial agent-relativity in everyday moral experience. From the fact that all wrongdoing and all responsibility is everyone's concern, it does not follow that one should be even-handed in one's efforts to avoid every wrong or to hold everyone responsible. Often one should begin by trying to put one's own house in order, for here one may perhaps be less prone to counterproductivity, self-defeatingness, overzealousness, and similar errors. I suspect that I did not make this point clearly enough in 'Complicity and Causality'—for I left Tatjana Hörnle with this worry:

[T]he amount of intrusion is limited only by the fact that it might sometimes be inefficient. If one takes this stance seriously, everybody would constantly be trying to be as efficient as possible in morally improving others.[46]

---

[46] T Hörnle, 'Commentary', above n 14, 148.

Actually, I said 'limited mainly' rather than 'limited only'. But leaving this quibble on one side, is it true that, on my view, 'everybody [should] constantly be trying to be as efficient as possible in morally improving others'? No. Indeed this is exactly the worry that I was trying to defuse by invoking the efficiency principle in the first place. That *ceteris paribus* everyone should minimize wrongdoing by everyone does not mean that *ceteris paribus* everyone should *try* to minimize wrongdoing by everyone. For much of this effort would be inefficient, i.e. would not succeed in reducing wrongdoing and might even increase it. Hörnle is making the common mistake of confusing what one should do with what one should try to do, forgetting that often it is the trying that is the problem.

To be fair, Hörnle has deeper worries about my agent-neutralism, and perhaps Duff shares them. Hörnle worries, in a neo-Kantian vein, that my agent-neutralism 'violates ... human dignity' by licensing 'trade-offs' of one person against another. I do not share this worry. I cannot speak for all agent-neutralists. It may be that some (e.g. classical utilitarians) leave little space for anything resembling human dignity. But if so I clearly part company with them. As 'The Wrongness of Rape' and 'The Functions and Justifications of Criminal Law and Punishment' (Chapter 10) both make clear, I share Kant's view that human beings have a value beyond price (i.e. a value beyond their use-value) that we might reasonably call their dignity. My difficulty is in seeing why this dignity should be valued agent-relatively, not agent-neutrally, and hence should not be traded-off between persons just like any other value. Fundamentally, the wrongdoing and responsibility of those who join death squads in Iraq, of those who traffic people in Albania, of those who attempt internet scams in Nigeria, and of those who preach pseudo-Biblical resentments in the USA are no less my concern than are my own wrongdoing and responsibility. That is precisely because these wrongdoers, just like me, have a value beyond price; they belong, just like me, to the Kingdom of Ends. I have no reason to regard their moral fates (which are bound up with their wrongdoing and their responsibility) as any less important than my own. I only have reason to make extensive allowances in what I do for my own relative impotence in improving the moral fates of others, and in particular for the risk that I will make those moral fates even worse in my bungled efforts to improve them. If I should avoid trading off one person's dignity against another's—if I should adopt superficial agent-relative conceits of the 'none-of-my business' variety, and thereby pass the buck for trade-offs onto somebody else—then that (I repeat) is mainly because and to the extent that I am not best-placed to do the trade-offs well.

9. Crimes and punishments

There are various applications of the efficiency principle in 'The Functions and Justifications of Criminal Law and Punishment' and also in 'Crime: in Proportion and in Perspective'. A central theme of the former paper is that a certain reason can contribute to the justification of criminal punishment even though it is not the case that a particular official (or indeed any official) should punish anyone for that reason. Normally this is because acting for that reason is not a good way for the official concerned to do what the reason would have him do. Highlighted in the latter paper, meanwhile, is the localized agent-relativity of the state's duties of humanity and justice, an agent-relativity which is said to have a deeper agent-neutral basis. Again, the efficiency principle plays the dominant role in explaining this.

These papers have not attracted as much critical attention in print as have the others in this volume. Perhaps they are more banal. It does not follow that their claims are more widely endorsed. In discussion, many of my colleagues and students have doubted my view that punishment calls for (or is even open to) a pluralistic, cumulative justification. This is thought by many to be an incoherent view, or at least a view that condemns the practice of punishment itself to incoherence. Several people have reminded me of HLA Hart's remark that

> … what is most needed is *not* the simple admission that instead of a single value or aim (Deterrence, Retribution, Reform or any other) a plurality of different values and aims should be given as a conjunctive answer to some *single* question concerning the justification of punishment. What is needed is the realization that different principles (each of which may in a sense be a called a 'justification') are relevant at different points in any morally acceptable account of punishment.[47]

Hart himself thought that deterrence (or more generally the prevention of wrongdoing) is the 'general justifying aim' of criminal punishment. He thought that guilt (culpability, fault) is relevant only to the distribution

---

[47] HLA Hart, 'Prolegomenon to the Principles of Punishment' in his *Punishment and Responsibility* (1968), 3.

of criminal punishment, coming into play only once it had been determined that criminal punishment in general is justified. Importantly, and unlike some who have cited Hart's remark to me, Hart agreed that it would be possible to hold a view according to which 'giving guilty people what they deserve' and 'preventing future wrongs' figure side-by-side as criminal punishment's twin general justifying aims. His resistance to doing so did not come of the thought that one could not reasonably endorse 'conjunctive' general justifying aims for criminal punishment. His objection was simply a moral objection to the view according to which a person's guilt is a reason in favour of punishing her. He thought that a person's innocence serves as a (powerful, usually decisive) reason for *not* punishing her, and hence that the importance of considering questions of guilt in connection with an anticipated punishment could only be negative: to limit and regulate the use of criminal punishment, granted that such punishment, as a general practice, is justified on other grounds.

Personally, I think that Hart's philosophical judgment here is sound, but his moral judgment is flawed. The principle of desert (as I will call it) cuts both ways. The fact that someone is innocent is a reason against punishing her; the fact that she is guilty is also a reason in favour of punishing her. So giving people what they deserve figures among the general justifying aims of punishment. Yet the justificatory importance of the principle of desert is not symmetrical. It justifies the non-punishment of the innocent much more readily than it justifies the punishment of the guilty. That is because, in general, it is much easier to justify not punishing than it is to justify punishing. Indeed, it is easier to justify that many guilty people go unpunished than that one innocent person is punished. And why, you may ask, is that? Primarily, it is because punishment involves the intentional infliction of disadvantage or suffering upon the person who is punished. The disadvantage or suffering is not a side-effect (as it is with the payment of reparative damages, the protective detention of the seriously mentally ill, the pre-trial custody of a suspect, and so on), but part of the punisher's plan. This morally repugnant feature—the wishing of evil upon another—makes punishment extremely hard to justify.

Because of the argumentative force of the other side of the desert principle (i.e. against punishing the innocent), guilt is usually a necessary condition of justified punishment, and when it is present it is also (without further ado) a reason in favour of exacting the punishment for the justification of which it is a necessary condition. So as well as neutralizing a major objection, it forms the first part of the positive case for punishing. But even though it is usually a necessary condition of justified punishment, guilt is rarely a sufficient condition. More than nominal punishment is almost never justifiable on the strength of guilt alone. There must be further benefits, which may either be consequences of honouring the principle of desert or independent benefits, before there is an adequate case for punishing any but the very guiltiest. That, at any rate, is my sense of how we are forced towards a generally pluralistic approach to the justification of punishment, and thus (*inter alia*) to the justification of criminal punishment.

This pluralistic approach is advocated in 'The Functions and Justifications of Criminal Law and Punishment' and echoed in 'Crime: in Proportion and in Perspective'. All the same, looking back on the latter paper, I now think that it starts off on a misleading note. The 'displacement function' of criminal law—its ability to interpose itself coolly between wrongdoers and those they have wronged—is presented as a key part of the case for criminal law's continuing existence. This was taken by some of my readers to entail that the displacement function is also a key part of the case for punishment. This interpretation was understandable in view of some of my remarks and examples, but it was not what I intended. I do not regard every argument for punishment as an argument for criminal law, or for that matter *vice versa*. In writing about the displacement function, I assumed that punishment of the wrongdoer, if justified at all, falls to be justified by an accumulation of other considerations, including the wrongdoer's guilt. What the paper was supposed to offer was an simple explanation of why, *assuming that the guilty wrongdoer should indeed be punished by someone*, the criminal law (as opposed to victims or their families or their sympathizers) should be the one to exact the punishment. I then tried to investigate what some of the consequences of this explanation would be for the criminal law itself, including its future legitimacy.

Clearly, in framing this investigation, I should have paid more attention to Hart's warning quoted above. As well as there being 'a plurality of different values and aims' that are needed to provide an adequate answer to the general question 'why punish?', it is also true that different considerations 'are relevant at different points' in the inquiry. Notably, some considerations are relevant mainly to the question 'who gets to punish?' rather than the prior question 'why punish?' Of course one can run the two questions together by asking 'why punish?' with a particular punisher (such as the criminal law) already in mind. But it is better to separate the two questions. Already, too much academic writing about the criminal law casually runs together questions about the justification of criminal law and questions about the justification of punishment. Such writing often harbours an excessively statist view of punishment and/or a too narrowly punitive view of the purposes of the criminal law. In real life, for better or worse, most punishments are exacted, not by the criminal law, but by parents, spouses and ex-spouses, friends and ex-friends, business partners and ex-business-partners, etc.[48] At the same time the criminal law should not be seen as a merely, or even a mainly, punitive institution. Rather, as I explained in 'In Defence of Defences', the criminal law

> ... is primarily a vehicle for the public identification of wrongdoing ... and for responsible agents, whose wrongs have been thus identified, to *answer for* their wrongs by offering justifications and excuses for having committed them. By calling this latter function 'primary' I do not mean to suggest that it is socially more important. I mean that the proper execution of the other functions depends upon it. Criminal law can be a proper vehicle for ... punishment only because it is a vehicle for responsible agents to answer for their wrongs.

This remains my view. It explains the emphasis, in many of the foregoing essays, on questions about responsibility, justification, and excuse. I am sorry if 'Crime: in Proportion and in Perspective' accidentally gave succour to a rival view according to which the purposes of the criminal law are primarily punitive, and according to which whatever justifies the criminal law also justifies (*pro tanto*) the practice of punishment.

---

[48] Hart relegates such punishments to the margins in ibid, 5, favouring (without argument) the view that official state punishment is the 'central case'.

Index

Reasons *(cont.)*
  guiding v explanatory 91–120,
    259–61
  legal regulation of 27–8, 73–4,
    114–15
  privileged 104–5
  protected 105–8, 147–8
Regret 81–2, 85–6, 97, 119, 145–6, 148,
    253–4, 272, 276
Responsibility 60–4, 69–71, 73, 131–4,
    161, 177–200, 251
  basic 84, 131–3, 181–200, 276–7
  consequential 83–4, 131–3, 177–81,
    191–2
  diachronic aspect 182–5
  diminished 133–4, 155, 171–2,
    180–1, 274
  distinguished from
    accountability 194–5
  importance of 80, 276, 283
  personal v vicarious 60, 250–1
  relational view of 185–8, 276–8
  residual view of 83–5
Rights 20, 31–2, 244, 277–8
  property 8–14
  to be punished 192
  to sexual autonomy 19–21, 31–2
Ripstein, Arthur 242–3
Robinson, Paul 100, 141–2
Roles 128–31, 134–7, 169–72, 195,
    265–7, 278
Rorty, Richard 185, 187–8
Rule of law 34, 43–55, 114–18, 137–9,
    219, 223–4, 239–41, 245, 247–8,
    251, 268–9
Rules 105–6 *(see also* norms)
  closure 117
  conduct v adjudication 114–18

Self-defence 120, 132, 178, 270
Self-respect 26, 85, 133–8, 170–2,
    272–6
Sentencing, *see* punishment
Shakespeare, William 22
Shute, Stephen 243
Solzhenitsyn, Alexander 57–8, 75–6
Stanton-Ife, John 240–1
Stewart, Hamish 258, 273–4
State, duties of 31, 209, 216–21
  duty of humanity 216–18, 220,
    232–8

duty of justice 218–19, 220
Subjectivism, *see* objective standards

Tadros, Victor 245, 258–63, 267, 273
Theft 42, 47, 121–2, 137, 150, 241, 245
Tort 31, 163, 197, 247, 252
Torture 16, 59, 60–1, 68, 69, 172, 245

Value
  intrinsic v instrumental 137, 188–92,
    237
  of humanity 20, 279–80
  of legal process 188–91, 235–8
  perfectionist 118–19
  pluralism 118, 193
  use v identification 9–12, 14–15,
    19–20
Vice, *see* character
Victim
  experiences 2–8
  perspective 225–31
  role in criminal trial 235–8, 282
Violence 16, 25, 36–40, 46
  domestic 133–4, 171, 180–1, 245–6
Virtue, *see* character

Westen, Peter 256–8
Williams, Bernard 254, 259–61
Wilson, William 267–9
Wounding 35, 37, 51–2, 229–31
Wrongs, wrongdoing 122–3, 231, 239,
    253, 277–80
  and criminalization 1, 30–1, 205–6,
    242–3
  closure view of 77–83, 253–6
  distinguished from harm 4–5, 8, 31,
    36, 39, 46
  fault-anticipating 80, 151–3, 259
  harmless 4–8, 11–12, 15, 29, 45, 119,
    215, 242, 244
  instrumental v non-instrumental 30
  paradigmatic 1, 16–17, 22, 150–1,
    239
  prima facie v all things
    considered 77–9, 95–7, 145–6, 255
  private v public 31–2
  right/wrong asymmetry 228–9 *(see
    also* reasons, for v against)
  subtractive view of 73–5
  variety of 16, 27, 228, 246 *(see also*
    crimes, variety of)